ESSAYS ON CONSTITUTIONAL
LAW AND EQUITY

VOLUME II

Da Capo Press Reprints in

AMERICAN CONSTITUTIONAL AND LEGAL HISTORY

GENERAL EDITOR: LEONARD W. LEVY

Claremont Graduate School

ESSAYS ON CONSTITUTIONAL LAW AND EQUITY

BY HENRY SCHOFIELD

VOLUME II

DA CAPO PRESS • NEW YORK • 1972

Library of Congress Cataloging in Publication Data

Schofield, Henry, 1866-1918.
  Essays on constitutional law and equity.

  (Da Capo Press reprints in American constitutional
and legal history)
    1. U.S. — Constitutional law — Addresses, essays,
lectures. 2. Equity — U.S. — Addresses, essays,
lectures. I. Title.
KF4550.A2S3 1972   342'.73   79-38814
ISBN 0-306-70450-1

This Da Capo Press edition of *Essays on Constitutional Law
and Equity* is an unabridged republication of the first
edition published in Boston in 1921.

Copyright 1921 by the Chipman Law Publishing Company

Published by Da Capo Press, Inc.
A Subsidiary of Plenum Publishing Corporation
227 West 17th Street, New York, N.Y. 10011

ESSAYS ON CONSTITUTIONAL
LAW AND EQUITY

VOLUME II

ESSAYS ON

CONSTITUTIONAL LAW AND EQUITY

AND OTHER SUBJECTS

BY

HENRY SCHOFIELD

LATE PROFESSOR OF LAW
IN NORTHWESTERN
UNIVERSITY

EDITED BY

THE FACULTY OF LAW

NORTHWESTERN UNIVERSITY

VOL. II

BOSTON

PUBLISHED FOR NORTHWESTERN UNIVERSITY LAW SCHOOL, BY
THE CHIPMAN LAW PUBLISHING COMPANY

1921

The Riverdale Press, Brookline, Mass., U. S. A.

CONTENTS

PART I

CONSTITUTIONAL LAW

TOPIC I

THE RELATIONS OF THE FEDERAL AND STATE COURTS UNDER THE CONSTITUTION

Topic II

The Full Faith and Credit Clause

Topic III

Trial by Jury

CONTENTS

Topic IV

Interstate Commerce

Topic V

Punishment

Topic VI

Religious Liberty and Liberty of the Press

Topic VII

The Obligation of Contracts Clause

Topic VIII

The Power of Appointment to Public Office

Topic IX
Due Process of Law

PART II
EQUITY
Topic I
Specific Performance

CONTENTS

TOPIC II

CONSTRUCTION, REFORMATION, AND RESCISSION OF WRITTEN INSTRUMENTS

TOPIC III

RELIEF AGAINST TORTS

TOPIC IV

RELIEF AGAINST PROCEEDINGS AT LAW

TOPIC V

SUBROGATION AND EXONERATION

Topic VI

Administration of Assets

Appendix

PART I

CONSTITUTIONAL LAW

(Continued)

TOPIC VI

RELIGIOUS LIBERTY AND LIBERTY OF THE PRESS

I. Religious Liberty and Bible Reading in Illinois Public Schools.

II. Freedom of the Press in the United States.

I

RELIGIOUS LIBERTY AND BIBLE READING IN ILLINOIS PUBLIC SCHOOLS[a]

In People *v.* Board of Education,[1] Dunn, J., writing the opinion, Hand and Cartwright, JJ., filing a dissenting opinion, the Supreme Court declared, by a vote of five to two, that the religious liberty guarantees of the Illinois constitution forbid the legislature to authorize reading the Bible in the public schools. That is a very broad and important proposition of state constitutional law, materially cutting down the power of the state legislature over the subject of public education. The proposition ultimately rests, not on the ground that reading the Bible in the public schools molests anybody in the exercise and enjoyment of his constitutional right of freedom of religious profession, worship, and opinion, but on the ground that reading the Bible in the public schools molests the taxpayer, without any regard to his religion or want of religion, in the exercise and enjoyment of his constitutional right of freedom from taxation to help support any clergy or church establishment.

In view of the references by the majority to the history of religious liberty as a personal right which government is bound to secure and protect, it seems appropriate, before entering upon an analysis of their opinion, to take a brief survey of the religious liberty guarantees in the

[a] [6 Ill. Law Rev., 17–33, 91–111, May and June, 1911.]
[1] 245 Ill., 334.

bill of rights of the constitution of Illinois, leaving out, for the present, the addition in the article on "Education" introduced in 1870, on which the case turned. The immediate legal source of those guarantees is section 16 of the bill of rights of the Virginia constitution of 1776, written by George Mason, and the famous Virginia religious liberty statute of 1785, written by Thomas Jefferson.[2] The Illinois guarantees, like the provisions of the Virginia constitution and statute, fall into three parts, viz.: (1) those provisions designed to secure the right of freedom of religious profession, worship, and opinion, and the duty of toleration; (2) those provisions designed to secure the right of freedom from civil and political disabilities on account of religion or want of religion; (3) those provisions designed to secure the right of freedom from taxation to help support any clergy or church establishment. Freedom from taxation to help support any clergy or church establishment stands to freedom of religious profession, worship, and opinion, and the duty of toleration, in the relation of temporal means to attain and preserve a spiritual end. Freedom of religious profession, worship, and opinion, and the duty of toleration, constitute the spiritual end; freedom from taxation to help support any church establishment is the temporal means; and freedom from civil and political disabilities on account of religion or want of religion is another temporal means to attain and preserve the spiritual end of freedom of religious profession, worship,

[2] 2 Tucker, Constitution, 668. See Gay's Madison, 16–18. The Virginia constitution and statute are not original, but go back directly through the laws of several of the states to the lawgiver of Rhode Island, in 1636, i. e., Roger Williams. It is easy to trace Mason's and Jefferson's sources in Thorpe's American Charters, Constitutions, and Organic Laws. "The first person in modern Christendom to assert, in its plenitude, the doctrine of liberty of conscience, the equality of opinion before the law," was Roger Williams. 1 Bancroft, Abridged History of the Colonization of the United States, Ch. 15.

and opinion, and the duty of toleration.[3]   George Mason's section of the bill of rights of the Virginia constitution of 1776 secured freedom of religious profession and worship, and the duty of toleration, and Thomas Jefferson's Virginia statute of 1785 secured freedom of religious opinion, freedom from taxation to help support any church establishment, and freedom from civil and political disabilities on account of religion or want of religion.   The Virginia constitutional and statutory provisions, together with the Illinois version of them, are printed in the margin.[4]

[3] "The magistrates [of Massachusetts in the winter of 1635] insisted on the presence of every man at public worship. [Roger] Williams reprobated the law; the worst statute in the English code was that which did but enforce attendance upon the parish church. 'No one should be bound to worship, or,' he added, 'to maintain a worship against his own consent.' 'What!' exclaimed his astonished antagonists, amazed at his tenets, 'is not the laborer worthy of his hire?' 'Yes,' replied he, 'from them that hire him.' The magistrates were selected exclusively from members of the church; with equal propriety reasoned Williams, might 'a doctor of physick or a pilot' be selected according to his skill in theology and his standing in the church."   1 Bancroft, Abridged History of the Colonization of the United States, Ch. 15.

[4] Virginia Bill of Rights of 1776, Sec. 16: "That religion, or the duty which we owe to our Creator, and the manner of discharging it, can be directed only by reason and conviction, not by force or violence, and therefore all men are equally entitled to the free exercise of religion, according to the dictates of conscience; and that it is the mutual duty of all to practise Christian forbearance, love and charity towards each other."

Enacting Clause of the Virginia Statute of 1785: "Be it enacted by the General Assembly, that no man shall be compelled to frequent or support any religious worship, place, or ministry whatsoever; nor shall be enforced, restrained, molested, or burthened, in his body or goods, nor shall otherwise suffer on account of his religious opinions or belief; but that all men shall be free to profess, and by argument to maintain, their opinions in matters of religion, and that the same shall in no wise diminish, enlarge, or affect their civil capacity."

Illinois Bill of Rights of 1818 and 1848, Secs. 3 and 4: "That all men have a natural and indefeasible right to worship Almighty God according to the dictates of their own consciences; that no man can of right be compelled to attend, erect, or support any place of worship, or maintain any ministry against his consent; that no human authority can, in any case whatever, control or interfere with the rights of conscience; and that no preference shall ever be given by law to any religious establishments or modes of worship." "That no religious test shall ever be required as a qualification to any office or public trust under this state."

Illinois Bill of Rights of 1870, Sec. 3: "The free exercise and enjoyment of

The part of the religious liberty guarantees designed to secure freedom of religious profession, worship, and opinion, and the duty of toleration, affirm the principle, as an eternal principle of justice, that every man has a right to worship God in the manner which seems to him the best. The words secure to every man freedom to deny, if he wants to, so far as he himself is concerned, the authority of any church as interpreter of the revealed will of God, as well as freedom to join any church, if he wants to, and to accept it, so far as he himself is concerned, as his authoritative interpreter of the revealed will of God, and freedom to reject religion altogether, if he wants to, so far as he himself is concerned.[5]

The notion of a church establishment includes:

(1) "A clergy, or an order of men secluded from other professions to attend upon the offices of religion; (2) a legal provision for the maintenance of the clergy; and (3) the confining of that provision to the teachers of a particular sect of Christianity."[6]

religious profession and worship, without discrimination, shall forever be guaranteed; and no person shall be denied any civil or political right, privilege, or capacity, on account of his religious opinions; but the liberty of conscience hereby secured shall not be construed to dispense with oaths or affirmations, excuse acts of licentiousness, or justify practices inconsistent with the peace or safety of the state. No person shall be required to attend or support any ministry or place of worship against his consent, nor shall any preference be given by law to any religious denomination or mode of worship."

Jefferson's Virginia Statute of 1785 has a preamble, too long to be reproduced here, explanatory of the reasons of the enacting clause given above; and the enacting clause is followed by a declaration, "that the rights hereby asserted are of the natural rights of mankind, and a repeal or modification of the statute "to narrow its operation, . . . will be an infringement of natural right." See Code of Virginia, 1887, Secs. 1394, 1395. The idea, form, and much of the substance of Jefferson's preamble go back to the Charter of Rhode Island and Providence Plantations of 1664, to William Penn's Frame of Government of Pennsylvania of 1682, and his Charter of Liberties of 1701. See Thorpe's American Charters, Constitutions, and Organic Laws, pp. 2537, 3053–5, 3063, 3077.

[5] 2 Story, Constitution, Sec. 1781, et seq.; Hackett v. Brooksville Graded School District, 120 Ky., 608, 619; Hegel, Philosophy of History, Part 6, Ch. 1; Guizot, History of Civilization in Europe, Lecture 12.

[6] Paley, Moral Philosophy, Bk. 6, Ch. 10.

There can be no doubt that such was the meaning of a church establishment in Virginia in 1784–5.[7]   An established church and individual freedom of religious profession, worship, and opinion may coexist, and do coexist to-day in England and in Germany, for example.   But they cannot coexist, either in fact or in law, in any state of the Union that has placed in its constitution Thomas Jefferson's Virginia religious liberty statute of 1785.[8]

The immediate cause of that statute was a bill introduced in the Virginia legislature in 1784 to lay a tax for the benefit of the clergy of all Christian sects in Virginia, leaving the taxpayer free to designate on the collector's warrant the particular sect the taxpayer wanted to give his money to.   This bill aroused the Virginia advocates of religious liberty as comprehending a complete separation of church and state, who had been struggling under the leadership of Thomas Jefferson, outside and inside the legislature, since 1777, to get their views on religious liberty enacted into law.   James Madison, who was in the legislature, got the bill put over to the next session, and meantime they appealed to the people of Virginia, Madison publishing his celebrated "Memorial and Remonstrance" against the bill.   At the session of 1785 the bill was beaten, and Jefferson's religious liberty statute, written in 1777, Jefferson being absent as minister to France from 1784 to 1789, was enacted into law.   Jefferson circulated the statute through Europe, where it made, and its principle still is making, a profound impression.   Jefferson's view of its importance to promote the happiness of mankind is shown by his epitaph, written by himself, wherein he passed over all his offices, honors, and other achievements, and noticed only that he was

[7] Curtis, The True Thomas Jefferson, 326 to 331.

[8] 2 Story, Constitution, Secs. 1781, 1782; Paley, Moral Philosophy, Bk. 6, Ch. 10.

(1) the author of the Declaration of Independence, (2) the author of the Virginia Religious Liberty Statute, (3) the founder of the University of Virginia.[9]

Whatever one may think of Thomas Jefferson, the great fact remains that he took up the religious liberty cause of Roger Williams and stood for religious liberty as one of the primordial rights government is instituted to secure and protect, and diffused the notion among the American people, so that his views on religious liberty as comprehending the separation of church and state, as expressed in a statute written by himself, have been accepted by the people in most of our states and made a part of their fundamental organic state law.   The key-note of Jefferson's statute divorcing the clergy of every church from the taxing power of the state, and securing to men the exercise and enjoyment of civil and political rights without regard to their religion or want of religion, is freedom, man's destiny to be free, which notion of freedom is founded on the sentence in St. John selected by Jefferson as the motto of the University of Virginia, viz.: "And ye shall know the truth, and the truth shall make you free."[10]   Montesquieu wrote in his "Spirit of Laws," published in 1748, the book, next after the Bible, the founders of our system of government consulted most, that the Christian religion is a stranger to mere despotic power.[11]   And Jefferson said: "I have sworn

[9] Reynolds v. United States, 98 U. S., 145, 162, 163, 164; 2 Watson, Constitution, p. 1379, n. 14; Curtis, The True Thomas Jefferson, Ch. 11.   The taxation plan of the rejected Virginia statute to support the clergy was in use in other states, as in Maryland, Constitution of 1776, and in Massachusetts, Constitution of 1780, and in New Hampshire, Constitution 1784.   Paley, Moral Philosophy, Bk. 6, Ch. 10, published in 1785, speaks of this American experiment as "The only plan which seems to render the legal maintenance of a clergy practicable, without the legal preference of one sect of Christians to others."

[10] John, 8, 32.

[11] 2 Story, Constitution, Sec. 1873.

upon the altar of God eternal hostility to every form of
tyranny over the mind of man." Jefferson's statute
was not aimed at the Christian religion; it draws a clear
line between the clergy and religion; it divorced the
church from the state, but not the state, i. e., the people,
from the Christian religion.[12] Jefferson's definition of a
church gives the principle on which his statute was
drawn:

"A voluntary society of men, joining themselves together of their
own accord, in order to the public worship of God, in such a manner
as they judge acceptable to Him, and effectual to the salvation of
their souls. It is voluntary, because no man is bound by nature
to any church. The hope of salvation is the cause of his entering
into it. If he finds anything wrong in it, he should be as free to
go out as he was to come in."[13]

In the case before the Supreme Court it appeared that
some of the teachers in the public schools in District
24, in Scott County, were in the habit of commencing
the daily session of their schools by causing the pupils
to rise in their seats, fold their hands, and bow their
heads while the teacher read from the King James Bible
and while teacher and pupils recited in concert the
Lord's Prayer as found in the King James Bible. As
part of the same mode of commencing the daily task,
teacher and pupils joined in singing a sacred hymn, one
entitled "Grace Enough for Me" being given as an

---

[12] "States and governments were made for man. . . . By a state I mean
a complete body of free persons united together for their common benefit, to
enjoy peaceably what is their own, and to do justice to others. . . . The
sovereign, when traced to his source, must be found in the man." Wilson, J., in
Chisholm v. Georgia, 2 Dallas, 419, 455, 458.

[13] Curtis, The True Thomas Jefferson, Ch. 11. The author concludes thus
on p. 398: "He [i. e., Jefferson] had one purpose that never wavered. He was
often inconsistent, but was never insincere in his anxiety and never faltered in
his determination to establish a democracy in the United States — a government,
as Lincoln said, of the people, for the people, by the people — and whatever he did
was done with the intention and the hope of promoting that end."

example. The teacher occasionally asked a pupil to explain the meaning of the passage read from the Bible. Five residents of the school district objected to this school exercise and applied to the Circuit Court of Scott County for a writ of mandamus directed to the board of education commanding the board to require the teachers who were in the habit of commencing their daily task in the way stated, to stop it. The complainants rested their claim of right to have the writ on two legal foundations, viz.: (1) the foundation of the rights of parental authority touching religious profession and worship by children; (2) the foundation of the rights of private property, i. e., specifically, freedom from taxation to help support any church establishment. All five complainants rested their claim to have the writ on the first foundation of the rights of parental authority, but only two of the complainants rested their claim to have the writ on the second foundation of the rights of private property, for only two of the five were taxpayers, The first claim touched and concerned the complainants' religious consciences only; the second claim touched and concerned their property only. The two parts of the case are so distinct and separate as to make two cases, and may be called: (1) the rights-of-conscience part, and (2) the freedom-from-taxation part. The majority mixed the two parts of the case together so that it is not easy to follow their argument without going over the same ground more than once, starting from a different point either in the religious liberty guarantees or in the majority opinion.

First. As to the rights-of-conscience part of the case:

The five complainants were parents, either father or mother, of children between the ages of seven and fourteen years, attending one or another of the public schools in question. By the law of the state parents must allow their children between those ages to go to school — not necessarily to a public school, but to some school — and in the school district in question there was no school but the public school. The complaining parents were members of the Roman Catholic Church. They said the school exercise in question was a Protestant mode of worship, and to compel their children to take part in it, or to attend school while it was being conducted in their children's presence, infringed their parental right to require their children to observe only Roman Catholic modes of worship, and to keep away from places wherein Protestant modes of worship are being conducted. Their reason for saying the school exercise in question was a Protestant mode of worship was that the teacher read the Protestant Bible, i. e., the King James Bible, and not the Catholic Bible, i. e., the Douay Bible, and the Lord's Prayer recited was the one as found in the King James Bible, and not the one as found in the Douay Bible. No objection to the sacred hymns commonly sung was specified.

We may pass by for the present the question whether the parental right to prescribe the religious profession and worship of children until they reach the age of discretion is a constitutional right, i. e., a right immune from legislative control and interference, flowing from, or protected by, the freedom-of-conscience guarantee, because that question is not specifically noticed anywhere in the case. Nor does it appear that any of the five complaining parents asked to have their children excused from attending or joining in this school exercise, and their request was refused. There can be no doubt whatever that the excusing of the children from this school exercise would have left nothing for the parents to complain about, so far as the constitutional right of freedom of religious profession and worship is concerned. There is nothing in the guarantee of freedom of religious profession and worship that enables a father or mother of a single pupil in a public school to use their freedom of religious profession and worship to destroy or abridge other people's freedom of religious profession and worship by the mode of silencing the teachers and all the other pupils in the public schools on the subject of the Bible. That is clearly the law, as is plain on the face of the freedom-of-conscience guarantee, and as is declared in Millard *v.* Board of Education,[14] North *v.* Trustees of the University of Illinois,[15] and in several cases in other states.[16]

Let us assume these complaining parents asked to have their children excused from this school exercise and the request was refused; and let us also assume that the parental right to prescribe the religious profession and worship of children is a constitutional right involved in the right of freedom of religious profession and worship. The question under the rights-of-conscience part of the case, then, is whether this school exercise encounters the guarantee securing and protecting Roman Catholic parents in the exercise and enjoyment of the right of freedom of religious profession and worship. The determination of the majority of the court that this school exercise

[14] 121 Ill., 227.

[15] 137 Ill., 296.

[16] They are cited in 245 Ill., on pp. 350, 358, 359. In 245 Ill., on p. 351, the majority reject the proposition stated in the text and the cases which they admit support it. But the majority overlook the difference between freedom of religious profession and worship, and freedom from taxation to help support a church. After it is judicially determined that reading the Bible in the public schools involves spending public money to aid a church, it is no answer to a taxpayer to say that this or that pupil was excused; but it is an answer to the excused pupil's parents objecting on religious grounds. The majority took their notion from the Wisconsin case in 76 Wis., 177, 199, 200, but they misapplied their authority, and do not see that the Wisconsin court gave a bad reason for a sound result — assuming the Wisconsin court's premise that Bible-reading is "sectarian instruction," within the meaning of the Wisconsin constitution and statute, is sound.

is a mode of worship cannot be criticized, as it seems to me. And their statement that it is a mode of worship "usually practiced by Protestant Christian denominations" may be accepted as correct in point of fact. But that is not enough in this case to put this school exercise, at the instance of Roman Catholic parents, under the ban of the guarantee securing freedom of religious profession and worship. You must go further in this case, and show that this school exercise, sanctioned and made compulsory by the state, as is now being assumed, discriminates in a religious matter between sects of the Christian religion, giving a preference to Protestant sects over the Roman Catholic sect, in such a way as to molest, unconstitutionally, Roman Catholic parents in their religious consciences, i. e., you must show it is not simply non-Roman Catholic, but anti-Roman Catholic. It was not claimed that this same mode of worship is not practiced by the Roman Catholic denomination. Only two conscientious religious objections were taken to the school exercise or mode of worship, viz.: (1) the reading of the King James Bible instead of the Douay Bible; (2) the reciting of the Lord's Prayer as found in the King James Bible instead of as found in the Douay Bible.

The precise way these conscientious religious objections arose in the minds of the complaining parents must be kept in view. They arose out of the complainants' membership in the Roman Catholic Church, and through their religious duty of obedience to its authority in matters of religion. That is a good constitutional foundation on which to rest a claim of the constitutional right of freedom of religious profession and worship. But unless the Roman Catholic Church has a religious doctrine that Roman Catholic parents endanger the salvation of their souls by allowing their children to attend or join in this school exercise, because of the use of the King James Bible instead of the Douay Bible, the conscientious religious objections of the complaining parents fall to the ground by their own admission.   Hence, the religious doctrine of the Roman Catholic Church on these objections was a proper subject for judicial inquiry. There is nothing in the case about it, except a general statement made by the complainants' counsel and admitted by the counsel for the defendant board of education "That said church believes the King James version of the Bible to be an incorrect and incomplete translation, and that it disapproves of its being read as a devotional exercise."   That statement falls far short of saying the Roman Catholic Church imposes a religious duty on its members, at the peril of loss of salvation, to refuse to allow their children to attend or join in this school exercise in a public school in Illinois because of the use of the King James Bible rather than the Douay Bible.   The rights-of-conscience part of the case ought to have been thrown out of court for want of a showing that the complaining parents had any conscientious religious objection at all, in point of fact, to the school exercise drawn in question.

But can the ancient and seemingly irreconcilable dispute between the Roman Catholic Church and Protestant Churches over the King James Bible and the Douay Bible influence or determine, at this date, the judicial construction and application of the freedom-of-conscience guarantee of the constitution of Illinois as a limitation on the legislative power of the state to provide a system of free public schools and to prescribe the curriculum therein to give the children of the state a good common school education?   The Lord's-Prayer feature of the school exercise may be dismissed out of view, because the Bible-reading feature was thought sufficient in itself to bring the school exercise into collision with the guarantee of freedom from taxation.[17]

A parent's conscientious religious objection to reading the Bible in a public school must be, and constitutionally can be, only his own, because the constitutional right of freedom of religious profession and worship is an individual, purely personal right. The guarantee of freedom of religious profession and worship dissolves all churches into their atoms, i. e., men and women, and deals only with them individually, not with the churches of which they are voluntary members. A parent's conscientious religious objection is his own, whether it arises from his own notion of his duty to God, or from his notion of his duty to God as prescribed by the spiritual authority of his church, as his accepted authoritative expounder of his duty to God. When a parent takes his conscientious religious objection to Bible reading in a public school into court, lays it before the judge, and asks the judge to give effect to it as a constitutional limitation on the legislative power of the state over the public-school curriculum, necessarily the constitutional merit of the objection is made a judicial question. The case devolves upon the judge the duty to make a definition of the line between church and state, to mark the line with a stake, stick, or stone, so to speak. When the objection is founded on the parent's own notion of his duty to God, clearly the judge must determine the constitutional merit of the parent's conscientious religious objection. If that is not so, then any parent has it in his power, by an

---

[17] As to the Lord's-Prayer feature of the exercise, see n. 40, infra. The Supreme Court might have, and probably ought to have, treated the school exercise in question as an indivisible unit. Then, accepting their determination that it was a Protestant mode of worship, the decision might have been, and probably ought to have been, restrained to a condemnation of this particular mode of using the King James Bible as one of a series of connected, inseparable acts, which, taken together as a unit, constituted a Protestant, or anti-Catholic, mode of worship.

exercise of arbitrary will, whim, or caprice, to limit, abridge, arrest, and destroy utterly the legislative power of the state over the public-school curriculum by simply telling the judge that instruction is going on in the public schools that troubles him in his religious conscience.

If a parent not a member of the Roman Catholic Church, as a result of his own investigation, study, and reflection, comes to the conclusion that the King James Bible is "incorrect and incomplete," and the Douay Bible is correct and complete, and also comes to the conclusion that his duty to God requires him to refuse to allow his children to attend or join in a school exercise in a public school wherein the King James Bible is used, and then goes into court to stop the school exercise for that reason, clearly the judge must determine the constitutional merit of his conscientious religious objection, and cannot allow him to draw the line between church and state by the simple arbitrary process of calling what he has in his mind a conscientious religious objection.

Under and agreeably to the constitution the case is no different when a Roman Catholic parent goes into court to stop the same public-school exercise because of the use of the King James Bible, founding his conscientious religious objection not on his own investigation and study of the Bible, but on the investigation, study, and conclusion of the learned authorities of his church. The objection is still the conscientious religious objection of the party, and constitutionally cannot be the objection of the party's church, and no superior constitutional merit attaches, or can attach, to the objection, because it is founded on, or backed by, the traditions, learning, and authority of the Roman Catholic Church. If that is not so, then the mere fact that the authorities of a church, i. e., of any church, say a book, i. e., any book, is incorrect and incomplete, and disapprove of its use in

the public schools, is enough to exclude that book from
the public schools without any reference to the contents
of the book, or the way it is used, or the purpose for which
it is used, in the public-school curriculum. That means
simply that the power of the churches, singly or in combination, is superior to the power of the state, i. e., the
people, over the public school curriculum, and results
in the very evil the people by their constitution have
forbidden, viz., interference in matters of state by any
church, or by all the churches. It must not be forgotten
that, in making the principle of the separation of church
and state a part of their fundamental organic state law,
the people reserved to themselves alone the sole and exclusive right to define and draw the line of separation
in all cases of conflict between church and state, and
charged their judges with the duty of defining and
drawing the line of separation when the conflict takes the
form of a controversy justiciable by the courts. The
judge called upon to perform that duty cannot dodge it,
or abdicate his duty, by the method of adopting the view
and conclusion of any church. This point is made and
enforced clearly by the Kentucky Court of Appeals,
speaking by Judge O'Rear, in Hackett v. Brooksville
Graded School District.[18]

[18] 120 Ky., 608, 617, 618, 619. The case arose chiefly on a Kentucky statute
saying: "No books or other publication of a sectarian . . . character shall
be used or distributed in any common school; nor shall any sectarian . . .
doctrine be taught therein." The court says: "The main question, we conceive
to be, is the King James translation of the Bible, or, for that matter any edition
of the Bible, a sectarian book?" The court answered the question in the negative,
saying that it is the inside, not the outside, of a book that determines its character
as sectarian or non-sectarian, within the meaning of the Kentucky statute. And
see the excellent opinion of Appleton, J., in Donahoe v. Richards, 38 Me., 379,
398. If the majority of the Illinois court mean to say (see 245 Ill., on pp. 345–
346) they cannot inquire, in a case like the one before them, into the constitutional
merit of a Catholic's objection to the King James Bible, or a Protestant's objection to the Douay Bible, they are plainly in error.

The majority of the Supreme Court say the mere fact alone that the Roman Catholic Church disapproves of reading the King James Bible is enough to make the reading of it in the public schools an unconstitutional invasion of the rights of conscience of Roman Catholic parents. But decided cases, and continuous custom and usage over a century in Illinois and throughout the United States, are against that view. The question whether the fact, alone, that the Roman Catholic Church regards the King James Bible as "incorrect and incomplete" and "disapproves of its being used" in a public-school exercise like this one before the Illinois court, constitutes a constitutional, conscientious religious objection to the school exercise in the part of Roman Catholic parents, under the freedom-of-conscience guarantee, has been before the highest courts of several of the states of the Union. The majority of the Illinois court admit that all of them but two, Wisconsin and Nebraska, have ruled that it is not; and when the Wisconsin and Nebraska cases are read with exclusive reference to the guarantee of the Illinois constitution securing freedom of religious profession and worship, they plainly do not rule that it is; they only hold, at the most, that Bible-reading may be so conducted in the public schools as to discriminate against the Roman Catholic faith and so give ground for a conscientious religious objection to it by Roman Catholic parents.[19] It is admitted by all that the Bible has been

[19] The Wisconsin case, State v. District Board, 76 Wis., 177, arose under a provision of the Wisconsin constitution saying: "No sectarian instruction shall be allowed" in the public schools; and under a Wisconsin statute of 1883 saying: "No text-books shall be permitted in any free public school which will have a tendency to inculcate sectarian ideas." The Nebraska case, State v. Scheve, 65 Neb., 853, arose under a provision of the Nebraska constitution saying: "No sectarian instruction shall be allowed in any school or institution supported, in whole or in part, by the public funds set apart for educational purposes." See the New York law in note 39, infra. The lex scripta of Illinois is different. And

read in the public schools of Illinois from the beginning, and the custom goes back into the time when Illinois was a territory under the ordinance of 1787. The third article of that ordinance said:

"Religion, morality, and knowledge being necessary to good government and the happiness of mankind, schools and the means of education shall forever be encouraged."

That ordinance was re-enacted August 7, 1789, by the same Congress that proposed the first amendment to the federal constitution, forbidding Congress to make any "law respecting an establishment of religion, or prohibiting the free exercise thereof; or abridging the freedom of speech or of the press."[20] That amendment was proposed in Congress by Madison, removed from Jefferson's mind a great source of disappointment over the terms of the federal constitution, and means the same thing as the Virginia religious-liberty constitutional and statutory provisions of 1776 and 1785, and the religious-liberty provisions in the bill of rights of the several constitutions of Illinois of 1818, 1848, and 1870.[21] None of the friends of the rights of conscience ever saw any repugnancy between the above clause of the ordinance of 1787 and the first amendment of the federal consti-

the minority of the Illinois court discriminate these cases correctly, as it seems to me. See 245 Ill., on pp. 357, 359, 366. See an article on the Wisconsin case in 29 Am. Law Reg., 321.

[20] 1 S. & C. Ann. Ill. Stat., 2d ed., pp. 36, 47, 45. The words of the religious-liberty clauses of the Northwest Ordinance come from Massachusetts. See articles 2, 3, and amendment 11, substituted for article 3 in 1833, of the Massachusetts constitution of 1780 in Thorpe's American Charters, Constitutions, and Organic Laws, 1889, 1914; and 1 Revised Laws of Massachusetts, 18, 43, 51. Nathan Dane wrote in 1830: "Generally, when persons have asked me questions respecting the [Northwest] Ordinance, I have referred to the Ordinance itself, as evidently being the work of a Massachusetts lawyer on the face of it."   3 Hart, Am. Hist. Told by Contemporaries, 155. But the substance of the Virginia notion of religious liberty prevails in the ordinance.

[21] Reynolds v. United States, 98 U. S., 145, 162–165.

tution. Indeed, the first article of the ordinance of
1787 says:

"No person demeaning himself in a peaceable and orderly manner
shall ever be molested on account of his mode of worship, or religious
sentiments in the said territories."

The rights of conscience never have lacked watchful
and aggressive friends in Illinois, but no one ever noticed
any collision between reading the Bible in the public
schools and the guarantee of freedom of religious profession and worship. A discussion in the convention of
1870 that wrote the present Illinois constitution over a
motion to put into the proposed constitution a provision
that "The Bible shall never be excluded from the common
schools in this state, nor shall sectarian doctrines be
taught therein," shows that not a man in the convention
entertained any idea whatever that the constitution of
1870, as it went to the people, was adopted by them,
and as it now stands, forbids the reading of the Bible in
the public schools. Indeed, it seemes to have been
agreed by all in the convention that a provision in the
proposed constitution excluding the Bible from the public schools would have caused the defeat of the whole
instrument by the people. Mr. Cameron seems to have
expressed the general sense and judgment of the convention when he said:

"Custom makes law, and custom has generally established the
Bible in our public schools. Why not leave the question in the
future, as in the past, to be determined by the same law, or by such
laws as the legislature may from time to time enact?"[22]

[22] 2 Debates in C. C. of 1870, 1739–1745; 1744; 1749–1761. The minority
opinion, 245 Ill., on p. 377, speaks of "the well-known historical fact that the
framers of the constitution of 1870 expressly refused to incorporate into the
constitution a provision excluding the Bible from the public schools when the
provision was offered in that convention." I have not been able to find any
notice of such a motion in the printed report of the proceedings of the convention.
The chief debate was on a motion to insert a provision forbidding the exclusion

The majority of the Supreme Court do not deny that the judicial decisions and century and a quarter of custom and usage referred to, affirming the consistency of reading the Bible in the public schools with the guarantee of freedom of religious profession and worship, are fatal to the rights-of-conscience part of the case, but they say the case before the court was a new case, calling for new judicial thought. The only thing about the case that can be called new in Illinois jurisprudence is the setting up by the two complaining taxpayers of the right of freedom from taxation to help support any clergy or church establishment, and the claim that reading the Bible in the public schools infringed that right. This brings us to the second part of the case, i. e., the freedom-from-taxation part.

Second. As to the freedom-from-taxation part of the case:

It requires a mental strain, to say the least, to affirm, and the majority opinion does not affirm, directly at least, that reading the Bible in the public schools helps to support any clergy or church establishment. Reading the Bible in the public schools, even as a mode of worship, does not transform the teachers into an order of clergy to attend upon the offices of religion; nor does it transform the appropriation to pay the salaries of the teachers into an appropriation to help support the clergy of any

of the Bible from the public-school curriculum. Mr. Medill cleared and cooled the atmosphere by drawing the convention's attention to the fact that the motion under debate was not a proposal to exclude the Bible but a proposal not to exclude it. 2 Debates in C. C. of 1870, 1757. If no proposal to exclude the Bible was made, it is plain the reason is that everybody knew it would have been useless to make such a proposal. The statement of the majority in 245 Ill. , on p. 343, that it was proposed to add a provision forbidding the exclusion of the Bible to section 3, article 8, may be correct, sed quaere. It was proposed to add such a provision to section 4 of article 8, and to the whole article as a new section. See 2 Debates in C. C. of 1870, 1739, 1745, 1749, 1753. The only reference to the Bible I can find in the debate on section 3 was by Mr. Browning as given in note 41, infra.

sect; nor does it transform the schoolhouses into churches
or places of worship; nor does it confine the occupation
of teaching in the public schools to the members of any
sect.   If proof is needed that reading the Bible in the public schools does not transform the schoolhouses into
churches or places of worship, or the teachers into a clergy
or ministry, in the sense of the freedom-from-taxation
part of the religious-liberty guarantees, enough proof
is furnished by the fact that the property of religious
denominations used for school purposes cannot be exempted from taxation on the theory that it is used
"exclusively for religious purposes," within the meaning
of the constitution, or "actually and exclusively for public
worship," within the meaning of the revenue statute, but
can be exempted from taxation only on the theory that it
is used "exclusively for school purposes," within the meaning of the constitution, and is "property of institutions
of learning" or "property of schools," within the meaning
of the revenue statute, though it is a fact of common
knowledge that God is publicly worshiped and religious
instruction is given in all denominational public schools
owned and controlled by churches.[23]   It is very plain, in
fact and in law, that a considerable percentage of the
public-school curriculum may be devoted to Bible-reading
before a court can say the schoolhouses have become
churches or places of worship, and the teachers have
become a clergy, or ministry, within the meaning of the
freedom-from-taxation part of the religious-liberty guarantee of the bill of rights.

[23] "Such property as may be used exclusively . . . for school, religious,
cemetery, and charitable purposes, may be exempted from taxation; but such
exemption shall be only by general law." Constitution, Art. 9, Sec. 3. See
Revenue Law, Sec. 2; Monticello Female Seminary v. People, 106 Ill., 398; People
v. Ryan, 138 Ill., 263; People v. St. Francis Academy, 233 Ill., 26; McCullough
v. Board of Review, 183 Ill., 373; Re Walker, 200 Ill., 566; People v. Deutsche
Evangelisch Lutherische Jehovah Gemeinde Ungeandeer Augsburgischer Confession, 249 Ill., 132.

The taxpayer's right of freedom from taxation to help support any clergy or church establishment is not a new thing in our American fundamental law; it is as old as the Virginia religious-liberty statute of 1785, and goes back to the Rhode Island of Roger Williams of 1636; and is secured in the several Illinois constitutions in like manner and by almost the same words as in the Rhode Island laws of Roger Williams and in the Virginia statute of Thomas Jefferson, i. e., in the constitutions of 1818 and 1848 by the words:

"No man can of right be compelled to . . . erect or support any place of worship or to maintain any ministry against his consent."

And in the constitution of 1870 by the words:

"No person shall be required to . . . support any ministry or place of worship against his consent."

It is not fair to their known intelligence and keen scent for an illegal tax to say that it took the people of Illinois over a century to grasp the thought that a taxpayer's right of freedom from taxation to help support any church establishment is infringed by reading the Bible in the public schools of the state for the purpose of giving the children a good common school education.

The present constitution of 1870 deals with the authority of the legislature to provide public schools in terms of legislative duty, not in terms of legislative power.[24] To prevent the legislature from impairing the state's monopoly of control of public schools and public education by turning the function of public education over to the clergy of churches and religous denominations, a new section was put into the constitution of 1870 forbidding

---

[24] "The General Assembly shall provide a thorough and efficient system of free schools, whereby all children of this state may receive a good common-school education."   Constitution, Art. 8, Sec. 1.

any appropriation or donation of money, and any grant or donation of land or other property, to help support any schools controlled by any church or sectarian denomination. The section was not designed to limit the power of the legislature to provide public schools and prescribe the curriculum, or define what shall constitute a good common-school education; its whole end and aim was just the other way, i. e., to compel the legislature to provide public schools under state control by disabling it to provide any substitute. The principle of state-ownership, state-control, or state-monopoly of public education, was thought to be ecclesiastically threatened by the establishment of Roman Catholic parochial schools, and the new section was designed to secure and protect that principle from impairment by the legislature. For example, as one illustration of the effect of the new section, it is idle to talk in this state, except with a view to securing an amendment to the state constitution, about turning over the school taxes paid by Roman Catholic taxpayers to help support Roman Catholic parochial schools, even on the terms of doing the same thing for all other denominational parochial schools established or to be established.[25]

[25] The new section is Sec. 3 of Art. 8, entitled "Education," and reads: "Neither the General Assembly, nor any county, city, town, township, school district, or other public corporation, shall ever make any appropriation or pay from any public fund whatever, anything in aid of any church or sectarian purpose, or to help support or sustain any school, academy, seminary, college, university, or other literary or scientific institution, controlled by any church or sectarian denomination whatever; nor shall any grant or donation of land, money, or other personal property, ever be made by the state or any such public corporation, to any church, or for any sectarian purpose."

This section came before the convention as section 40 of the proposed legislative article, and was then debated. The debate shows that the two things directly and immediately within the vision of the convention were the rising Roman Catholic parochial schools in Illinois, and the New York practice of appropriating money to aid the parish-schools of all denominations in New York. The introduction of this practice into Illinois was feared. As the debate on the

This new section in the present constitution of 1870 contains a general provision forbidding any appropriation or payment of money out of any public fund "in aid of any church or sectarian purpose." It is on this provision chiefly, and especially on the words "sectarian purpose," that the majority of the Supreme Court rest their ruling that the framers of the present constitution of 1870 did unwittingly, by way of subtle implication or construction of law, the very identical thing they did not want to do, tried not to do, and knew they could not do honorably, by way of plain English words, because they knew it would have been a betrayal of the confidence of the people who sent them to the constitutional convention, and that the people of 1870 would have voted the whole constitution down, if they did it, i. e., exclude reading the Bible altogether from the public schools.[26]

It is not necessary here to attempt to exhaust the construction and application of the words "sectarian

---

Bible shows, some feared the Roman Catholic parochial school as an educational plan to undermine freedom of conscience by holding it up as a form of American political deliramentum. The word "church" was not in the section at first, but seems to have been inserted so as to make the phrase "church or sectarian," to meet a suggestion made by Mr. Hayes, for a different purpose, that a Roman Catholic majority might construe the word "sectarian" as having no application to Roman Catholics, on the ground that they constituted "the church." See 1 Debates in C. C. of 1870, 490, 492, 617 to 626; 617, 678; 2 Debates in C. C. of 1870, 1742. The section was before the Supreme Court in County of McLean v. Humphreys, 104 Ill., 378; Cook County v. The Chicago Industrial School for Girls, 125 Ill., 540; Stevens v. St. Mary's Training School, 144 Ill., 336. It may be noticed that the constitution of 1870 is not strictly logical. While it forbids any affirmative use of the taxing power to help support any denominational school or church, it expressly permits a negative use of the taxing power by way of exemption for the same purpose. See the provision set out in note 23, supra.

[26] In its "Address to the People," the convention said nothing about excluding the Bible from the public schools, though it devoted a paragraph to the subject of "common schools," saying: "We have forbidden the General Assembly and all public corporations from donating money or property to any church, or for any sectarian purpose, or for any school controlled by any church or sect." 2 Debates in C. C. of 1870, 1883, 1864.

purpose," in this provision of the new section put into the constitution of 1870, prohibiting any appropriation or payment of money out of any public fund in aid of any "church or sectarian purpose." It is enough here to exhibit and examine the intellectual process by which the majority of the Supreme Court brought reading the Bible in the public schools within the scope of the phrase, "sectarian purpose." They did not do it by the simple, direct, violent process of holding that the word "sectarian" means "religious"; their intellectual process is indirect, circuitous, and involved. They begin by assuming that the new "sectarian-purpose" tax provision in the present constitution of 1870 puts a new and expanded meaning on the old guarantee of religious profession, worship, and opinion, as a limitation on the power of the legislature to prescribe the public-school curriculum. By means of that assumption the freedom-from-taxation part of the case was drawn back under the old guarantee of freedom of religious profession, worship, and opinion in the bill of rights, where the rights-of-conscience part of the case stood, necessitating a new judicial exposition of the guarantee of freedom of religious profession, worship, and opinion, which the majority proceed to give.

There are two fallacies in this process of the majority. The first is the assumption that the new "sectarian-purpose" tax provision put in the constitution of 1870 operates as an additional and revolutionary limitation on the power of the legislature to prescribe the public-school curriculum. The new provision was not aimed directly at the public-school curriculum at all, and if the new provision reaches the curriculum at all, then, as more fully shown hereafter, it is only in case of abuse of the legislative power and duty to prescribe the public-school curriculum to gain a religious advantage for one Christian sect over others. Clearly, it cannot be sound constitutional law to adjudge that the continuation of reading the Bible in the public-school curriculum after the adoption of the constitution of 1870 just the same as before, is an unconstitutional abuse of the legislative power and duty to prescribe the public-school curriculum when reading the Bible was an old, established, commonly known and well-understood part of the public-school curriculum when the constitution of 1870 was adopted, and the constitutional convention of 1870 debated at length the question of fixing reading the Bible irrevocably in the public-school curriculum by constitutional provision, and decided to leave the legislature free, as it always had been, to exclude reading the Bible from the public-school curriculum, or to keep it in the curriculum, as might seem best to the legislature as the constitutional organ of changing public opinion.[27]

The second fallacy in the process of the majority is the one commonly called putting the cart before the horse. They missed the point that the right of freedom from taxation to help support any church establishment was intended to stand, always has stood from the days of Roger Williams in 1636 down to date, and must stand, to the right of freedom of religious profession, worship, and opinion, in the relation of means to attain and preserve an end.   If there is any relation or connection at all between the new "sectarian-purpose" tax provision in the present constitution of 1870 and the old guarantee of freedom of religious profession, worship, and opinion in the bill of rights, in respect of their application as limitations on the power and duty of the legislature to prescribe the public-school curriculum, then the latter controls the former, and not vice versa.   The taxpayer's right of freedom from taxation to aid "any church or

----

[27] See the minority opinion, 245 Ill., on pp. 372, 373, 354.

sectarian purpose" is the means of attaining and preserving the end of freedom of religious profession, worship and opinion; the end controls and determines the
means, not the means the end. In so far as they may
be related or connected, the new "sectarian-purpose"
tax provision does not enlarge and expand the meaning
of the old guarantee of freedom of religious profession,
worship, and opinion, but, on the contrary, the old guarantee of freedom of religious profession, worship, and
opinion controls, defines, and limits the meaning of the
new "sectarian-purpose" tax provision, when the two
are applied in combination, as the majority opinion applies them, to limit the power and duty of the legislature
to prescribe the public-school curriculum. As already
shown, decided cases, and unchallenged usage and custom of over a century, established and fixed the law to be,
that the old guarantee of freedom of religious profession,
worship, and opinion does not forbid the legislature to
authorize reading the Bible in the public schools. And, as
stated above, the majority of the court do not deny that,
in express words at least.

But through the fallacious intellectual process indicated the majority did in fact bring the freedom-from-
taxation part of the case within and under the old guarantee of freedom of religious profession, worship, and opinion
in the bill of rights; and to decide the freedom-from-
taxation part of the case they entered upon a new and
original exposition of the old guarantee of freedom of
religious profession, worship, and opinion, expanding it
beyond its former meaning and scope as a limitation on
the legislature. They say "Protestant, the Catholic, the
Mohammedan, the Jew, the Mormon, the free-thinker,
the atheist," "all stand equal before the law," and "the
law knows no distinction between the Christian and the
Pagan, the Protestant and the Catholic." As a general

statement, no exception can be taken to that; but when it comes to the practical application of the general statement, a distinction must be taken in respect of its application (1) to the taxpayer's right of freedom from taxation to aid "any church or sectarian purpose," and (2) to the individual's right of freedom of religious profession, worship, and opinion. The general statement applies and is true, when the law is dealing with people as taxpayers, seeking the aid of the courts to protect their freedom from taxation to aid "any church or sectarian purpose." But the general statement does not apply and is not true, when the law is dealing with people as professors of their religion and worshipers, and maintainers of their opinions about religion, seeking the aid of the courts to protect their freedom of religious profession, worship, and opinion. The atheist has no religion to profess and nothing to worship; the freedom the law secures to the atheist is freedom of opinion and speech on the subject of religion, not freedom of religious profession and worship. A like rule applies to the Pagan. The Pagan's public worship of his gods may be suppressed by the legislature as a thing "inconsistent with the peace or safety of the state." No man or association of men can make a thing, belief, or practice, "religious profession and worship" by calling it so.[28] The guarantee of freedom of religious profession, worship, and opinion enacts into the law of the land the principle of Christian toleration, not the principle of Pagan toleration of the ancient Greeks and Romans. The principle of toleration as practiced by the Greeks and Romans rested upon the thought, as Gibbon says, that all gods and religions are equally true to the people, equally false to the philosopher, and equally

[28] Mormon Church v. United States, 136 U. S., 1, 49, 40; Davis v. Beason, 133 U. S., 333; Ill. Const. of 1870, Art. 2, Sec. 3.

useful to the statesman.[29] The principle of Christian toleration, on the other hand, made a part of our fundamental law by the guarantee of freedom of religious profession, worship, and opinion, is widely different, and rests upon the thought that there is but one God and one religion — the Christian religion — one truth, which every man is free to search and find out for himself in the way that seems to him the best, unmolested by any other man, human power, or authority whatsoever. The atheist and the Pagan have the benefit and protection of that principle, for it allows and protects freedom of opinion for or against the Christian religion.[30]

The majority say "the free enjoyment of religious worship includes freedom not to worship.[31] They use that doctrine to put atheists, Pagans, free-thinkers, Mohammedans, Jews, and all non-Christians into the same class with Christians, compounding them all up together into one consolidated mass under the guarantee of freedom of religious profession, worship, and opinion, to enable them to use that guarantee to complain as taxpayers that any mention of the Bible in the public

[29] Milman's Gibbon, Decline and Fall of the Roman Empire, Ch. 2.

[30] See Sec. 16, Virginia Bill of Rights of 1776, in n. 4, supra; Bacon's Essays on Truth, Unity in Religion, Atheism.

[31] 245 Ill., on p. 340. In the Girard Will Case, 2 How., 127, 198, in 1844, after quoting the religious-liberty guarantees in the Pennsylvania Constitution of that date, which are substantially the same as those in the Illinois bill of rights, Story, J., said the words were broad enough to include "all sects whether they believe in Christianity or not, and whether they were Jews or infidels." The passage is obiter. Judge Story evidently did not mean that infidels have the right of freedom of religious profession and worship, of which they can make no use. Judge Story's generality is erroneously used by Cassoday, J., as I think, in his separate opinion in 76 Wis., 177, 210; and the generality has traveled through the courts far and wide, but always as obiter dictum. See In re Walker, 200 Ill., 566, 573. The reason is the pseudo-liberal sound of the generality, there being a current opinion that a denominationalist must be narrow-minded, and a man who is against religion must be liberal-minded, though the men who put through the religious-liberty guarantees were denominationalists.

schools constitutes an appropriation or payment of money out of a public fund in aid of a "church or sectarian purpose." This judicial doctrine that freedom to worship means freedom not to worship cannot be accepted without proof. The majority of the court persistently decline to draw any distinction in their practical application to men and things between freedom of religious profession and worship, and freedom of religious opinion; between freedom of religious profession, worship, and opinion, and freedom from civil and political disabilities on account of religion or religious opinion; between freedom of religious profession, worship, and opinion, and freedom from taxation to aid any "church or sectarian purpose."

Taking the guarantee of freedom of religious profession and worship, standing by itself in connection with the legally-enjoined duty of Christian toleration, as it stood in the Virginia constitution of 1776, and as it stands in the Illinois bill of rights, what does the guarantee mean as a limitation on the power of the legislature? What do the people mean by "religious profession and worship" as a limitation on the power of the legislature? In their ordinary, natural signification, the words of the guarantee of freedom of religious profession and worship denote an affirmative right, not a negative right; a right to do (facere) not a right not to do (non facere); a right exercisable and enjoyable by affirmative act or acts, and not a right exercisable and enjoyable by a negative forbearance or forbearances. There can be no doubt that, historically, the object of the right of freedom of religious profession is one certain, determinate religion, i. e., the Christian religion; and the object of the right of freedom of worship is equally certain and determinate, i. e., God, Almighty God, the jealous God, worshiped by all Christians. The words of the bill of rights of the constitutions of Illinois of 1818 and 1884 leave no room to think that the historical meaning was changed. They declare:

"That all men have a natural and indefeasible right to worship Almighty God according to the dictates of their own consciences."

"And that no preference shall ever be given by law to any religious establishments or modes of worship."

The bill of rights of the Illinois constitution of 1870 changes the words of the declaration, saying:

"The free exercise of religious profession and worship, without discrimination, shall forever be guaranteed."

"Nor shall any preference be given by law to any religious denomination or mode of worship."

There is no direct reference to Almighty God, but the constitution of 1870 begins with an expression of gratitude "to Almighty God for the . . . religious liberty which He hath so long permitted us to enjoy," and looks "to Him for a blessing upon our endeavors to secure and transmit the same unimpaired to succeeding generations." The rights of conscience of Christians and non-Christians under the guarantee of freedom of religious profession, worship, and opinion, are unquestionably sacred and equal before the law as individual, purely personal rights; all Christians and non-Christians alike are equally secure and are equally protected, all are equally under the shield and panoply of the state, in the exercise and enjoyment of their rights of conscience; but all do not stand in one compounded, consolidated class, for all cannot, and do not, exercise the rights of conscience in the same way; as they do, and must, stand in different classes in point of fact, so they do, and must, stand in different classes in point of law, and the lines between the classes lawfully may be made visible in the management of state affairs and state institutions and in the discharge of state powers, duties, and functions, when the state has to spend money on religion in the proper conduct of its affairs, institutions, powers, duties, and functions and has to select the religion or mode of worship.[32]

If the guarantee of freedom of religious profession and worship secures to men, as it unquestionably does, the positive affirmative right to profess the Christian religion and to worship God in all usual Christian modes, subject to the legally-enjoined duty of Christian toleration, then its operation and effect as a limitation on the legislature is plain, viz.: it forbids the legislature to discriminate between Christian sects; to give one sect a preference over others; it requires the legislature to stand neutral on the points that divide the Christian sects; to treat them all with absolute equality and impartiality; it secures equal rights to all Christian sects and special privileges to none; it does not require the legislature to give a preference to any non-Christian religion, to infidelity, to atheism, or to Paganism; it leaves the legislature free to raise and unfurl the banner of Christianity stripped of the divisive points and bearing all the non-divisive points common to all Christians; or bearing all the divisive points with absolute equality and impartiality, as the American flag bears a star for each state. The guarantees of freedom from civil and political disabilities

[32] Jefferson's statute of 1785 emphasized freedom of opinion, and the Virginia bill of rights of 1776 emphasized freedom of religious profession and worship. The terms of all of the prior and contemporaneous constitutional and statutory provisions in the several states guarding the rights of conscience show clearly they were intended to denote an affirmative, equal right to profess the Christian religion; and show clearly that the idea was the state may deal impartially with the Christian religion without being against it or without excluding it altogether from state functions. It is an easy matter to find and examine them in Thorpe's American Charters, Constitutions, and Organic Laws, taking each of the original thirteen states separately. Advanced liberals like Roger Williams and Jefferson saw clearly that it was necessary to add freedom of religious opinion and speech to freedom of religious profession and worship in order to protect completely the rights of conscience.

on account of religious opinion, and freedom from taxation to help support any church establishment, come into play as practical temporal prohibitions, incapacitating and disabling the legislature to uphold and advance the banner of united Christendom by the un-Christian mode of imposing civil or political disabilities on account of religious opinions, whether for or against the Christian religion, or by the mode of taxing people to help support any church establishment, Christian or non-Christian.

It is very plain that a Christian taxpayer can have no constitutional ground for complaint to a court, under the original Virginia religious-liberty guarantees of 1776 and 1785 as they appear in the Illinois bill of rights, when the legislature authorizes a Christian mode of worship in the conduct of the affairs of the state into which religion may enter, if the legislature does not discriminate against his own religious profession and modes of worship; if it imposes no civil or political disability upon him; and if it does not tax him to support any church establishment. Can a non-Christian taxpayer have any constitutional ground for complaint to a court in such case? If he can, it must be the ground that the Christian mode of worship authorized by the legislature and employed by the state in the conduct of its affairs infringes his freedom of religious profession and worship, or his freedom of opinion. It is believed the non-Christian taxpayer has no constitutional ground for complaint to a court, under the original Virginia religious-liberty guarantees as they appear in the Illinois bill of rights, of a Christian mode of worship authorized by the legislature and employed by the state in the conduct of its affairs, when the sole ground of his complaint is that the mode of worship is Christian. There is nothing in the text or history of the original Virginia religious-liberty guarantees as they appear in the Illinois bill of rights, nor is there any judicial authority, that lends any support whatever to the view that a non-Christian taxpayer is not getting the full measure of his constitutional individual personal rights under those guarantees so long as he is left free to profess and maintain his opinion about the Chirstian religion, is not subjected to any civil or political disability on account of his religious opinion, and is not taxed to help support any church establishment, Christian or non-Christian. The Virginia leaders of the political movement that resulted in the incorporation of the religious-liberty guarantees in the Illinois bill of rights had no intention to divorce the state, i. e., the people, altogether from the Christian religion, to impose upon the state an intolerant policy of silence and suppression as to the Christian religion, or to put the state into a position of constitutional hostility or indifference to the Christian religion. If anything like that had been the intention or plan of the Virginia leaders they never could have caried the people with them as they did. It must be remembered the Virginia leaders were not originators of anything new; they were but followers of Roger Williams, an ordained minister and teacher of the Christian religion.[33] Mr. Justice Story concisely expresses in his work on the Constitution the effect of the guarantees of religious liberty, as they appear in the Virginia constitution of 1776 and in the Virginia statute of 1785, in the Illinois bill of rights, and in the first amend-

---

[33] In 2 Story, Constitution, Sec. 1874, it is said:

"Probably at the time of the adoption of the [federal] constitution, and of the [first] amendment to it now under consideration, the general if not the universal sentiment in America was, that Christianity ought to receive encouragement from the state, so far as was not incompatible with the private rights of conscience and the freedom of religious worship. An attempt to level all religions and to make it a matter of state policy to hold all in utter indifference, would have created universal disapprobation, if not universal indignation."

ment of the federal constitution, as limitations on the power of organized government, as follows:

"The real object . . . was, not to countenance, much less advance Mohametanism, or Judaism, or infidelity, by prostrating Christianity; but to exclude all rivalry among Christian sects, and to prevent any [governmental] ecclesiastical establishment, which should give to a hierarchy the exclusive patronage of . . . the government. [They] thus cut off the means of religious prosecution (the vice and pest of former ages), and of the subversion of the rights of conscience in matters of religion, which had been trampled upon almost from the days of the Apostles to the present age."[34]

Public education is, by our Illinois constitution, historically and by express words, a state function, and is not an ecclesiastical function. And the truth is, none of the original religious-liberty guarantees as they appear in the Virginia constitution and statute and in the Illinois bill of rights, either the one for freedom of religious profession, worship, and opinion, or the one for freedom from civil and political disabilities on account of religion, or the one for freedom from taxation to help support any church establishment, ever had any serious application or force as limitations on the power of the legislature to provide public schools and prescribe the public-school curriculum. That is brought out very pointedly and plainly by the fact that the framers of the present constitution of 1870 thought a new section was necessary to keep the legislature from displacing state-ownership, state-control, or state-monopoly of public education by substituting church-ownership, church-control, or church-monopoly of public education. There can be no question

[34] 2 Story, Constitution, Sec. 1877. In Sec. 1875 Judge Story says: "It yet remains a problem to be solved in human affairs, whether any free government can be permanent where the public worship of God and the support of religion constitute no part of the policy or duty of the state in any assignable shape. The future experience of Christendom and chiefly of the American States, must settle this problem as yet new in the history of the world, abundant as it has been in experiments in the theory of government." This was written in 1833.

whatever that, before the insertion of the new "sectarian-purpose" tax provision in the present constitution of 1870, the legislature was perfectly and completely free to spend money on reading the Bible either in the state-owned public schools or in church-owned denominational public schools, as might seem best to the legislature.   In many states, though it had never been the practice in Illinois, the legislature used to appropriate money to help support church-owned denominational public schools, i. e., parochial schools or parish-schools, giving religious instruction in the divisive elements or doctrines peculiar to their own faith.   Such legislative expenditure of public money never was thought to be repugnant to the principle of separation of church and state in the religious-liberty guarantees in the ordinary and usual form of the Virginia constitution of 1776 and statute of 1785, so long, at least, as the legislature treated all Christian sects equally and impartially.

The Virginia guarantees of religious liberty as they appear in the Illinois bill of rights deal with adults and church establishments and religious profession, worship, and opinion, not with little children and public schools and common school education.   Children have no free-dom of religious profession, worship, and opinion, in the sense of those religious liberty guarantees, either in fact or in law, from the very nature of the case, until they reach "the age of discretion."   Exactly what age that is has not been determined, so far as I know, in a way that operates as a limitation on the power of the legislature to prescribe the public-school curriculum.   The school laws and usages of a Christian state, as Illinois is judicially declared to be, in so far as they authorize reading the Bible in the public schools, cannot be viewed as it seems to me, as the majority of the Superme Court view them, viz., as laws and usages, compelling religious profession,

worship, and opinion by children, but rather must be
viewed as laws and usages forbidding adults to put obstructions in the way of the religious instruction of children.   That view is not inconsistent with the letter of the
religious-liberty guarantees, but is, on the contrary, in
entire accord and harmony with their letter, history, and
spirit, for they declare political principles that are not
against the Christian religion, that were founded upon
it, and were drawn out of it, and were not drawn from
any other source, though whether they were rightly
drawn from the pure fountain is not for the lawyer or
judge to stop to inquire.[35]

It is through the medium of parents' rights that the
Virginia religious-liberty guarantees as they appear in the
Illinois bill of rights must operate to limit, if they limit
at all, the power of the legislature to put reading the
Bible in the public-school curriculum.[36]   The courts occa-
sionally say, and always tacitly assume,[37] that the Virginia

[35] It is sometimes said the American notion of religious liberty as a right government must protect is of French origin.   That is because Thomas Jefferson was in
France from 1784 to 1789.

[36] By the common law, the father has the right as against third persons to
prescribe the religious profession and worship of the child; and the mother on
the death of the father; as between parent and child, the religious education of the
child is a parental duty.   See 21 Am. and Eng. Ency. of Law, 2d Ed., 1057;
29 Cyc., 1585.   In exercise of the parens-patriae power of the state over infants
lodged in them by the legislature, the courts generally — exceptions to the rule
being rare — require a guardian to educate the ward in the religion of the ward's
father.   2 Story, Equity Jurisprudence, Ch. 35; Cowls v. Cowls, 3 Gilman, 435;
29 Cyc., 1585.   The parens-patriae power of the state over infants is a very
extensive power.   Modern juvenile court acts are a striking example of its
plenary scope.   How far the legislature may disregard the wishes of parents
in prescribing Bible-reading as a part of the public-school curriculum is perhaps
not now a very practical question, because parents can control the legislature
quite as effectively as a written constitution through their political right to vote.
Parents have practically no voice as to the strictly secular part of the public-
school curriculum.

[37] See Spiller v. Woburn, 12 Allen, 127, 129; Donohoe v. Richards, 38 Me., 379,
398.   All the decided cases bearing directly on reading the Bible in the public
schools are cited in the majority and minority opinions in 245 Ill., 334.

religious-liberty guarantees as they appear in the Illinois bill of rights have a "spirit," and, in the view of the courts, it is this supposed "spirit " of the religious-liberty guarantees, rather than the letter of them, that limits the exercise by the legislature of its power to put reading the Bible in the public-school curriculum. It is very plain, and is firmly established constitutional law, as already shown, that the religious-liberty guarantees, in their ordinary and usual form, as in the Virginia constitution of 1776 and Virginia Statute of 1785, and in the Illinois bill of rights, do not absolutely forbid the legislature to put reading the Bible in the public-school curriculum. But by their terms, as applied to adults and church establishments, they do forbid the legislature to discriminate between Christian sects; to give one sect a preference over others; and they do enjoin upon the state a policy of absolute equality and impartiality toward all Christian sects, i. e., a policy of equal rights to all Christian sects, and special privileges to none; in other words, they expressly require the religious policy of the state to be "non-sectarian," so far as adults and church establishments are concerned. In obedience to this equal, impartial, "non-sectarian" religious policy expressly enjoined upon the state by the religious-liberty guarantees in the bill of rights, the state of Illinois always has rested its religious policy upon two principles, viz.: (1) The principle of authorizing the practice of the modes of worship, and the teaching of the doctrines, peculiar to each Christian sect, without any discrimination, i. e., the divisive, denominational principle, as in the state penitentiary, state reform schools, state charitable institutions, state militia, and state legislature; and the principle has been extended and applied to embrace Jewish modes of worship and doctrines; (2) The principle of excluding all the divisive, denominational elements or doctrines of the Christian faith, and authorizing only modes of worship and instruction in elements or doctrines of the faith common to all Christians, i. e., the non-divisive, non-denominational, united-Christian principle, as in the public schools. This latter principle applied by the state in exercise of its control of public education is, as the courts are in the habit of saying, agreeable to, and enjoined by, the "spirit" of the religious-liberty guarantees, rather than by their letter. But this judicially-supposed "spirit" of the religious-liberty guarantees restraining the legislative power to put Bible-reading in the public-school curriculum is nothing more nor less than the political-religious opinion of the parents of the pupils in the public schools manifested and made effective by the parents through their exercise of their political rights to vote and to hold office. There is nothing in the religious-liberty guarantees in the ordinary and usual form, as in the Illinois bill of rights, that forbids the legislature to extend and apply the former divisive, denominational principle to the matter of reading the Bible in the public schools, leaving parents free to select the denominational instruction they wish their children to have; the opinion of parents is what always has stood in the way; but if the opinion of parents changes, favors the divisive, denominational principle, and wants it tried in the public schools, there is nothing in the religious-liberty guarantees of the bill of rights that forbids the legislature to give effect by law to that change of parental opinion.

Turn now to the new "sectarian-purpose" tax section put into the present constitution of 1870; fit the section into the old religious-liberty guarantees in the bill of rights; harmonize it with those guarantees and with the section allowing the legislature to exempt from taxation by general law property used exclusively for school purposes

or for religious purposes, and its effect as a limitation
on the power of the legislature over the public schools
becomes plain enough. It forbids the legislature to abolish
state control, state ownership, or state monopoly of public schools and public education, by substituting church
ownership or church control, or ecclesiasticism, in public
education. It forbids the legislature in the management
of the state-owned public school or state monopoly of
control of public education to discriminate. against any
Christian sect, or to give one Christian sect a legal preference over others; in other words, to use the concise,
classical phrase, it compels the legislature to give equal
rights to all Christian sects and special privileges to none,
in the state-owned monopolistic public schools. It does
not forbid the legislature to put reading the Bible in the
public-school curriculum; not does it forbid the legislature
to base reading the Bible in the public schools either
on the non-divisive, non-denominational, united Christian
principle, or on the divisive, denominational principle,
leaving parents free to elect the divisive, denominational
instruction they wish given to their children. But it
does forbid the legislature to spend public money to aid
church-owned schools giving denominational religious
instruction; if the state wants to give denominational
religious instruction, it must do it in its own schools or
not at all. A different conclusion cannot be reached
without affirming that the word "sectarian" as used in
the phrase in the section, "in aid of any church or sectarian purpose," means "religious"; but the majority
of the Supreme Court do not say, and never can say
upon any basis of reason, that the word "sectarian"
as used in that phrase in the section means "religious,"
though the logic of their opinion necessarily leads to the
result, as hereinafter shown, of striking out the word "sectarian" and substituting the word "religious" in its place.

Agreeably to the "sectarian-purpose" tax section, and without violating it, the Illinois legislature, i. e., the people of Illinois acting through the legislature, may deal with the educational problem of reading the Bible in the public schools on any one of three different principles of political, religious, or non-religious policy, viz.: (1) The principle of secularism, excluding reading the Bible altogether; (2) The non-divisive, non-denominational, united Christian principle, letting in reading the Bible or religious instruction in elements or doctrines of the faith common to all Christians; (3) The divisive, denominational principle, letting in reading the Bible or religious instruction in elements or doctrines peculiar to each Christian sect, leaving parents free to elect the divisive, denominational instruction they wish their children to enjoy. Each of these principles is "non-sectarian"; not one of them is "sectarian" within the meaning of the phrase "in aid of any church or sectarian purpose" in the new section put into the present constitution of 1870.

It may be admitted there is room for doubt on the non-sectarianism of the third principle, i. e., the divisive, denominational principle. On the question whether the third principle is "sectarian" within the meaning of the phrase, "church or sectarian purpose," put in the constitution of 1870, it need not be doubted, and is not doubted, that the framers of the present constitution of 1870 intended to say this, viz.:

"The legislature may authorize or forbid reading the Bible in the public schools, as it likes; but if the legislature authorizes reading the Bible in the public schools, it is forbidden to authorize the teaching of any divisive, denominational tenet or doctrine peculiar to any Christian sect and not common to all Christian sects."

The only quest'on of law is, however, whether the framers of the constitution used words apt and proper

to express that intention.   It is an axiomatic rule of law
that courts are permitted to deal only with the bare
existence of legislative power, the question of the propriety, wisdom, justice, and policy of the use of legislative power being carefully and jealously reserved to the
people acting through the legislature; and it is an equally
axiomatic corollary of that rule that the words of the
written state constitution do not strip the state of legislative power unless they do so plainly or by fair intendment and construction of law; and doubt as to the fair
legal effect of the written words is fatal to a claim that
they cut off legislative power.   The words of the section
in hand are broad enough to embrace all privately and
publicly owned and controlled institutions as well as
schools and institutions of learning privately or publicly
owned and controlled; and it has been decided that
charitable and reformatory institutions owned or controlled by churches are embraced by the words of the
section.[38]   It is not sound constitutional law, as it seems
to me, to say the word "sectarian" excludes the divisive,
denominational principle of religious instruction from
the public schools for the same reason that it is not sound
constitutional law to say that the word "sectarian" excludes denominational religion from other public institutions like the penitentiary, charitable institutions, etc.,
or to say the policy of the federal government is "sectarian," because it spends money to provide the soldier

[38] Chicago Industrial Schools for Girls *v.* Cook County, 125 Ill., 540.   It is
hard to determine all the court intended this case to stand for, but I think it rules
the point stated in the text, and rules it correctly.   The court goes near to saying
that the word "sectarian" in the phrase "church or sectarian denomination whatever" means "religious."   See the remarks of Mr. Browning in n. 41, infra.
The case certainly does not rule that an expenditure of money to provide the
inmates of state-owned and state-controlled charitable and reformatory institutions with denominal religious worship and instruction is an unconstitutional
appropriation of money in aid of a "church or sectarian purpose."

in the army or the sailor in the navy with the denominational religious worship and instruction he calls for. If
the denominational principle of religious instruction is
excluded from the public schools altogether by the constitution, that result must flow from the word "church,"
and not from the word "sectarian," in the phrase, "church
or sectarian purpose." It is practically impossible, and
hardly would be consistent with the rights of conscience,
for the state to provide denominational religious instruction in the public schools by teachers fairly and reasonably
deemed incompetent and unfit by the spiritual heads of
the several religious denominations or churches. But a
power in the spiritual heads of denominations or churches
to object to the competency and fitness of teachers
selected by the state to give instruction in the public
schools in the peculiar doctrines of their faith as a part
of a good common-school education, is not clearly repugnant to the principle of state control of public education.
A court ought to decline to rule, as it seems to me, especially in the face of a clear constitutional declaration
in favor of state control, and against ecclesiastical control, of public· education, that an ambiguous, equivocal
word in the state constitution is enough to strip the
state of the important power to supervise and control the
giving of religious instruction as part of a good common
school education inside or outside the public schools.[39]

[39] The section put into the present New York Constitution of 1894 corresponding to the section in hand of the Illinois Constitution of 1870 clearly forbids the
New York legislature to authorize denominational instruction in New York
public schools, and restricts the New York legislature to non-denominational
religious instruction, or to the principle of secularism excluding religious instruction altogether as the only alternative.   The New York section reads: "Neither
the state, nor any subdivision thereof, shall use its property or credit or any public
money, or authorize or permit either to be used, directly or indirectly, in aid or
maintenance, other than for examination or inspection, of any school or institution of learning wholly or in part under the control or direction of any religious
denomination, or in which any denominational tenet or doctrine is taught."

It is now easy to exhibit clearly the essential simplicity, in point of law, of the freedom-from-taxation part of the case the Supreme Court had to decide. The Illinois legislature has never undertaken since the present constitution of 1870 to authorize or forbid reading the Bible or religious instruction or worship in the public schools; it has devolved its power and discretion in that regard upon the local school boards throughout the state. Sometimes, as in Chicago for example, the local school board, adopting the principle of secularism, either does not provide for or forbids reading the Bible or religious instruction or worship in the public schools under its jurisdiction. The local school board in the case before the Supreme Court authorized religious instruction and worship in the public schools under its jurisdiction to the extent of the school exercise in question. The principle of equality and impartiality toward all Christian sects the local school board tried to apply evidently was the principle of non-divisive, non-denominational, united

New York Constitution, Sec. 123. Corresponding constitutional provisions in twenty-three states are set out chronologically in 8 Am. State Rep., 414. Illinois is one of the first, if not the first. Quaere, whether the men who wrote these new provisions were not sometimes loose in their choice of words to express the popular thought. Our loose, long-winded state constitutions, plus fierce and erratic state judicial construction and application of them, is the mother of the referendum. Logically, state courts ought not to be allowed to pass on the constitutionality of acts approved by the electors, and probably will not be if the referendum gets a firm footing.

Religious education in public schools is under able and cool discussion in England at the present time. A committee appointed to consider the subject, called "The Educational Settlement Committee," has reported a plan of religious instruction. The committee agreed on these three general propositions: (1) Religious instruction and training form a necessary part of national education; (2) Denominational instruction should be under teachers approved by the spiritual head of the denomination; (3) Denominational schools and training colleges belonging to the great organic religious bodies should be part of the national educational system. See articles in the Contemporary Review for October, 1910, and February, 1911, and in The Tablet of February 11 and February 18, 1911. For a brief statement of the present English plan under the Birrell Act of 1906, see 1 Hall, Educational Problems, 191, note.

Christian teaching and worship. The chief objection, the one thought fatal, urged against the local school board was that the selection of the King James Bible, of itself and necessarily in a constitutional sense, because the Roman Catholic Church disapproves .of the King James Bible, injected a divisive, denominational element or doctrine, and made the school exercise anti-Roman Catholic, i. e., a discrimination against the Roman Catholic faith and in favor of the Protestant faith. The answer is, the objection only shows, at the most, that the King James Bible is non-Roman Catholic, not that it is, of itself and necessarily in a constitutional sense, anti-Roman Catholic. In the same way the Douay Bible is non-Protestant, but it is not, of itself and necessarily in a constitutional sense, anti-Protestant. The selection of the Douay Bible for use in the public schools would not necessarily give a preference to the Roman Catholic faith over the faith of all Protestant sects.[40]

[40] See Hysong v. School District, 164 Pa., 629, where all the members of the school board and most of the pupils were Catholics. If the Bible "teaches the doctrine of some sect .   .   . we ought to be able to say what sect." —Minority opinion, 245 Ill., on p. 375. The reciting of the Lord's Prayer as found in the King James Bible seems an error of judgment under the circumstances; but it is difficult to understand how a court could say it was unconstitutional, or even unreasonable as an exercise of delegated discretion by a subordinate body like a school board. The idea of the majority of the Supreme Court that the teachers in the public schools are not competent or fit to read the Bible fairly and impartially (245 Ill., on pp. 347, 348), may be true enough in point of fact; but in point of constitutional law and in the case before it, the court was legally bound to presume them competent, impartial, and fair.

The minority of the Supreme Court say on p. 359: "We think it apparent that it must be held, from a constitutional standpoint, that all parts of the Bible can be read in the public schools or that it must be excluded as an entirety from the public schools." But when the non-denominational principle of reading or instruction is adopted, it very well may become a judicial question, under constitutional and statutory provisions in some states, whether parts of the King James Bible not in the Douay Bible,or differently translated, or parts of the DouayBible not in the King James Bible, or differently translated, can be read without giving a legal preference to one sect, or making a discrimination against another. The statement of Sullivan, C. J., in State v. Scheve, 65 Neb., 853, 884, seems to me to

The majority cite the case of the Jew, and say both the King James Bible and the Douay Bible are certainly anti-Jew, or "the Bible, in its entirety, is a sectarian book as to the Jew and every believer in any religion other than the Christian religion and as to those who are heretical or who hold beliefs that are not regarded as orthodox." There can be no doubt that the legislature of Illinois cannot make an adult Jew read the Bible or take instruction in the Christian religion, if he does not want to. But that was not a question in the case. Nor was it a question in the case whether the legislature of Illinois can compel the children of Jewish parents to read the Bible or take instruction in the Christian religion in the public schools against the wishes of their parents. The case of a Jew complaining to a court of reading the Bible or instruction in the Christian religion in the public schools raises the question whether the constitution vests in a Jew, not as a Jew, but as a taxpayer, a constitutional right to command the intellectual and physical force of the state, exerted by its courts, to exclude reading the Bible or instruction in the Christian religion from the public-school curriculum altogether, merely because it is the Bible or the Christian religion. The answer is, the constitution does nothing of the kind. The Jew may complain to a court as a taxpayer just exactly when, and only when, a Christian may complain to a court as a taxpayer, i. e., when the legislature authorizes such reading of the Bible or such instruction in the Christian religion in the public schools as gives one Christian sect

---

be sound under Nebraska lex scripta, viz.: "Whether the practice of Bible-reading has taken the form of sectarian instruction in a particular case is a question for the courts to determine upon evidence." In the case before the Illinois Supreme Court there was no claim that denominational parts of the Bible were read or that the Bible was read with unfair denominational emphasis. The whole claim was that the King James Bible, in its entirety, is anti-Roman Catholic.

a preference over others. The religious case of the Jew against the state for reading the Bible or instruction in the Christian religion in the public schools, is simply this: If the state puts reading the Bible or instruction in the Christian religion in the public-school curriculum for the benefit of children of Christian parents, then the state ought to spend some more money to put instruction in the Jewish religion in the public-school curriculum for the benefit of children of Jewish parents; and in any event children of Jewish parents ought to be excused from the Bible-reading part of the curriculum. But the religious case of the Jew is for the people and the legislature, not for the Supreme Court, to deal with as becomes a Christian religious-liberty state.

The majority's argument, though purporting to be an argument against a union of church and state, really comes round to the old, obsolete argument in favor of a union of church and state, i. e., a state not united with any church is in germ an atheistic state — the argument the religious-liberty guarantees and the state's practice under them always have been supposed to overthrow as sophistical. In the view of the majority of the Supreme Court the Christian religion is "sectarian" as to the Jew, and the Jewish religion is "sectarian" as to the Christian; and so on down the catalogue of religions, each one is "sectarian" as to every other. There is nothing left for the religious-liberty state of Illinois but atheism; and the legislature is free to spend the taxpayers' money on that, unless atheism also is "sectarian," and the majority appear to say that it is. In short, the majority hold the word "sectarian" means "religious"; if a thing is "religious," it is "sectarian"; and the constitution forbids the legislature to have anything to do with it if it involves any expense, however microscopic; as the minority say, nothing is left "except that which has been sterilized," as the French school-books, by striking out the name of God and substituting the word "reason" or "humanity." Logically and practically, under this decision, the constitution excludes the Bible, the Christian religion, and every other religion, from every state-owned and state-controlled institution as well as from the state-owned public schools.   There is no escape from that result.[41]

The central thought of the opinion of the majority, around which the whole opinion revolves, is in the following sentence: If reading the Bible or religious instruction is allowed in the public schools, "a religious contest may be expected at each election of a school director, to determine which sect [i. e., specifically, Roman Catholic or Protestant] shall prevail in the school."   The legal error in the sentence is obvious.   The constitution does not allow any sect to "prevail in the school," but requires that all sects be allowed to "prevail in the school" equally and without discrimination.   A school director, elected on a denominational religious platform, can do nothing, if the courts do their duty, to make the denominational religious views of his party "prevail in the

[41] In the constitutional convention of 1870, Mr. Browning, described as "admittedly a profound lawyer" by Hand, J., in Burke v. Snively, 208 Ill., 328, 363, took up the clause forbidding any appropriation to help support any school "controlled by any church or sectarian denomination whatever," and subjected it to "a very brief analysis," as follows: "What is a sectarian denomination, and how is the question to be settled?   Is it a characteristic of a sectarian school that the Bible is introduced into it and read and its principles inculcated there?   What constitutes sectarian control?   Is it the reading of the Bible, or the religious opinions of those who govern or those who teach?   Who is to determine it?   What rule of law is there by which it is to be determined?   Is it intended to exclude all the control of all Christian denominations in our schools?   Then who is to have control of them?   Is it that class of the community alone who scoff at all revealed religion, who repudiate all Christian teaching, who denounce the truths of the Bible?   Are they to have the control of all the schools of this country?   The section does not exclude them.   On the contrary, the state, and every municipal corporation of the state, may make appropriations of public money for the support of schools under the control of avowed infidels, but not a dollar in support of those controlled by religious denominations." 1 Debates in C. C. of 1870, 625.

school," i. e., to force them on to the children of parents who object.[42]

In so far as the majority say the division of Christians into organized churches or sects is the cause of the exclusion of reading the Bible from the public schools, they are probably correct in point of fact. There is no element of law in the position, however. But the way that practical result has come about, wherever it has come about in Illinois, as a consequence of the division of Christians into organized churches or sects, may be noticed, to the end of showing the net constitutional result of the opinion of the majority of the Supreme Court. The principle of non-divisive, non-denominational or united Christian Bible reading in the public schools always has been tolerably satisfactory to the members of most Protestant churches or sects, and the principle worked well in practice in the public schools until the entrance of children of Roman Catholic parents in considerable numbers. The Roman Catholic Church has stood since the Council of Trent, 1545–1563, for the divisive, denominational principle in public education. It has been reinforced, to some extent, but for different reasons, to the extent that establishing parochial schools is reinforcement, by the Lutheran Church, and by the High Church Episcopalian party, and, upon grounds of their own, by the Jews. For reasons commonly supposed to be legal and constitutional, flowing from the religious-liberty guarantees in the bill of rights, but being in truth only practical political reasons flowing from changeable, but seemingly unchangeable,[43] public opinion,

[42] The majority's "religious-contest" idea on p. 347 is singled out and replied to by the minority on pp. 346, 347.

[43] The religious-liberty guarantees have reacted powerfully on men's minds and turned them to the points of the faith common to all Christians. Non-denominational Bible-reading in public schools has contributed to this current of opinion.

the only alternative to uncompromising or uncompromised adherence to the divisive, denominational principle always has been, and is now, the principle of secularism excluding the Bible altogether from the public schools. The principle of secularism, applied in that way, enters and prevails in public schools, wherever it has entered and prevailed, not because the members of any Christian church or sect like it or want it, but ex necessitate as the easiest practical political solution of a very difficult, explosive problem in public education.[44]

The precise constitutional effect of the opinion of the majority of the Supreme Court is, then, to change the principle of secularism, excluding the Bible from the public schools, from a principle of state governmental policy to a principle of state governmental power, i. e., to a rule of fundamental organic state law, expressed by the people in the state constitution, cutting down the scope of the power of the legislature over the subject of public education   The opinion makes Illinois the only state in the Union, I think, that puts a constitutional padlock on the Bible in public schools.

The exact legal criticism of the opinion of the majority of the Supreme Court is that it carries the Supreme Court's authority to determine the scope of legislative power far out on the wide sea of governmental policy, with nothing to guide and restrain the course of the

---

The fear that it may ultimately obliterate the lines separating Christian sects seems to be one of the grounds of opposition to united Christian teaching in English public schools.

[44] Perhaps the exclusion of the Bible from our public schools is only a technical exclusion after all, like the exclusion of English law-books from the courts of some of the states at an early date. See the articles on "moral training" in public schools in Religious Education for February, 1911. In the Girard Will Case, 2 Hoℵ., 126, 133, 153, 199–201, the testator expressed a wish that "the purest principles of morality" be taught in Girard College. Mr. Binney argued that this affirmatively recommended the Bible, saying: "Where are they found? Whoever searches for them must go to the source from which a Christian man derives his faith — the Bible." The court accepted the argument.

Supreme Court but the crooked cord of the private
opinion of the judges for the time being.   In other words,
it substitutes the will of the judges for the time being for
the expressed will of the people.[45]   It may be quite true
that the rule, "The truths of the Bible . . . do not
come within the province of the public school,"[46] is the
wisest present-day rule of educational policy for Illinois —
the one best suited to existing conditions everywhere
throughout Illinois, as well as in Chicago and other large
cities.   But the Supreme Court had no right to concern
itself with that question of policy.   The only question
before the court was the question of law, whether the
people of Illinois expressed that rule, "The truths of the
Bible . . . do not come within the province of the
public school," by any written words in their state constitution of 1870 as a legal limitation on the power and
duty of the legislature to prescribe a public-school curriculum "whereby the children of this state may receive a
good common-school education.[47]

[45] In 245 Ill., on p. 377, the minority directly charge the majority with usurpation of the power of the people to amend the state constitution.

[46] 245 Ill., on p. 349.

[47] "The scope of judicial inquiry in deciding the question of power is not to be
confused with the scope of legislative considerations in dealing with the matter
of policy. . . . The earnest conflict of serious opinion does not suffice to
bring [the matter of policy] within the range of judicial cognizance." C., B. &
Q. R. Co. v. McGuire, 31 Sup. Ct. Rep., 259, 263; 219 U. S., 549, Hughes, J.

"It is therefore no mere technicality to point out that the American judges do
not, as Europeans are apt to say, 'control the legislature,' but simply interpret
the law. . . The will that prevails is the will of the people, expressed in the
constitution they enacted. . . . To construe the law, that is, to elucidate
the will of the people as the supreme lawgiver, is the beginning and end of their
duty." Bryce, Am. Com. (Ed. of 1910), 253.

"The candid citizen must confess that if the policy of the government upon
vital questions affecting the whole people is to be irrevocably fixed by decisions
of the Supreme Court the instant they are made in ordinary litigation between
parties in personal actions, the people will have ceased to be their own rulers,
having to that extent practically resigned their government into the hands of
that eminent tribunal." — Lincoln's First Inaugural, quoted in 1 Story, Constitution, ed. 5, p. 276, note a, by Judge Cooley.

It is very evident the majority of the Supreme Court have not settled for all time the educational problem they went outside their sphere to meddle with; at the most they have only changed the form of the problem from a legislative and administrative one to a constitutional one, to be solved, sooner or later, by a general public discussion and a vote of the electors of the state on a proposal to amend the state constitution by reversing this judicial opinion and restoring the freedom of the people, acting through their legislature and local school boards, unvexed by the Supreme Court, to put reading the Bible in the public-school curriculum or to leave it out, as seems to them the best for the children, i. e., the future state.[48]

[48] The matter of the Bible in public schools long has been a troublesome political question in Australia.   The ordinary referendum was applied to it in South Australia in 1895, in Victoria in 1904, in Queensland in 1908.   See an article on The Referendum in Operation in Switzerland, Australia, and the United States, The Quarterly Review, April, 1911, 509, 535–537.

The opinion of the majority of the Supreme Court, in addition to being wrong in itself, as I think, in its sweeping condemnation of reading the Bible in public schools as being forbidden by the state constitutions, goes far beyond the facts of the case, as suggested in note 17, supra, and on that account ought to be classed as extra-judicial, agreeably to the familiar maxim thus stated by Marshall, C. J.: "It is a maxim not to be disregarded, that general expressions, in every opinion, are to be taken in connection with the case in which those expressions are used.   If they go beyond the case, they may be respected, but ought not to control the judgment in a subsequent suit where the very point is presented for decision," as, e. g., in this instance, Bible-reading disconnected with reciting the Lord's Prayer and singing sacred hymns.   Cohens v. Virginia, 6 Wheat., 264, 399.

II

FREEDOM OF THE PRESS IN THE UNITED STATES[a]

Immediately after the Declaration of Independence, the several states reorganized under written constitutions, most of them containing declarations or bills of rights, and liberty of the press among the rights declared. To-day all state constitutions declare in some phrase the right of liberty of the press, and the bill of rights of the federal constitution, as the first ten amendments are commonly called, has a declaration of the right of liberty of the press. Side by side with the declaration, preceding or following it closely, we find in the earliest and present state constitutions and in the federal constitution a declaration of the twin-sister right of religious liberty. The First Amendment to the federal constitution declares:

"Congress shall make no law respecting an establishment of religion or prohibiting the free exercise thereof; or abridging the freedom of speech, or of the press."

This federal declaration is typical of the declaration in the original state constitutions, as, for example, that of Massachusetts in 1780, still in force, which says:

"The liberty of the press is essential to freedom in a state. It ought not, therefore, to be restricted in this commonwealth."

Very many state constitutions to-day adopt the definition of liberty of the press given by Hamilton in his

[a] [Am. Sociol. Soc. Proc., 1914, IX, pp. 67–116.]

argument in Croswell's case in New York in 1804.[1] As fairly typical of these present Hamiltonian state constitutions, we may take the declaration of liberty of the press in the present Illinois constitution of 1870, which reads as follows:

"Every person may freely speak, write, and publish on all subjects, being responsible for the abuse of that liberty; and in all trials for libel, both civil and criminal, the truth, when published with good motives and for justifiable ends, shall be a sufficient defense.[2]

The nearly if not quite unanimous expressed view of our judges always has been, and is, that the constitutional declarations of liberty of the press are only declaratory of the English common-law right protected by the English courts at the time of the Revolution, like, for example, the declaration of the right of trial by jury, and are not expansive of that right or creative of a new right unknown to the English common law. They accept the definition of the right given by Blackstone, Lord Mansfield, and Lord Kenyon as the right line of constitutional law separating liberty from license. Blackstone said in the fourth book of his Commentaries, first published in 1769:

"The liberty of the press is indeed essential to the nature of a free state; but this consists in laying no previous restraints upon publications; and not in freedom from censure for criminal matter when published.[3]

[1] People v. Croswell, 3 Johns. Cas., 337.

[2] See Thorpe, American Charters, Constitutions, and Organic Laws, Poore, Federal and State Constitutions. New York and New Jersey had no constitutional declarations of liberty of the press until 1821 and 1844. Connecticut and Rhode Island lived under Charles II's charters of 1662 and 1663 until 1818 and 1842.

[3] 4 Bl. Co., 151–53. Lord Mansfield, like Blackstone, thought a man's mind could be free though the law forbade him to publish his thoughts. See citations on p. 519, note 14.

In 1784 Lord Mansfield said:

"The liberty of the press consists in printing without any previous license, subject to the consequences of law.

"The licentiousness of the press is Pandora's Box, the source of every evil. Miserable is the condition of individuals, dangerous is the condition of the state if there is no certain law (or what is the same thing), no certain administration of law to protect individuals or to guard the state."[4]

In 1799, seven years after Fox's Libel act of 1792, Lord Kenyon said:

"The liberty of the press is dear to England. The licentiousness of the press is odious to England. The liberty of it can never be so well protected as by beating down the licentiousness. I said that the liberty of the press was dear to Englishmen, and I will say that nothing can put that in danger but the licentiousness of the press.

"The liberty of the press is neither more nor less than this, that a man may publish anything which twelve of his countrymen think is not blameable, but that he ought to be punished if he publishes that which is blameable.[5]

American judges early took the view that this English common-law definition that "liberty of the press consists in printing without any previous license, subject to the consequences of law," is a correct definition of the right of liberty of the press declared in our first constitutions, and that, therefore, those constitutional declarations left standing the English common law of libel as declared by the English courts after 1694, when the last English licensing act expired and Parliament refused to renew it, and before the American Revolution. This view was first expressed by Chief Justice McKean of Pennsylvania in 1788 in Oswald's case, wherein the editor

---

[4] Dean of St. Asaph's case, or Rex v. Shipley, 4 Douglas, 73, 170.

[5] Rex v. Cuthill, 27 St. Tr., 674. See the comment in 2 Stephen, History of the Criminal Law of England, 348, note 1, concluding: "Hobbes is nearly the only writer who seems to me capable of using the word 'liberty' without talking nonsense."

of a newspaper was punished by the summary criminal process of contempt of court for a publication censuring his adversary and one of the judges in a pending case to which the editor was the defendant.[6] The same judge expressed the same view in 1797 in his charge to the grand jury in Philadelphia that indicted Cobbett for an alleged seditious publication in Porcupine's Gazette censuring the administration at Washington.[7] The view lies at the base of the federal Sedition act of 1798 and its judicial administration by Judges Chase and Patterson of the United States Supreme Court and Judges Griffin, Hitchcock and Peters of the United States District Court, as appears from their summing up to the juries in the prosecutions of Callender, Cooper, Haswell, and Lyon under that act for alleged seditious publications censuring the administration of John Adams.[8] The view was expressed by Chief Justice Parker of Massachusetts in 1825 in Blanding's case, which was a criminal prosecution for a publication in a newspaper defamatory of an innkeeper in his calling.[9] And the view was expressed more or less directly by the judge in prosecutions for blasphemous publications in the courts of different states, by Chief Justice Kent in Ruggles' case in New York in 1811, Judge Duncan in Updegraph's case in Pennsylvania in 1824, by Chief Justice Clayton in Chandler's case in Delaware in 1837, and by Chief Justice Shaw in Kneeland's case in Massachusetts in 1838.[10] The view forms the whole of the foundation of the modern and rather numerous cases in state courts wherein

[6] Respublica v. Oswald, 1 Dallas, 319.

[7] Cobbett's case in Wharton's St. Tr.

[8] The cases of Callender, Cooper, Haskins, and Lyon are in Wharton's St. Tr. and in Federal Cases, Nos. 8646, 14704, 14865, 15834.

[9] Commonwealth v. Blanding, 3 Pick., 304.

[10] 8 Johns. Rep., 290; 11 Serg. and R., 394; 2 Harr., 553; 20 Pick., 206.

strangers to pending and not pending lawsuits were fined or imprisoned under the summary criminal process of contempt of court for publications censuring judges for their administration of the law. And the view perhaps accounts in part for the common judicial classification of the right of liberty of the press under the head of "qualified privilege" in the ordinary law of libel along with the privilege of an employer giving the character of a servant to publish defamatory falsehood about the servant in the honest belief it is truth. One of the latest judicial expressions of the view is by Mr. Justice Holmes speaking for the majority of the United States Supreme Court in 1906 in Senator Patterson's case, on error to the Colorado Supreme Court under the Fourteenth Amendment, wherein the learned Justice said :

"The main purpose of such constitutional provisions [declaring liberty of the press] is 'to prevent all such previous restraints upon publications as had been practiced by other governments,' and they do not prevent the subsequent punishment of such as may be deemed contrary to the public welfare."[11]

The work which the constitutional declarations threw upon the judges was to draw the line of law that separates liberty from license, and the question here is whether the judges are right in saying Blackstone, Lord Mansfield, and Lord Kenyon did the work for them by anticipation.

At the time of the Revolution the English common law divided unlawful publications into four species of libel, viz.: defamatory libels, or publications defamatory of personal or professional reputation; seditious libels, or

---

[11] 205 U. S., 454. Text-writers state the law in the same way. See, e. g., Willoughby, Constitution, student's ed., pp. 327–28; Townshend, Slander and Libel, 2d ed., sec. 252. That constitutional liberty of the press means more than freedom from previous censorship, see State v. McKee, 73 Conn., 19, 28, and carrying it much further and perhaps too far, see Louthan v. State, 79 Va., 196; Ex parte Harrison, 212 Mo., 88.

publications defamatory of existing public officers, government, institutions, and laws; blasphemous libels, or publications defamatory of the Christian religion; obscene and immoral libels, or publications defamatory of England's existing standard of public morality. If a given publication did not encounter any one of these four species of libel, then it was a lawful publication in exercise of the right of liberty of the press. By that negative process of exclusion, the sphere of liberty of the press was outlined.

The great subjects of public discussion in England at the time were religion and politics, and especially politics. The King's Bench was the criminal court of practically exclusive jurisdiction of all criminal prosecutions for libel. Lord Mansfield became its lord chief justice in 1756, holding the office until 1788, when he was succeeded by Lord Kenyon, who held the office until 1802. Lord Mansfield laid it down clearly that the English common-law test to be applied to determine the seditious character of publications on politics was their tendency as opinion-makers to create and diffuse among the people an ill opinion of existing public officers, government, institutions, and laws. The same rule governed publications on religion; their tendency to create and diffuse among the people an ill opinion of the Christian religion was the test to be applied to determine whether they were unlawful as blasphemous libels. Likewise publications were unlawful as obscene and immoral libels if their tendency was to create and diffuse among the people an ill opinion of existing standards of morality; and publications were unlawful as defamatory libels if their tendency was to create and diffuse among the people an ill opinion of the personal or professional reputations of the persons referred to, though here it seems actual objective tendency as a matter of fact was more emphasized and important than in the other cases of seditious, blasphemous, and obscene and immoral libels, where supposed tendency as a matter of abstract, subjective speculation seems to have been controlling and decisive. The remedy for a publication alleged to be a defamatory libel was either a civil action for damages by the person whose personal or professional reputation was involved, or a criminal prosecution by the Attorney-General. The remedy for a publication alleged to be a seditious libel, a blasphemous libel, or an obscene and immoral libel, was a criminal prosecution. In a civil action for a defamatory libel the truth of the publication was a decisive answer, the burden of proving the truth being on the defendant author and publisher. In all criminal prosecutions, whether for defamatory libel, seditious libel, blasphemous libel, or obscene and immoral libel, the truth or falsity of the publication was of no importance. "The greater the truth the greater the libel" was the maxim in all criminal prosecutions.

When the legal test of the lawfulness of a publication is its tendency as an opinion-maker to create and diffuse among the people an ill opinion of existing things, the tribunal to apply the test is a matter of great importance. Lord Mansfield laid it down with his usual simplicity and lucidity of expression that the exclusive tribunal to apply the test of tendency was the judges of the King's Bench sitting in banc to hear and decide a motion by the defendant in arrest of judgment after the verdict of a jury finding the defendant guilty; that the jury had nothing whatever to do with the tendency of the publication as an opinion-maker, and consequently that the trial had no right to leave the question of tendency to the jury in any shape or form, but must withdraw that question from the jury by directing the members of the jury that they had nothing to do with it and must not assume to pass on it. Erskine's fight for liberty of the press at the bar of the King's Bench was from a legal point of view a procedural fight to substitute the twelve men in the jury-box in the place of the judges on the bench on the issue of libel or no libel. Taking his stand on the maxim dividing the province of the jury from the province of the judge, assigning questions of fact within the issue to the jury and questions of law to the judge, Erskine first contended for the substantive-law point that the "intent" or "criminal intent" of the author and publisher was the true test of libel or no libel, and the question of "intent" or "criminal intent" was a question of fact for the jury exclusively. Erskine was defeated by the opinion of Lord Mansfield in the Dean of St. Asaph's case in 1784, Mr. Justice Willes alone dissenting but disagreeing with Erskine. The fight for the tribunal was transferred to Parliament. In Fox's Libel act of 1792 Parliament declared in favor of Mr. Justice Willes' view of the English common law on the procedural point of the tribunal authorized to apply the test of tendency. The act required the trial judge to submit the question of tendency to the jury, and declared the jury was the exclusive tribunal on the question of tendency only when it decided the question in favor of the defendant, but left the judges as the exclusive tribunal when the jury found the question against the defendant. In short, after Fox's act the prosecution had to convince both the jury and the judges of the bad tendency of the publication as an opinion-maker, while the defendant had to convince only the jury of its good or indifferent or harmless tendency as an opinion-maker. The result of the fight for the tribunal was, as Lord Kenyon expressed it, that before Fox's act liberty of the press in England meant nothing more nor less than that a man could publish anything the judges sitting in banc as subsequent or ex post facto censors of the press thought was not blamable, while after Fox's act a man could publish anything a jury sitting as subsequent ex post facto censors of the press thought was not blamable; but if the jury thought the publication was blamable, there was a second thought coming from the judges, who could set aside the verdict of the jury against the defendant and substitute in its place their own verdict in his favor if they thought the publication was not blamable, meaning by "not blamable" having no bad tendency as an opinion-maker to excite and move the people to change existing things, and by "the people" the multitude or "the masses."

Lord Mansfield and his associates did fine men and send them to jail for their published political opinions because they thought the published political opinions in question had a bad tendency to excite the people to put men out of office and put others in their places, to subvert the existing government, institutions, and laws of the country as it was called by creating and diffusing through the community an ill opinion of them. And they did in fact fine men and send them to jail for their published opinions on the Christian religion, because they thought the published opinions in question had a bad tendency to subvert Christianity by creating and diffusing an ill opinion of it among the people.[12]

---

[12] For the English common law of libel at the time of the Revolution, see 2 Stephen, History of the Criminal Law of England, chaps. 24 and 25, on "Sedition" and "Blasphemy"; the first editions of Starkie on Libel and Holt's Libel Laws. And see 1 May, Constitutional History of England, chaps. 9 and 10, on "The Press, and Liberty of Opinion"; Bury, A History of Freedom of Thought, in "Home University Library" published by Henry Holt & Co. Fox's Libel act is 32 Geo. III, c. 60, and is in Stephen's History, supra, p. 344. See Lord Blackburn's explanation of the legal effect of Fox's act, in Capital and Counties Bank v. Henty (1882), 7 App. Cas., 741, 770–76.

As to publications on religion at the time of the Revolution, the English judges were pronouncing them blasphemous under the law laid down by Lord Hale in 1676, viz.:

"Christianity being parcel of the laws of England, therefore to reproach the Christian religion is to speak in subversion of the law."[13]

In 1767 Lord Mansfield said:

"The eternal principles of natural religion are part of the common law; the essential principles of revealed religion are part of the common law; so that any person reviling, subverting, or ridiculing them may be prosecuted at common law."[14]

In 1797 Lord Kenyon told the jury in the prosecution of a publisher of Paine's Age of Reason that "the Christian religion is part of the law of the land."[15] As it was popularly put, the English judges were proceeding on the view that God had a reputation to maintain and needed the help of the English common law to support it.

At the time of the Revolution, then, the line of English common law separating liberty of the press from licentiousness was the opinion of the judges of the King's Bench on the tendency of publications, true or false, to excite and move the people to change the existing order; and that meant the opinion of Lord Mansfield, whose influence in the King's Bench was commanding and controlling. Is it true, as our judges keep telling us, that the original declarations of liberty of the press did nothing but forbid previous censorship, putting American judges into the shoes of Lord Mansfield as subsequent or ex post facto censors of publications, true or false?

---

[13] Rex v. Taylor, 3 Keble, 607.

[14] Chamberlain of London v. Evans, cited by C. J. Clayton in State v. Chandler, 2 Harr. (Del.), 556, and in Odgers, Libel and Slander, 2d ed., 443.

[15] Rex v. Williams, 26 St. Tn., 653, 704.

With reference to the English common law of seditious publications, Sir James Fitzjames Stephen begins his story of it in his History of the Criminal Law of England with these observations:[16]

"Two different views may be taken of the relation between rulers and their subjects. If the ruler is regarded as the superior of the subject, as being by the nature of his position presumably wise and good, the rightful ruler and guide of the whole population, it must necessarily follow that it is wrong to censure him openly; that even if he is mistaken his mistakes should be pointed out with the utmost respect, and that whether mistaken or not no censure should be cast upon him likely or designed to diminish his authority.

"If on the other hand the ruler is regarded as the agent and servant, and the subject as the wise and good master who is obliged to delegate his power to the so-called ruler because being a multitude he cannot use it himself, it is obvious that this sentiment must be reversed. Every member of the public who censures the ruler for the time being exercises in his own person the right which belongs to the whole of which he forms a part. He is finding fault with his servant. If others think differently they can take the other side of the dispute, and the utmost that can happen is that the servant will be dismissed and another put in his place, or perhaps that the arrangements of the household will be modified. To those who hold this view fully and carry it out to all its consequences, there can be no such offence as sedition There may indeed be breaches of the peace which may destroy or endanger life, limb, or property, and there may be incitements to such offences, but no imaginable censure of the government, short of a censure which has an immediate tendency to produce such a breach of the peace, ought to be regarded as criminal.

Sir James goes on to say that the present English law of seditious publications as stated by him in his Digest of the Criminal Law of England is the result of a "compromise" between these two "extreme views" of the relation between governors and the governed.[17] The

---

[16] II, 299.

[17] II, 298, note 1, and 300.

second view, however, that the governed are the master and the governors are the servants, cannot be regarded as "extreme" by an American judge. That view was promulgated in the Declaration of Independence, was vindicated by the Revolutionary War, and was made the foundation stone of the law of the land by our written constitutions. The supreme power of the people always has been a fixed legal fact in the United States, admitting of no discussion inside the courts. As related to this fixed legal fact, the constitutional declarations of liberty of the press do not involve any theory that the people are "wise and good" as Sir James Stephen suggests. They simply involve the idea that power denotes duty, expressed over and over again in English law books, commencing with the second one by Bracton, saying that the holder of the supreme power in the community ought to use it to display his reason and judgment rather than the vigor of his power.[18] When the supreme power is definitely lodged by law in the people, to enable them to exercise their power and perform their duty with reason and judgment and not with the vigor of mere power, they must have education and the means of education. The framers of our written constitutions did not leave this legal idea to rest for security on a necessary legal inference from the legal fact of the supremacy of the people, but expressly declared it in the constitutional declarations of the right of liberty of speech and of the press.

Many of the publications on politics in the Colonies before the Revolution were seditious and even treasonable under the English common law and its administration. One of the objects of the Revolution was to get

---

[18] 1 Bracton, Laws and Customs of England, trans. by T. Twiss, 39, 41; Coke's report of his interview with James I telling him that the king cannot sit on the bench to decide cases in his own proper person, Prohibitions Del Roy, 12 Coke's Rep., 63.

rid of the English common law on liberty of speech and of the press. The first Continental Congress in 1774 enumerated the right of liberty of the press as one of five invaluable rights without which a people cannot be free, and declared its importance consisted

"in the advancement of truth, science, morality, and arts in general, and in the diffusion of liberal sentiments on the administration of government, the ready communication of thought between subjects, and the consequential promotion of union among them whereby oppressive officers are shamed or intimidated into more honorable and just modes of conducting affairs."[19]

This declaration evidences the view that the right of liberty of the press is confined to matters of public concern such as those enumerated, viz.: the arts and sciences, morality, public officers and their conduct of public affairs, and does not extend to matters of private concern.

The declaration also evidences the view that truth and the right of liberty of the press are one and inseparable, the duty to publish the truth being the right expressed in terms of duty. As obedience to law is liberty, so obedience to truth is liberty of the press.

The Virginia Religious Liberty statute of 1777 declared not only the right of liberty to profess religion and to worship God, but also the right of liberty of opinion, of speech, and of the press on the subject of religion, and eliminated the English common-law subjective test of supposed bad tendency in the following words:

"It is time enough for the rightful purposes of civil government for its officers to interfere when principles break out into overt acts against peace and good order."

This distinction is brought out more fully in one of Dr. Furneaux's letters to Blackstone published in

---

[19] Cited by Kent, J., in People v. Croswell, 3 Johns. cases, 337, 391.

England and in Philadelphia before the Virginia Religious Liberty statute, wherein Dr. Furneaux said:

"If it be objected, that when the tendency of principles is unfavorable to the peace and good order of society, as it may be, it is the magistrate's duty then, and for that reason, to restrain them by penal laws; I reply, that the tendency of principles, though it be unfavorable, is not prejudicial to society, till it issues in some overt acts against the public peace and order; and when it does, then the magistrate's authority to punish commences; that is, he may punish the overt acts, but not the tendency, which is not actually hurtful; and therefore his penal laws should be directed against overt acts only, which are detrimental to the peace and good order of society, let them spring from what principles they will; and not against principles, or the tendency of principles.

"The distinction between the tendency of principles, and the overt acts arising from them is, and cannot but be, observed in many cases of a civil nature, in order to determine the bounds of the magistrate's power, or at least to limit the exercise of it, in such cases. It would not be difficult to mention customs and manners, as well as principles, which have a tendency unfavorable to society; and which, nevertheless, cannot be restrained by penal laws, except with the total destruction of civil liberty. And here the magistrate must be contented with pointing his penal laws against the evil overt acts resulting from them . . . . Punishing a man for the tendency of his principles is punishing him before he is guilty, for fear he should be guilty."[20]

While this distinction between the tendency of principles and overt acts arising from principles had special reference to the subject of religion and to nonconformists in the Christian religion, yet it applies equally to any

---

[20] Cited and quoted by Clayton, C. J., in State v. Chandler, 2 Harr. (Del.) 553, 576. For an account of Dr. Furneaux, see the Dictionary of National Biography, edited by Leslie Stephen. See Locke's first "Letter concerning Toleration" in 1689. As Jefferson himself said, there is not an original thought or word in the Virginia Religious Liberty statute. Jefferson drew it from the laws of Rhode Island, Maryland, and Pennsylvania, and from the best English literature on religious liberty and liberty of the press. I do not know that Jefferson used Dr. Furneaux's letter to Blackstone, but he was looking for literature like that.

matter of public concern within the sphere of the right of liberty of the press. There is no difference between principles and opinions. And as respects the phrase "overt acts," since speaking is acting, and writing, printing, and publishing are acting, all publications are overt acts. But publications are not overt acts against peace and good order simply because of their supposed bad tendency as opinion-makers. As illustrating the practical application of the distinction, reference may be made to the Mormon cases in the United States Supreme Court holding the practice of polygamy, and publications teaching and advising the practice of polygamy, to be overt acts against peace and good order though arising out of opinions called religious,[21] and to Most's case in the New York Court of Appeals holding anarchists' publications teaching and advising the use of force to be overt acts against peace and good order.[22]

Reading the original declarations of the right of liberty of the press in the light of their history and without reference to judicial opinions, evidently they obliterated the English common-law test of supposed bad tendency to determine the seditious or blasphemous character of a publication, and hence obliterated the English common-law crimes of sedition and blasphemy; shifted the law of obscene and immoral publications from the region of libel to the region of public nuisance;[23] and left standing

[21] Davis v. Beason, 133 U. S., 333; Mormon Church v. United States, 136 U. S., 1.

[22] People v. Most, 171 N. Y., 423. It has been decided that constitutional religious liberty protects "eternity celestial polygamy" in the next world (Hilton v. Roylance, 25 Utah, 129); that it does not protect a Salvation Army drummer beating his drum out of season (State v. White, 64 N. H., 48), nor a Christian Scientist healing the sick without a doctor's license (State v. Marble, 72 Oh. St., 21; People v. Pierson, 176 N. Y., 201) nor a fortune teller (State v. Neitzel, 69 Wash., 567).

[23] A standard English lawbook, 2 Russell, Law of Crimes, 7th English and 1st Canadian eds., 1875, classifies indecent, obscene, and immoral publications as public nuisances, not as libels as in former editions.

only the law of defamatory publications, materially modifying that. Separating publications as they do into those on matters of public concern and those on matters of private concern, and applying only to the former, and truth being the dividing line between lawful and unlawful publications, the declarations wiped out the English common-law rule in criminal prosecutions for defamatory libel, "The greater the truth the greater the libel.' The declarations threw on American judges in civil and criminal actions for defamatory libel the new work of drawing the line between matters of public concern and matters of private concern, and of determining what is truth in a publication on a matter of public concern.[24]

When, as ordinarily happens, a publication on a matter of public concern reflecting on personal or professional reputation, as by imputing disgraceful motives and conduct, contains both statements of fact and expressions of opinions, the two have to be separated. It is not true that liberty of the press makes lawful every published expression of opinion on matters of public

---

[24] It must be remembered that the accepted judicial view is that the constitutional declarations did not touch the English common-law rules making truth a defense to a civil action for defamatory libel, and of no importance in a criminal action. See Com. v. Blanding, 3 Pick., 304, in 1825; Patterson v. Colorado, 205 U. S., 454, in 1906. In most if not all the states constitutional or statutory provisions, following the New York statute of 1805, hereinafter referred to, expressly make truth a defense in criminal as well as civil actions for defamatory libel, many putting on the defense of truth Hamilton's rider, hereinafter considered, viz., "truth, with good motives, for justifiable ends." There is a wide difference between a rule of substantive law shutting out the truth altogether, and a procedural rule placing the burden of proving truth on the defendant, instead of making the plaintiff prove falsity, the latter being the more natural and logical procedural rule. The true reasons for the English common-law rules about truth in libel cases are unknown, so far as I can see. Reasons as plenty as blackberries are given in the lawbooks, but they are obvious inventions. Lord Campbell's act in 1843, 6 and 7 Vict., c. 96, s. 6, provides that in a criminal prosecution for a defamatory libel, "the truth of the matters charged may be inquired into, but shall not amount to a defense, unless it was for the public benefit that the said matters charged should be punished."

concern. Published opinions may be true, or false and
defamatory, just as published statements of facts may be
true, or false and defamatory. If published opinions on
matters of public concern are false and defamatory because of their tendency to infuse into the minds of men
suspicion, distrust, and dislike for other men, and so influence their conduct, such published false opinions are
just as unlawful as false statements of facts having the
same tendency. An opinion ordinarily is but an inference from facts. The correct test of the truth or falsity
of an opinion on a matter of public concern seems to be
the one laid down by the better modern English judges
in the law of fair comment on matters of public concern,
viz.: Assuming the facts to be true, is the inference or
opinion an allowable one?   Is it an inference or opinion
capable of being drawn from those facts?   In other words,
could or might a fair-minded average man draw the
inference or opinion in question from the facts proved
or admitted to be true?   This leaves a wide margin for
the play and action of conflicting opinions on matters of
public concern, leaving the restraint of truth as to matters
of fact until removed by the legislature.[25]

The true view of the original declarations of liberty of
the press would appear to be, then, that they wiped out
the English common-law test of supposed bad tendency as

[25] Campbell v. Spottiswoode, 3 B. and S. 769 (1863), especially the opinion
of Blackburn, J., Hunt v. Star Newspaper Co. [1908], 2 K. B., 309. The right
of liberty of the press originated outside the English courts, for all practical purposes in Milton's "Speech for the Liberty of Unlicensed Printing," in 1644, but
it did not really begin to become a legal right protected by the English courts
until the opinions of Lord Ellenborough in Tabbert v. Tipper, 1 Campbell, 350,
in 1808, and in Carr v. Wood, 1 Campbell, 354, note, in 1813, commencing what
is called the law of "fair comment on matters of public concern," on which see
generally the article on "Fair Comment" by W. Blake Odgers, Q. C., in 6 Encyc.
of the Laws of England, 2d ed., 5, and Pollock, The Law of Torts, 9th ed., 262.
Note that it has been written in civil actions for defamatory libel exclusively.
where the rule that truth, simpliciter, is a defense has obtained for a long time.

opinion-makers, and substituted the test of truth, as the dividing line between lawful and unlawful publications on matters of public concern, the restraint of truth being inflexible as applied to matters of fact until altered by the legislature,[26] but flexible enough as applied to matters of opinion to legalize any allowable opinion on any matter of public concern which any fair-minded average man could or might form from the facts, thus securing to every man the right to publish truth on any matter of public concern, the right of the editor and owner of a newspaper being no greater than the right of any other individual; and making the right to own and operate a printing press a common private-property right, because the public-education right can be exercised practically and conveniently only through the printing press.

The practical securities provided by existing law to compel observance of the restraint of truth in publications on matters of public concern, are the English common-law civil action for damages and criminal prosecution for defamatory publications. Unless published falsehood on matters of public concern has a tendency to defame personal or professional reputation or to cast suspicion on the title or quality of property, it cannot be the foundation of either a civil action for damages or a criminal prosecution. Published truth on matters of public concern cannot be defamatory, under the original declarations at least, as distinguished from the Hamiltonian declarations. But the adequacy of the power of government in the United States to punish those who fabricate and spread non-defamatory false news having a tendency to mislead the people on matters of public concern is not open to doubt. Coke says that before the Norman

---

[26] The constitutional declarations only forbid the abridgement of liberty of the press, and a legislative removal of the restraint of truth enlarges the liberty, and hence is constitutional.

Conquest "the author and spreader of false rumors amongst the people had his tongue cut out if he redeemed it not by the estimation of his head." The statute of Westminster I, in 1275, made the spreading of false news or tales a misdemeanor punishable by fine and imprisonment.[27]

Striking out some of the reasons for this old law and substituting new ones suited to the times, it gives a fairly correct measure of the power of government in the United States to stop the fabrication and spreading of non-defamatory false news likely to mislead the people on matters of public concern, without abridging the constitutional right of liberty of the press, which only requires the government to leave plenty of room for the allowable opinions of original authors and publishers like Dr. Johnson, taking "good care to see that the Whig dogs do not get the better of the argument."

The constitutional declarations did not legalize indecent, obscene, and immoral publications, however true, because of their want of educational value. Criticism of judicial decisions sustaining state statutes prohibiting such publications, and of acts of Congress excluding them from the mails, only shows a misunderstanding of the meaning of liberty of the press as a public-education right.[28] The test of indecent, obscene, and immoral publications under such state statutes and acts of Congress commonly adopted by the state and federal courts is the one laid down in England in 1868 by Lord Chief Justice Cockburn, viz., "whether the tendency of the

---

[27] Encyc. of the Laws of England, 2d ed., 640, title "News."

[28] Schroeder, Obscene Literature and Constitutional Law, is devoted to the thesis that such statutes unconstitutionally abridge liberty of the press, but the contrary always has been assumed in the courts, and is expressly decided in United States v. Harmon, 45 Fed. Rep., 414; In re Banks, 56 Kan., 242; State v. McKee, 73 Conn., 18; State v. Van Wye, 136 Mo., 227; State v. Warren, 113 N. C., 683.

matter charged as obscenity is to deprave and corrupt those whose minds are open to such immoral influences, and into whose hands a publication of this sort may fall."[29] The test may be open to fair criticism as being too subjective in point of form, offensive to Americans devoted to equality as savoring too much of the Star-Chamber previous censor morum of the "masses" as distinguished from the "classes." In actual judicial administration, however, the test seems to work down to whether the publication in question has a tendency to shock the moral sense of the average, normal head of a family, which is more objective in point of form at least, and shifts indecent, obscene, and immoral publications into the region of public nuisance. It may be that the existing test prevents truthful and useful publications of educational value on sex hygiene, commercialized vice, and other subjects, heretofore tabooed, but now thought by many fit topics for public discussion. If the courts decline to change their administration of the existing test enough to support those who are of that opinion the legislatures are there to supply the remedy. The constitutional declarations only forbid the abridgment, not the enlargement, of the right to publish on matters of public concern.

A picture, or play, including a moving-picture show, may be an exercise of the right of liberty of the press if its subject is a matter of public concern. But statutes or municipal ordinances creating previous censors of moving-picture shows to prevent the exhibition of indecent, obscene, and immoral pictures and plays for private profit would not be unconstitutional abridgements of the right of liberty of the press. No doubt it is possible for previous censors of moving-picture shows, as it is possible for previous censors of mailable matter, to become

[29] Regina v. Hicklin, L. R., 3 Q. B., 360.

too officious and to abridge the freedom of the press under the guise of guarding the public morals and promoting the general welfare. But the evil or foolish administration of statutes is not enough to make them unconstitutional; when it invades private rights, the courts are there to correct it.

Publications advertising lotteries and other devices to make easy and quick money are not exercises of the right of liberty of the press, for that does not include the right to advertise, and if it does under the Hamiltonian state constitutions, then the right to advertise must be exercised "with good motives, for justifiable ends," which does not include getting rich quick without work. State statutes prohibiting such publications, and acts of Congress excluding them from the mails, do not abridge the freedom of the press.[30]

Though liberty of the press is a legal right of American origin, to get anything like a correct view of the true meaning of it as an affirmative right, outside the ordinary law of libel, to publish truth on matters of public concern, we have to go to the modern English judicial opinions concerning fair comment on matters of public concern commencing in 1808 and 1813.[31] Our own judges seem to have forgotten that the founders of the government are not distinguished for their reception of the English common law but for their adaptation of the democratic leaning and tendency of the constitutional side of it to a new career of popular freedom and equal justice. We

---

[30] Re Jackson, 96 U. S., 727; Re Rapier, 143 U. S., 110; Champion v. Ames, 188 U. S., 321; American School of Magnetic Healing v. McAnnulty, 187 U. S., 94; Public Clearing House v. Coyne, 194 U. S., 497. The remark in Taylor, The Origin and Growth of the American Constitution, p. 230, that Re Rapier "removed from the Constitution, so far as the mails are concerned," the freedom of the press prohibition, is an extravagance of a defeated lawyer before he has cooled off.

[31] See note 25, p. 526.

must look at the cases wherein American judges got into the habit of treating the constitutional declarations of liberty of the press as only declaratory of the English common law of seditious, blasphemous, defamatory, obscene, and immoral libel as it stood before the Revolution.

The four blasphemy prosecutions in the state courts, the case of Ruggles in New York in 1811, of Updegraph in Pennsylvania in 1824, of Chandler in Delaware in 1837, and of Kneeland in Massachusetts in 1838, resulted in convictions.[32] It appears that in the New York and Delaware cases the publications used indecent, vulgar, and vile language concerning the birth of Christ. In the Pennsylvania case the publication pronounced the Holy Scriptures "a fable, containing a number of good things, but a great many lies." And in the Massachusetts case the publication announced the author did not believe in God, saying: "Universalists believe in a god which I do not; but believe that their god with all his moral attributes (aside from nature itself) is nothing more than a chimera of their own imagination:" The New York prosecution was founded on the English common law in force in the colony on April 19, 1775, continued in force by the New York constitution of 1777, the constitution containing a declaration of the right of religious liberty, but no declaration of the right of liberty of the press. The other prosecutions were founded on local blasphemy statutes first passed in Colonial days. In each of the four prosecutions the chief reliance of the defendant was on the constitutional declaration of the right of religious liberty; only in the Massachusetts prosecution was the declaration of the right of liberty of the press relied on or considered by the court. In all of the cases the religious-liberty

[32] Citations in note 10, p. 513.

point was rejected, and rightly so in all of them except the Pennsylvania case, though upon labored and involved reasoning, owing to the fact that the judges went to the English common law to find out what religious liberty is not, without looking at the written state constitution to find out what religious liberty is, the right being of pure American origin in Rhode Island.

The declared right of religious liberty is an affirmative right to profess some religion and to worship God. A man who has no religion, rejects all religion, and denies the existence of God cannot have the right or exercise and enjoy it, because he has no practical use for it. And a man who uses indecent, vulgar, and vile language concerning any religion is not professing religion or worshiping God. The usual religious-liberty declaration, standing by itself unsupported by the declaration of liberty of speech and of the press, is not enough to secure complete freedom of the mind on the subject of religion against hostile action by the government. Indecent, vulgar, and vile language concerning any religion, Christian or non-Christian, is not an exercise of the right of liberty of speech or of the press, but shocks the general sense of fair argument and debate on religion, and is an overt act against peace and good order, punishable as a public nuisance. The publications in the Pennsylvania and Massachusetts cases were exercises of the right of liberty of the press, and the convictions can be sustained only on the view of the judges that the constitutional declarations are only declaratory of the English common law. In the Delaware case Chief Justice Clayton went out of his way to lay down that doctrine, taking up and denying at length Jefferson's well-known challenge of the doctrine of Lord Hale and his successors down to and including Lord Kenyon, that Christianity is a part of the English common law.

So far as I know there has been no prosecution for blasphemy in the United States since the case of Kneeland in Massachusetts in 1838. But these four judicial decisions are set forth in our text-books on the law of libel as correctly declaring the law, and are cited to this day by the courts to the point that the constitutional declarations of liberty of the press only prohibit previous censorship, the courts usually putting the word "previous" in italics as Blackstone did, thus following anti-republican precedent verbatim, literatim, et punctuatim.[33]

The federal Sedition act of 1798, in its second section, changed the English common-law test of tendency, and, following Erskine, prescribed as the test of a seditious publication: "the intent to defame the said government, or either house of Congress or the said President or to bring either of them into contempt or disrepute, or to excite against them the hatred of the good people of the United States." The third section also changed the English common law by allowing the defendant to show the truth of the publication, and by authorizing the jury to "determine the law and the fact under the direction of the court, as in other cases." The publications printed in the four reported prosecutions of Callen-

[33] "Mr. Justice Blackstone, we all know, was an anti-republican lawyer." Mr. Justice Willes in 1784 in Dean of St. Asaph's case, 4 Douglas, 73, 172, 173. Nobody calls Blackstone a good authority on a point in constitutional law.

Blasphemy is not extinct in England. See 2 Stephen, History of the Criminal Law of England, chap. 25; article entitled "Blasphemy" by W. Blake Odgers, Q. C., in 2 Encyc. of the Laws of England, 292. How the law of fair comment affects it is hard to say. Pollock, The Law of Torts, 9th ed., 243, note a, says, "the definition of blasphemous libel and the grounds on which it is punishable are questions of great difficulty," which the author leaves to the experts on criminal law and procedure, who apparently handle the subject as if there were no such thing as the law of fair comment on matters of public concern, leaving that to the experts on the civil law and procedure in defamatory-libel cases. I do not see how the fair-comment law and the blasphemy law can co-exist in the same system except upon artificial grounds.

der, Cooper, Haswell, and Lyon[34] censured the measures of the administration of John Adams and his official connection with them as President. The statements of fact were not false, and the expressions of opinion were allowable. The motives and intent of the authors unquestionably were to create and diffuse among the people an ill opinion of the administration of Adams and to move the people at the next election to put Adams out and put Jefferson in. And that was the tendency of the publications, whatever may have been the motives and intent of the authors. The publications did not teach or advise the use of force to get rid of John Adams or the Federalist party; nor did they assail the personal reputation of John Adams so far as to be defamatory. The cases resulted in verdicts of guilty and in sentences of fine and imprisonment. The judges reduced the test of intent prescribed by the statute to a fiction by inferring bad intent from the tendency of the publications as opinion-makers; and their summing up to the juries left nothing for honest jurors to do but return verdicts of guilty. They are clear cases where men were fined and imprisoned for the published political opinions, or for the supposed bad tendency of their published political opinions to move the people at the next election to change the administration at Washington. The judicially supposed bad tendency of the publications to create an ill opinion of the administration at Washington was regarded and enforced as decisive evidence of the bad intent prescribed by the Sedition act as the test of sedition.

The judges held the Sedition act constitutional, or rather declined to hold it unconstitutional, inviting the defendants to take the question of constitutionality to

[34] Citations in note 8, p. 513. The Sedition act is in 1 U. S. Stat., 596, and is printed in the report of Callender's case.

the Supreme Court of the United States; but happily for the country the invitation was not accepted. The constitutionality of the act was questioned on two grounds; first, that it was outside the powers delegated to Congress; second, that it was prohibited by the First Amendment forbidding Congress to pass any law abridging the freedom of speech or of the press. Assuming that the act was within the powers delegated to Congress, there can be no question that the Sedition act as construed and enforced by the judges was an unconstitutional abridgment of the freedom of the press. Liberty of the press as declared in the First Amendment and the English common-law crime of sedition cannot co-exist; and it makes no difference whether the prescribed test of sedition is in form the tendency of the publication or the intent of the author and publisher, for tendency and intent come around to the same identical thing in practical application, the tendency constituting the evidence of the intent.[35]

There have been no prosecutions for seditious publications in the United States since those under the Sedition act of 1798. The attempt of the legal advisers of President Roosevelt in 1908 to bring to the bar of justice for crime against the United States the New York World and Indianapolis News for publications concerning the payment of forty million dollars for the Panama rights of the French company seems to have been based on the idea that there are spots in the United States where the

[35] The destruction of the Federalist party chiefly on account of the Sedition act is decisive of the common underatanding that the original declarations wiped out the English common law of seditious libel, as also blasphemous libel. The attempt to make the English common law of sedition common criminal law of the United States was defeated by United States v. Hudson, 7 Cranch 32,, in 1812, holding that crime against the United States can be only statutory. It seems Cobbett was once taken up, but not tried, for the common-law crime of sedition against the United States. See Cobbett's case in Wharton St. Tr.

crime of sedition against the United States may exist.[36]
The publications were not seditious, and could not be,
because the crime of sedition and liberty of the press
as declared in the First Amendment cannot co-exist.
If the publications were true, they were lawful comment
on a matter of naional public concern; but if false and
defamatory of the personal reputation of Mr. Roosevelt,
he had at his disposal like any other citizen the remedy
of a civil action for damages or a criminal prosecution
in a state court by the state acting through its prosecuting attorney or attorney-general.   There is no statute
of the United States making a false publication on a matter
of public concern defamatory of the personal reputation
of an officer of the United States a crime against the
United States.   For reasons stated hereinafter I think
such a statute would be constitutional, if Congress should
see fit to pass one.   In the case of Most[37] in New York in
1902, where the publication taught and advised the
murder of public officers, riot, and arson, the publication
was an overt act against peace and good order, and Most
was rightly convicted, not for a seditious publication, but
under a section of the New York criminal code providing
for the punishment of any person "who wilfully and
wrongfully commits any act which seriously endangers
the public peace."   And there can be no doubt that it
was within the power of Congress to pass the act proposed in 1901 providing for the punishment of any person
advocating and teaching the duty of killing any officer of
the United States.[38]   That proposed act differs widely

[36] United States v. Press Publishing Co., 219 U. S., 1.

[37] 171 N. Y., 423.

[38] 35 Cong. Rec., Pt. 1, 314, and in Rogers, "Federal Interference with the
Freedom of the Press," 23 Yale Law J., 559, 567.   The Postal Appropriation
Act of 1911, sec. 2 (36 U. S. Stat., Part I, p. 1339), adds the following to the U. S.
Penal Code of 1909: "The term 'indecent' shall include matter of a character tend-
ing to incite arson, murder, assassination."

from the Sedition act of 1798 as construed and applied by the federal courts in the cases of Callender, Cooper, Haswell, and Lyon.

Hamilton's verson of the original declarations of liberty of the press in his argument in Croswell's case [39] in 1804 is a landmark in the law, because of its wide acceptance by the makers of the present constitutions of the several states. The case is a by-product of the federal Sedition act. Croswell was the editor of a newspaper called The Wasp and published the following:

"Holt says, the burden of the federal song is that Mr. Jefferson paid Callender for writing against the late administration. This is wholly false. The charge is explicitly this: Jefferson paid Callender for calling Washington a traitor, a robber, and a perjurer; for calling Adams a hoary-headed incendiary, and for most grossly slandering the private characters of men whom he well knew were virtuous. These charges, not a democratic editor has yet dared, or ever will dare, to meet in open and manly discussion."

At the time of the publication Jefferson was President. Callender was one of the men fined and imprisoned under the Sedition act and afterward went over to the Federalists, making "confessions," as the Federalists insisted on calling them, of his past relations with Jefferson. Hamilton, Harrison, and Van Ness defended Croswell. The prosecution was treated throughout as one for a seditious libel, though plainly it was for an old-fashioned defamatory libel. The case was governed by the English common law of libel in force in New York on April 19, 1775, there being no declaration of liberty of the press in the New York constitution at that time. Chief Justice Lewis presided at the trial and made these two rulings in accord with the English common law as declared and enforced in the only applicable case in New York, viz., Zenger's case in 1735: first, the truth of the publication

[39] 3 Johns. Cas., 337.

is of no legal importance; and, second, the tendency of
the publication is not for the jury but for the court.
The jury found Croswell guilty and the case came up
in the Supreme Court on Croswell's motion for a new
trial.   Hamilton and his associates challenged those two
rulings of the trial judge.   The court divided equally,
Judges Kent and Thompson agreeing with Hamilton
in toto, Chief Justice Lewis and Judge Livingston disagreeing in toto.   Hamilton formulated the following
definition of liberty of the press:

> "The liberty of the press consists in the right to publish, with
> impunity, truth, with good motives, for justifiable ends, though
> reflecting on government, magistracy, or individuals."

He professed that he found or discovered this definition
in the English common law.   But it was not there.
The definition must be viewed and judged for what it
really is, viz., Hamilton's original version of the declarations of liberty of the press.   So viewing the definition,
its chief merit lies in making truth the cardinal restraint
on the right.   The definition does not separate matters
of public concern from matters of private concern and
has been accepted as an extension of liberty of the press
to all matters of private concern as well as matters of
public concern, obliterating the distinction between the
two.   It is not clear that Hamilton so intended.   The
facts of Croswell's case made it expedient for him as an
advocate to glide over the distinction without bringing
it into prominence, for perhaps there is a fair question
whether the publication in question was on a matter of
public concern, though I think it was.

The next original thing about the definition is its
good-motives-for-justifiable-ends limitation on truth.
There was no support for that in the English common
law.   All the lawbooks were against it solidly, almost

without exception. Its chief support was Erskine's rejected argument that intent and not tendency is the test of sedition. The English judges unanimously advised the House of Lords when Fox's Libel act was under consideration that the intent of the author and publisher of the publication was of no legal importance under the common law on the question of libel or no libel.[40] Hamilton like Erskine confused and identified the tendency of a publication as an opinion-maker with the 'motives of the author and publisher, his intent and ends, when plainly they are widely different things.[41] Aside from a reference to the Roman law and to the Dutch jurist Vinnius, the only English book besides Erskine's argument in the Dean of St. Asaph's case cited to support the good-motives-for-justifiable-ends limitation on truth was Paley's Moral Philosophy.[42] To a certain extent Paley does support it, when the matter under discussion is one of private concern.

There can be no question that Hamilton's good-motives-for-justifiable-ends limitation on truth has no place in the original declarations of liberty of the press. When they are confined, as they should be, to matters of public concern, and assuming the publications to be true, as they must be, in the absence of contrary legislation, to come within the protection of liberty of the press, the original declarations did not overthrow the English common-law rule that the motives, intent, or ends of authors and publishers are of no consequence on the question of libel or no libel, but they did substitute new reasons for the English common-law rule. They

[40] 22 St. Tr., 296; 2 Stephen, History of the Criminal Law of England, 343.

[41] Erskine's argument for intent as the test of seditious libel is carefully considered and ably criticized in 2 Stephen, History of the Criminal Law of England, 33–58.

[42] Book 3, chap. 12 on "Slander."

made the right of liberty of the press a common right, exercisable by any man and by every man, publicly and truthfully to discuss all matters of public concern, not for his own private profit and benefit, but for the educational profit and benefit of the public. Assuming a publication on a matter of public concern to be true in respect of its facts, and true in respect of its opinions in the sense that the opinions are allowable inferences from the facts, they make the publication lawful without any reference whatever to the good or bad motives, justifiable or unjustifiable ends of the author and publisher, because to make good motives for justifiable ends the test of the lawfulness of truth published on a matter of public concern is to cut off allowable argument and debate and to deprive the public of the educational benefit of the publication. In addition to this legal reason, there is the practical reason of the great danger, illustrated by the prosecutions under the federal Sedition act, that men will be fined and imprisoned, under the guise of being punished for their bad motives, or bad intent and ends, simply because the powers that be do not agree with their opinions, and spokesmen of minorities may be terrorized and silenced when they are most needed by the community and most useful to it, and when they stand most in need of the protection of the law against a hostile, arrogant majority. The common right publicly and truthfully to discuss matters of public concern is not like the common right of ownership of an acre of land. The common right of ownership exists for the private profit and benefit of the owner, whereas the common right of public and truthful discussion of public affairs exists as a right held in trust for the educational profit and benefit of the public. When an owner of an acre of land builds a spite fence on it, not to advance any private interest of his own, but only to molest his neighbor, it is proper in morals and permissible in law to make his spiteful act unlawful simply because of his bad motives or bad intent and ends to make his neighbor's life miserable without doing himself any good as owner of the acre of land in question.[43] It is very different, however, when a man exercises the common right of public and truthful discussion of public affairs under the inspiration of ill will and hatred for the men and things he censures. If the publication is on a matter of public concern and is true, strictly so as to its facts and allowably so as to its opinions, then it is lawful, and bad motives, intent, or ends cannot make it unlawful without impairing and abridging the right of the public to have the educational profit and benefit of the publication. The right of liberty of the press is a sanctioning or remedial right, preservative of all other rights, and was classified by Milton as the most important right we have. It is, like the right to sue and defend in the courts, the alternative of force to protect other rights, and when the constitution requires litigants to have good motives, for justifiable ends, it might as well shut up and abolish the courts. Hamilton was so situated politically with reference to liberty of the press when he undertook to defend Croswell that he had to say something plausible to save the federal Sedition act from collision with the

---

[43] The courts have ruled quite uniformly that a spite fence is not an unlawful use of property unless made so by statute. See cases in the notes in 40 L.R.A., 181, and 25 L.R.A. (N.S.), 733. Generally, apart from statute, bad motives, intent, or ends cannot create a civil liability for an act done in exercise of a common right like the right of private property; the law, apart from statute, looks to the practical effects, consequences, or results of acts, not the motives, intent, or ends of the actor, refusing to let an actor say he did not intend the natural consequences of his act. For exceptions see Ames, "How Far an Act May Be a Tort Because of the Wrongful Motive of the Actor," 18 Harvard Law Rev., 411; Walton, "Motive as an Element in Torts in the Common and in the Civil Law," 22 ibid., 501. On "intent" as distinguished from "motive," see Smith, "Crucial Issues in Labor Litigation," 20 Harvard Law Rev., 256–59.

declaration of liberty of the press in the First Amendment of the federal constitution.[44]

When liberty of the press is extended to all matters of private concern, Hamilton's good-motives-for-justifiable-ends limitation on truth is commendable as being potential for good in the hands of judges, if confined to publications on private matters, because it enables judges to prevent that extension of the right from operat-

[44] Hamilton's "truth, with good motives, for justifiable ends" in a constitution is potentially rather than actually dangerous in the existing state of public opinion. Under it the legislature may revive the common-law crimes of sedition and blasphemy by making the author's or publisher's bad motives and unjustifiable ends the test of sedition or blasphemy, which almost inevitably will come down in practice to a fiction inferred from the supposed bad tendency of the publication. The Greeks had liberty of the press but they made Socrates drink the hemlock for the "intent or tendency" of his teaching to corrupt the youth of Athens. See the account of the political side of the prosecution of Socrates in Professor Bury's History of Freedom of Thought, 30–32. After Fox's libel act the English judges shifted the test of sedition to Erskine's intent, though there was nothing in the act requiring them to do it. Sedition is not legally extinct in England, though there has been no prosecution for the crime since the Reform Bill of 1832. The definitions of sedition in Stephen, Digest of the Criminal Law of England, and in Paterson, Liberty of the Press, Speech and Public Worship, are drawn from the English sedition cases after Fox's act of 1792 and before 1832, and cannot be used, as Paterson's definition is used in Rogers, "Federal Interference with the Freedom of the Press," 23 Yale Law J., 559, to throw light on the meaning of liberty of the press in the First Amendment, or on any constitutional declaration of liberty of the press except a Hamiltonian one. 2 Stephen, History of the Criminal Law of England, chap. 25, gives an excellent review of the English sedition cases from 1792 to 1832.

As to an author's or publisher's motives, intent, or ends in the modern English civil law of fair comment on matters of public concern: In the recent case of Thomas v. Bradbury, Agnew & Co. [1906], 2 K. B., 627, the Court of Appeal in a considered opinion by Collins, M. R., decided that "proof of malice may take a criticism that is prima facie fair outside the limits of fair comment"; i. e., in other words, that an author's or publisher's bad motives, intent, or ends may make his publication of truth in exercise of the right of liberty of the press an unlawful publication, i. e., the foundation of an action for defamatory libel, though it would be lawful but for the author's or publisher's bad motives, intent, or ends. Pollock, The Law of Torts, 9th ed., 264, criticizes the opinion on principle, as an unwarranted exception to "the general rule that the law will not examine the motive of an act done in exercise of a common right." This criticism I have adopted and emphasized in the text by pointing out that the common right in question

ing to legalize what Sir J. F. Stephen calls the occupation of the spy who invades private affairs and the home to pick up gossip, to put in it the papers for the black-mailing pecuniary profit of their owners, and who steals photographs to use them to advertise tobacco, whiskey and other commodities. But I am not aware that Hamilton's good-motives-for-justifiable-ends limitation ever has been used in the courts to reach and support such desirable results.[45]

is a public-education right existing for the benefit of the public and not a merely private right existing for the benefit of the one who uses it — and on authority, as being contrary to precedents binding on the court. The court plainly did not correctly read the opinions in Campbell v. Spottiswoode and especially the observation of Blackburn, J., which Collins, M. R., quotes, viz.: "Honest belief may be an ingredient to be taken into consideration by the jury in determining whether the publication is a libel, that is, whether it exceeds the limits of a fair and proper comment, but it cannot in itself prevent the matter being libellous" — which Blackburn, J., explained by citing two striking cases overlooked by Collins, M. R., showing that a bona fide belief sometimes may be an ingredient in the annals of facts supporting the inference on opinions exposed. The restraint of "good motives, for justifiable ends," on authors and publishers of truth on mat-ters of public concern is but a metaphysical cobweb for "wild boars of the forest" like Junius to break through with impunity, for juries to-day will not enforce it against them except unequally and spasmodically. Something can be said, though I do not agree with it, however, for the political wisdom of leaving room for the majority, through the jury, lawfully to suppress spasmodically truth they do not like, as they are likely to do it anyway.

[45] In Ruhstrat v. People, 185 Ill., 133, the court seems to say that advertising is an exercise of the right of liberty of the press, and not merely a private-property right, under the Illinois constitution extending liberty of the press to "all sub-jects." I do not see why that is not a correct interpretation of "all subjects." "Truth, with good motives, for justifiable ends," in connection with "all subjects," is capable of use to support actions for the unauthorized use of photographs for advertising purposes, though it has not been so used, and was used the other way without success in Pavesich v. N. E. Life Ins. Co., 122 Ga., 190, 202–5. See Roberson v. Folder Box Co., 171 N. Y., 538. The phrase "right of privacy," used to describe the right invaded in these cases, is too ambitious, suggesting a new elastic legal "institute" like "trust" and "contract." The right to veto the publication of one's photograph for advertising purposes is a property right of pecuniary value, worth as much as you can make the man who wants to use it pay for it, like the right to veto your neighbor's desire for a right of way across your front lawn. In Peck v. Chicago Tribune, 214 U. S., 185, which arose in Illinois, the advertising photograph publication was false, of possible defamatory

After Croswell's case, on April 5, 1805, the New York legislature passed a statute, in form declaratory of the true English common-law test of "truth, with good motives, for justifiable ends" invented by Hamilton. The statute was drawn by Van Ness, associate of Hamilton in Croswell's defense.[46] This New York statute of 1805 and Hamilton's argument are the source and model of the declarations of liberty of the press in most of the present-day constitutions of the several states. Only five of the states, Massachusetts, New Hampshire, Vermont, North Carolina, and South Carolina, retain in their present constitutions the original short form of the declaration as in the First Amendment to the federal constitution. Most of the other states extend the right to "all subjects" or to "every subject" or use some other like phrase comprehensive enough to include private concerns as well as public concerns. Hamilton's "truth, with good motives, for justifiable ends" is expressed by

tendency, falsely stating that the subject of the photograph used and recommended Duffy's malt whiskey, and hence was not an exercise of the Illinois right of liberty of the press; but if the publication had been true, then applying the Illinois restraint of "good motives, for justifiable ends," note that the motives and ends of the advertiser hardly could be the same as the motives and ends of the defendant newspaper company. In Sperry & H. Co. v. Rhodes, 220 U. S., 502, and Fifth Avenue Coach Co. v. New York, 221 U. S., 467, New York statutes regulating and limiting the right to advertise were held constitutional, though liberty of the press on "all subjects" in the New York constitution was not relied on, counsel and court viewing the right to advertise in New York as only a private-property right.

[46] The statute is printed at the end of the report of People v. Croswell, 3 Johns. Cas., 337. It seems to be a combination of Fox's Libel act and the federal Sedition act of 1798. Note that it is not a constitutional declaration of liberty of the press, but an ordinary libel statute changing the English common law of libel in force in New York on April 19, 1775. Hamilton's argument made the restraint of "truth, with good motives, for justifiable ends," an essential and inseparable part and parcel of the right of liberty of the press, but the statute makes it a defense to a criminal prosecution for libel, leaving untouched the English common-law rule in civil actions for defamatory libel making truth, simpliciter, a defense.

way of a defense in a libel case in the present constitutions of at least twenty states, some confining it to
criminal prosecutions, and others applying it to civil
and criminal cases alike.   There has been a vast amount
of tinkering with the constitutional declarations in the
several states and to-day there is no uniformity in them.
In states where the constitution-makers have not
altered the phraseology of the original declarations, one
is very likely to find that the legislature has altered it.
The generally prevailing rule in the several states, declared either in the state constitution or in a statute,
is that the right of liberty of the press extends to all
subjects, subject to the Hamiltonian defense of "truth,
with good motives, for justifiable ends."   Nobody really
knows or seems to care very much about the true meaning and application of "truth, with good motives, for
justifiable ends"; there is nothing that fairly may be
called a judicial construction of the phrase as it stands
in present state constitutions and statutes.   The courts
appear to be administering the ante-Revolution English
common law of defamatory libel without much if any
reference to the state constitutions and statutes, or
respect for them.

Another result of Croswell's case and the consequent
New York statute of 1805 is a constitutional or statutory
provision in several of the states making the jury "judge
of the law and the fact" in libel cases, sometimes adding
"as in other cases," sometimes confining the provision
to criminal cases, and sometimes extending it to civil
cases.[47]   I am not aware that the provision has received

---

[47] The first section of the New York statute declared the functions of judge and
jury in a libel case.   It has been incorporated into the constitutions of at least
twenty states.   Some three or four states by constitution make the jury judge
of the law and fact in all criminal cases, and Illinois does that by statute, on which
see Sparf v. U. S., 154 U. S., 51, and the use made of the libel cases by Gray, J.,
dissenting.

much attention at the hands of state courts bound by it. When the provision is read in the light of its history, as it must be, it cannot be taken literally as eliminating the judge and giving to the jury the whole power of decision on law and fact in the issue of libel or no libel. The tendency of a publication as an opinion-maker always was the English common-law test of libel or no libel, and to-day is the test of defamatory libel. Perhaps it was in its nature according to modern ideas of law and fact in jury trials a question of fact and not of law, but by way of an anomaly in jury trial it never was a question of fact for the jury exclusively. The early English judges who separated the province of the judge from that of the jury withdrew the question of tendency from the jury, not wholly but partially, on grounds of policy. The earliest cases for libel were for civil defamatory libel. They began to come into the English common-law courts when jurors decided issues of fact as witnesses upon their own knowledge of the facts in controversy, and not as now and for about two centuries past as judges of the weight of evidence produced before them in open court, and when the class from which jurors came ordinarily could neither read nor write. Partly for that practical reason, and partly for the additional practical reason of the necessity of discouraging frequent and frivolous civil actions for defamatory libel, the question of the tendency of the writing charged to be a defamatory libel was withdrawn partially from the jury. There was no mode of procedure for withdrawing the question wholly from the jury, the present motion for a directed verdict being a very modern invention between 1800 and 1825, so that the trial judge had to and did let the question go to the jury, subject to a motion in arrest of judgment addressed to the full court in banc by the defendant if the jury found against him. If the jury found in favor of the defendant, there was no mode of procedure for setting aside their verdict except the process of attaint in civil cases, until the motion for a new trial came in after 1655. The question of tendency in a civil case for defamatory libel early came to be described as "a question of law for the judge" simply because it was for the judges on the defendant's motion in arrest of judgment after a verdict against him, though in its nature according to modern ideas of law and fact it probably was "a question of fact for the judge." After the printing press brought along or made more common and dangerous to the existing order publications called seditious, blasphemous, obscene, and immoral libels, the question of their tendency to shake the existing order went to the Star Chamber as previous censor of the press until its fall in 1641, when it came before the ordinary criminal court of King's Bench. That court, on the analogy of civil cases for defamatory libel, should have left the question of tendency to the jury, subject to the defendant's motion in arrest of judgment if the jury found against him, as Fox's Libel act prescribed in 1792, but for some reason or other the King's Bench did not do that but began the practice of instructing the jury that the question of tendency was not for them to pass on at all, thus making itself the exclusive subsequent or ex post facto censor of the press, as the Star Chamber had been previous censor. In all the discussions ending in Fox's Libel act the question of tendency, or "libel or no libel," was spoken of as "a question of law," though in truth perhaps a question of fact. Lord Mansfield gave new reasons of policy for the practice he found established in the King's Bench of instructing the jury not to pass on the point of tendency in criminal prosecutions for libel, viz., that it would be—"an absurdity," "a solecism in politics," to confide that question, which he called one of law, to a jury "under all the bias of interest in this town where thousands more or less are concerned in the publication of newspapers, paragraphs, and pamphlets."[48] When after 1800 the right of liberty of the press in the sense of a right to publish truth on matters of public concern was recognized and established, practically overthrowing the old English common law of seditious libel and blasphemous libel, and relegating the law of obscene and immoral libel to the region of public nuisance, a new question in addition to the question of tendency was injected into a civil case for defamatory libel for a publication on a matter of public concern, viz., whether the opinions expressed in the publication reflecting on personal and professional reputation are allowable inferences from the facts. This new question is probably in its nature a question of law, as it concerns a rule or standard of conduct, but at any rate, whether a question of law or of fact, it is for the judge and not for the jury in the English courts to-day, at least when it arises on the face of the publication.[49]

In the light of history, then, when a state constitution or statute makes the jury "judge of the law and the fact" in a criminal case for libel, and stops there, it is only

[48] Dean of St. Asaph's case, or Rex *v.* Shipley, 4 Douglas, 73, 171.

[49] McGuire *v.* Western Morning News Co. [1903], 2 K. B., 100; Thomas *v.* Bradbury Agnew & Co. [1906], 2 K. B., 627. In Dakyl *v.* Labonchere, in the House of Lords in 1907, reported in a note in [1908], 2 K. B., 325, where the publication called a doctor "a quack of the rankest species," Lord Atkinson said on p. 329: "Whether the personal attack in any given case can reasonably be inferred from the truly stated facts upon which it purports to be a comment is matter of law for the determination of the judge before whom the case is tried, but if he should rule that the inference is capable of being drawn, *it is for the jury to determine whether in that particular case it ought to be drawn.*" When that is taken as a generality separated from the facts of the case before the court, it seems clear to me that the words I have put in italics ought to be cut out. It seems, however, that the Court of Appeal accepted it as a correct abstract general statement of the functions of judge and jury in a fair comment case, in Hunt *v.* Star Newspaper Co. [1908], 2 K. B., 309.

Fox's Libel act extending to criminal cases for libel the functions of judge and jury in civil actions for defamatory libel on the question of the defamatory tendency of the publication. And when a state constitution or statute goes further, making Erskine's intent of the author or Hamilton's "truth, with good motives, for justifiable ends" the test of criminal libel, then the provision making the jury "judge of the law and the fact" in criminal cases for libel is only declaratory of what would be the law anyway, for no one ever doubted that Erskine's test of the author's or publisher's intent was a question for the jury. And when a state constitution or statute goes further still, extending the test of intent to civil cases for defamatory libel, and making the jury "judge of the law and the fact" in civil as well as criminal cases for libel, there is no good reason to think it radically altered the English common law separating the function of the judge from the function of the jury on the issue of libel or no libel, though it does alter the issue. Neither Erskine nor Hamilton intended to apply the test of motives, intent, or ends in civil actions for defamatory libel. But when a state constitution or statute plainly so extends it there is nothing for the judges to do but enforce it. Altering the English common-law division of labor between judge and jury on the issue of libel or no libel, by extending the function of the jury at the expense of the judge, does not necessarily make for freedom of public discussion of matters of public concern, either in normal times or in excited times, especially when the subject is politics, religion, a literary or scientific work, or a work of art. "The man on the Clapham omnibus," as Lord Bowen phrased it,[50] is not the man to have the whole power to decide

---

[50] McGuire v. Western Morning News Co. [1903], 2 K. B., 100, quoted in opinion of Collins, M. R.

whether public discussion of such topics is truthful, allowable, and fair, and not false and defamatory. At any rate, the English common law of jury trial never gave it to him, whatever may be the true meaning of the Hamiltonian constitutions and statutes of several of our states.[51]

The judicial habit of assuming that the constitutional declarations, original and Hamiltonian alike, only prohibit previous censorship, leaving all publications subject to the English common law of libel, comes out in the numerous cases creating what may be called a judge-made liberty of the press, wherein it has been held that matters of public concern are "privileged occasions" making the publication of falsehood of defamatory tendency permissible and lawful if the falsehood is published in good faith in the honest belief that it is truth. Our judges, without exception so far as I can see, classify publications on matters of public concern in the same group with an employer's comment on the character of a servant looking for a situation made to a person thinking of employing him. The English common law of defamatory libel has been for a long time back, and is now, that an employer in giving the character of a servant may publish what he honestly believes to be truth, though it may be in fact false and defamatory; and judges now say this rule is the judicial expression of the moral and social duty of the employer, at least when the character is solicited. The case is typical of a class of cases where

[51] The subject of the division of labor between judge and jury in a libel case is historical, technical, and hard, but of great practical importance. It is enough to refer generally to Thayer, Preliminary Treatise on the Law of Evidence, the chapters on "Jury Trial and Its Development" and "Law and Fact in Jury Trials," and to Lord Blackburn's opinion in Capital and Counties Bank v. Henty [1882], 7 App. Cas., 741, and to the opinions in Sparf v. U. S., 154 U. S., 51. As a matter of fact the English common-law rules separating the functions of judge and jury are not well observed in any kind of a case in our courts, and the neglect of these rules is one of the chief causes of the unsatisfactory and uncertain adminis-. tration of justice.

false defamatory publications on matters of private concern are permissible under the English common law of libel by way of guarded exceptions to the general rule of the English common law of libel that a person makes a false defamatory publication at his peril just as a person keeps a dog that bites mankind and lets him out at his peril. Such false defamatory publications are said to be cases of "qualified privilege," the privilege consisting in permission to publish defamatory falsehood, and the qualification consisting in the requirement that the publisher must honestly believe the falsehood to be truth, and must publish it with good motives, for justifiable ends, and must not spread the publication too widely. When publications on matters of public concern are classified under the head of "qualified privilege" in the law of libel, side by side with an employer's publication giving a character to a servant, the conception of liberty of the press is that it is a judge-made privilege in the ordinary law of libel to publish, with impunity, falsehood in the honest belief it is truth, with good motives, for justifiable ends. As expounders of liberty of the press the judges have eclipsed Hamilton. When liberty of the press meant the right to publish with impunity truth on matters of public concern, without reference to motives or justifiable ends, Hamilton extended the right, or has been understood as extending the right, to matters of private concern, and attached to the restraint of truth the qualification "with good motives for justifiable ends." The judges have struck out the word "truth," have substituted in its place "falsehood in the honest belief it is truth," and have attached to the substitute Hamilton's qualification "with good motives, for justifiable ends," thus getting the result: "Liberty of the press is a privilege to publish, with impunity, falsehood on matters of public concern, in the honest belief it is truth, with good motives, for justifiable ends." This judge-made liberty of the press in the ordinary law of libel to publish defamatory false-hood on matters of public concern is consistent with, and perhaps is necessitated by, the other judicial view that the constitutional declarations, in the original and Hamiltonian forms, only prohibit previous censorship. The declarations forbid the abridgment of freedom of the press, permitting its enlargement, and the judge-made privilege to publish defamatory falsehood enlarges freedom of the press, emancipating it from the restraint of truth.

In 1908 in Kansas, the state constitution being Hamil-tonian, the Kansas Supreme Court declared the Kansas rule of qualified privilege to publish defamatory false-hood concerning a candidate for public office as follows:

"If the publisher of a newspaper circulated throughout the state publish an article reciting facts and making comment relating to the official conduct and character of a state officer, who is a candi-date for re-election, for the sole purpose of giving to the people of the state what he honestly believes to be true information, and for the sole purpose of enabling the voters to cast their ballots more intelligently, and the whole thing is done in good faith, the publica-tion is privileged, although the matters contained in the article may be untrue in fact and derogatory to the character of the candidate."

The highest courts of some of the states limit the quali-fied privilege to publish defamatory falsehood concerning a candidate for public office to publications that circu-late only within the state or election district. With reference to this limitation on the qualified privilege the Kansas Supreme Court said in the case referred to:

"Generally, publications should be no wider than the moral or social duty to publish. If it be designedly or unnecessarily or negligently excessive, privilege is lost. But if a state newspaper published primarily for a state constituency have a small circula-tion elsewhere, it is not deprived of its privilege in the discussion of subjects of state-wide concern because of that fact."[52]

[52] Coleman v. MacLennan, 78 Kan., 711.

The present constitution of Pennsylvania of 1873 provides in its liberty-of-the-press clause:

"No conviction shall be had for the publication of papers relating to the official conduct of officers or men in public capacity, or to any other matter proper for public investigation or information, where the fact that such publication was not voluntarily or negligently made shall be established to the satisfaction of the jury."

In 1878 the Pennsylvania Supreme Court thought that this provision extended to original publications and decided that this provision applies only in criminal prosecutions for libel, and not in civil actions for libel.[53]   In 1886, however, the Pennsylvania Supreme Court declared a broader rule of qualified privilege to publish defamatory falsehood concerning public officers and candidates for public offices, saying:

"If a respectable citizen honestly believes and states that a candidate for a public office is guilty of official misconduct or is a person of evil repute, in the sense that it affects his fitness for the office which he seeks, such statement is privileged and may be repeated by another in a meeting assembled to inquire into the merits of the candidate, though it be absolutely false, and upon inquiry its falsity might have been ascertained; for the voter has the right to canvass and discuss the qualifications of the candidates who seek his suffrage openly and fully."[54]

Some text-writers on the law of libel say the Kansas and Pennsylvania rules are extreme or exceptional, and that the prevailing rule in our various jurisdictions is that judge-made qualified privilege to publish on matters of

[53] Barr *v.* Moore, 87 Pa. St., 385.

[54] Briggs *v.* Garrett, 111 Pa. St., 404. A Pennsylvania statute passed in 1903 made "negligence. . . . in the ascertainment of facts and in making publications affecting the character, reputation, or business of citizens," the test of liability. Pa. Laws, 1903, 349, also printing a long message by Governor Pennypacker approving the act, which was repealed in 1907. Pa. Laws, 1907, 124. See Ex parte Harrison, 212 Mo., 88.

public concern does not legalize defamatory falsehood.[55] It seems, however, they take as the true rule the modern English judiciary law classifying fair comment on matters of public concern as an exercise of the right of liberty of the press, or the right to publish truth on matters of public concern. When American reported cases are looked into, it must be admitted that the law evidenced by them is in an extremely loose and fluid state. It is not easy to locate and name the American court that has clearly and pointedly made either truth alone, or Hamilton's "truth, with good motives, for justifiable ends," the dividing line between lawful and unlawful publications on matters of public concern.[56]

With reference to "privilege" in the ordinary law of libel, there is a clear distinction between publications originating defamatory falsehood and publications of defamatory falsehood originated by others in judicial, legislative, and other official proceedings, and in unofficial proceedings, and in unofficial public meetings on matters of public concern. Under the rule of the English common law making everyone who repeats defamatory falsehood liable, as well as the original author and publisher, and even though the original author and publisher may not be liable, the publishers of true reports of

[55] Burdick's Law of Torts, 331–36; Newell, Slander and Libel, 3d ed., 643–51; 25 Cyc., 401–6.

[56] The opinions by Holmes, J., in Burt v. Boston Advertiser, 154 Mass., 238, in 1891, and by Taft, J., in Hallam v. Kentucky Post, 59 Fed. Rep., 530, in 1893, are the best American opinions I know of. Both deal with the publications — one censuring the plaintiff in connection with frauds in the New York Custom House, and the other censuring the plaintiff as a candidate for Congress — as exercises of the qualified privilege of an employer to give a character to a servant, and speak of the judicial function as a legislative one "to draw a line between conflicting interests" (Holmes, J.), and "balancing the needs and good of society against the right of an individual to enjoy a good reputation" (Taft, J.). So far as our constitutions are concerned, there can be no conflict between the right of liberty of the press and the right of personal reputation.

defamatory falsehood in official and unofficial public proceedings are liable to the persons defamed.[57] Such true reports properly fall under the head of "privilege" in the ordinary law of libel, because liberty of the press does not sanction either the original publication or subsequent repeating and spreading of defamatory falsehood.[58] The office of a newspaper libel law is to expand for the protection of editors and owners of newspapers more than the judges have been able to expand it, the doctrine of "privilege" so as to enable them to publish with impunity true reports of official and unofficial public proceedings. As the English judiciary law already legalized true newspaper reports of defamatory falsehood in judicial and legislative proceedings, the English Newspaper Libel Law of 1881 was extended by Parliament in 1888 to protect editors and owners of newspapers from liability for defamatory falsehood in fair and accurate newspaper reports of the proceedings of public meetings. It defined a public meeting as "any meeting bona fide and lawfully held for a lawful purpose, and for the furtherance or discussion of any matter of public concern, whether admission thereto be general or restricted."[59] The legislative

[57] The immunity of legislators from civil and criminal liability for defamatory falsehood in legislative proceedings goes back to the English Bill of Rights in 1688, and usually is expressly declared in our constitutions. The like immunity of those engaged in the judicial administration of justice rests on the common law. Liberty of the press does not per se extend the immunity to those who repeat and report such defamatory falsehood. On a distinction between slander, or oral defamation, and libel, or written defamation, making words not actionable when spoken but actionable when written, that has come down from the remote past, falsehood orally uttered by a speaker at a public meeting may not be actionable defamation as against the speaker, but may be actionable defamation as against the newspaper that prints and publishes it correctly.

[58] Publicity, as opposed to Tudor and Stuart secrecy, in the conduct of governmental affairs does not necessarily entail the legal consequence of a right to report, publish, and spread defamatory falsehood originated in the conduct of government affairs by public officers.

[59] See Odgers, Slander and Libel, 2d ed., 373–93, 725–29; and same author, An Outline of the Law of Libel, 137–64.

limitation of the privilege to editors and owners of newspapers rests on their peculiar relation to the work of giving wide publicity to official and unofficial discussions of public affairs. Newspaper libel laws are rare in the United States. I do not know of any except in California and Texas.[60] Such laws are not needed in the United States because of the judicial view of liberty of the press as a qualified privilege in the ordinary law of libel to originate defamatory falsehood, as well as to report defamatory falsehood originated by others, on matters of public concern. The Illinois legislature passed a newspaper libel law in 1895 which was repealed by the next legislature in 1897.[61] It went so far beyond the proper function of a newspaper libel law, giving editors and owners of newspapers a special privilege to originate as well as to report defamatory falsehood, that it probably encountered the constitutional rule of equality before the law, and the usual declaration in the Bill of Rights that every person ought to find a certain remedy in the laws for every injury and wrong he may receive in his person, property, or reputation.

Labor leaders complain that liberty of the press is unconstitutionally abridged by injunctions forbidding publications to make a strike or boycott more effective, like the "Unfair" and "We don't patronize" publications in the recent boycott case of Gompers v. Buck's Stove and Range Company in the courts of the District of Columbia and United States Supreme Court. Whether the courts were right or wrong in extending the remedy of injunction to strikes and boycotts, instead of leaving he striking and boycotting workmen to the ordinary

[60] Deering, Civil Code of California, 1909, sec. 47; McEachin, Civil Statutes, Texas, Art. 5597, subdiv. 3; Newell, Libel and Slander, 3d ed., 682–83.

[61] Ill. Session Laws, 1895, 315, and 3 Starr & Curtis, Ann. Ill. Stats., 2d ed., p. 3799; Ill. Sess. Laws, 1897, 297.

remedies of damages in civil actions and fine and imprisonment in criminal actions, is a question in the law of procedure with which liberty of press has nothing to do. Preliminary to that question in the law of procedure, distinct and separate from it, is the question in substantive law whether strike and boycott "peacefully persuasive" publications like "Unfair" and "We don't patronize" are unlawful acts, or can be unlawful acts. Under the original as distinguished from the Hamiltonian constitutional declarations of liberty of the press, like the First Amendment to the federal constitution, which governed Gompers' case, and which confines the right to matters of public concern, publications like "Unfair" and "We don't patronize" to make a strike or boycott more effective are not exercises of the right of liberty of the press any more than "U-Need-a-Biscuit," or "Drink Schlitz, the beer that made Milwaukee famous," are exercises of the right, because they are only advertising publications to promote private welfare and not educational publications to promote the general welfare. When, rightly or wrongly, the judiciary or statutory law of the land declares the strike or boycott an unlawful conspiracy, then advertising publications employed as means to make the unlawful conspiracy more effective are themselves unlawful, under the original declarations of liberty of the press.[62]

Under the Hamiltonian state constitutions, however, the legal situation is different. Those constitutions, verbally at least, put all publications of truth on matters of private concern as well as on matters of public concern

[62] 221 U. S., 418. With due respect to those who take the opposite view, there is nothing to the idea of Walworth, C., in Brandreth v. Lance, 8 Paige, 24, in 1839, repeatedly judicially echoed since, that liberty of the press forbids the extension of the remedy of injunction to stop a threatened publication of falsehood defamatory of property, or business, or even personal or professional reputation.

under the protection of liberty of the press, if the truth is published "with good motives, for justifiable ends." Falsehood is not an ingredient in strike and boycott publications like "Unfair" and "We don't patronize." There is nothing in them but truth of more or less persuasive tendency to move sympathetic readers to do what they have a perfect right to do, viz., refuse to buy goods from a particular dealer. The ultimate motives and ends of the striking and boycotting authors and publishers are to better their working conditions, which are not bad motives nor unjustifiable ends. To say that the motives and ends of the striking and boycotting authors and publishers are to put unlawful economic pressure on their employers begs the whole question by confusing means with ends, substituting the immediate means employed for the ultimate end to be attained. When a constitution speaks of "truth, with good motives, for justifiable ends," presumably at least it means ultimate motives and ends. It is not easy to see and articulate clearly and convincingly just wherein the labor leaders are wrong in point of law under the Hamiltonian state constitutions on which they rely when they say their strike and boycott publications like "Unfair" and "We don't patronize" do not differ from the publications before the Revolution to move people to refrain from using George III's tea and stamps. True, the tea and stamp publications were used to promote a political matter of public concern, while the strike and boycott publications are used to promote a private-property matter of private concern; but it must be borne in mind that the Hamiltonian state constitutions, on which the labor leaders rely, verbally at least, put matters of private concern on the same constitutional footing as matters of public concern with reference to the right of liberty of the press. The answer the courts commonly give to the

labor leaders, and the United States Supreme Court,
overlooking the difference between the First Amendment
and the Hamiltonian state constitutions, adopted the
answer in Gompers' case, brackets the publications of
the striking and boycotting workmen with the publications of anarchists teaching and advising the use of force,
riot, arson, and murder. The bracketing phrase of the
courts is "verbal acts."[63] There is nothing to the phrase,
because all publications are "verbal acts." The publications of striking and boycotting workmen like "Unfair"
and "We don't patronize" are not "verbal acts" or
"overt acts" against peace and good order like the
publications of anarchists teaching and advising the use
of force. When judges in solemn and deliberate opinions
bracket striking and boycotting workmen with anarchists, then the tu quoque hot retort of the workmen that
the judges are tools of the corporations is essentially
human. The legal argument of the workmen deserves
a better answer than the judges are giving; and if there
is no better answer the argument should prevail when a
Hamiltonian state constitution governs.

The judicial practice of fining and imprisoning strangers
to litigation like editors of newspapers in summary criminal proceedings for criminal contempt of court for publications censuring judges, imputing to them disgraceful
motives and conduct in their administration of the law
in particular pending and ended cases and generally, has
become rather common in the courts of several of the
states.[64] The practice is justly criticized as re-establishing

[63] Enough cases are cited in Gompers' case, 221 U. S., 418. See opinions
reaching the opposite result in Marx & Haas Clothing Co. v. Watson, 168 Mo.,
133; Lindsay & Co. v. Montana Federation of Labor, 37 Mont., 264, on the untenable ground that liberty of the press forbids the prevention of publications.

[64] McDougall v. Sheridan, 23 Idaho, 191, is one of the latest cases and cites the
precedents.

the jurisdiction of the Star Chamber in violation of the constitutional right of liberty of the press and the constitutional right of trial by jury in criminal cases. A declaratory act of Congress first passed in 1831, adopting the argument of Mr. Storrs, one of the managers for the House in the impeachment of Judge Peck, forbids the practice in all federal courts below the Supreme Court.[65] There are like statutes in some of the states, going back to the one in Pennsylvania in 1809 resulting from impeachment proceedings against the judges of the Pennsylvania Supreme Court in consequence of Passmore's case.[66] Without distinguishing between publications by strangers, parties, and attorneys, between those concerning pending cases and ended cases, or between the civil wrong to parties by depriving them of a fair trial, and the criminal wrong to the public, whether seditious libel, defamatory libel, or obstructing justice, but bundling all publications together as like criminal acts of contempt of court, the practice goes back to Oswald's case[67] in Pennsylvania in 1788, spread to the federal courts and to other state courts, but was checked by the impeachment proceedings against Judge Peck and the above-mentioned act of Congress of 1831, until its revival in 1855 by an opinion of Judge English of the Arkansas Supreme Court.[68] In most of the modern cases

---

[65] The statute is now R. S., U. S., sec. 725, re-enacted as sec. 268, Fed. Jud. Code; Cuyler v. R. R. Co., 131 Fed. Rep., 95. Doubt whether the statute applies to the Supreme Court was expressed in Ex parte Robinson, 22 Wallace, 505, in 1873, and in United States v. Shipp, 203 U. S., 506, in 1906, and has not been resolved. The doubt rests on the wrong idea that "judicial power" and "contempt" are "coeval."

[66] Respublica v. Passmore, 3 Yeates., 441, and argument of Mr. Buchanan in Judge Peck's case, published by Arthur Stansbury, Boston, 1833, pp. 432–33.

[67] 1 Dallas, 319.

[68] State v. Morrill, 16 Ark., 384. He goes so far as to intimate a publication scandalizing a judge is beyond the reach of the pardoning power.

the publications are of the kind called "scandalizing judges" by imputing to them disgraceful conduct in their administration of the law, and what is here said is confined to publications of that sort. There can be no question that the English common law before the Revolution made such publications, whether true or false, criminal seditious libels when their tendency was to create and diffuse an ill opinion of the law and its judicial administration, and criminal defamatory libels when their tendency was to create and diffuse an ill opinion of the personal or professional reputations of the judges, and, whether true or false, criminal acts obstructing justice when their tendency was to prejudice the right of parties to a pending case to a fair and impartial trial on the law and on the evidence produced in open court, punishable by fine or imprisonment in the ordinary course of the criminal law, i. e., by indictment or information and trial by jury. The view that such publications by strangers scandalizing judges are criminal acts of contempt of court rests on nothing in the English common law before the Revolution but a dubious opinion of Lord Chancellor Hardwicke in 1742, first published in 1765–1768,[69] and on uncertain passages in Blackstone's fourth book, probably taken from Mr. Justice Wilmot's celebrated undelivered opinion in 1756, first published in 1802,[70] in contempt proceedings in the King's Bench against the bookseller Almon for publishing a pamphlet, approved if not written by Lord Camden, censuring Lord Mansfield for amending behind Wilkes' back the information against him for sedition for writing and publishing North Briton, No. 45, and for changing a standing rule of the King's Bench so as to require an

[69] St. James Evening Post Case, 2 Atkyns, 469.

[70] Wilmot's Reports by his son. Blackstone submitted proofs of his fourth book to Wilmot, J.

affidavit in support of a petition for the writ of habeas corpus. Mr. Storrs showed clearly in his argument against Judge Peck, and the same thing has been shown more clearly recently by Mr. Fox, master in chancery of the English High Court of Justice, Chancery Division, in two historical articles on Mr. Justice Wilmot's unde-livered opinion in Almon's case,[71] that publications by strangers scandalizing judges in pending cases or in ended cases were not criminal acts of contempt of court within the reach of the criminal process of contempt according to the English common law as it stood at the time of the Revolution, but were criminal misdemeanors, i. e., seditious libels or defamatory libels or criminal acts obstructing justice in pending cases, punishable summarily in the Court of Star Chamber until its fall in 1641, and thereafter only in the King's Bench in the ordinary course of the criminal law, i. e., by indictment or information and trial by jury. In the modern cases in the state courts the whole of the wrong as the judges view it and describe it is the defamatory and seditious character of the publications, and not the criminal wrong to the public, much less the civil wrong to the parties, of obstructing justice in a pending case. In some of the cases it is laid down that there is nothing to the distinction between publications scandalizing judges in pending cases and in ended cases, and that is correct when the scandaliz-ing publications are viewed as defamatory and seditious libels as distinguished from acts obstructing justice. As Mr. Justice Wilmot's undelivered opinion in Almon's case said that to censure Lord Mansfield is to censure the king who employs him, so it is said that to censure state judges is to censure the people who employ them. The practical reason assigned for extending the criminal process

___

[71] 24 Law Quarterly Rev., 194, 266.

of contempt to publications by strangers scandalizing
judges is that jurors cannot be relied on to do their duty
in civil actions or criminal prosecutions for defamatory
libel where judges are the victims. The reason is bad in
law, even if true in fact. The true reason probably is,
however, that the scandalized judges do not like to meet
their critics face to face before a jury on the footing of
the judge-made liberty of the press or "qualified privilege"
to publish defamatory falsehood on matters of public
concern with good motives, for justifiable ends. It is
likely that jurors could and would honestly find from the
evidence that the authors of the scandalizing publications
were actuated by good motives for justifiable ends.
The judge-made "qualified privilege" is good enough for
other people's officers, but not for judges.

The criminal contempt-of-court process for dealing
with publications scandalizing judges is seen complete in
Senator Patterson's case. As editor of a Denver newspaper he censured the judges of the Colorado Supreme
Court for a decision in a case held to be pending at the
time of the publication because the defeated party could
and subsequently did apply for a rehearing, charging that
the decision was the fruit of a conspiracy between the
judges and Denver capitalists to employ the judicial
power to nullify a vote of the people amending the state
constitution to take from the state legislature and vest in
the city of Denver the control of Denver public utilities.
In seeming admitted violation of the written text of the
state constitution and statutes, on the spurious historical
theory that the criminal process of contempt of court to
fine and imprison the authors of publications scandalizing
judges is "coeval" with the English common-law judicial
power granted to the Colorado Supreme Court by the
state constitution, reaching back of and uplifting all the
rest of the written text of the state constitution and

statutes, the Colorado Supreme Court caused the attorney-general to put into play and action against the editor the summary criminal process of contempt, refused to let the editor show the truth of his publication, and fined him $1,000.00. On error to the Supreme Court of the United States under the Fourteenth Amendment, that court said the Colorado Supreme Court's administration of the state constitution and statutes, refusing to let the editor show the truth and denying jury trial, even if wrong, was not wrong enough to be such a purely personal and arbitrary exercise of the state judicial power as could shock the reason of mankind and so be wanting in "due process of law." Over the protest of Brewer, J., and the dissent of Harlan, J., the court dodged the point whether liberty of the press as declared in the First Amendment is included in the word "liberty" in the Fourteenth Amendment, by conceding it for the sake of argument. Then viewing the publication as a defamatory libel or seditious libel, the court decided the First Amendment does not make truth an answer, because it only prohibits previous censorship, leaving authors liable for criminal matter after publication, even though true, which is wrong, for, as already shown, if liberty of the press in the First Amendment means anything it legalizes published truth on all matters of public concern. Next viewing the publication as an act obstructing justice in a pending case, i. e., prejudicial to the right of parties in a pending case to a fair and impartial trial on the law and on the evidence, and without distinguishing between the civil wrong to the parties and its appropriate remedies and the criminal wrong to the public and its appropriate remedies, but treating the wrong as manifestly a criminal act of contempt of court within the reach of the criminal process of contempt, the court decided that the truth of the publication was no answer to the charge that it criminally obstructed or tended to obstruct justice in a pending case. Perhaps it is correct to say that the truth of a publication scandalizing judges is no answer to a charge that the publication criminally obstructed or tended to obstruct justice in a pending case, but the difficulty is to harmonize the rule with liberty of the press as a right to publish truth on matters of public concern, which may be done, perhaps, on the view that the right to sue and defend in the courts is a matter of private concern and not of public concern until the case is ended, and so falls outside the sphere of liberty of the press, except under the Hamiltonian state constitutions extending liberty of the press to all subjects, where it may be said published truth scandalizing judges and obstructing or tending to obstruct justice in a pending case cannot be the Hamiltonian "truth, with good motives, for justifiable ends." The decisive answer to this part of the opinion of the court, however, is that it is abstract jurisprudence in the air, because it is hard to see how it is possible to read the opinion of the Colorado Supreme Court without being convinced that the Colorado judges fined the editor, not because his publication obstructed or tended to obstruct justice in a pending case, but because it was a defamatory and seditious libel. It is hard to see why the opinion of the Colorado Supreme Court was not binding on the United States Supreme Court as a finding of fact that the publication neither obstructed nor tended to obstruct justice in a pending case, because the Colorado judges found as a fact they were incapable of deciding a case on anything but the law and the evidence, leaving nothing but a defamatory and seditious libel and the question whether truth was an answer. No doubt the court "scrutinized the case," as they say, but at the same time the opinion is far from satisfactory, and it is by no means certain that it will stand as the last

word on the subject.   Brewer, J., was right in saying the
court had no business to try to dodge the question whether
the word "liberty" in the Fourteenth Amdenment includes liberty to publish truth on matters of public
concern.[72]

The practice of dealing with publications scandalizing
judges under the criminal process of contempt of court
ought to be stopped, voluntarily by the judges or under
the compulsion of impeachment.   If the practice is
desirable, then the constitutional declarations of liberty
of the press and jury trial in criminal cases ought to be
amended in the regular way by the people themselves, and
not in the irregular way of spurious judicial interpretation
following Mr. Justice Wilmot's obsolete idea in Almon's
case that "the underlying principle is to keep a blaze of
glory around the courts, and to deter people from attempting to render them contemptible in the eyes of the public."   Under a Hamiltonian state constitution published
truth about judges may be sedition, if published with bad
motives for unjustifiable ends, but under ordinary jury
clauses a man cannot be punished for the crime of sedition except on the verdict of a jury.

The First Amendment to the federal Constitution
declaring the right of liberty of the press seems to be
regarded as of little practical importance.   This idea
seems to be a survival of the argument for and against
the propriety of a bill of rights in the federal Constitution.[73]   The usage and practice of Congress from the
beginning has been that the right of liberty of the
press there declared includes the right of circulation

---

[72] 205 U. S., 454; 35 Colorado, 253.   It is not easy to believe Senator Patterson's offer to show the truth was not "a bluff."   But that makes no difference.

[73] 2 Watson, Constitution, 1351–70, 1399.   The rule is that the first eight
amendments restrain only the delegated powers of the federal government, not
the reserved powers of the states.

through the post-office within each state and across state lines. This view of Congress has the support of a dictum of the United States Supreme Court, and seems to me sound in law.[74] And as the Constitution of the United States divides matters of public concern into those that are national and those that are state or local, the right of liberty of the press declared in the First Amendment would appear to be a distinct, separate, and independent right arising out of and protected by the Constitution of the United States, to punish truth on all matters of national public concern. In that view, Congress was right in 1835 and 1836 in thinking it had no power, and President Jackson was wrong in thinking Congress had power, to prohibit totally the sending of abolition literature through the post-office from the free states into the slave states, as there can be little doubt that slavery was a matter of national public concern under liberty of the press.[75] To-day the question of a uniform law on marriage and divorce, the liquor-prohibition question, the woman-suffrage question, and many other questions are in one aspect or another questions of national public concern as related to liberty of the press in the First Amendment. And it follows that the right to publish truth on matters of national public concern is one of the privileges and immunities of citizens of the United States protected from abridgment by any state by the first prohibition in the Fourteenth Amendment.[76] And it

[74] Ex parte Jackson, 96 U. S., 727, 733.

[75] For the federal precedents, see Rogers, "Federal Interference with the Freedom of the Press," 23 Yale Law J., 559. If Jackson's message was limited to abolition literature teaching the use of force, it was constitutionally sound. Jackson had very able official and unofficial legal advisers.

[76] Slaughter-House cases, 16 Wallace, 36. In United States v. Hall, 26 Fed. Case No. 15282, Woods, J., decided that liberty of the press is a privilege and immunity of national citizenship under the first prohibition of the Fourteenth Amendment. As stated, whether it falls under the word "liberty" in the second prohibition was left undecided in Patterson v. Colorado, 205 U. S., 454.

results from this view of the First Amendment that
Congress has the power to make defamatory falsehood concerning public officers of the United States or
candidates for public office under the United States the
foundation of a civil action for damages in the federal
courts or a criminal prosecution for crime against the
United States, just as Congress has power to protect
officers of the United States from murderous assaults,
or to protect the right to vote for representatives in
Congress and presidential electors.[77]

The act of Congress of 1912 excluding from the low
rate for second-class mail matter newspapers, magazines, periodicals, and other publications unless the names
of the owners and secured creditors are filed with the
Postmaster-General and published in the second issue
after filing, and unless paid-for reading-matter is marked
"advertisement," was assailed outside and inside the
courts as an abridgment of the freedom of the press in
the First Amendment. The assailing arguments only
show a misunderstanding of the constitutional right.
The act was sustained by the United States Supreme
Court as promotive rather than restrictive of liberty
of the press, on the ground that Congress has the power
to manage the post-office, as it always has managed it,
as a means for "the wide dissemination of intelligence as
to current events," and any act of Congress adapted
to advance that policy is constitutional, the degree of
the adaptation falling outside the range of the judicial
power.[78] As the owners of newspapers, magazines,

[77] Re Neagle, 135 U. S., 1; Wiley v. Sinkler, 179 U. S., 58. The view taken
of the First Amendment makes it of great practical importance, enabling Congress
to make the law of liberty of the press on all matters of national public concern
uniform throughout the United States, leaving to the United States Supreme
Court the judicial duty to draw the line between matters of national and local
public concern as related to the federal right of liberty of the press.

[78] Lewis Publishing Co. v. Morgan, 229 U. S., 288.

periodicals, and other publications are operating public educational institutions in exercise of the right of liberty of the press to educate the public on matters of public concern, of course the public, i. e., the scholars, are not idly curious when they want to know who owns the institutions. A like statute passed in Pennsylvania in 1903 was repealed in 1907.[79] The state legislatures and Congress may carry the principle further to let the scholars know the names of the teachers or editorial staff now working anonymously behind the mask of the wonder-working corporate cloak. Since 1899 the California penal code has required every article, statement, or editorial reflecting on personal or professional reputation to be supplemented by the true name of the writer.[80]

The constitutional declarations of liberty of the press are original work of the American people in the sphere of law and government. Their chief practical bulwark always has been the overthrow of the Federalist party because of the Sedition act of 1798. As guardians and expounders of the declarations the courts are a failure up to date. They cannot be a success until judges get rid of the notion that the declarations are only declaratory of the anti-republican English common law of the days of Blackstone, Lord Mansfield, and Lord Kenyon, only prohibiting previous censorship of publications on matters of public concern, leaving untouched the English common law of seditious, blasphemous, defamatory, obscene, and immoral libel. The judge-made liberty of the press to publish defamatory falsehood on matters of public

[79] Citations in note 1, p. 102, supra.

[80] Deering, Penal Code of California, 1909, sec. 259. The provisions of the California civil and penal codes on slander and libel, taken together, are interesting and instructive. See Ex parte Harrison, 212 Mo., 88, holding Missouri liberty of the press forbids the legislature to require reports of a cross league on candidates to give the names of those who furnished information.

concern is unauthorized judicial legislation destructive of men's reputations and property, inviting and encouraging the owners and editors of newspapers and periodicals to found their educational power on falsehood, whereas the declarations require them to found it on truth, except when the legislature sees fit to remove the restraint of truth. And the judge-made law of contempt of court for publications censuring judges is simply intolerable in a land of equality before the law where judges are no more important to the universe than executives and legislators. The complete immunity from legislation regulating the exercise of the right of liberty of the press owners and editors of newspapers and periodicals and all others have enjoyed since the Sedition act of 1798 does not rest on anything in the state and federal constitutions, but rests entirely on sufferance by the people, and their state and federal legislative representatives, who in their respective spheres have ample power to prescribe and enforce the rudiments of fair play involved in the restraint of truth in publications on matters of public concern, and on matters of private concern as well. Such legislation, state and federal, seems desirable and necessary, at least for the better protection by the courts of personal reputation and property from defamatory falsehood. It is not easy to get a bill of particulars of other evils comprehended in the popular phrase "trust press." No doubt the owners and editors of newspapers and periodicals, like everybody else, have fallen victims to the "dollar culture" or "fierce game of money," but it may be doubted whether they are worse victims than others, or less desirous than others to keep the dollar from taking up so much room on the driver's seat. I do not know what ought to be done, or can be done, by legislation to squeeze the dollar out of its usurped place on the driver's seat in any existing scheme of public education, whether through the printing press or the classroom. But the signs of the times are that the people are about ready to demand and support state and federal legislation regulating the newspaper and periodical business of the country. The constitutional right of liberty of the press does not make the owners and editors of newspapers and periodicals "the sovereigns of the state," but leaves them subject to the general rule: "The state subordinate to the people, and everything else subordinate to the state."[81] Indeed, constitutional liberty of the press in the United States is nothing more nor less than a fine popular attempt to employ the law and its machinery to realize the great saying: "And ye shall know the truth, and the truth shall make you free."

[81] Wilson, J., in Chisholm v. Georgia, 2 Dallas, 419, 455, 456.

TOPIC VII

THE OBLIGATION OF CONTRACTS CLAUSE

The Street Railroad Problem in Chicago

THE STREET RAILROAD PROBLEM IN CHICAGO

ITS SOLUTION MUST BE SOUGHT UNDER THE SETTLED LAW OF ILLINOIS, AND NOT UNDER THE DOCTRINE OF THE DARTMOUTH COLLEGE CASE, OR UNDER THE PRINCIPLE AND POLICY OF MUNICIPAL OWNERSHIP[a]

During the past eight years the principal street railroad corporations of Chicago, the Chicago City Railway Company and the Chicago Union Traction Company, have been seeking an extension or renewal of their franchises at the hands of the city council. They have not yet got the extension or renewal, and perhaps a majority of the electors of Chicago are opposed to the granting of street railroad franchises by the city council.

I. WHAT IS A STREET RAILROAD FRANCHISE GRANTABLE BY THE COUNCIL OF CHICAGO?

What is a street railroad franchise grantable by the council of Chicago, and what is there about it to make some people want to get the thing so badly and to make other people so strongly oppose their getting it?

Blackstone, speaking of franchises, says: "Franchise and liberty are used as synonymous terms, and their definition is, a royal privilege, or branch of the king's prerogative, subsisting in the hands of a subject. Being, therefore, derived from the crown, they must arise from the king's grant" (2 Com., 37). He classes franchises as "incorporeal hereditaments," whose existence, he says, "is merely in idea and abstracted contemplation; though their effects and profits may be, frequently, objects of our bodily senses" (2 Com., 20).

[a] [Northwestern University Bulletin, Vol. 4, No. 4, February–April, 1906.]

If we strike out of Blackstone's definition the words "king," "crown," "royal" and subject," and substitute therefor "people of Illinois" and "citizen," Blackstone's definition of a franchise is good to-day in Illinois, and will read thus: "Franchise and liberty are used as synonymous terms; and their definition is, a privilege of the people of Illinois, or branch of the prerogative of the people of Illinois, subsisting in the hands of a citizen. Being, therefore, derived from the people of Illinois, they must arise from that people's grant."

In the case of California v. Central Pacific Railroad Company, 127 U. S., 1, 40, Mr. Justice Bradley, speaking for the Supreme Court of the United States, said: "What is a franchise? . . . Generalized and divested of the special form it assumes under a monarchial government based on feudal traditions, a franchise is a right, privilege, or power of public concern, which ought not to be exercised by private individuals at their mere will and pleasure, but should be reserved for public control and administration, either by the government directly or by public agents, acting under such conditions and regulations as the government may impose, in the public interest, and for the public security. Such rights and powers must exist under every form of society. They are always educed by the laws and customs of the community. Under our system, their existence and disposal are under the control of the legislative department of the government, and they cannot be assumed or exercised without legislative authority. No private person can establish a public highway, or a public ferry, or railroad, or charge tolls for the use of the same, without authority from the legislature, direct or derived. These are franchises. No private person can take another's property, even for a public use, without such authority; which is the same as to say, that the right of eminent domain can only be exercised by virtue of a legislative grant. This is a franchise. No persons can make themselves a body corporate and politic without legislative authority. Corporate capacity is a franchise. The list might be continued indefinitely."

The right to occupy public streets and other public grounds with railroad track is a franchise. (Davis *v.* Mayor of New York, 14 N. Y., 506, 523; New Orleans, etc., R. Co. *v.* Delamore, 114 U. S., 501, 507; see also Memphis and Little Rock R. Co. *v.* Railroad Commissioners, 112 U. S., 609, 619; Louisville, etc., R. Co. *v.* State Board of Assessors, 55 N. J. Law, 529, 537.)

In order that private citizens may carry on the business of constructing and operating street railroads over and along public streets in Chicago, as a corporation, they must obtain several different kinds of franchises, or special privileges, or powers. They must get first the franchise to be a corporation; that is to say, the right of a collective and changing body of men to act as an individual (Providence Bank *v.* Billings, 4 Peters, 514, 562). This franchise to be a corporation belongs to the natural persons who compose the corporation and not to the corporation itself. The franchises which belong to the corporation grow out of the power, or capacity, conferred upon the corporation to do things that a natural person gets the capacity or power to do from his Creator; that is to say, in the case of a street railroad corporation, to construct the railroad, to operate cars over it, and to take tolls or fares from the people carried. But these corporate powers or franchises, when granted, so far as street railroad corporations are concerned, exist only "in abstracted contemplation," until the power or franchise to enter upon and use public streets is obtained. When this latter franchise is obtained, the effects of a use of the other franchises, or powers, become immediately "objects of our bodily senses" in the shape of iron rails, street cars, conductors, motormen, and all the other paraphernalia of a going street railroad.

It has always been, and is now, one of the powers, liberties, privileges, or prerogatives of the people of Illinois to do the work of carrying people in street cars over and along the streets of Chicago either directly, or by a delegation of the power, liberty, privilege, or prerogative to the people of Chicago, with street railroads owned by the people, and operated by their own officers and employees (16 Harv. Law Rev., 172, and case cited). Hitherto they have not used that power, liberty, privilege, or prerogative simply because a majority of the electors of the whole State and of Chicago have been of the opinion that they could get the work done better by granting that power, liberty, privilege, or prerogative to private individuals associated together as a corporation, requiring them to use it with material property owned by themselves and operated by their own officers and employees, and allowing them to get their pay or compensation out of the fares paid by the people carried.

A street railroad franchise in Chicago grantable by the council is, and always has been, therefore, only that power, liberty, privilege, or prerogative of the people of Illinois to carry passengers for hire over and along the streets of Chicago by means of street railroads, subsisting in the hands of private individuals under and by virtue of a grant made by the people of Illinois. A street railroad franchise is just like a public office in this: the holder of it enjoys the privilege of wielding a portion of the sovereign power of the people of Illinois, and of using a portion of their property, the public streets, in trust for the ultimate benefit of the people. But, instead of furnishing the holders of a street railroad franchise with all the material property necessary to enable them to use it beneficially, and paying them for their services out of the public treasury, the people of Illinois require them to get the necessary material property, except the public streets, with their own money, and to earn their pay or compensation out of the fares paid by the people carried.

II. THE CONSTITUTIONAL MODES OF MAKING GRANTS OF STREET RAILROAD FRANCHISES IN ILLINOIS PRIOR TO, AND AFTER AUGUST 8, 1870.

August 16, 1858, marks the introduction of street railroads in Chicago (199 Ill., 488). Illinois was then organized under her second State Constitution, in force April 1, 1848, which was superseded by the present State Constitution, in force August 8, 1870 (Hurd's R. S., 1903, p. 37; p. 53. Neither of those Constitutions, nor any statute passed in pursuance thereof, except the Mueller Act of 1903, uses the word "franchise" as that word is used every day in Chicago, but describe the same thing as the right to lay down and use street railroad tracks in public streets, the right of user consisting of the right to operate street cars over and along the tracks, to carry people in them, and to exact tolls or fares from the people carried.

Under the Constitution of 1848 the people of Illinois, acting in their State Legislature, had the power either to make a direct grant of the right, or to authorize a municipal corporation to make such grant.

But under the present Constitution the State Legislature has no power to make a direct grant of the right, and can only authorize municipal corporations to make the grant. Article XI, Section 4, of that Constitution says: "No law shall be passed by the General Assembly granting the right to construct and operate a street railroad within any city, town, or incorporated village, without requiring the consent of the local authorities having the control of the street or highway proposed to be occupied by such street railroad."

This provision makes the operation and management of street railroads in Chicago a subject or object exclusively of local government. Under this provision it is very clear that all that a number of individuals combined together in a corporation to own and operate a street railroad over and along the streets of Chicago can get from the people of Illinois, acting in their State Legislature, is the bare power to carry on the business as a corporation. In 1899 the State Supreme Court said: "While it is true the charter of a street railway corporation is granted under the general laws of the State, yet a charter so obtained gives but the bare power to exist. In order to enable such a corporation to carry out the sole purpose for which it has existence, it must have a further exercise of sovereign power in its behalf. Some city or village clothed, by delegation, with authority to exercise sovereign power possessed by the State, must grant such corporation authority to enter upon its streets and alleys and construct and operate its road there" (The People v. Suburban R. Co., 178 Ill., 594, 605).

The city council of Chicago is the local authority in Chicago having control of the streets of Chicago. The right, liberty, privilege, franchise, or prerogative, or whatever else one may choose to call it (but being, as above stated, in the last analysis, only the special privilege, created, and bestowed upon private individuals by some competent authority chosen by the people, of doing work the people can do themselves by their own officers and employes whenever a majority of the electors want to), to lay down and use street railroad tracks in the streets of Chicago is, therefore, under the present law of Illinois, obtainable only by a grant made by the city council of Chicago, and the making of such grant is an exercise, by the city council, of the sovereign power of the people of Illinois, delegated to it, for purposes of local government, by the Constitution and Legislature of the State.

III. STREET RAILROAD FRANCHISES AND CABMEN'S LICENSES.

Obviously, so far, what is commonly called in Chicago a street railroad franchise differs in no material respect from what is commonly called a cabman's license. ' Such a license is but a grant by the city council of Chicago, under a power delegated to it by the State Legislature, of the right or privilege to carry people in cabs over and along the streets of Chicago, and to take tolls or fares from the people carried. It is the law of Illinois, and always has been, that street railroad companies and cabmen pursue like occupations. The State Supreme Court has said: "The only distinction which can be called substantial between the two classes of occupation is that one carriage goes upon iron rails, in a regular track, with wheels, and the other carriage goes with wheels upon the ordinary street way" (Allerton v. Chicago, 6 Fed. Rep., 555; Union Traction Co. v. Chicago, 199 Ill., 484, 517 to 522).

But the word "license" at once raises in the mind of everyone the thought that it is revocable, and certainly will be revoked, at least for good cause, by the city council, so no one is afraid to let the city council of Chicago grant a license to a cabman. The word "franchise," however, at once raises in the mind of nearly everyone the thought that it is irrevocable by the city council, and that thought is confirmed by the fact that no one has ever heard of the city council of Chicago revoking a franchise of a street railroad company even for a good cause, though occasions for exercising the power have not been wanting, as everyone in Chicago knows. And so very many think that the city council of Chicago should not be allowed to grant a street railroad franchise for a fixed term of years.

IV. THE CONCEPTION OF THE IRREVOCABILITY, BY LEGISLATIVE ACT, OF A STREET RAILROAD FRANCHISE.

Right there, in that thought that a street railroad franchise, once granted for a fixed term of years, and accepted, is irrevocable by the city council of Chicago at any time and for any cause before the expiration of the fixed term of years, lies the peculiar charm to some, and the peculiar odium to others, of a street railroad franchise. Is that thought correct?

It is, no doubt, true that, in England, before and at the time Blackstone wrote his definition of a franchise as being a branch of the king's prerogative, subsisting in the hands of a subject, under a royal grant, the king could not revoke a franchise granted by him unless he expressly reserved the right so to do in the grant. But the people of England, assembled in Parliament, always could revoke the king's grant, and their own grant as well, and can do it to-day, whenever a majority of them make up their minds the thing ought to be done (8 Am. Law Rev., 189). A few years after Blackstone wrote they began to talk about revoking the franchises of the great East India Company, and finally did it, after some fifty years or more of discussion (May's Constitutional History of England, Vol. II, pp. 540-546; New York, 1874, W. J. Widdleton, Publisher).

In the United States, in 1819, in the famous Dartmouth College case (4 Wheaton, 518), the Supreme Court of the United States extended the English doctrine of irrevocability by the king to a grant of a franchise made by the people of a State in this Union, assembled in their State Legislature, and, in consequence, held a grant of a franchise made by one State Legislature, and accepted by the grantee, to be irrevocable by the people of the

State acting in a subsequently convened Legislature, unless power to revoke the grant of the franchise, or to alter or amend the law making the grant of it had been previously reserved, either in the law itself making the grant, or in a general law in force at the date of the passage of the law making the grant, not repealed, or not repealable, by the latter law.

This doctrine of the irrevocability of a franchise granted by the people of a State acting in their State Legislature has never been extended, and, no doubt, cannot be extended, by judicial decision, to a franchise granted by the people of the United States, assembled in Congress (Sinking Fund Cases, 99 U. S., 700, 747), but it has been extended to a franchise granted by any subordinate, local, municipal body, of even lowest degree, sitting under a State Legislature, if the State Legislature had, in apt and clear words, delegated to such body power to grant franchises by the irrevocable method of the Dartmouth College case (Freeport Water Co. v. Freeport City, 180 U. S., 587, 593). And the doctrine has been carried so high, or so low, that a franchise granted by a State, or by a municipal body sitting under a State, is so under the "protection" of the Constitution of the United States, ordained to "establish justice" and "promote domestic tranquility" (Constitution of the United States, Preamble), that it is irrevocable by the people of the whole State, even though obtained by fraud and corruption of their elected representatives, and even though the people, by their Legislature, should offer to turn over to the grantees of the franchise everything of value received by them in exchange for, or in consideration of, the grant, together with every dollar bona fide expended in using the franchise granted (Fletcher v. Peck, 6 Cranch, 87; New Orleans v. Warner, 175 U. S., 120, 145).

Such is "the supreme law of the land," and such it has been now for nearly a century, maintained, in a large measure, I think, by sheer force of the fact that the great name of John Marshall is subscribed to it. That it is not now, and has not been for several years back, in harmony with the general sense of right of a majority of the American people is fully attested by statutes and constitutional amendments,[1] in force in nearly every State in the Union designed to get rid of it, in the way pointed out by Mr. Justice Story in his concurring opinion in the Dartmouth College case itself (4 Wheaton, 708) — that is to say, as above indicated, by reserving power to alter, amend, or repeal laws making grants of special privileges or franchises (Greenwood v. The Freight Company, 105 U. S., 13).

V. The legal basis of the Chicago street railroad tangle.

It is very evident to everyone that the street railroad war in Chicago has been, and is being, waged upon the basis of the accepted legal opinion that this doctrine of the irrevocability of a franchise granted by the Legislature of a State in this Union always has applied, and applies to-day, in Illinois to street railroad franchises granted by the city council of Chicago. And it is largely, if not wholly, because of this accepted legal opinion that, on the one hand, the managers of the two largest street railroads in Chicago want so badly to get street railroad franchises from the city council, and that, on the other hand, perhaps a majority of the electors of Chicago appear to be even angrily determined that they must not get what they want so much.

Is that accepted legal opinion sound? Is it true, so far as street railroad franchises in Chicago are concerned,

---

[1] They are gathered in 3 Cook on Corporations, Ed. 4, 1898, Sections 946, et seq.

that the people of Chicago ever were subject to, or are not yet emancipated from, what Chief Justice Ryan of Wisconsin in 1874 called the "thralldom" of the doctrine of the Dartmouth College case (Attorney-General *v.* Railroad Companies, 35 Wis., 425, 574)?

I think that, so far as street railroad franchises are concerned, the people of Chicago never were subject to, or bound by, the doctrine of the Dartmouth College case, and I also think the people of Chicago were emancipated from the possibility of being bound by the doctrine of that case in and by the present State Constitution, in force August 8, 1870, so far as all laws making grants of franchises, passed subsequent to that date, are concerned.

VI. THE DOCTRINE OF THE DARTMOUTH COLLEGE CASE.

Under the doctrine of the Dartmouth College case, certain provisions of a municipal ordinance making a grant of street railroad privileges, such as, for example, the part of the ordinance making the grant and the part of it fixing the rate of fare to be charged, may become, when the ordinance has been accepted by the grantee, irrevocable by act of the legislative authority of the municipality, or by act of the Legislature of the State, because such provisions may become "contracts," within the meaning of the word "contracts," in that clause of the Constitution of the United States which says that "No State shall pass any law impairing the obligation of contracts," and, consequently, any subsequent act of the legislative authority of the municipality, or of the State Legislature, altering, amending, or repealing or revoking such provisions, without the consent of the grantee, might be void, as a State law impairing the obligation of contracts, in contravention of the prohibition in the Constitution of the United States against the passage of any such State law.

But, as above indicated, it is settled that, in order that that constitutional prohibition, as interpreted and applied in the Dartmouth College case, may operate down upon any of the provisions of a municipal ordinance making a grant of street railroad privileges, it must appear, first, that the Legislature of the State, in apt, clear, and unambiguous words, has delegated to the municipal legislative authority that passed the ordinance power to bind itself and the State Legislature by the irrevocable contract method of the Dartmouth College case not to use the legislative power to alter, amend, or repeal, or revoke, because a municipal corporation of a State has only such powers of government as are expressly granted to it by the State Legislature, or by the State Constitution, and because the power to bind, by irrevocable contract, the people of a State not to use their legislative power is so very extraordinary a power that it cannot arise in a municipal body by mere inference. (Chicago v. Rumpf, 45 Ill., 90; People's Railroad v. Memphis Railroad, 10 Wallace, 38, 51; Birmingham St. R. Case, 79 Ala., 465, 470; Lake Roland El. R. Co. v. Baltimore, 20 L. R. A., 126; Providence Bank v. Billings, 4 Peters, 514; Charles River Bridge v. Warren Bridge, 11 Peters, 420.) And it must appear, secondly, that the Legislature of the State was not forbidden by the State Constitution, in force at the date of the passage of the ordinance, to part with the power, or to divest itself of the right to use the power, to alter, amend, or repeal or revoke laws making grants of rights, privileges, franchises, or immunities within the gift of the State, because such a State constitutional prohibition becomes part and parcel of the ordinance, and, therefore, a subsequent State law, altering, amending, or repealing the ordinance is consistent with the contract evidenced by it, and cannot, therefore, impair its obligation. (Greenwood *v.* Freight Co., 105 U. S., 13; New Jersey *v.* Yard, 95 U. S., 104, 111; Hamilton Gas Light and Coke Company *v.* Hamilton City, 146 U. S., 258, 270.)

VII. HAS THE DOCTRINE OF THE DARTMOUTH COLLEGE CASE EVER HAD ANY APPLICATION AT ALL TO ORDINANCES OF THE COUNCIL OF CHICAGO MAKING GRANTS OF STREET RAILROAD FRANCHISES?

The questions arising are: First, has the Legislature of Illinois ever made a direct, irrevocable grant of the right to lay down and use street railroad tracks in the streets of the city of Chicago? Second, has the Legislature of Illinois ever made an express grant of power to the council of Chicago to bind itself, and the State Legislature, by irrevocable contract, not to use, for a fixed period of time, the legislative power to alter, amend, repeal or revoke an ordinance making a grant of the right to lay down and use street railroad tracks in the streets of Chicago? Third, could the Legislature of Illinois, consistently with the State Constitution, in force at the time, make an express grant of such power to the council of Chicago?

In considering these questions, the legislative history of Illinois must be divided into two periods — first, April 1, 1848, to August 8, 1870, during which Illinois was organized under the Constitution of 1848, and, second, August 8, 1870, to the present time, the present State Constitution having gone into force on August 8, 1870.

VIII. THE CONSTITUTION OF 1848 DID NOT FORBID THE STATE LEGISLATURE TO ITSELF MAKE, OR TO AUTHORIZE CHICAGO TO MAKE, IRREVOCABLE GRANTS.

As above stated, August 16, 1858, marks the beginning of street railroads in Chicago, because on that date the common council of Chicago made its first grant of a street railroad franchise. Illinois was then organized under her second State Constitution, in force April 1, 1848, and continued to operate under that Constitution, as above stated, until the present Constitution took effect on August 8, 1870. For present purposes, it may be conceded that, under the Constitution of 1848, the Legislature of Illinois could itself pass a law making a direct, irrevocable grant of the right to lay down and use street railroad tracks in the streets of Chicago, or could delegate the power to make such irrevocable grant to the common council of Chicago. Under that concession, the sole inquiry here now is, whether the Lesigla-ture ever did pass a law prior to August 8, 1870, making such an irrevocable grant, or ever passed a law delegating to the council of Chicago power to make such an irrevocable grant.

IX. CHICAGO'S SPECIAL CHARTER OF 1851 NEITHER MADE, NOR DELEGATED POWER TO CHICAGO TO MAKE, IRREVOCABLE GRANTS.

At the date (August 16, 1858) of the making of the first grant of a street railroad franchise Chicago was operating as a municipal corporation under a special charter granted by the State Legislature, in force February 14, 1851 (Private Laws, Illinois, 1851, p. 40). This charter gave the common council a most extensive legislative power to regulate and control the use of the streets of Chicago, and specifically enumerated this legislative power: "To regulate and prohibit the use of locomotive engines within the city, and may require the cars to be used thereon, within the inhabited portions thereof, to be drawn or propelled by other power than that of steam; to direct and control the location of railroad tracks and depot grounds, and prohibit railroad companies from doing storage and warehouse business and collecting pay for storage" (Clause 49, Private Laws, 1851, p. 146). The charter of 1851 also gave the common council power "to license, regulate, and suppress hackmen, draymen, carters, porters, omnibus drivers, cabmen, packers, carmen, and all others who may pursue like occupations with or without vehicles, under other cognomens, and prescribe their compensation" (Ch. 4, Sec. 4, Cl. 9, Act of 1851; 199 Ill., 517), as well as a sweeping power to make, amend, and repeal all such ordinances "as may be necessary or expedient to carry into effect the powers vested in the common council . . . by this act" (Ch. 4, Cl. 62, Act of 1851; 199 Ill., 517).

At the April term, 1859, the Supreme Court of the State decided that the common council of Chicago had power, under this charter of 1851, to pass any ordinance making a grant to a steam commercial railroad company of the right to lay down and use tracks in a public street, deriving the power of the council by implication from the power to regulate the use of streets and from the express power to regulate and control the location of railroad tracks within the city. Mr. Chief Justice Caton, to illustrate and explain the ruling of the Court, said that a contrary ruling would require the Court to hold that the common council did not have power, under the charter of 1851, to grant the right to lay down and use street railroad tracks for the operation of street cars propelled by horses, a result which he thought would be a manifest absurdity (Moses *v.* Pittsburg, Ft. Wayne and Chicago R. Co., 21 Ill., 511, 523).

Under the said ruling of the State Supreme Court in April, 1859, the common council clearly had the power, under Chicago's charter of 1851, to pass the said ordinance of August 16, 1858 (see also 199 Ill., 523).

That ordinance made a grant to certain individuals, Henry Fuller, Franklin Parmelee, and Liberty Bigelow, of the right to lay down and use, with animal power only, street railroad tracks in certain streets in the south and west divisions of Chicago, for twenty-five years (199 Ill., 488). That ordinance was not void, because the common council had the power to pass it. And natural persons were then, and are now, just as competent to receive, exercise, and enjoy a grant of the right to use a public street by operating a street railroad over and along it with horses and mules as a fictitious person, or corporation (New Orleans, Spanish Fort and Lake Erie Railroad Co. v. Delamore, 114 U. S., 501, 507–8).

But did that ordinance of August 16, 1858, when accepted by the grantees, become an unalterable, unamendable, and irrevocable grant or contract? That it did not is clear, I think, because, plainly, the common council had no power, by delegation from the Legislature, in Chicago's charter of 1851, in clear, apt, and unambiguous language, to give that legal effect to the ordinance, and because it had express power in the charter of 1851 to alter or repeal that ordinance.

In 1902, in reply to a contention made on behalf of the Chicago Union Traction Company, claiming that ordinance by assignment, that that ordinance of August 16, 1858, operated as an irrevocable contract, binding the council of Chicago not to cut the rate of street car fares below five cents by compelling that corporation to give transfer tickets, the Supreme Court of the State said: "At the time of the passage of the ordinance of August 16th, 1858, there was no law or statute in Illinois conferring upon the common council of any city the power to make a contract with any person, firm, or corporation, engaged in the business of carrying passengers for hire, obligating the city never to change the rates once fixed, or to make a contract with any such person, firm, or corporation in relation to a maximum rate of fare to be charged. Hence, the common council could not have passed Section 6 of the ordinance of 1858 in pursuance of any act of the Legislature, granting the power to make such contract. The only act of the Legislature then existing, which conferred upon the common council the power to pass Section 6 of the ordinance of 1858, was the act of February 14th, 1851," that is Chicago's charter of 1851 (Union Traction Company *v.* Chicago, 199 Ill., 484, 523–4).

That ordinance of August 16, 1858, was, therefore, primarily a law. The State Supreme Court has said: "When an incorporated town or city has been invested with power to pass an ordinance, by the Legislature, for the government or welfare of the municipality, an ordinance enacted by the legislative branch of the corporation, in pursuance of the act creating the corporation, has the same force and effect of a law passed by the Legislature, and cannot be regarded otherwise than a law of, and within, the incorporation. An ordinance is a law of the inhabitants of the municipality" (Mason *v.* City of Shawneetown, 77 Ill., 533, 537; Tudor *v.* Rapid Transit R. R. Co., 154 Ill., 129, 136).

That ordinance being primarily a law, and the common council being without power to turn it into an irrevocable and unalterable contract, necessarily each and every provision of it was alterable and repealable by the common council, within the limits of its delegated power of legislation, under its express power to alter and repeal in the charter of 1851, or by the State Legislature.

But it should be observed that that ordinance was also a contract, though not an irrevocable contract. An individual or a corporation never could be compelled, and never can be compelled, under our written Constitutions, against his or its will, to do the work of carrying people in street cars over and along a public street. The right and duty of an individual or corporation to perform that work can arise, and be imposed upon an individual or corporation, only with his or its consent. Hence an ordinance creating the right and imposing the duty necessarily must, in a large measure, take the form of a grant, or contract, to be accepted or assented to by the individual or corporation proposing to build and operate a street railroad under the ordinance. And such ordinance is, in substance, a contract, even when the municipality has no power, by delegation from the Legislature, or because of a reservation of power, to make the ordinance unalterable and irrepealable, but it is an alterable and revocable contract, that is to say, alterable and revocable by one of the parties to it, the people, by their agents, the legislative authority of the municipality acting within the limits of its delegated power of legislation, or the Legislature of the State. Until the right to alter and revoke is excerised, the contract, though revocable, is just as binding and obligatory upon the parties to it, and upon the whole world, as it would be if made irrevocable. Such alterable and revocable contracts are not unusual in private transactions. For example, a lease of a house for a fixed term of years, terminable before the expiration of the term at the will of the landlord, is a contract binding upon tenant, landlord, and all the world, until the landlord elects to put an end to it and to enter into the possession, use, and enjoyment of his own. Obviously, had the Supreme Court of the United States reached a different result in the Dartmouth College case, and it probably would have done so had the cause been argued differently at the bar (8 Am. Law Rev., 210, 210, and Note 2; 28 ib., 336, 440), no state law and no municipal ordinance making a grant of the right to use a street for street railroad purposes could operate as an irrevocable contract, and the grantees would have to rely, as they have always done, and must now do, all over the world, "for the perpetuity and integrity of the franchises granted to them, solely upon the faith of the sovereign grantor" (Cooley, Const. Lim., Ed. 6, 472).

This difference between revocable contracts or grants, and irrevocable contracts or grants, respecting the use of streets for street railroad purposes, under the doctrine of the Dartmouth College case, must ever be kept in mind to avoid falling into the fallacy, not unusual in such cases, of non sequitur, by drawing the conclusion, "the ordinance is irrevocable," from the premise, "the ordinance is a contract."

That ordinance of August 16, 1858, was, therefore, in one aspect a law and in another a contract, but, by reason of the lack of power in the common council to make the ordinance unalterable, unamendable, and irrepealable, and by reason of its express power to alter, amend, and repeal, and under the rule in the Dartmouth College case, it was a law or a contract which the common council or the State Legislature could alter or determine. (Attorney-General v. R. R. Companies, 35 Wis., 424, 574; Monongahela Navigation Co. v. United States, 148 U. S., 312, 343; Slaughter House Co. v. Slaughter House Co., 111 U. S., 746; The Slaughter House Cases, 16 Wallace, 36; Cooley, Const. Lim., Ed. 6, 472.)

X. CHICAGO'S SPECIAL CHARTER OF 1863 NEITHER MADE, NOR DELEGATED POWER TO CHICAGO TO MAKE, IRREVOCABLE GRANTS.

Chicago's special charter of 1851 was superseded by a special charter, in force February 13, 1863 (Private Laws, Illinois, 1863, Vol. 1, p. 40), very considerably amended by an act, in force March 9, 1867 (Private Laws, Illinois, Vol. 1, p. 754). Express power to regulate and control the use of streets and to amend and repeal ordinances is given in the charter of 1863 in much the same words as in the charter of 1851. Clause 64, p. 60, of the charter of 1863 grants power "to regulate the running of horse railway cars, the laying down of tracks for the same, the transportation of passengers therein, and the kind of rail to be used." In the act of 1867, clause 9, page 771, gives power "to authorize the use of streets and alleys in said city by railroad companies or city railroad companies, for the purpose of laying tracks and running cars thereon"; provides that such "permission and authority" shall not be given, nor shall any such "grant or permission" already given be extended, unless upon a vote of three-fourths of all the aldermen elected, and provides that "no grant, consent, contract, or permission heretofore given or made, or hereafter to be made or given, shall in any case be extended until within one year of the expiration of such grant, consent, contract, or permission." Clause 23, p. 773, gives power "to allow dummies or steam engines to be used on the street railways of the city by ordinance or contract"; also, "at any time to order a partial or total discontinuance of the use of such dummies and engines in said city." An act, in force March 10, 1869 (Private Laws, Illinois, 1869, Sec. 1, p. 335), amended said clause 9 so as to read: "To allow dummies or steam engines to be used on the street railways of said city upon such terms and conditions as said common council may by contract with said railway companies determine."

Wholly aside from the express grant of power to amend and repeal all ordinances, it is impossible to affirm, upon the settled rules of interpretation for such cases, that any of the aforesaid words are apt and proper, either to make, or to delegate power to the common council of Chicago to make, irrevocable grants or contracts respecting the operation and management of street railways in public streets. The multiplicity of words used to designate the effect of an ordinance granting the right to lay down and use street railroad tracks in a street — grant, consent, contract or permission and authority, ordinance or contract —

indicate clearly that there was no legislative intent to grant power to make irrevocable contracts. The word franchise is avoided.

The uncertainty of conception evidenced by these various words used as equivalents, and the avoidance of the word franchise, is explained, I think, by two decisions of the Court of Appeals of New York, one in December, 1856 (Davis v. The Mayor of New York, 14 N. Y., 506), and the other in September, 1863 (Milhau v. Sharp, 27 N. Y., 611), wherein it was ruled that a New York municipal ordinance passed December 29, 1852 (quite like the first Chicago street railroad ordinance of 1858), in the now usual form, granting to Jacob Sharp and his associates the right to lay down and use street railroad tracks in Broadway, New York City, was utterly void under New York's charter, as an irrevocable grant of a franchise; one Judge, Wright, holding the ordinance good as "a license, revocable at pleasure, although in form a grant or contract"; and another Judge, Comstock, holding that the board of aldermen of New York City had power, under the city charter, to authorize "by mere license" individuals to construct and operate a street railroad in Broadway, but holding the ordinance void, because, on its true construction, it was an attempt to make an irrevocable grant of a franchise in perpetuity. As above stated, the Supreme Court of Illinois ruled, in 1859, that the council of Chicago had power, under the charter of 1851, to authorize the use of streets for railroad purposes.

Chicago continued to operate under the charter of 1863, as amended in 1867, until, pursuant to a popular vote cast April 23, 1875, she organized as a city on the first Monday in May, 1875, under the general Cities and Villages Act, in force July 1, 1872. The Constitution of 1870, in force August 8 of that year, by Section 1 of the Schedule, continued said charter of 1863 and its amendments in force, so far as not inconsistent with the provisions of that Constitution.

XI. THE SPECIAL ACTS OF THE LEGISLATURE OF 1859, 1861, AND 1865, RELATING TO HORSE RAILROADS IN CHICAGO, NEITHER MADE, NOR AUTHORIZED CHICAGO TO MAKE, IRREVOCABLE GRANTS.

It has never been contended by anyone, so far as I know, that by said charters of 1851 and 1863 the Legislature either made, or gave the common council of Chicago power to make, irrevocable grants to, or irrevocable contracts with, anyone respecting the operation and management of street railroads in the streets of Chicago. The assumption has been, that the common council of Chicago had no power at all, under those charters, to deal with the subject of laying down and using street railroad tracks in the streets of Chicago (Opinion of Corporation Counsel, July 17, 1883, Council Proceedings, 1883–4, p. 77; Govin v. Chicago, 132 Fed. Rep., 848), an assumption that is manifestly irreconcilable with the aforesaid ruling of the State Supreme Court in 1859. Those who maintain that the Legislature either made, or authorized the common council of Chicago to make, prior to August 8, 1870, irrevocable grants or contracts respecting the operation and management of street railroads in the streets of Chicago, point only to certain special acts passed by the Legislature in 1859, 1861, and 1865, the primary purpose of which was to empower certain individuals to carry on the street railroad business in Chicago as corporations.

February 19, 1859, the Legislature passed a special act creating the individual grantees named in the said ordinance of August 16, 1858, a body politic and corporate by the name of the Chicago City Railway Company for twenty-five years. Section 2 provided as follows:

"The said corporation is hereby authorized and empowered to construct, maintain, and operate a single or double track railway, with all necessary and convenient tracks for turnouts, sidetracks, and appendages, in the city of Chicago and in, on, over, and along such street or streets, highway or highways, bridge or bridges, river or rivers, within the present or future limits of the south or west divisions of the city of Chicago, as the Common Council of said city have authorized said corporators, or any of them, or shall authorize said corporation so to do, in such manner and upon such terms and conditions, with such rights and privileges as the said Common Council has or may by contract with said parties, or any or either of them, prescribe; but said corporation shall not be liable for the loss of any baggage carried on said railways, kept in and under the care of its owner, his servant or agent."

The tenth section of the act created certain named individuals a body politic and corporate by the name of the North Chicago City Railway Company, with the same powers and privileges in the north division of Chicago as were given to the Chicago City Railway Company in the south and west divisions. The act was entitled "An act to promote the construction of horse railways in the City of Chicago" (Private Laws, Illinois, 1859, p. 530).

February 21, 1861, "an act to authorize the extension of horse railways in the City of Chicago" was passed, creating certain individuals a body politic and corporate under the name of the Chicago West Division Railway Company, with substantially all the powers for constructing and operating street railroads in the west division of Chicago that were conferred by the Act of 1869 upon the two corporations thereby created (Private Laws, Illinois, 1861, p. 340).

July 29, 1863, the Chicago City Railway Company agreed to sell to the Chicago West Division Railway Company all its property, privileges, and franchises in the west division of Chicago, and the agreement was executed by a deed of conveyance on July 20, 1863 (199 Ill., 498–499).

February 6, 1865, "an act concerning horse railways in the City of Chicago" was passed (Private Laws,

Illinois, 1865, p. 597). It extended the corporate life of said three horse railway corporations from twenty-five to ninety-nine years, and amended Section 2 of the Act of 1859 by making some slight verbal changes in it and by adding to it the following words:

"And any and all acts or deeds of transfer of rights, privileges, or franchises, between the corporations in said several acts named, or any two of them, and all contracts, stipulations, licenses, and undertakings made, entered into, or given, and as made or amended by and between the said common council and any one or more of the said corporations, respecting the location, use, or exclusion of railways or in upon the streets, or any of them, of said city, shall be deemed and held and continued in force, during the life hereof, as valid and effectual, to all intents and purposes, as if made a part, and the same are hereby made a part, of said several acts" [of 1859 and 1861].

The Chicago City Railway Company, created by said act of 1859, operated horse railways in the south division of Chicago up to some time after the year 1880, when horses began to give way to the cable and electricity as a motive power, that company, and all other street railway companies in Chicago, obtaining the right to change their motive power under ordinances passed by the city council of Chicago after 1880, or, at least, after the taking effect of the present State Constitution on August 8, 1870. The North Chicago City Railway Company, created by the act of 1859, operated horse railways in the north division of Chicago up to about the year 1886, when it made a lease of all its property and franchises to the North Chicago Street Railroad Company, a corporation organized under the Illinois General Incorporation Act, in force July 1, 1872. This latter company operated horse, cable, and electric railways in the north division of Chicago up to about June 1, 1899, when it made a lease to the Chicago Union Traction Company, organized under the Illinois General Incorporation Act, in force July 1, 1872.

The Chicago West Division Railway Company, created by the act of 1861, operated horse railways in the west division of Chicago up to about the year 1889, when it made a lease to the West Chicago Street Railroad Company, organized under the Illinois General Incorporation Act, in force July 1, 1872. This latter company operated horse, cable, and electric railways in the west division of Chicago up to June 1, 1899, when it made a lease to the said Chicago Union Traction Company. The latter company claims, without any reason (199 Ill., 500–503), the right to use and enjoy whatever rights the North Chicago City Railway Company and the Chicago West Division Railway Company got under the said acts of 1859, 1861, and 1865, just as fully as the Chicago City Railway Company, which was one of the original corporations named in said acts.

XII. THE WORDS ABOVE QUOTED FROM THE ACT OF 1865, IN CONJUNCTION WITH THE WORDS ABOVE QUOTED FROM THE ACT OF 1859, DID NOT OPERATE TO TURN ALTERABLE AND REVOCABLE ORDINANCES PASSED BY THE COMMON COUNCIL INTO IRREVOCABLE CONTRACTS FOR TWENTY-FIVE OR NINETY-NINE YEARS.

The words quoted from the act of 1865 are wholly retrospective. They touch and affect only past transactions, and have no prospective operation whatever; that is to say, they do not affect any transactions that took place after February 6, 1865, the date of the passage of the act in which they are found. One of the main purposes of the men interested in those acts evidently was to confine each of the corporations created by the acts of 1859 and 1861 to a particular division or side of the city of Chicago, and to prohibit one corporation from invading the territory, side, or preserve of the other. They attempted, prior to February 6, 1865, to do that by agreements and deeds among themselves, running for a much

longer period than twenty-five years, the allotted span
of life given the corporations by the acts of 1859 and 1861
(199 Ill., 498, 530). Under the acts of 1859 and 1861
those agreements and deeds were of extremely questionable validity, and the common council of Chicago, however much it may have tried by "contracts, stipulations,
licenses, and undertakings," had no power to inject
validity into such "acts or deeds of transfer of rights,
privileges, or franchises between the corporations . . . or
any two of them, respecting the location, use, or exclusion of street railways in or upon the streets or any of
them of said city" (Chicago Gas Light and Coke Company v. People's Gas Light & Coke Co., 121 Ill., 530).
The Legislature alone had the power to do that, and
attempted to do it on February 6, 1865, by laying down a
rule for the guidance of the courts in effect saying: You
must hold all those acts, deeds of transfer, contracts,
stipulations, licenses, and undertakings, parceling out
Chicago between these three horse railway corporations
"valid and effectual," "during the life hereof," "as made
or amended" by the parties to them, just as if the State
Legislature, sitting in 1859 and 1861, had written out the
whole of them in words in the acts of 1859 and 1861 and
had then passed those acts. Assuming that the Legislature, sitting in 1865, could, consistently with the mandate of the Constitution of 1848 that "every bill shall
be read on three different days, in each house" (Article
III, Section 23), thus in 1865 stuff tons of unknown and
unknowable literature into the bosoms of acts passed by
a former Legislature in 1859 and 1861, the words above
quoted do not, so far as I can see, necessarily alter the
legal effect of ordinances passed prior to February 6,
1865. That is to say, if an ordinance granting the right
to lay down and use tracks in a street, passed prior to
February 6, 1865, operated as an alterable, amendable

and revocable contract, the said words of the act of 1865 did not operate retrospectively upon such previously passed ordinance to turn it into an unalterable, unamendable and irrepealable, or irrevocable, contract for ninety-nine years, because the act of 1865, if it says anything at all about such ordinances, says they shall be held "valid and effectual as made or amended," and if you carry them back "as made or amended" to 1859 and 1861 and then insert them "as made or amended" into those acts of 1859 and 1861, necessarily you must carry into those acts the reserved legislative power to alter and revoke, otherwise you do not carry them back and insert them "as made or amended" into those acts, but you carry back and insert into those acts something widely and totally different from the thing previously made. The intent of the framers of the act of 1865, as evidenced by the retrospective words used in the act, was, I think, that those retrospective words should apply to, and operate upon, only such past "acts," "deeds of transfer," "contracts, stipulations, licenses, and undertakings," as were of questionable validity, or wholly invalid, under the powers granted in the acts of 1859 and 1861, and in Chicago's charters of 1851 and 1863. An intent to change the legal effect of a valid ordinance previously passed from a revocable contract into an irrevocable contract certainly is not clearly made manifest. As above stated, an ordinance making a grant of the right to lay down and use street railroad tracks in a street may very well be "valid and effectual," though in legal effect an alterable and revocable contract.

A question left is whether the words first above quoted from the act of 1859, in so far as retrospective in their operation, and carried forward into the acts of 1861 and 1865, operated to change previously passed ordinances making grants of the right to lay down and use street railway tracks in public streets, which, if passed solely under the powers granted in Chicago's charters of 1851 and 1863, could operate only as revocable contracts, into irrevocable contracts.

The acts of 1859 and 1861 gave certain named individuals the right to be a corporation. They then stated the purposes for which the corporation was formed, by giving the corporation certain specified powers, or, in other words, by assigning to it a very limited sphere of human activity and endeavor, to wit: "to construct, maintain, and operate a single or double track railway in the city of Chicago." Then, recognizing that the railway would have to be constructed and operated in, on, over, and along streets, highways, bridges, and rivers, of which the common council, under the city's charter, had exclusive control, and that the operation and management of street railways in Chicago was a purely local affair, it restricted the corporation to the use of only "such" streets, highways, bridges, and rivers "as the common council of said city have authorized said corporators . . . or shall authorize said corporation so to do." But the common council was not restricted to a mere grant or refusal of authority, to saying merely yes or no, to use the streets, highways, bridges, and rivers of the city, but the corporation was required to construct and operate its railway in streets authorized to be used by the common council "in such manner and upon such terms and conditions, with such rights and privileges, as the said common council has or may by contract . . . prescribe."

In 1902, the Supreme Court of Illinois said that the words, "as the said common council has or may by contract prescribe," are elliptical, and mean, "as the said common council has prescribed, or may by contract prescribe," and that, therefore, in so far as the words are retrospective, they did not change the legal effect of a

valid ordinance passed prior to the date of the act of
1859 from a revocable contract into an irrevocable contract, whatever might be their effect upon ordinances
passed subsequent to the date of the act, February 19,
1859 (199 Ill., 484, 524). The Court said: "The last
clause is elliptical and the word 'prescribed,' to which
the word 'has' applies, was accidently omitted. If the
word thus omitted be supplied, the clause should read as
follows: 'With such rights and privileges as the common
council has prescribed, or may by contract with said
parties, or any or either of them, prescribe? The words,
'by contract with said parties, or any or either of them,'
qualify the words 'may prescribe.' That is to say, the
right to contract was a right to be exercised in the future.
The words 'with such rights and privileges as the said
common council has prescribed' refer to the past." That
view is certainly permissible (Freeport Water Co. *v.* Freeport City, 180 U. S., 587, 598). If it "be not clear, as I
think it is, yet any other construction is certainly not so,
and doubt is fatal to the claim" of a legislative intention
to turn a past municipal revocable contract or grant into
an irrevocable contract or grant (Mobile, etc., R. Co. *v.*
Tennessee, 153 U. S., 486, dissenting opinion).

XIII. THE SAID SECTION 2 OF THE ACT OF 1859, IN SO FAR AS
IT IS PROSPECTIVE IN ITS OPERATION, DID NOT MAKE A DIRECT
IRREVOCABLE GRANT OF THE RIGHT TO USE THE STREETS OF CHI-
CAGO FOR STREET RAILROAD PURPOSES.

The words, in so far as prospective, are: "The said
corporation is hereby . . . empowered to construct,
maintain, and operate a single or double track railway
. . . in the city of Chicago, and in, on, over, and along
such . . . streets . . . of the city of Chicago
as the common council of said city . . . shall authorize
said corporation so to do, in such manner, and upon
such terms and conditions, and with such rights and

CONSTITUTIONAL LAW

privileges as the said common council may by contract
. . . (with said corporation) prescribe."

Manifestly, the words of the act do not authorize and empower the corporation to enter upon any street in Chicago and locate and construct its railway there. The only granted power is the abstracted corporate power, or capacity, to build and operate a street railroad in Chicago. The act virtually prohibits the corporation to use that power in or upon any street in Chicago, for the corporation is allowed to use the power only in "such streets" "as the common council shall authorize." Plainly, the words of the section do not make a direct grant of the franchise to enter upon a street in Chicago and build and operate a street railroad there. The council, under the act, clearly could refuse to authorize the use of a street by the corporation. Could the corporation lawfully, in the face of such refusal, enter upon a street? Plainly not.

XIV. Said section 2, in so far as it is prospective in its operation, did not delegate power to the common council of Chicago to make irrevocable grants of the right to lay down and use street railroad tracks in the streets of Chicago.

The only words manifesting such legislative intent are the words "by contract." Acts of a Legislature must be construed according to the rules of English grammar. The words "by contract" form an adverbial phrase. Looking at the sentence in which they are found, obviously they must qualify the preceding verb "shall authorize," or the verb whose parts they split, that is, "may . . . prescribe." "The strict rule of grammar would seem to require, as a general thing, a limiting clause or phrase, following several expressions to which it might be applicable, to be restrained to the last antecedent" (Endlich, Interpretation of Statutes, Sec. 414). Applying that rule of grammar, the words "by contract" must qualify only the antecedent "may prescribe." The application of this rule of grammar is expressly enjoined by the fact that the words "by contract" are placed between "may" and "prescribe." That position of the words appears to demonstrate that the intent of the Legislature was to restrict the qualifying phrase, "by contract," to the verb "may prescribe." It is true that "this technical grammatical rule is liable to be displaced whenever the subject matter requires a different construction" (Endlich, supra). But there is nothing about the subject matter of this act rendering it necessary to displace this grammatical rule. The question being whether the act authorizes the making of contracts irrevocably binding a State not to use its legislative power, the law requires that the words used be so construed as to preserve the legislative power of the State intact as a continuing, unsold power, unless an intention to sell it out by contract is shown in clear, grammatically constructed sentences (Providence Bank v. Billings, 4 Peters, 514; Charles River Bridge v. Warren Bridge, 11 Peters, 420). Besides, as above stated, the Legislature itself restricted the qualifying words "by contract" to the verb "may prescribe" by placing them between "may" and "prescribe." Besides, the Supreme Court of Illinois has said, as above shown, that the words "by contract" cannot be carried back and made to qualify the elliptical verb "has prescribed" (Union Traction Co. v. Chicago, 199 Ill., 484, 524). And the Circuit Court of the United States has said that the words "by contract" cannot be carried back and made to qualify the verb "shall authorize" (Govin v. Chicago, 132 Fed. Rep., 848, 856).

The words, "in such streets as the common council shall authorize," are not, in form at least, a grant of power to the council. In form they are a restriction or limitation upon the use of power granted to the street railroad corporation created by the act to construct a street railroad, forbidding that corporation to use that power on a particular part of the earth's surface — the streets of Chicago — except when authorized "so to do" by the common council of Chicago. The words recognize the council as the existing legislative authority of the local government of Chicago, organized by and under Chicago's municipal charter. The words, therefore, refer us to that charter to ascertain in what manner the council may act when it sets out to authorize the street railroad corporation to enter upon a street in Chicago and construct a street railroad in, on, over, and along that street. That charter shows that the council must act "by ordinance"; that the council cannot make the ordinance irrevocable for a fixed term of years; that the council has express power to alter, amend, and repeal the ordinance.

It is plain, therefore, that the words of this Section 2 of the acts of 1859, 1861, and 1865 did not clothe the common council of Chicago with power to give the street railroad corporations, organized under those acts, an irrevocable right, or franchise, to lay down and use street railroad tracks in the streets of Chicago for a fixed term of years.

Taking up now the words, "in such manner, and upon such terms and conditions, and with such rights and privileges as the said common council . . . may . . . by contract prescribe," evidently they also subject the street railroad corporation to a further restriction or limitation upon the use of its power to construct, maintain, and operate a street railroad in the streets of Chicago by compelling the corporation to use the power agreeably to such rules and regulations touching the mode of construction, operation, and management of its street railroad in the streets of Chicago as the common council "may by contract prescribe." Is it permissible to insert the word "irrevocable" before the word "contract"? Manifestly it is not permissible, without violating settled rules of statutory interpretation for such case. The word "contract" is sufficiently comprehensive to include revocable and irrevocable contracts. But the word here occurs in a clause at once limiting the power of a street railroad corporation, and enlarging the power of the legislative authority of a municipal corporation. To insert the word "irrevocable" before the word "contract" would give the clause a capacity, or potentiality, to operate as an enlargement of the power of the street railroad corporation, and as a limitation upon the power of the municipal corporation, by enabling the legislative authority of the municipal corporation to divest itself, and the State Legislature as well, of a portion of the legislative power of the State in favor of the street railroad corporation. Besides, if, as above shown, the essence and quintessence of an ordinance making a grant of the right to use a street, the granting part of it, cannot, under the act, operate as an irrevocable contract, what sense would there be in making the parts of such ordinance touching the construction, operation, and management of the road operate as irrevocable contracts? Ninety-nine per cent. of all legislative regulations of the operation and management of a street railroad in the streets of a city, affecting as they do the health and safety of the people, cannot, by any possibility, be brought within the application of the doctrine of the Dartmouth College case (cases cited infra).

The words of this clause here in hand "purport to enlarge, not to diminish the powers vested" in the common council by Chicago's existing charter (McCulloch v. Maryland, 4 Wheaton, 311, 420): "It is a rule of construction, acknowledged by all, that the exceptions from a power (granted or delegated) mark its extent; for it would be absurd, as well as useless, to except from a granted power that which was not granted, that which the words of the grant could not comprehend" (Gibbons *v.* Ogden, 9 Wheaton, 1, 191). Now the part of Section 2 of the act of 1859 in question here being, in substance, a present grant of more power to the common council, note the subject or object of legislative power excepted from the grant: "but said corporation shall not be liable for the loss of any baggage carried on said railway kept in and under the care of its owner, his servant, or agent." The subject or object evidently is a subject or object of what is commonly called the police powers of a State government. A State Legislature never could, as hereinafter shown, by irrevocable contract, under the doctrine of the Dartmouth College case, bind itself not to use its police powers over some subjects or objects of government. The exception, therefore, would appear to be irreconcilable with an expressed intent, by use of the phrase "by contract," to clothe the common council of Chicago with the extraordinary power to bind itself, and the State Legislature as well, by irrevocable contract, not to use for ninetynine years the legislative power of the State to its fullest extent over the operation and management of street railroads in Chicago by the corporations created by the acts of 1859 and 1861.

Viewing the grant of power to the street railway corporations, in the act of 1859, "to construct, maintain, and operate a single or double track railway . . . in the city of Chicago, and in, on, over, and along such . . . streets . . . as the common council of said city . . . shall authorize said corporation so to do, in such manner and upon such terms and conditions, and with such rights and privileges as the said common council . . . may by contract . . . prescribe," as a present grant of more power to the common council of Chicago, the grant evidently did enlarge the pre-existing powers of the council by enabling it to prescribe regulations, in the form of terms and conditions in the ordinance authorizing the use of streets and to grant rights and privileges in such ordinance, that it could not have prescribed or granted under the powers then vested in the common council by Chicago's charter. For example, it could and did (revocably) exempt the street railway corporations from liability to pay a special assessment for curbing and paving streets (Chicago v. Sheldon, 9 Wallace, 50), a thing the council could not possibly have done under any power vested in the council by Chicago's charter, as it stood in 1859 (Chicago v. Baer, 41 Ill., 306). And it is familiar law in Illinois, that a city council can impose regulations upon a street railroad company, a gas company, or a telephone company in the form of terms and conditions in an ordinance making a grant of the right to use streets, that it cannot impose by a general ordinance passed pursuant to its other grants of powers from the Legislature, and that an acceptance of the ordinance estops the grantee to deny the reasonableness of its terms. For example, a city council can, in such an ordinance, prescribe a rate to be charged for telephones, though it is highly probable a city council has no power to regulate telephone rates by a general ordinance. (Cities and Villages Act of 1872, Part 1, Article V, Section 1, Clause 13; Horse and Dummy Act of 1874, Section 3, R. S., 1874, 571; Session Laws, 1897, 282; Session Laws, 1899, 337; Decatur Gas Light & Coke Co. v. Decatur, 120 Ill., 67; Suburban R. Co. v. People, 178 Ill., 594; People's Gas Light & Coke Co. v. Hale, 94 Ill. App., 406; Chicago Telephone Co. v. Illinois Manufacturers' Association, 106 Ill., App., 54.)

This construction gives complete force and effect to the words "by contract" without attributing to the State

Legislature an intent to tie its own hands, and the hands of the common council of Chicago, acting under powers delegated and to be delegated, for ninety-nine years, respecting the regulation and control of the operation and management of street railroads in Chicago.

It is difficult indeed to make out that the State Legislature intended to, and did, in and by the acts of 1859, 1861, and 1865, divest itself of power to add to, and take from, the delegated powers of the common council of Chicago over the operation and management of street railroads. If the man who drew those acts and the Legislatures that passed them intended to deprive the common council of the power that it had under Chicago's charters of 1851 and 1863 to make revocable contracts, and to give the council a new power, and to restrict the council to a use of that new power, that is to say, to make irrevocable contracts respecting the laying down and use of street railroad tracks in the streets of Chicago, why did they not say it in plain language?   In 1902, the Supreme Court of Illinois, in reply to the argument that two ordinances passed May 23, 1859, giving the Chicago City Railway Company and the North Chicago City Railway Company, incorporated by the special act of 1850, a right to use certain streets, created irrevocable contracts, binding the council not to change the five cent rate of fare specified in them, said: "Again, in the ordinance of May 23, 1859, the language shows that the common council, which passed that ordinance, relied upon its power to do so under said clause 9 of the charter of 1851. Section 1 of the ordinance of May 23, 1859, recites that, under and by virtue of the act of the Legislature approved February 14, 1859, 'and by virtue of the powers and authority in the said common council otherwise by law vested,' the council thereby granted permission to the Chicago City Railway to lay a single or double track for a railway, etc. In other words, the ordinance of May 23, 1859, was not only passed in pursuance of the act of February 14, 1859, but also by virtue of the power and authority vested by law in the common council otherwise than by the act of February 14, 1859. Necessarily, the power, referred to in Section 1 of the ordinance as otherwise by law vested in the council, was the power so vested by virtue of clause 9, section 4 of chapter 4 of the charter of 1851. . . . The fixing of a maximum rate of five cents for each fare for any distance can as well be attributed to an exercise of the power to prescribe the compensation under the charter of 1851, as to any power to make a ·contract upon the subject, embodied in the act of February 14, 1859" (Union Traction Co. v. Chicago, 199 Ill., 484, 525–6). In other words, the Court said, conceding, for the sake of argument, but not deciding, that the act of 1859 gave the common council power to make an irrevocable contract, the act did not take away its power, under the city's charter, to make a revocable contract; a given ordinance expressly passed in exercise of both powers cannot be at once a revocable contract and an irrevocable contract; under the rule for such cases the Court had to say that the ordinance must operate in the way most favorable to the people, that is, as a revocable contract (Providence Bank v. Billings, 4 Peters, 514; Charles River Bridge v. Warren Bridge, 11 Peters, 420).

If the man who drew the acts of 1859, 1861, and 1865, and the Legislature that passed them, did really want to give the common council power to make irrevocable contracts with the corporations created by them, why did they leave untouched the power of the common council, under the city's charter of 1851 and 1863, to amend and repeal all ordinances? Why did they not take these corporations and the construction and operation of street railroads by them in the streets of Chicago out from under the scope and application of that power to amend and repeal? It is impossible to get rid of that express power to amend and repeal by mere inference.

Again, if the man who drew those acts, and the Legislature that passed them, really wanted to give the common council of Chicago power to make irrevocable contracts with the corporations created by those acts, why was no limitation placed upon the sweeping power to prescribe "terms and conditions," except the dubious limitation, "by contract," when the Legislature, at or about the same time, constantly used the word "contract" in the same connection as an alternative for "ordinance" (Charter of 1863, supra)? In 1867, when the State Legislature intended the word "contract," in connection with the subject of the municipal control of street railroads, to mean irrevocable contract, it used the word "irrevocable" (Clause of Charter of 1867, supra, respecting use of dummies on street railroads).

And why were those corporations so carefully limited to the use of horses as a motive power on the street railways they were empowered to construct and operate (North Chicago City Railway v. Lake View, 105 Ill., 207, 213; Constitution, 1848, Art. 111, Sec. 23)? The men of 1859 and 1865 were perfectly aware that horses would not continue to be used on street railways in Chicago for ninety-nine years. This is evidenced by the grants of power in the acts of 1867 and 1869 to the common council to authorize the use of dummies and steam engines. In April, 1859, Mr. Chief Justice Caton said: "Cars upon street railroads are now generally, if not universally, propelled by horses, but who can say how long it will be before it will be found safe and profitable to propel them with steam, or some other power besides horses" (21 Ill., 523)? The doctrine of the Dartmouth College case has never been extended so far as to empower a State Legislature, or a municipal corporation, sitting under a State Legislature, to grant an irrevocable right to drive, for ninety-nine years, mules and horses between two iron rails laid down in a street in a growing city such as Chicago was in 1859 and 1865. It is established by the Federal Supreme Court that a State Legislature cannot grant an irrevocable right to make and sell beer (Beer Co. v. Massachusetts, 97 U. S., 25), to maintain a lottery and sell lottery tickets (Stone v. Mississippi, 101 U. S., 814), to manufacture and sell manure in a city (Fertilizing Co. v. Hyde Park, 97 U. S., 659), to maintain and operate a slaughter house in a city (Slaughter House Co. v. Slaughter House Co., 111 U. S., 746), or to operate a railroad in a city over tracks laid even with the grade of a street (N. Y. & N. E. R. Co. v. Bristol, 151 U. S., 556). The principle of these cases, that the doctrine of the Dartmouth College case does not extend so far as to authorize a State Legislature, or a municipal corporation, to bind itself, by irrevocable contract, not to use its legislative power to protect the lives, health, and morals of the people of the State, would appear to apply to the propelling of cars over the streets of Chicago with horses and mules for ninety-nine years (McCartney v. Chicago & Evanston R. Co., 112 Ill., 611).

The truth is, I think, that the man who drew those acts of 1859, 1861, and 1865, and the Legislature that passed them, had no intention whatever to give the common council power to make irrevocable contracts with the corporations created by those acts. If they thought about the matter at all, I think they had a doubt in their minds whether the State Legislature could constitutionally delegate such power to the council. The sole purpose of using the words "by contract," was, I think, to prevent the possibility of a court decision, such as was made by the Court of Appeals of New York in 1856, and again in

1863, and by a lower court in Cook County in 1858 or 1859 prior to the decision of the Supreme Court of Illinois in 1859, above cited, holding the ordinances passed, and to be passed, void because expressed in the form of contracts (Davis *v.* Mayor, 14 N. Y., 506; Milham *v.* Sharp, 27 N. Y., 611; Council Proceedings, 1883–4, 77).

XV. THE EFFECT OF CHICAGO'S CHARTER OF 1863, AS AMENDED IN 1861, ON THE POWERS VESTED IN CHICAGO'S COUNCIL BY THE ACTS OF 1859, 1861, 1865.

But if it be conceded that the said special acts of 1859 and 1861 did clothe the common council with power to make irrevocable grants to, or irrevocable contracts with, the street railway corporations created by them, for twenty-five years, a question arises whether the common council was not stripped of the right to use that power by the taking effect of the city's charter on February 13, 1863. And if the taking effect of that charter did strip the council of the right to use that power, and the council was reinvested by the act of February 19, 1865, with power to make irrevocable grants to, or irrevocable contracts with, the street railway corporations, to which the act applied, for ninety-nine years, a question arises whether the common council was not stripped of the right to use that power by the taking effect, on March 9, 1867, of the act amendatory of the city's charter of 1863.

As has already been shown, under the city's charter of 1863, and under the amendatory act of 1867, the common council was clothed with power to deal with the operation and management of street railroads in Chicago by the legislative method of passing ordinances making only alterable and revocable contracts or grants. In 1904 the Circuit Court of the United States for the Northern District of Illinois ruled that whatever power the common council got out of the said special acts of 1859, 1861, and 1865 was extinguished utterly when Chicago organized on the first Monday in May, 1875, as a city under the Illinois general Cities and Villages Act, in force July 1, 1872, because that act of 1872, "delegated to the city plenary power to grant or withhold franchises." But the city's charter of 1863, and the amendatory act of 1867, also "delegated to the city plenary power to grant or withhold franchises," and, therefore, on the ratio decidendi of the ruling referred to, the taking effect of the charter of 1863 on February 13 of that year stripped the common council of the right to look to the special acts of 1859 and 1861 as a source of power, and the taking effect of the amendatory act of 1867 on March 9 of that year stripped the common council of the right to look to the act of 1865 as a source of power (Govin v. Chicago, 132 Fed. Rep., 548).

It is simply impossible, as the ruling referred to in effect says, to construe the said special acts of 1859, 1861, and 1865 as irrevocable contracts, binding the Legislature of the State not to alter, amend, repeal, or revoke those acts, in so far as they made grants of power to the common council of Chicago. It is true, that the said ruling of the Circuit Court of the United Sates was made under the influence of the conception, that "plenary (State legislative) power to grant . . . franchises" is State legislative power to make the grant irrevocable for a fixed period of time. But that conception is clearly erroneous and the result of a confusion of thought respecting the doctrine of the Dartmouth College case. Irrevocability by legislative act is not a necessary ingredient of a franchise granted by a State. The legislative power of a State, under the doctrine of the Dartmouth College case, to make a grant of a franchise irrevocable by a contract binding the State Legislature not to alter or revoke the grant is not plenary legislative power at all, but is in derogation of plenary legislative power under the common law to grant franchises. The Parliament of England never could make an irrevocable grant of a franchise, yet its legislative power to grant franchises is plenary. The Congress of the United States, in exercising its delegated powers "to establish postoffice and post roads"; "to regulate commerce with foreign Nations, and among the several States, and with the Indian tribes"; "to exercise exclusive legislation in all cases whatsoever over" the District of Columbia; and "to . . . make all needful rules and regulations respecting the territory . . . belonging to the United States," cannot make irrevocable grants of franchises, yet its power to grant franchises "necessary and proper for carrying into execution the foregoing powers" is a plenary or complete power. "When the power to establish postoffices and post roads was surrendered to the Congress, it was a complete power, and the grant carried with it the right to exercise all the powers which made that power effective." And so, when in and by the city's charter of 1863, and the amendatory act of 1867, the State Legislature delegated to the common council power to regulate the use of the streets of Chicago, and power to regulate and control the laying down and use of street railway tracks in those streets, the powers delegated were complete, plenary powers, and all the more so because the council was forbidden to bind itself, and the State Legislature, by irrevocable contract, not to use the legislative power of the State by altering, amending, or repealing an ordinance making a grant of a street railroad franchise. And the charter of 1863 may very well be held, just as the act of 1872 was held, to be a command to the council of Chicago not to act "by contract," under the acts of 1859 and 1861, and the amendatory act of 1867 may very well be held, just as the act of 1872 was held, to be a command to the council of Chicago not to act "by contract," under the act of

1865, if the words, "by contract," in the acts of 1859, 1861, and 1865, do really mean "by irrevocable contract." The Illinois Cities and Villages Act of 1872 is but a redraft, in the form of a general law, of Chicago's special charters of 1851, 1863, and 1867.

It should be noted that the Circuit Court of the United States, in addition to overlooking Chicago's charters of 1863 and 1867, also entirely overlooked the question as to what effect the present Illinois State Constitution, in force August 8, 1870, had on the subsequent use of the powers granted in and by the said acts of 1859, 1861, and 1865, and entirely overlooked the Illinois Horse and Dummy Act, in force July 1, 1874, which was a general law, applicable to Chicago, although Chicago was then organized under a special charter, and which act unquestionably did, quite as much as, and indeed more than, the Cities and Villages Act of 1872, delegate to Chicago "plenary power to grant or withhold franchises." (Govin v. Chicago, 132 Fed. Rep., 848, 854, 860; Chicago City Railway Co. v. The People, 73 Ill., 541, 550; People's Gas Light & Coke Co. v. Chicago, 194 U. S., 1; Pearsall v. Great Northern Railroad, 161 U. S., 646; Louisville & Nashville Railroad v. Kentucky, 161 U. S., 677; Illinois Rev. Stat., 1874, Preface, and Horse and Dummy Act, p. 571; In re Rapier, 143 U. S., 110; McCulloch v. Maryland, 4 Wheaton, 316; Munn v. Illinois, 94 U. S., 113, 124; Cooley, Const. Lim., Ed. 6, 200.)

XVI. THE CASE OF CHICAGO v. SHELDON DOES NOT HOLD THAT THE STATE LEGISLATURE DID, IN AND BY THE ACTS OF 1859, 1861, AND 1865, EITHER MAKE, OR AUTHORIZE CHICAGO TO MAKE, IRREVOCABLE GRANTS.

The chief basis of support for the proposition that ordinances, passed by the common council of Chicago prior to August 8, 1870, making grants of the right to lay down and use street railroad tracks in the streets of

Chicago, operate as irrevocable contracts, under and by virtue of the said special acts of 1859, 1861, and 1865, appears to be not the language used in those acts, expounded under the guidance of the established rule of resolving all reasonable and rational doubts against the claim of power in a municipal body to make irrevocable contracts, but a judgment rendered by the Supreme Court of the United States at the December term, 1869, in the case of Chicago v. Sheldon, 9 Wallace, 50, a case that arose out of the judgment of the Supreme Court of Illinois, rendered at the April term, 1866, in the case of Chicago v. Baer, 41 Ill., 306.   Does that case of Chicago v. Sheldon support the proposition?   Let it be examined.

May 23, 1859, the common council of Chicago passed an ordinance making a grant to the North Chicago City Railway Company, created, as above stated, by the said special act in force February 19, 1859, of the right to lay down and use horse railroad tracks in North Clark street. July 27, 1865, the common council passed an ordinance requiring North Clark street to be curbed with stone and paved with wooden blocks known as the Nicholson pavement, the cost of the improvement to be paid by special assessment levied against the property benefited. The commissioners of the board of public works of Chicago fixed the district that would be benefited by the improvement, and apportioned the cost of it upon the parcels of property lying within the district.   The common council approved the report, and on October 16, 1865, a warrant was issued for the collection of the assessment.   At the February term, 1866, of the Superior Court of Chicago, the collector applied for a judgment against the parcels of property the assessment on which had not been paid. The owners appeared and objected to the entry of judgment, on the ground that the roadway of the North Chicago City Railway Company in North Clark street would be benefited by the new curbing and paving of the street, but no part of the cost had been assessed against the roadway of that company. The Superior Court of Chicago sustained the objection, and on appeal the Supreme Court of the State affirmed the judgment (Chicago v. Baer, 41 Ill., 306). The company claimed an exemption or immunity from the assessment on the ground that the said ordinance of May 23, 1859, on its true construction, was a contract binding the company to keep the pavement between their tracks on North Clark street in good condition and repair in consideration of an exemption or immunity from any special assessment to pay the cost of an entirely new pavement. The Supreme Court of the State did not stop to consider whether such was the true construction of the ordinance of May 23, 1859, but held the ordinance, so construed, to be utterly void, because prohibited by the Constitution of 1848, as expounded in the case of Chicago v. Larned, 34 Ill., 265, in 1864, wherein it was ruled that, under the Constitution of 1848, a special assessment is not a tax, but an exercise of the power of eminent domain, but, in ascertaining the just compensation enjoined by the Constitution, the rule of equality and uniformity by which the taxing power was expressly limited by the Constitution of 1848 must be observed. It was also ruled in Chicago v. Larned that the levying of a special assessment under the Constitution of 1848 must be a judicial, and not a legislative, proceeding. On the rendition of the judgment in Chicago v. Baer, a portion of the cost of the new curb and pavement for North Clark street was assessed against the roadway of the North Chicago City Railway Company, the amount of the assessment being $28,677. Thereupon, one Sheldon, a stockholder in the company, the company itself having declined to act, filed a bill in the Circuit Court of the United States to enjoin the collection. The

Court enjoined it, and Chicago took the case into the Supreme Court of the United States on writ of error. It does not expressly appear, but it may be safely assumed, that Sheldon was not a citizen of Illinois and that the jurisdiction of the courts of the United States rested on the ground that the controversy was between citizens of different States. It is stated (9 Wallace, 52) that the "main question" was "whether under their contract to keep the road, for a certain number of feet 'in good condition and repair,' the company could be made to pay for what was a new curbing, grading, and paving, altogether, there being also some minor questions as to the decisions" of the Supreme Court of Illinois in Chicago *v.* Larned, and Chicago *v.* Baer. The "main question," the construction of the ordinance of May 23, 1859, was decided in favor of the company. Then the "minor question whether the Federal Supreme Court was bound to follow the decision of the State Supreme Court in Chicago *v.* Baer came up. It was said that the Federal Supreme Court was not concerned to deal with the question whether the Illinois Constitution of 1848 was rightly or wrongly expounded in 1866 by the State Supreme Court in Chicago *v.* Baer, because in three cases, decided in 1855 and 1863 (Illinois Central R. Co. *v.* McLean County, 17 Ill., 291; Hunsaker *v.* Wright, 30 Ill., 146; Newstadt *v.* Illinois Central R. Co., 31 Ill., 484), the Supreme Court of the State had decided that the State Legislature could, consistently with the State Constitution of 1848, exempt corporations and individuals from general taxation in consideration of a payment of money, or other equivalent, into the public treasury, the Legislature being the exclusive judge of the value of the equivalent exacted. These State decisions were standing unreversed at the date of the passage of the ordinance of May 23, 1859, and that ordinance operating as a contract, it was held that the contract could not be invalidated by a decision of the highest court of the State, made after its passage, in effect, in the view of the Federal Supreme Court, overruling the earlier State decisions.

Does that case of Chicago v. Sheldon hold that the ordinance of May 23, 1859, was an unalterable and irrevocable contract?   How could it?   That it was a contract was not, and could not have been, denied either by counsel or by the Court.   But the question whether the contract was revocable or irrevocable could not possibly have arisen unless the State Legislature, or the common council of Chicago, by virtue of delegated power, had passed a law altering or revoking some part of it. The ordinance authorizing the improvement was passed July 27, 1865, after the taking effect of an amendment of Chicago's charter of 1863, on February 15, 1865 (Private Laws, Ill., 1865, Vol. 1, p. 274, Sec. 1), designed to give the spreading of a special assessment the character of a judicial proceeding enjoined by the decision in Chicago v. Larned, by requiring the commissioners "to assess the amount directed by the common council to be assessed upon the real estate by them deemed benefited by any such improvement, in proportion, as nearly as may be, to the benefit resulting thereto," instead of "on the real estate fronting or abutting on the contemplated improvement" under a front foot rule of apportionment (Charter of 1863, Ch. VII, Sec. 21; 1 Private Laws, 1863, p. 89; Chicago v. Larned, 34 Ill., 403; Chicago v. Baer, 41 Ill., 306, 314).   Now, when it is remembered that the levying of this special assessment under the ordinance of 1865 was a judicial, and not a legislative proceeding, there was no subsequent State law before the court that could impair the obligation of the contract, nor was any such point advanced by counsel for Sheldon, Mr. Benjamin R. Curtis, formerly Mr. Justice Curtis of the Supreme Court of the

United States, and Mr. William C. Goudy. Their contention was: "Such contract is valid" (Chicago *v.* Sheldon, 19 L. Ed., 594, 595). The rendition of a judgment by a State court is not the passage of a law, within the meaning of the prohibition that "No State shall pass any law impairing the obligation of contracts" (Railway Co. *v.* Rock, 4 Wallace, 177; Weber *v.* Rogan, 188 U. S., 10). Chicago *v.* Sheldon is, therefore, but an example of the application of the rule in the case of Gelpcke *v.* Dubuque, 1 Wallace, 175, decided in 1863, that when the meaning of the Constitution of a State is established by a decision of the highest court of the State, at the time a contract is entered into, in favor of the validity of the contract, the contract cannot afterwards be held invalid, even by a court which should be of opinion that the former construction of the State Constitution by the highest court of the State was wrong (the case of Gelpcke *v.* Dubuque, 4 Harv. Law Rev., 311; Prettyman *v.* Tazewell County, 19 Ill., 406; Marshall *v.* Silliman, 61 Ill., 218, 221). Whether the rule was rightly applied in Chicago *v.* Sheldon may perhaps be doubted, if for no other reason, in view of the wide difference that has always existed in Illinois between the subject of general taxation, involved in the earlier State decisions, and the subject of special assessment, involved in the later State decisions. (Illinois Central R. Co. *v.* Decatur, 147 U. S., 190; West River Bridge Co. *v.* Dix, 6 Howard, 541; Village of Hyde Park *v.* Cemetery Association, 119 Ill., 141, 148; Chicago *v.* Chicago Union Traction Co., 199 Ill., 259, 270.) But, necessarily, the Federal Supreme Court must have reached the same result in Chicago *v.* Sheldon whether the contract evidenced by the ordinance of May 23, 1859, was revocable or irrevocable, because, until revoked by legislative act, it was just as valid, obligatory, and binding, and just as much entitled to enforcement by a court, as if it was irrevocable. No one can affirm that the act of 1859 of the Legislature of Illinois, involved in Hunsaker v. Wright, 30 Ill., 146, one of the earlier State decisions cited in Chicago v. Sheldon, exempting real and personal property within the limits of the city of Cairo, on certain conditions, from taxation for county purposes, constituted an irrevocable contract (City of Worcester v. Worcester Street R. Co., 196 U. S., 539), yet that act being held good, had to be enforced by the court until the Legislature saw fit to alter or repeal it. It is true that Mr. Justice Nelson did say in Chicago v. Sheldon that "it is not competent for its (the State's) Legislature to pass an act impairing its obligation," (i. e., of the contract, evidenced by the ordinance of May 23, 1859,) but this was only to illustrate and enforce the main proposition that the Federal Supreme Court would not give effect to the later State decisions invalidating the contract. Mr. Justice Nelson also said: "A point is made that the Legislature have not conferred, or intended to confer, authority upon the city to make this contract. We need only say that full power was not only conferred (by the said special act of 1859), but that the contract has been since ratified by this body" (by the said special act of 1865). But, for the reasons stated, it is not permissible, I think, to insert the word "irrevocable," rather than the word "revocable," before the word "contract," in this language of the learned Justice.

I think, therefore, that the case of Chicago v. Sheldon lends no support at all to the proposition that the common council of Chicago got power, out of the said special acts of 1859, 1861, and 1865, to make irrevocable contracts respecting the use of the streets of Chicago for street railroad purposes.

XVII. THE DOCTRINE OF THE SUPREME COURT OF ILLINOIS
APPEARS TO BE THAT CHICAGO COULD GRANT ONLY LICENSES
UNDER SAID ACTS OF 1859, 1861, 1865.

In Chicago v. Baer, 41 Ill., 306, 312, Mr. Justice Lawrence did say that "it is true, as urged by counsel, that
the (North Chicago City) railway company . . . has
certainly, through its charter from the Legislature, and its
contract with the city, acquired a property in these streets
of the most valuable character, which neither the Legislature nor the city can take away against the consent of
the company, and capable, like other property, of being
sold and conveyed" (pp. 313, 312). Counsel for the city
apparently urged this in reply to the argument of oppos-
ing counsel that the company's property was not of a
nature to be assessable for a local improvement. But
the statement plainly is not decision. The Court said:
"It is wholly unnecessary to define, for the purpose of this
case, what is the precise extent or nature of its property"
(p. 313). The position of this sentence in the opinion
makes it look very much as if it was inserted by the writer
of the opinion at the instance of the Court.

Those special acts were before the Supreme Court of
Illinois at the September term, 1874, in the case of Chicago
City Railway Company v. The People, 73 Ill., 541. The
question was as to the validity of, that is to say, the
power of the council to pass, an ordinance passed by the
common council of Chicago on November 13, 1871, after
the taking effect of the present Constitution on August 8,
1870, making a grant to the Chicago City Railway Company of the right to lay down and use street railroad
tracks in Indiana Avenue. The ordinance was clearly
valid, because, as above shown, the council had express
power to pass it under Chicago's charter of 1863, as
amended in 1867. But neither Court nor counsel noticed
Chicago's charter, and both Court and counsel assumed

that the common council's sole and exclusive source of power to pass the ordinance was the said special acts of 1859 and 1865, and so, as the case was viewed, the validity of the ordinance hinged entirely upon its legal effect. Counsel on both sides assumed that the legal effect of the ordinance was to make an irrevocable grant of a franchise, and the issue debated at the bar was, whether the Constitution of 1870 stripped the council of power to make irrevocable grants of street railroad franchises under those acts. Three Justices ruled that it did. Four Justices, of their own motion, apparently, ruled that the ordinance of November 13, 1871, was only a waiver of a forfeiture of a prior ordinance, passed August 22, 1864, of like import, the forfeiture having accrued by reason of the non-performance by the railway company of a condition in the ordinance of August 22, 1864, that the track be laid in Indiana avenue within fifteen months after the passage of the ordinance, and that the common council had the power, on November 13, 1871, to waive the forfeiture, even without any act of the Legislature, in force on November 13, 1871, delegating to it power, or "enabling" it, to waive such forfeiture. The majority also ruled that the taking effect of the new State Constitution on August 8, 1870, did not destroy the right of the company to use, after August 8, 1870, the rights and privileges granted by the ordinance of August 22, 1864, because that ordinance, though perhaps a contract, within the meaning of the word "contract" in said special Acts of 1859 and 1865, was yet only a grant of "a mere license." The reason given for this last result was that, under Blackstone's definition of a franchise, the sovereign law-making power in the State alone, i. e., the State Legislature, can grant a franchise, and, under the ruling of the Court of Appeals of New York in the case of Davis v. The Mayor, above referred to, "a municipal body, it is understood, possesses no power to confer a franchise" (Chicago City Railway Co. *v.* The People, 73 Ill., 541, 547, 548, 549).

Here, then, in September, 1874, is at least a clear expression of opinion by a majority of the highest court of the State of Illinois to the effect that, on August 22, 1864, the common council of Chicago had no power, under and by virtue of the special act of 1859, to grant to the Chicago City Railway Company, created by that act, anything more than "a mere license" to lay down and use horse railway tracks in Indiana avenue in Chicago, which means, if it means anything, that the license was revocable, and was not, and could not be made, irrevocable by the council because the ordinance granting it did not "emanate from any source competent to grant a franchise." It is not clear, and it is not very material, I think, whether the majority meant to say that the State Legislature merely did not, or whether they meant to say that the State Legislature could not, in 1859, delegate power to the common council of Chicago to make an irrevocable grant to a street railroad company of the right to use a public street.

XVIII. THE DOCTRINE OF THE CIRCUIT COURT OF THE UNITED STATES RESPECTING ORDINANCES PASSED BY CHICAGO UNDER THE ACTS OF 1859, 1861, 1865, IS IN ACCORD WITH THE DOCTRINE OF THE STATE SUPREME COURT, AND ITS DOCTRINE THAT SAID ACTS MADE A DIRECT IRREVOCABLE GRANT IN THE NATURE OF A FLOAT IS EITHER WRONG OR OF LITTLE PRACTICAL IMPORTANCE.

In 1904, in the case of Govin *v.* Chicago, 132 Fed. Rep., 848, the question of the legal effect of ordinances passed by the common council of Chicago prior to August 8, 1870, making grants of the right to lay down and use street railway tracks to the North Chicago City Railway Company and the Chicago West Division Railway Company, organized under said Acts of 1859, 1861 and 1865, was considered by the Circuit Court of the United States for the Northern District of Illinois. The Court ruled that all the power the common council of Chicago got out of those acts was power to designate the streets in which the corporations organized under those acts might exercise and use their abstract corporate power or capacity, conferred by the acts, to construct, maintain, and operate street railroads, and when, pursuant to such designation by the council, the corporations acted by making the effects of the abstract power visible in the shape of iron rails, cars moving thereon with wheels, propelled by horses and mules, the result was the same as if the State Legislature had named the streets in words in the Acts of 1859, 1861, and 1865. The Court said: "The language used in the section under consideration (Section 2 of the Act of 1859, above quoted) constituted a clear and definite grant of authority to the companies to occupy the streets, a grant direct, and not by circumlocution; a grant by the Legislature to the companies, not the grant of power to the city to grant in turn to the companies. True, the streets to be used are not set out by name; but they are set out by description, a description that fixes with certainty their identity as to the then past, and with equal certainty the means of identity as to the then future (the index finger of the common council of Chicago), and it is a universal maxim of law that that is certain that can be made certain. True, also, that the grant is in the nature of a float, not attaching to any specific street until such street has been designated (by the common council), but when the street has been designated, the grant attaches as of the date of the act. In that sense the grant is in praesenti" (as of February 19, 1859).

The Court, by implication at least, concedes that its result is not justified by the words of the acts alone, but maintains that its result is warranted by the words of

CONSTITUTIONAL LAW

the acts read in the light of "the then (1859–1865) prevailing idea respecting railway grants." The Court said: "In the interpretation of all statutes that come to us from a considerable past, we must look not only to the language actually used but to the historical relation out of which the language comes, as also the interpretation put upon like language by courts speaking at, or about, that period." The Court then states the results of its researches into "the historical relation, out of which the language" of the Acts of 1859, 1861, and 1865 came, and into "the interpretation put upon like language by courts speaking at, or about, that period," as follows: "At first it was thought that under their general power over streets, the municipalities in whose streets street railways were to be laid might have power to authorize the construction of such roads. But this view was quickly dissipated by the courts; with unanimity, the courts decided that the Legislatures of the States, alone, possessed such power; that the municipality had no such power; and that the power could be exercised by the Legislature without the consent of the municipality, or even a reference to its wishes. State v. Mayor of New York (1854), 3 Duer., 119; Chicago v. Evans (1860), 24 Ill., 52; People's R. Co. v. Memphis R. Co. (1869), 10 Wall., 38. In the latter case, the Supreme Court of the United States said:" Then follows a quotation from the opinion of Mr. Justice Clifford, and the Court concludes: "In general, the Court (in the case last cited) held that the municipality (Memphis, Tenn.) had no power, in virtue of the ordinary powers possessed by such municipality, to grant a franchise to a street railway company to use its streets; and even doubted whether such power could be constitutionally delegated by the Legislature to the municipality. Those and other cases (not cited) show the ideas of public policy then held, relative to the sources from which street railway companies obtained their rights to use streets for railway purposes."

The error the Court fell into, I think, was this: In its researches into the past, it failed to discriminate between the power of a municipal corporation to make an irrevocable grant of the right to use a public street for street railroad purposes, and its power to make a revocable grant. Power in a municipal corporation to make such an irrevocable grant was denied by the courts, "with unanimity," unless a statute passed by the State Legislature delegating to a municipal corporation the power, in clear and unambiguous words, was produced. But power in a municipal corporation to make a revocable grant was not denied by the courts, "with unanimity." In April, 1859, the Supreme Court of Illinois, speaking by Mr. Chief Justice Caton, ruled, as above stated, that the common council of Chicago had the power, under its charter of 1851, to grant the right to lay down and use both steam and horse railroad tracks in the streets of Chicago, and said though there were contrary rulings in other States, yet the "weight of authority, and certainly, in our apprehension, all good reasoning" supports the ruling made (see Davis v. The Mayor, 14 N. Y., 506, 508, 523, 529, 533; Memphis R. Co. v. People's R. Co., 10 Wallace, 38, 50–53, and cases cited, 56; Chicago's Charters of 1851, 1863, and 1867; Birmingham Street R. Cases, 79 Ala., 465, 470, and citations).

In Chicago v. Baer, 41 Ill., 306, 313, in April, 1866, the State Supreme Court said that the North Chicago City Railway Company got its right to occupy a certain portion of North Clark street in Chicago by its ties, rails, and cars, so far as may be necessary for operating the railway, out of ordinances of the council of Chicago, and not out of the Acts of 1859 and 1865 (see Chicago City Railway v. The People, 73 Ill., 541; Chicago v. Sheldon,

9 Wallace, 50; Opinion of Mr. Justice Curtis, cited 114 U. S., 507–8; State *v.* Gas Co., 18 Ohio State, 262, 293, cited in 172 U. S., 9).

So far as I can find, the theory that the acts of 1859, 1861, and 1865 made a direct irrevocable grant, "in the nature of a float," of the right to use a street in Chicago for street railroad purposes was not developed until the case of Govin *v.* Chicago was decided in May, 1904.

In this connection, it is worthy of notice that the Legislature of New York, in 1860, when it wanted to make a direct irrevocable grant of the right to use streets in New York city for street railroad purposes, specifically enumerated the streets in the act that it passed (People *v.* Kerr, 27 N. Y., 188; compare, Davis *v.* Mayor 14 N. Y., 506; Malhau *v.* Sharp, 27 N. Y., 611).

But in Govin *v.* Chicago the Court did, as I think, rule strongly that the common council of Chicago had no power whatever, under and by virtue of the acts of 1859, 1861, and 1865, to make irrevocable grants of the right to lay down and use street railroad tracks in the streets of Chicago for a fixed period of ninety-nine years.

The Court conceded, as I think, that the language of the acts alone, unaided by extrinsic considerations, would not justify its ruling that the Legislature made "a direct grant in the nature of a float," and pinnacled the legal merit of its ruling upon the question of the correctness of the Court's conception of "the then (1859–1865) prevailing idea respecting railway grants." With all due deference, I think the Court's conception is not only not supported by the printed evidence, but is directly contradicted by the evidence of the principal reported decision cited in its support — People's R. Co. *v.* Memphis R. Co., 10 Wallace, 38, 19 L. Ed., 844, and by the very words of the acts the Court was construing.

It may be that there are expressions in the majority opinion in Chicago City Railway Co. *v.* The People, 73 Ill., 541, which could be used to support the proposition that the said acts made a direct irrevocable grant in the nature of a float, but they have not been so used, and the result reached in the case is against the proposition.

Then, as above stated, if the acts did make a direct irrevocable grant, in the nature of a float, one is brought face to face with the question whether Chicago's charters of 1863 and 1867 and the State Constitution of 1870, in force August 8, 1870, did not end, or revoke, the capacity of the grant to float over the streets of Chicago any longer. That such was the effect of the said charters and of the Constitution would appear to be a sound proposition (Govin *v.* Chicago, 132 Fed. Rep., 848, 858–860; Chicago City Railway Co. *v.* The People, 73 Ill., 541, minority opinion).[2]

XIX. The doctrine of the Dartmouth College case has little, if any, application to the street railroad corporations of Chicago down to August 8, 1870.

For the reasons aforesaid, the State Legislature did not, at any time prior to the taking effect of the present State Constitution on August 8, 1870, make irrevocable grants or contracts respecting the right to lay down and use street railroad tracks in the streets of Chicago, either directly or indirectly, by delegating power to the common council of Chicago to make such irrevocable grants. But if the special acts of 1859 and 1861 did authorize the common council to make irrevocable grants, the authority was taken away by the charter of Chicago of 1863, and if the act of 1865 restored the authority, that restored authority was taken away by the amendment of the

---

[2] It is not clear that the opinion in Govin *v.* Chicago is entitled to rank as a judicial opinion, because the record in the case raises a grave doubt as to whether the Court had any jurisdiction.

charter in 1867. And on any view, irrevocable grants, if made prior to August 8, 1870, being few in number are negligible things.

Revocable grants made prior to August 8, 1870, may be revoked by the State Legislature, at its own will and pleasure, and by the city council of Chicago for good and just cause. The reason for the difference between the State's power of revocation and the city's power of revocation by legislative act will appear hereinafter.

XX. August 8, 1870, the date of the taking effect of the present State Constitution, the doctrine of the Dartmouth College case ceased to be the law in Illinois.

It only remains to inquire whether, under the present State Constitution, the State Legislature can make, and has made, or can authorize, and has authorized, the city council of Chicago to make irrevocable grants or contracts respecting the right to use the streets of Chicago for street railroad purposes for a fixed term of years.

Section 14 of Article II, the Bill of Rights, of the Constitution of 1870 says: "No . . . law making any irrevocable grant of special privileges or immunities shall be passed." The whole section reads: "No ex post facto law, or law impairing the obligation of contracts, or making any irrevocable grant of special privileges or immunities, shall be passed." What does that short, general mandate, "No law making any irrevocable grant of special privileges or immunities shall be passed," mean? Can there be any rational doubt as to its meaning? Noscitur a sociis, it is known from its associates. It excepts from the operation of the obligation of contracts clause all laws thereafter passed making grants of special privileges, and, by prohibiting only irrevocable grants, sanctions revocable grants, of special privileges. That a law making a grant of the right to lay down and use street railroad tracks in the streets of Chicago makes a grant of a special privilege cannot be doubted (Bank of Augusta *v.* Earle, 13 Peters, 519, 595; Davis *v.* The Mayor, 14 N. Y., 506). That an ordinance of the city council of Chicago making such a grant is a law cannot be doubted (Tudor *v.* Rapid Transit R. Co., 154 Ill., 129, 136; People *v.* Suburban R. Co., 178 Ill., 594; Hayes *v.* Railroad Co., 111 U. S., 228; Davis and Farnum Mfg. Co. *v.* Los Angeles, 189 U. S., 207, 216). The Supreme Court of the United States has decided that a mandate in the Constitution of Ohio of 1851 that "No special privileges or immunities shall ever be granted that may not be altered, revoked, or repealed by the General Assembly," as applied to corporations, is at least the equivalent of the more usual provision reserving power to alter, amend, or repeal corporate charters (Shields *v.* Ohio, 95 U. S., 319, 324; Hamilton Gas Light and Coke Company *v.* Hamilton City, 146 U. S., 258, 269; see also The Birmingham Street Railroad Cases, 79 Ala., 465, 473; City of Houston *v.* Houston Street R. Company, 19 So. W. Rep. (Texas), 127, 129; Atchison St. R. Co. *v.* Missouri Pacific R. Co., 3 Pac. Rep., 284, Kansas, Brewer, Judge; North Springs Water Co. *v.* Tacoma, 58 Pac. Rep., 773, 775, column 1, 778, column 2, Washington), and the same Court has also decided that the Legislature of Massachusetts could, under such reserved power to alter or repeal in existence at the date of the grant, revoke and annul the right of a street railroad company, resting upon a direct grant of the State Legislature, to lay down and use street railroad tracks in the streets of Boston, and could authorize the laying down of new tracks by a new company over identically the same ground occupied by the old tracks of the old company (Greenwood *v.* The Freight Co., 105 U. S., 13; see also Bridge Co. *v.* U. S., 105 U. S., 470; Sinking Fund Cases, 99 U. S., 700).

The mandate in the Illinois Constitution is not confined to grants of special privileges to corporations, but applies as well to such grants to individuals; nor does it, like that in the Ohio Constitution, mention any lawmaking authority, but it is addressed to every authority in the State clothed with any part of the legislative power of the people of the State. As originally proposed the mandate was directed to the General Assembly. In the Report of the Committee on Bill of Rights, it read: "The General Assembly shall not . . . make any revocable grant of special privileges or immunities" (2 Debates in C. C. of 1870, 1558), was so adopted (2 Debates, 1586), was so referred to the Committee on Revision and Adjustment (2 Debates, 1590), but came out of that Committee, and was ordered enrolled, in the form in which it now appears in the Constitution (2 Debates, 1778).

By this mandate, and by inserting it in the Bill of Rights, the framers of the Constitution intended to affirm the rule of equality before the law-making power of the State, the most striking exceptions to which, in this country, prior to 1870, after the abolition of slavery, were holders of special privileges granted by a State irrevocably placed upon a pedestal above and beyond the reach of the State by the doctrine of the Dartmouth College case. "The State was stripped, under this interpretation (of the obligation of contracts clause of the Federal Constitution in the Dartmouth College case) of prerogatives that are commonly regarded as inseparable from sovereignty, and might have stood, like Lear, destitute before her offspring, had not the police power (and the reserved power to alter or repeal or revoke) been dextrously declared paramount, and used as a means of rescinding improvident grants" (1 Hare, Am. Const. Law, 606, 607). Speaking in opposition to a motion made in the Illinois Constitutional Convention to change the mandate so as to prohibit the making of irrevocable grants of special privileges only "by special law," Mr. Church said: "I regard the amendment offered by the gentleman from Adams (Mr. Skinner) as striking at the very heart of the Constitution that we propose to make, so far as regards the relations we propose to allow to exist between the people of this State and corporations hereafter to be created. I concede that for one, that in the insertion of this clause in the Bill of Rights, I did mean, and such I believe to have been the meaning of the whole Committee, to strike out the very power of the Legislature hereafter to ever grant any corporate privileges whatever, but such as should be subject to law" (2 Debates, 1585). Mr. Skinner's motion was lost by a vote of ten yeas to thirty-eight nays; absent and not voting, thirty-five (2 Debates, 1586). To enforce his said view of what this mandate would do for Illinois, and his further view thus expressed — "It, sir, is a very fatal error that the gentleman has fallen into, and that many other public spirited men have fallen into . . . that to reserve the control of . . . corporations in the sovereign power of the State will be to discourage the investment of capital. . . . I do not believe, sir, that such will be, or ever has been, the effect" — Mr. Church referred to "our sister State of Wisconsin" as a State where the people had long ago done what this mandate would do for Illinois, and where invested capital was just as secure as it ever was in Illinois. Turning to the Wisconsin Constitution of 1858, we find therein this provision: "All general laws or special acts enacted under the provisions of this section (for the formation of corporations) may be altered or repealed by the Legislature at any time after their passage" (Article XI, Section 1). In 1874 we find the great Chief Justice of Wisconsin, in the case of Attorney-

General v. Railroad Companies, 35 Wis., 425, 569–574, reviewing the previous decisions of the Supreme Court of Wisconsin expounding this clause of the Constitution, and stating "the unanimous opinion of this Court, always, in all cases before it" thus: "By force of the constitutional power reserved and of the uniform construction and application of it, the rule in the Dartmouth College case, as applied to corporations, never had place in this State, never was the law here. The State emancipated itself from the thralldom of that decision, in the act of becoming a State; and corporations since created here have never been above the law of the land. Subject to this reserved right, and under the rule in the Dartmouth College case, charters of private corporations are contracts, but contracts which the State may alter or determine at pleasure. Contracts of that character are not unknown in ordinary private dealings; and such we hold to be the sound and safe rule of public policy. It is so in England. It is so under the Federal Government itself. The material property and rights of corporations should be inviolate, as they are here; but it comports with the dignity and safety of the State that the franchises of corporations should be subject to the power which grants them, that corporations should exist as the subordinates of the State, which is their creator, durante bene placito" (p. 574; see also Peik v. Chicago and N. W. R. Co., 94 U. S., 163, 175).

In order to bring as nearly as possible to the "common level" enjoined for the future by this general mandate in the Bill of Rights, all those who might have previously got above it by grants of franchises and privileges, "improvidently yielded by the State," the framers of the Constitution of 1870 inserted into it many particular and special provisions to discourage and stop any further growing up of "a growth within us that has risen above

STREET RAILROAD PROBLEM   637

us" (2 Debates, 1586). Article IV, Section 22, provides:
"The General Assembly shall not pass local or special
laws granting to any corporation, association, or individual the right to lay down railroad tracks, or amending
existing charters for such purpose; granting to any corporation, association, or individual any special or exclusive privilege, immunity, or franchise whatever." Article
IX prohibits the granting of any irrevocable exemption
from taxation; Article XI, Section 1, provides that "No
corporation shall be created by special laws, or its charter
extended, changed, or amended. . . . but the General
Assembly shall provide, by general laws, for the organization of all corporations to be hereafter created;" and
Section 2 provides: "All existing charters or grants of
special or exclusive privileges, under which organization
shall not have taken place, or which shall not have been
in operation within ten days from the time this Constitution takes effect, shall thereafter have no validity or
effect whatever." Section 12 declares railways heretofore or hereafter constructed to be "public highways,"
and Section 14 says: "The exercise of the power and the
right of eminent domain shall never be so construed or
abridged as to prevent the taking, by the General Assembly, of the property and franchises of incorporated companies already organized, and subjecting them to the
public necessity the same as individuals." This limitation to companies "already organized" is significant.
Under the prohibition in the Bill of Rights that "No law
making any irrevocable grant or special privileges or
immunities shall be passed," the franchises of corporations subsequently organized could be taken by a legislative revocation, but those of companies already organized might "require the exercise of a power based upon
other contingencies than the more common principles
of legislation" (2 Debates, 1586). It was not an unusual

argument in the '70s that a State does not need the power to revoke franchises or privileges granted by it, "because all the power which the State needs, she posesses under the power of eminent domain; that is to say, that a State having been deprived by fraud of her prerogatives, has the privilege of buying them back" (8 Am. Law Rev., 238). Section 15 says: "The General Assembly shall pass laws to correct abuses and prevent unjust discrimination and extortion in the rates of freight and passenger tariffs on the different railroads in this State, and enforce such laws by adequate penalties, to the extent, if necessary for that purpose, of forfeiture of their property and franchises."

Can there be any doubt whatever that "Equality of privilege is the principle of the Constitution of 1870" (Mr. Justice Sheldon in Chicago City Railway Company v. The People, 73 Ill., 541, 558)? And the meaning of that principle is that irrevocable special privileges cannot arise and exist in Illinois after that Constitution took effect. In other words, that the doctrine of the Dartmouth College case is not the law in Illinois, except as respects irrevocable grants of privileges made before, and put in operation within ten days after, August 8, 1870. Every one knows that no corporation organized in Illinois since the taking effect of the present Constitution can get from the Legislature directly any powers, privileges, or franchises that the Legislature may not alter or revoke by a general law. The State's power of alteration or revocation is commonly rested upon the ninth section of the General Incorporation Act of 1872, which says: "The General Assembly shall, at all times, have power to prescribe such regulations and provisions as it may deem advisable, which regulations and provisions shall be binding on any and all corporations formed under the provisions of this act. And, provided, further, that this act shall not be held to revive or extend any private charter or law heretofore granted or passed concerning any corporation." But this section is only a contemporaneous legislative enactment of the rule of the Constitution as applied to corporations. Is it possible to believe that the people of Illinois, on August 8, 1870, stripped their State Legislature of power to make irrevocable grants of special privileges, but left it with power to authorize the legislative authorities of cities, towns, and villages throughout the State to make such irrevocable grants to local public service corporations?

The mandate, "No law making any irrevocable grant of special privileges or immunities shall be passed," as above stated, sanctions the passage of laws making revocable grants of them. What authority may exercise the power of revocation? It must be a legislative authority, because, even under the doctrine of the Dartmouth College case, special privileges are revocable by the courts after a judicial inquiry establishing gross misuse or abuse of them, and the Constitution, therefore, would be meaningless, if construed as authorizing a judicial authority to exercise the power of revocation. There can be no doubt whatever that the highest legislative authority of the State, the General Assembly, can exercise the power. But it must act by a "general" law (Constitution of 1870, Art. IV, Sec. 22; Art. XI, Secs. 1, 2).

As respects the particular special privilege of laying down and using street railroad tracks in the streets of Chicago, would an act of the General Assembly revoking a particular grant made by the council of Chicago to a particular street railroad company since August 8, 1870, be a general law? I think it would be, unless a court could say that any man of average sense in the community at the date of the act of revocation would pronounce it repugnant to the principle of equality before the law.

A single street railroad company in a single city may, by its own conduct, put itself into a class by itself as respects the question whether its privileges should be revoked by legislative act. Events over which it has no control, and for which it may not be at all responsible, may single it out for legislative decapitation, as, for example, the expressed wish of the required number of the electors to have the city avail itself of a delegated power to own street railroads and to operate them by public officers and employees.

But if the Constitution of Illinois forbids the State Legislature to exercise its power of revocation of grants of the right to lay down and use street railroad tracks in public streets by using it from time to time in single instances in single cities or towns in the State, then it follows that the mandate to act by a general law operates practically to strip the State Legislature of the right to use the power of revocation justly and beneficially at all in the case of street railroad companies, except by a general law delegating the right to use the power to municipal corporations.

But if it be conceded that the State Legislature can revoke the privileges of a single street railroad company in a single city, it does not follow that a similar power of revocation does not reside in the legislative authority of the city. The Constitution of 1870 itself makes the laying down and use of street railroad tracks in public streets a local matter, a subject of local government, because it forbids the Legislature to grant the right without requiring the consent of the local authorities (Article XI, Section 4). In the case of a corporation, as above stated, the Legislature only creates an abstract person and qualifies that abstract person to ask for, and to receive, the consent of the local authorities, and it is the giving of that consent by ordinance which creates or grants the right to lay down and use street railroad tracks in public streets. Since the local authorities, under the Constitution, alone can grant the right by the passage of a law, and since the Constitution says that "No law making any irrevocable grant of special privileges or immunities shall be passed," it results that the Constitution itself gives the local authorities power to revoke the grant, and that the State Legislature cannot take that power of revocation away from them. Hence, the Constitution itself clothes the city council of Chicago with power to revoke a grant made by it of the right to lay down and use street railroad tracks in the streets of Chicago, and forbids the council to bind itself by irrevocable contract not to use that power for twenty years, twenty days or twenty minutes. It is a continuing and inalienable power of legislation. Besides, the State Legislature has never attempted to take that power of revocation away from cities, but has delegated the power to them by statutes hereinafter referred to.

There is, however, I think, this difference between the State Legislature's reserved power of revocation and the city council's reserved power of revocation. When the State Legislature uses the power in a given instance, the causes or abuses which induced the exercise of the power cannot be drawn in question before any court. The reserved power of the Legislature is a political power, and it results from the separation of the three departments of the government, and from the independence of each, that the judicial department must presume conclusively that the occasion was sufficiently grave and solemn to justify the legislative department in putting forth its reserved power of revocation (Greenwood v. Freight Co., 105 U. S., 13; Hamilton Gas Light Co. v. Hamilton City, 146 U. S., 258, 269; Bridge Company v. U. S., 105 U. S., 470). But when the city council uses its reserved power

of revocation in a given instance, the causes and abuses
which induced the exercise of the power may be inquired
into by a superior court of justice of the State. Such
court and the city council are not co-ordinate authorities,
but the relation is that of a superior, paramount authority
and an inferior, subordinate authority. The city council
acts only by delegation from the central State government, and is at all times accountable to its superior for
the use that it makes of its delegated powers. This is
because of the principle of the omnipotence or supremacy
throughout the whole State of the central State government, except where the State or Federal Constitution
lays down a different principle (Chicago v. Cicero, 210
Ill., 290; Dicey, Law of the Constitution, Ed. 4, Ch. IV,
173). It results from this principle that the superior
courts of the State, representing the central State government, have power to guard the peace and quiet of cities,
towns, and villages in the State and the inhabitants thereof
against abuses by local officials of their delegated powers
held in trust. And it is familiar law that a State court
in Illinois has the power to declare a municipal ordinance
void, even though the municipality had the mere power
to pass it, and even though the ordinance is not repugnant to the letter of any written constitutional or statutory
provision, if it will yet be, in actual operation and effect,
repugnant to a generally accepted standard of right
and justice, works considerable harm and plainly does no
one in the world any substantial good whatever.

XXI. THE SUPREME COURT OF ILLINOIS AND THE DARTMOUTH
COLLEGE CASE.

The only reply I have ever heard made to the proposition that the doctrine of the Dartmouth College case
ceased to be the law in Illinois on August 8, 1870, so far
as all laws passed after that date making grants of special
privileges or immunities are concerned, and that, there-

fore, any ordinance heretofore passed, or hereafter to be passed, by the city council of Chicago, subsequent to the date specified, making a grant of the right to lay down and use street railroad tracks in the streets of Chicago, is alterable, amendable, and repealable, or revocable, by the State Legislature, and by the city council, acting within the limits of its delegated powers, is the reply that the Supreme Court of Illinois is against the proposition (Chicago General Railway Company v. Chicago City Railway Company, 62 Ill. App., 502, 513, 518). Is that true?

It is true that, so far as I can find, the Supreme Court of the State has never, in words, construed and applied the aforesaid constitutional mandate that "No law making any irrevocable grant of special privileges or immuities shall be passed." But the Court has frequently construed and applied the aforesaid reservation of power in Section Nine of the General Incorporation Act of 1872. Of this section the Supreme Court of the United States has said: "The statute reserves to the General Assembly the power to prescribe in the government of corporations 'such regulations and provisions as it may deem advisable.' The language is very comprehensive. Regarding it alone, it is difficult to conceive what objects of legislation are not covered by it. The Supreme Court of the State has construed it to be of greater import than the usual reservation of the power to alter and amend the charters of corporations" (Freeport Water Company v. Freeport City, 180 U. S., 587, 596).

As above stated, while Chicago was organized under its special charter of 1863, as amended in 1867, the State Legislature passed a general act respecting the laying down and use of street railroad tracks in streets, the purpose of the act having been to carry out the policy of the State Constitution of 1870. The act is the Horse and

Dummy Act, approved March 19, 1874, in force July 1, 1874, modeled upon the basis of the said special Acts of 1859, 1861, and 1865. That act, in all its substantial features, has remained in force continuously since July 1, 1874 (R. S., 1874, p. 571; Laws, 1897, p. 282; Laws, 1899, p. 331). That act became part and parcel of the charter of all street railroad companies formed in Illinois after August 8, 1870, and, so far as applicable consistently with the Federal Constitution, of all street railroad companies previously formed under special charters. (Chicago Union Traction Co. *v.* Chicago, 199 Ill., 484, 531–546; West Chicago Street R. Co. *v.* The People, 203 Ill., 551; 214 Ill., 1; Constitution, 1870, Article IV, Section 22, Clauses 22, 23; Article XI, Sections 1, 2, 4; General Incorporation Act of 1872, Section 9; Laws, 1871–2, p. 296.)

That act, in its first section, authorizes street railroad companies, incorporated under the general laws of the State, to locate and construct their roads upon or over streets, "subject to the provisions contained in this act." Section two provides that no street railroad company shall have the right to locate or construct its road upon or along any street in any incorporated city "without the consent of the corporate authorities of said city"; that "said consent may be granted for any period, not longer than twenty years . . . upon such terms and conditions, not inconsistent with the provisions of this act, as such corporate authorities . . . shall deem for the best interests of the public. . . ." Section Four provides: "Every grant to any such company of a right to use any street, alley, road, highway, or public ground shall be subject to the right of the proper authorities to control the use, improvement, and repair of such street, alley, road, highway, or public ground, to the same extent as if no such grant had been made, and to make all necessary police regulations concerning the management and operation of such railroad, whether such right is reserved in the grant or not."

As above stated, Chicago organized as a city under the general Cities and Villages Act, in force July 1, 1872 (Laws, 1871–2, p. 218), completing the organization on the first Monday in May, 1875, pursuant to a popular vote cast April 23, 1875. That act, copied in a large measure from Chicago's charters of 1851 and 1863, delegated to the city council in cities complete power to regulate and control the use of streets; "to permit, regulate, or prohibit the locating, constructing, or laying a track for any horse railroad in any street, alley, or public place; but such permission shall not be for a longer time than twenty years"; "to provide for and change the location, grade, and crossing of any railroad"; "to license, tax, and regulate hackmen, draymen, omnibus drivers, carters, cabmen, porters, expressmen, and all others pursuing like occupations, and to prescribe their compensation"; "the city council . . . shall have no power to grant the use of, or the right to lay down, any railroad tracks in any street of the city, to any steam or horse railway company, except upon petition of the owners of the land representing more than one-half of the frontage of the street, or so much thereof as is sought to be used for railroad purposes"; "to pass all ordinances, rules, and make all regulations, proper or necessary to carry into effect the powers granted to cities . . . with such fines or penalties as the city council . . . shall deem proper; provided no fine or penalty shall exceed $200.00, and no imprisonment shall exceed six months for one offense." (Cities and Villages Act of 1872, Part 1, Article V, Section 1, Clauses 24, 25, 42, 90, 96.)

In cases arising under these statutory enactments, the Supreme Court of the State has decided that the city council of Chicago has no power, in an ordinance making

a grant of the right to lay down and use street railroad
tracks in public streets, by irrevocable contract, to divest
itself of delegated power, so far as any street railroad
company organized after August 8, 1870, is concerned,
to compel a street railroad company to cleanse the
space between its tracks once a week (Chicago Union
Traction Co. *v.* Chicago, 199 Ill., 259); to compel a
street railroad company to give transfer tickets, and
to regulate the rates of street railroad fares (Union
Traction Co. *v.* Chicago, 199 Ill., 484); to compel a street
railroad company to lower a tunnel constructed by it
under the Chicago River (West Chicago Street Railroad
Co. *v.* The People, 214 Ill., 1; 203 Ill., 551). It has also
decided that a street railroad company organized under
the General Incorporation Act of 1872 cannot acquire,
by assignment from a street railroad company organized
under the aforesaid special Acts of 1859, 1861, and 1865,
an irrevocable right to exercise and enjoy any irrevocable
right, privilege, or immunity, that may have been acquired under and by virtue of those acts, if any such
exist (Chicago Union Traction Company *v.* Chicago, 199
Ill., 484, 536–546).

It is true that, in the case of West Chicago Street Railroad Company *v.* Chicago, 189 Ill., 339, the State Supreme
Court did decide that the city council of Chicago could,
by an ordinance passed July 30, 1883, exempt the West
Chicago Street Railroad Company from liability to pay
a special assessment for paving a street, in consideration
of a condition in the franchise ordinance that the company keep a portion of the street in repair. The ruling,
however, is based solely on the authority of the case of
Chicago *v.* Sheldon, 9 Wallace, 50, above considered, and,
obviously, unduly extends the application of the ruling
in that case. Three Justices dissented. The ruling of
the Supreme Court of the United States, in Chicago *v.*

Sheldon, manifestly can have no application whatever to ordinances passed subsequent to the date of the State decision in Chicago *v.* Baer, holding that the rule of equality in taxation prescribed by the State Constitution of 1848 forbade the council of Chicago to exempt anyone from liability to pay a special assessment levied to defray the cost of a local improvement, and the decision in Chicago *v.* Sheldon left the State Supreme Court perfectly free to apply its own ruling in Chicago *v.* Baer to all ordinances passed after the date of that decision, and the State Supreme Court was bound to adhere to its own ruling to the extent stated, unless it was persuaded that its own ruling was not in harmony with the State Constitution of 1848. Besides, the State Constitution of 1870 expressly ratified and confirmed the State Court's rule of decision in Chicago *v.* Baer (Constitution of 1870, Article IX, Sections 1, 3, 6, 9, 10). The decision of the majority of the Illinois Supreme Court in West Chicago Street Railroad Company *v.* Chicago, 178 Ill., 339, was, therefore, I think, with deference, wrong, and ought to be expressly overruled.

Clearly, under the foregoing decisions of the State Supreme Court, the doctrine of the Dartmouth College case·has no application to any of the usual and ordinary provisions of an ordinance passed by the city council of Chicago after August 8, 1870, making a grant of the right to lay down and use street railroad tracks in the streets of Chicago.

A provision in such an ordinance obligating Chicago to purchase the material property of the grantee, in the event of the putting into effect of the policy of the municipal ownership of street railroads, I do not class as a usual and ordinary provision. Such a provision would, I think, constitute a contract, private in its nature, Chicago could not avoid by a use of its delegated sovereign powers of legislation, for the same reason that Chicago cannot avoid a contract to buy one thousand tons of coal for use in the operation of its municipally owned water works plant (Walla Walla v. Walla Walla Water Co., 172 U. S., 17; National Water Works Co. v. Kansas City, 62 Fed. Rep., 853, C. C. A., per Mr. Justice Brewer).

The only question left, then, is whether the doctrine of the Dartmouth College case applies to the usual and ordinary part of such an ordinance called "the granting part," passed after August 8, 1870. Is that part of such an ordinance repealable, or revocable, by legislative act? What is the doctrine of the State Supreme Court upon this subject?

The grantee in such an ordinance does get a right of private property of such a nature that it is taxable by the State (State Board of Equalization v. The People, 191, Ill., 528) and that special assessments for local improvements may be levied against it (Cicero and Proviso Street Railway Co. v. Chicago, 176 Ill., 501). But that, obviously, for reasons already stated, has no bearing whatever upon the question whether the granting part of the ordinance is revocable by the State otherwise than by a judicial proceeding. (But see Los Angeles v. Los Angeles Water Co., 177 U. S., 558, 576; People v. O'Brien, 111 N. Y., 41; and see the phrase "chartered right," in Monongahela Navigation Co. v. United States, 148 U. S., 312, 344; see Knoxville Water Co. v. Knoxville, 189 U. S., 434, 438; Carlyle v. Carlyle Water, Light and Power Co., 52 Ill. App., 577; East St. Louis v. East St. Louis Gas Co., 98 Ill., 415.) All the interest in a street in Chicago that a street railroad company ever could get is a right to use the street (Special Acts of 1859, 1861, 1865; Constitution of 1870, Article XI, Section 4; Horse and Dummy Act; Turnpike Company v. Illinois, 82 Ill., 174; affirmed, 96 U. S., 63). Such an ordinance does not grant a freehold

(Harlan *v.* R. R. Co., 198 Ill., 337; R. R. Co. *v.* People, 203 Ill., 551; 214 Ill., 1). Where Chicago is the owner of the fee of a street, under a statutory dedication, the city council has no power to alienate the title. And of course the council has no such power where, under a common law dedication, the fee remains in the abutting owners. And upon the vacation of a street, the fee must revert to the original dedicators, their heirs or assigns, where the dedication was statutory, and, where the dedication was at common law, the abutting owners, at the date of the vacation, take the fee freed from the public easement. (People *v.* Harris, 203 Ill., 272, and cases cited; Act in force July 1, 1874, Hurd's R. S., 1903, p. 1897; 5 Ill. Cyclopaedic Dig., p. 570. See Illinois Central R. Co. *v.* Illinois, 146 U. S., 387.)

It was stated above that the Supreme Court of Illinois decided at the April term, 1874, that all that a street railroad company organized under the special acts of 1859, 1861, and 1865 got out of an ordinance of the common council of Chicago, passed August 22, 1864, was "but a mere license" to use a public street in Chicago, and that such ordinance did not grant "a franchise." The Court has adhered to that doctrine ever since, and it is familiar law in Illinois, popular speech in Chicago to the contrary notwithstanding, that all that any public service corporation gets out of an ordinance making a grant of the right to use a public street, passed since the decision above referred to, is a license, and not a franchise (Chicago *v.* Rothschild & Co., 212 Ill., 590, 592, and cases cited). March 29, 1883, and again on October 31, 1889 (City of Quincy *v.* Bull, 106 Ill., 337; Gas Co. *v.* Town of Lake, 130 Ill., 42) the State Supreme Court said that such an ordinance, when accepted by the grantee, constitutes a contract between the grantee and the municipality.

Does this doctrine mean that the license, or contract, is irrevocable by legislative act? The circumstances under which the doctrine originated show, I think, that the substantive thought underlying this doctrine is that the license, or contract, is revocable by legislative act. The case referred to, where this doctrine originated, is Chicago City Railway Co. *v.* The People, 73 Ill., 541, and, though stated supra, it must be re-examined here. The validity of an ordinance passed by the common council of Chicago on November 13, 1871, purporting to amend a previous ordinance, passed August 22, 1864, making a grant of the right to lay down and use street railroad tracks in Indiana Avenue, and extending the time for performance, was assailed in an information in quo warranto filed by the Attorney-General, and in a bill for an injunction filed by owners of land abutting on Indiana Avenue. Counsel and Court alike assumed that the ordinance of November 13, 1871, was invalid, unless power to pass it could be got out of the said special acts of 1859, 1861, and 1865. Counsel also assumed that the legal effect of the ordinance was to make an irrevocable grant of the right, or franchise, to lay down and use street railroad tracks in Indiana Avenue for ninety-nine years. On the basis of these two assumptions, the ordinance was assailed by counsel as a local or special law, granting to a corporation the right to lay down railroad tracks, or amending an existing charter for that purpose, and granting to a corporation a special privilege or franchise in contravention of Article IV, Section 22, clauses 22 and 23, of the Constitution of 1870. Apparently no other part of that Constitution was relied on. It is not possible to believe, however, that Court and counsel were all unaware of other applicable provisions in that Constitution above set forth. Two of the majority Justices, Scholfield and Craig, had been members of the Constitutional Convention that framed that Constitution, and one of the counsel for the railroad company, Mr. Hitchcock, had been its president (1 Debates in C. C. of 1870, page next after title page). The main reply of counsel to the assault made upon the ordinance was this: "A valuable franchise of the railway company lies in its power to contract with the city for the use of the streets; . . . such a grant implies an obligation not to withdraw the power, which is protected by the Constitution of the United States, and . . . therefore, it is not competent for the people of the State, by their Constitution, to take away from the city the power to so contract with the company." Three Justices, accepting the views of counsel that the ordinance did make an irrevocable grant of a franchise, held that the State Constitution of 1870 could, and did, take away from the city power to make such a grant. Four Justices, however, held that the ordinance of August 22, 1864, was a grant of "but a mere license," and the ordinance of November 13, 1871, was a waiver of a forfeiture of the license for failure to comply with a condition that the road be built within fifteen months after August 22, 1864, which waiver the council could make without any enabling act The reason given for this result was, that a franchise could not emanate from the council of Chicago; it could emanate only from the State Legislature. The majority, after citing Blackstone's definition of a franchise and the New York case of Davis v. The Mayor, above referred to, went on and said: "It is a misconception of the law to suppose the railway company derives its power to construct a railroad from any ordinance of the city. All its authority is from the State and is conferred by its charter. The city has delegated to it the power to say in what manner and upon what conditions the company may exercise the franchise conferred by the State, but nothing more. . . . Whether it is in the power of the State to revoke that authority, is a question that does not arise for decision, and upon which we refrain from expressing an opinion.   It is sufficient it has not been done by any provision of the Constitution, nor by any general law enacted by the Legislature." The specific thing drawn in question in the case was, it should be observed, the power of the railway company to enter upon Indiana Avenue and locate its road there, and not its abstract "power to construct a railroad," two widely different powers, or franchises.   The majority did not affirm that the railway company got its power to enter upon Indiana Avenue and locate its road there out of the act of 1859, but the majority did in words affirm that the company got its power to enter upon Indiana Avenue and locate its road there from a license granted by the common council of Chicago on August 22, 1864.   The reason given for saying that the ordinance did not grant a franchise, but did grant a license, namely, that a franchise must come direct from the sovereign law-making power in the State, is not, necessarily, a good one.   A right to use a public street for street railroad purposes is a franchise when granted by the State Legislature directly (Greenwood v. Freight Co., 105 U. S., 13), and such right does, indirectly at least, emanate from the State Legislature when granted by the council of Chicago under a power delegated by the Legislature (Walla Walla v. Walla Walla Water Co., 172 U. S., 1, 9; Chicago v. Baer, 41 Ill., 306, 313; People v. Suburban R. Co., 178 Ill., 594, 605; State v. Gas Co., 18 Ohio St., 262, 295).   I think the majority decided that the trouble with the case was that the irrevocable grant of a right to use Indiana Avenue for ninety-nine years, on which the whole case was founded and argued on both sides, had no existence at all; that the Attorney-General and the abutting land owners were attacking a windmill, because the so-called irrevocable franchise was "but a mere license." The majority of the court did not expressly say that the license was revocable. All they said was that no one has attempted to revoke it. But if the ruling is in any way responsive to the case as discussed at the bar, namely, on the basis that the validity of the ordinance in issue hinged upon its admitted legal effect as an irrevocable grant, it clearly means that the license was revocable by legislative act."[3]

As above stated, the Attorney-General and the owners of land abutting on Indiana Avenue really had no case at all. The ordinance assailed was clearly valid, that is to say, the common council of Chicago had power to pass it under and by virtue of Chicago's charter of 1863, as amended in 1867, whatever may have been the legal effect of the ordinance, whether it operated as a revocable or as an irrevocable contract.

In 1883, in the case of the City of Quincy v. Bull, 106 Ill., 337, the State Supreme Court ruled that an ordinance of the city council of Quincy, passed August 7, 1873, making a grant to certain individuals of the right to lay down and use water pipes in the streets of Quincy, became, on acceptance, a valid and binding contract, and the Court enjoined the officials of the city from enforcing an ordinance subsequently passed revoking the grant. Mr. Justice Sheldon said: "We see no more to be involved here than the simple law of contract, whether a municipal corporation may at its will repudiate the obligation of a fair contract which it has made, and which it was authorized to make. The attempt is to take back a grant which the city has made under a contract. The State itself may not revoke a grant it has made. The city must be bound by the contract and grant it has made, and had

---

[3] One of the majority justices, Mr. Justice McAllister, was one of the original incorporators of the Chicago West Division Railway Company. See his opinion in Hickey v. Chicago & W. I. R. Co., 6 Ill. App., 172.

authority to make, the same as would an individual," citing Burlington *v.* Burlington Street Railway Company, 49 Iowa, 144. The facts of the case, and the Iowa decision cited, make it quite plain, I think, that all the Court could affirm was that the council of Quincy had no power to revoke the grant at its own will and pleasure, and that the justice of the cause of revocation is reviewable by a court. The revocation in this case, if sustained, would have left the people of Quincy without any water supply, and appears to have been an ill-considered act, doing no one any good, and injuriously affecting a large number of people. The case, I think, falls very short of holding that the city council of Quincy could not, for any cause whatever, revoke that water pipe grant.

In the case of Chicago Municipal Gas Light Co. *v.* Town of Lake, 130 Ill., 42, in 1889, it appears a bill was filed by the gas company on May 14, 1885, to enjoin the officials of the town, acting under authority of the town board of trustees, from preventing the laying down of gas pipes in the streets of the town under authority of an ordinance passed March 25, 1884, and accepted March 29, 1884. On May 25, 1884, the town board of trustees repealed the ordinance. Counsel for the town contended, first: "The ordinance was not a contract. It was a mere license"; and, second: "The complainant has not shown performance of the conditions imposed by the ordinance (to commence supplying gas within one year from the date of the passage of the ordinance); but even if it be assumed that a legal contract, and performance of its conditions, had been shown, the complainant has failed to establish such a case as entitles it to the writ of injunction, which is a negative specific performance of the contract." The case was decided in favor of the town on this second point advanced by counsel. The Court did, however, rule against their first point, saying: "The contract between the town and appellant being a valid and binding contract, the repealing ordinance of May 23, 1884 (two months after the passage of the ordinance), adopted by the town, was ineffectual to abrogate it, and said last mentioned ordinance was consequently null and void."

In 1894, in the case of Belleville v. Belleville Citizens, Street Railway Company, 152 Ill., 171, the Court upheld the right of the city council of Belleville to repeal ordinances previously passed, making grants of the right to lay down and use street railroad tracks in the streets of Belleville, when it appeared the grantees had neglected persistently to keep the road in good condition and to give good service, and a power of revocation was reserved in the granting ordinance. The case does nearly, if not quite, hold that a city council has the power to revoke a grant of the right to use a public street for street railroad purposes for good and just cause. It will be remembered that the Horse and Dummy Act saves all the powers of the council of a city whether the right to use them is expressly reserved in the granting ordinance or not.

In 1901, in the case of The People v. Central Union Telephone Co., 192 Ill., 307, 311, the Court said: "It is true, as said by counsel for the relator, that the grant made by the city of Pontiac of the right to use the streets, etc. (made April 7, 1899), is not a franchise, but a license or contract; but it is equally clear that when the corporation accepted the privileges and entered upon the right to use the streets, etc., it became a binding contract between the city and company, which could not be revoked or rescinded except for cause."

In 1904, in the case of Chicago v. Rothschild, 212 Ill., 590, the Court said: "The court has repeatedly held that a franchise is a privilege which emanates from the sovereign power — that is, in a case like this, from the State —

and that the power conferred upon a railroad company, by ordinance, to locate and maintain a railroad in the streets of a city is a license, which, after the road is built, may be irrevocable, but that such an ordinance does not create or confer upon the railroad company constructing the railroad in the street, a franchise."

I, for one, cannot see that it is true, that the State Supreme Court is against the proposition, that the city council of Chicago has had no power, since the taking effect of the present Constitution of Illinois on August 8, 1870, to make an irrevocable grant of the right to lay down and use street railroad tracks in the streets of Chicago for a term of years. The doctrine of the Court is, I think, that the council's grant is revocable by the council for good and just cause; the goodness and justice of the cause being a judicial question.

XXII. The State Legislature and the Dartmouth College case since August 8, 1870.

It would seem to be very clear from the statutes above cited that the State Legislature has never delegated any power to the council of Chicago to make irrevocable grants of street railroad franchises or licenses. The only words in any act passed by the State Legislature since August 8, 1870, that could be construed to clothe the council with that power are the words in the Cities and Villages Act of 1872, and in the Horse and Dummy Act of 1874, limiting the period of the grant to a term not exceeding twenty years. When these acts are considered in all their parts, and it is remembered that no time limitation is imposed upon municipal grants of privileges to other public service corporations, I think that is too slight a basis on which to engraft by mere implication so important a power (but see Freeport Water Co. v. Freeport City, 180 U. S., 587, 615; Cleveland St. R. Case, 194 U. S., 517, 536). Just why the State Legislature hit upon twenty years for the life of a municipal street railroad grant is not esay to make out. There is no sense underlying the limitation, if it be true, as I think it clearly is, that under the Constitution the grant is revocable by legislative act. It has been said by some one somewhere that twenty years was selected by analogy to that section of the State Constitution which requires the principal and interest of municipal bonds to be paid within twenty years (Article 1, Sec. 12). But even if each generation of men in Chicago ought to pay the public debts they incur, it does not clearly follow that each generation of men in Chicago ought to be required to pay the cost of building the street railroads of Chicago together with a reasonable rate of interest thereon. It should be observed, that the Horse and Dummy Act of 1874 was passed while the case of the Chicago City Railway Company v. the People, 73 Ill., 541, was pending in the State Supreme Court. It seems not unlikely that that act was a legislative answer to the irrevocable ninety-nine-year contract claim advanced in that case on behalf of the railway company, of which Mr. Justice Sheldon, for the minority, said (p. 558): "It appears to be a claim that ought not to be admitted." The twenty-year limitation may possibly have been intended only as a warning and notice to the authorities of municipal corporations, that they must stop looking to special acts chartering corporations, passed before the taking effect of the Constitution of 1870, as a source of legislative power.

XXIII. The Supreme Court of the United States is the final authority on the question whether the doctrine of the Dartmouth College case has had any place in the law of Illinois since 1870, and is not necessarily bound by state decisions.

But suppose the Supreme Court of Illinois has decided

that, under the Constitution of 1870, and under the statutes enacted pursuant thereto, the city council of Chicago has authority to make irrevocable grants of the right to use the streets of Chicago for street railroad purposes, what of it? The final judicial authority on the question is, admittedly, the Supreme Court of the United States. In the exercise of its jurisdiction over this question that tribunal has original, independent, judicial power granted to it by the Constitution of the United States. It is in no way whatever bound by a State decision holding that such an ordinance makes an irrevocable grant or contract. The Federal Supreme Court cannot, rightfully and constitutionally, adopt such a State decision, if it is not in harmony with its own independent judgment on the question (N. O. Waterworks Co. *v.* La. Sugar Ref. Co., 125 U. S., 18; McCulloch *v.* Virginia, 172 U. S., 102).

By a line of adjudications running back, as above stated, to the Dartmouth College case itself, the Supreme Court of the United States is irrevocably and finally committed to the doctrine that no State legislative body has the power to pass a law making a grant of powers, franchises, rights, privileges, or immunities that can operate as a contract irrevocably binding the State, acting by its Legislature, not to alter, amend, or repeal, or revoke, the grant, where, at the time of the passage of the law, the State Constitution prohibited the State Legislature from parting with any of the legislative power of the State, by a clause therein reserving power to alter, amend, or repeal, or by a clause at least equivalent thereto, such as that "No law making any irrevocable grant of special privileges or immunities shall be passed." That Court has recently said that a State's reserved power to alter, amend, or repeal should not be frittered away by refinements of reasoning (Covington *v.* Kentucky, 173

STREET RAILROAD PROBLEM   659

U. S., 231, 239). That Court also recently refused to adopt the opinion of the highest court of Kentucky holding (by reason of an inadvertent overlooking of a State statutory reservation of power to alter, amend, or repeal) an exemption from taxation to be an irrevocable contract. The Federal Supreme Court said: "As we conclude that the State decision in the Bank Tax case above cited (97 Kentucky, 597) upon the question of contract was not only in conflict with the settled adjudications of this court, but also inconsistent with sound principle, we will not adopt its conclusions" (Citizen's Savings Bank *v.* Owensboro, 173 U. S., 636, 648).

XXIV. THE POSITION OF THE SUPREME COURT OF THE UNITED STATES ON THE QUESTION OF THE APPLICATION OF THE DARTMOUTH COLLEGE CASE IN ILLINOIS SINCE AUGUST 8, 1870.

In the Water Rate cases that went up to the Supreme Court of the United States on writs of error to the Supreme Court of Illinois the general question was whether municipal ordinances regulating water rates, passed by cities and villages in Illinois under and pursuant to the Illinois Water Rate Act of 1891, impaired the obligation of contracts evidenced by municipal ordinances passed prior to 1891 but subsequent to the taking effect of the Illinois Constitution on August 8, 1870, making grants of the right to lay down and use water pipes in public streets, the grantees being in one case individuals, but subsequently organized as a corporation under the Illinois General Incorporation Act of 1872, and in other cases corporations organized under that act, the said granting ordinances containing provisions fixing the water rates to be charged. The Supreme Court of the United States, by a majority of one vote, sustained the ordinances passed after 1891 reducing water rates previously fixed in the franchises or license ordinances, on the ground that the municipalities had no power by delegation from the

State Legislature to bind themselves and the State Legislature by irrevocable contract not to regulate water rates (Illinois Water Rate cases, 180 U. S., 587, 619, 624). But Mr. Justice McKenna, speaking for the majority, said (180 U. S., 593): "It is not clear from the opinion of the (Illinois) Court whether it intended to decide that municipal corporations could not be invested with power to bind themselves by irrevocable contract not to regulate water rates. If so, we cannot concur in that view. We have decided to the contrary many times, and very lately in Los Angeles v. Los Angeles City Water Co., 1900, 177 U. S., 558. See also Walla Walla v. Walla Walla Water Co., 172 U. S., 1, 7, where the subject is more extensively discussed and the cases reviewed. See also New Orleans Water Co. v. Rivers, 115 U. S., 674. We do not mean to say that if it was the declared policy of the State that the power of alienation of a governmental function did not exist, a subsequently asserted contract would not be controlled by such policy." The attention of the Court was not, however, directed to that provision of the Constitution of Illinois of 1870 which says that: "No law making any irrevocable grant of special privileges or immunities shall be passed," which, as I think, effectually declared the policy of Illinois to be, for the future, that the power of alienation of a governmental function does not exist in Illinois. Had the Court's attention been directed to this prohibition, it seems certain that the Court would have unanimously affirmed the judgments of the Supreme Court of Illinois upon a line of reasoning widely different from what appears in the majority and minority opinions. Mr. Justice White, for the minority, said (180 U. S., 607): "In logical sequence, the questions which arise are these: Was there power in the Legislature to confer upon the municipality authority to contract for water for public use and fix by (irrevocable) contract the rates to be paid by the city for a stated period? . . . It is not even intimated in the opinion below that there was an express limitation in the Constitution of the State of Illinois restricting the power of the Legislature to authorize a municipality to contract for water for public use for a fixed period, and to agree upon the rates to be paid therefor for such time."

In several instances recently, however, where the question was whether an ordinance of a municipal legislative body sitting under the Legislature of a State impaired the obligation of a contract evidenced by provisions in a previous ordinance making a grant to a public service corporation of the right to use streets, the Supreme Court of the United States has appeared to ignore State Constitutions and statutes reserving power to alter, amend, or repeal. One explanation appears to be that counsel did not rely upon the State Constitution or statutes reserving such power. The Detroit and Cleveland Street Railroad Rate cases, though they affirmatively hold that the city councils of Detroit and Cleveland could make irrevocable contracts binding themselves and the State Legislatures of their respective States not to regulate street railroad rates, only mean, I think, that the city councils of Detroit and Cleveland had no power by delegation from the State Legislature to fix street railroad rates otherwise than by way of a condition in an ordinance making a grant of the right to use streets. In both cases, the State Constitution in force at the date of the passage of the ordinances relied on as irrevocable contracts reserved power to alter, amend, or repeal (Detroit Case, 184 U. S., 368; Cleveland Case, 194 U. S., 517; see Knoxville Case, 189 U. S., 434). In the Walla Walla Case, 172 U. S., 1, the contract evidenced by the ordinance and drawn in question in the case was a contract by the city to buy the water plant of the company, a contract not affected, I think, as above stated, either by the reservation of power to repeal or by the prohibition to make irrevocable grants in the Constitution of the State of Washington. The ordinance relied on as an irrevocable contract was passed March 15, 1887, while Washington was organized as a territory of the United States. The ordinance assailed as impairing the alleged irrevocable contract was passed June 10, 1893. Washington was admitted into the Union as a State in 1889. The question of the power of Congress to delegate power to the government of a territory to make irrevocable contracts, under the doctrine of the Dartmouth College case, was not considered, nor was the question whether the admitted State was irrevocably bound by such contracts made as a territory of the United States, when the State Constitution adopted on becoming a State is against irrevocable contracts. The Los Angeles Water Rate case, 177 U. S., 558, holding that the city council of Los Angeles could, and did, on July 22, 1868, bind itself by irrevocable contract not to use the powers subsequently derived from the State Constitution of 1879 and an act of the State Legislature passed in 1881 to regulate water rates is, I think, with all due deference, wrong, because the State Constitution in force July 22, 1868, expressly reserved power to amend or repeal charters of corporations. The decision seems directly at variance with the decision of the same Court in the case of Spring Valley Water Works v. Schottler, 110 U. S., 347 (61 Cal., 3, 18), overlooked apparently by Court and counsel, unless the circumstance in the Los Angeles case that the provision fixing rates in 1868 is found in a lease of the city's own water works to individuals, who at once transferred the lease to a corporation, is sufficient to reconcile the two decisions, and I cannot see how it can be.

The opinion in this Los Angeles case suggests the possibility of an extension by the Federal Supreme Court of the rule in Gelpcke v. Dubuque, above stated as having been applied in Chicago v. Sheldon, to a new subject. The same possibility is slightly hinted in the Cleveland Street Railroad case (194 U. S., 517, 594). The question suggested is this: If the Supreme Court of Illinois, in the face of State contitutional and statutory prohibitions, has ruled that an ordinance of the council of Chicago making a grant of the right to lay down and use street railroad tracks in the streets of Chicago, becomes, when accepted by the grantee, an irrevocable contract or grant, under the doctrine of the Dartmouth College case, will the Supreme Court of the United States hold all such ordinances, passed and accepted while such ruling of the Supreme Court of the State stood unreversed, to be irrevocable contracts or grants, although that ruling of the Supreme Court of the State is admittedly inconsistent with very many rulings of the Supreme Court of the United States itself?

An authoritative affirmative answer to this question would evidently involve a complete abdication of a part of its constitutional functions by the Supreme Court of the United States. Surely its function as an independent judicial tribunal is not to decline to adopt State decisions refusing to find irrevocable contracts or grants, and to adopt without question all State decisions finding them in manifest disregard of the plain meaning, settled by itself, of language, suggested by itself, used in a State Constitution or a State statute (See the dissenting opinion of Mr. Justice Miller in Washington University v. Rouse, 8 Wall., 439, 441). The reason for the rule in Gelpcke v. Dubuque, to wit: The acquisition of rights of private property presumably on the faith of the decision of the highest court of a State expounding a State Constitution and State statutes cannot possibly apply where the highest court of the State renders a decision directly contrary to a doctrine, established at the time of the State decision, of the Supreme Court of the United States. The letter and spirit of the rule in Gelpcke v. Dubuque ought to require men to read and to rely solely upon the settled adjudications of the Supreme Court of the United States alone expounding the legislative power of a State to make irrevocable contracts under the obligation of contracts clause of the Federal Constitution. Upon those decisions as they stand at a given time, and upon those alone, can men rightfully be permitted to rely in their dealings with State and municipal governments (The case of Gelpcke v. Dubuque, 4 Harv. Law Rev., 511; Bank v. Owensboro, 173 U. S., 636, 648).

Is there anything in the Los Angeles case really against this view? An examination of the case will show that there is not.

In that case it appeared that on July 22, 1868, the city council of Los Angeles leased its municipally owned water works to certain individuals for thirty years, granted the right to extend the works, and reserved the right to regulate the rates to be charged for water, "Provided they shall not so reduce such water rates or so fix the price thereof as to be less than those now charged.". . . In August, 1868, the lessees and grantees organized a corporation under the laws of California by the name of the Los Angeles City Water Company. April 2, 1870, the Legislature of California confirmed the lease and grant of July 22, 1868. The Constitution of the State in force on said dates provided that "corporations may be formed under general laws, but shall not be created by special act except for municipal purposes. *All general laws and special acts passed pursuant to this section may be altered from time to time or repealed.*" A new State Consti-

tution took effect in 1879, which retained said provision of the earlier Constitution (California Constitution of 1879, Art. I, Sec. 21; Art. XI, Sec. 19). Article
XIV of the new Constitution of 1879 expressly provided
that city councils should have power to regulate water
rates, and on March 9, 1881, the State Legislature passed
an act to enable city councils to regulate water rates.
February 23, 1897, the council of Los Angeles passed an
ordinance reducing water rates below the rates charged
July 22, 1868. This ordinance of 1897 was held void, as
impairing the obligation of the provision respecting water
rates in the lease and grant made in 1868. The question whether, under and by force of the above quoted
words·in italics in the State Constitution in force July 22,
1868, such ordinance could be an irrevocable contract, was
not considered very much, if at all. Counsel for the city
did contend that "the city did not have power to bind
the State," to which the court replied: "The contention
as expressed is very comprehensive and seems to deny
the competency of the State to give the city the power
to bind it. We do not, however, understand counsel as
so contending, nor could they. Walla Walla v. Walla
Walla Water Co., 172 U. S., 1; see also People v. Stephens,
62 Cal., 209. (But see Spring Valley Water Works v.
Schottler, 110 U. S., 347; Spring Valley Water Works v.
San Francisco, 61 Cal., 3, 18; which say counsel could,
and should, so contend.) We understand the argument
to be that the power, if not expressly given, will not be
presumed unless necessarily or fairly implied in or incident
to other powers expressly given, not simply convenient
but indispensable to them. . . . The rule is familiar."
The Court said that the rule did not apply to the case
in hand, because the State Legislature ratified the acts
and ordinances of 1868 on April 2, 1870. Then this act
of April 2, 1870, was assailed as being repugnant to the

first part of the above set forth provision of the State Constitution in force in 1870, because "the act of 1870 conferred franchises on the company by a special act instead of by a general law, and thereby infringes the constitutional provision, and against the existence of such power in the Legislature the following (California) cases are cited." The Court then said that under the decisions of the highest court of California, as they stood on April 12, 1870, the State Legislature did have power to confer franchises on the water company by a special act. But whether the franchises were revocable or irrevocable, in view of the expressed reserved power to repeal, was not expressly considered by the Court or argued by counsel. Then the Court said: "It follows, therefore, that at the time of the contract of 1868 and of the passage of the ratifying act of 1870 it was established by the decisions of the highest court of the State that the Constitution of the State permitted a grant of special franchises to persons and corporations, and permitted the latter to receive assignments of them from such persons or grants of them directly from the Legislature. This law was part of the contract of 1868, as confirmed by the act of 1870, and could not be affected by subsequent decisions." But the reserved power to alter and repeal also "was a part of the contract of 1868, as confirmed by the act of 1870." A grant of a revocable franchise by a special law is one thing, and a grant of an irrevocable franchise by a special law is another and different thing. The Court does not say that, nor did it enquire whether, under the State decisions, as they stood in 1870, the State Legislature of California could either directly, or indirectly by a grant of power to a municipal corporation, make a grant of an irrevocable franchise, and, hence, obviously, it is not, and could not have been, judicially affirmed in this case that the Supreme Court of the United

States would follow such State decisions, if they exist, rather than its own decisions to the contrary.

The Los Angeles case is, therefore, no authority at all in favor of extending the doctrine of Gelpcke *v.* Dubuque so as to make it the rule for the decision of a case involving the question whether a State Legislature has the power to make, or to authorize a municipal corporation to make, an irrevocable contract or grant bestowing an irrevocable franchise, when the State Constitution, in the mode and manner pointed out to the people by the Supreme Court of the United States itself, forbids it so to do.   Nor do I see how the Cleveland Street Railroad Rate case, 194 U. S., 517, 594, can be so regarded, when the learned Justice who wrote the opinion in that case, Mr. Justice White, dissented in Muehlker *v.* Harlem Railroad, 197 U. S., 544, where that doctrine was extended to a new subject, and apparently expressed, or hints, a contrary view in the Owensboro Case, 173 U. S., 636.

In the last analysis, the cases above referred to in the Federal Supreme Court and many others involving the same questions to be found in the reports of the highest courts of States rest upon the proposition, no doubt quite generally accepted in these days outside of courts, that State Legislatures are incompetent and untrustworthy, if not actually dishonest.   But that would seem to be a proposition for the electors to deal with, rather than a rule of decision for the courts.   "Some play must be allowed for the joints of the machine, and it must be remembered that legislatures are ultimate guardians of the liberties and welfare of the people in quite as great a degree as the courts" (Mr. Justice Holmes, in Missouri, K. & T. R. Co. *v.* May, 194 U. S., 267, 270).   "Under no system can the power of courts go far to save a people from ruin; our chief protection lies elsewhere" (James B.

Thayer, "The Origin and Scope of the American Doctrine of Constitutional Law," 7 Har. Law Rev., 129, 156).

It seems to me that the decisions of the Supreme Court of the United States have settled the proposition that, under the Illinois Constitution of 1870, and statutes passed pursuant thereto, the city council of Chicago has no power to pass an ordinance making an irrevocable grant of the right to lay down and use street railroad tracks in the streets of Chicago for a fixed period of time, and, if it be true, and I think it is not true, that the Supreme Court of Illinois is against that proposition, that makes no difference whatever, because the Supreme Court of Illinois has no commission to set aside the State Constitution under which it sits, and, if it has done so, it is, in the instance in hand, the duty of the Supreme Court of the United States to give effect to the State Constitution as it was written and adopted by the people of the State, agreeably to that Court's own suggestion as to how to write it in order to get a certain legal result.

XXV. THE NEW YORK CASE OF PEOPLE v. O'BRIEN.

The judicial authority most relied on to support the proposition that, under the Constitution of 1870, a twenty-year street railroad franchise or license to use streets in Chicago is irrevocable by legislative act before the expiration of the twenty years, is the judgment of the New York Court of Appeals in People v. O'Brien, 111 N. Y., 1. In that case Jacob Sharp and his associates finally did get street car tracks irrevocably laid down in Broadway, New York City. In that case the New York Court of Appeals decided that an act of the Legislature of New York, passed pursuant to a reserved power in the State Constitution to alter, amend, and repeal charters of corporations, revoking all the powers, privileges, franchises, rights, and immunities of The Broadway Surface Railroad Company, had no effect, except to take away the bare power of the corporation to live, or to exist, and that, as applied to the right of the corporation to lay down and use street railroad tracks in Broadway obtained from the common council of New York City, the act was void as an impairment of the obligation of contracts, and as a taking of private property without due process of law. The reserved power to alter and repeal was in the State Constitution in force at the time the corporation got its charter from the State, and at the time it got its right to use Broadway from the city of New York.

In so far as the ruling in this case is predicated upon the circumstance that, at the time of the passage of the act of repeal or revocation, the corporation had outstanding mortgages, bonds, and stocks, traffic agreements with other street railroad corporations, construction and equipment contracts and other merely private contracts, it is manifestly wrong, because it is plainly apparent that men cannot, by entering into contracts with each other, divest a State or the National Legislature of its legislative power of altering or revoking grants of special privileges (Greenwood v. Freight Co., 103 U. S., 13; Knoxville Water Co. v. Knoxville, 189 U. S., 434, 438; Buffalo East Side R. Co. v. Buffalo Street R. Co., 111 N. Y., 132).

In so far as the case rules that under the law of New York as it stood at the time in question (May to December 5, 1884) a grant by the local government of New York City to a corporation of the right to lay down and use street railroad tracks in a street in that city stands upon the same footing as a grant of an acre of land made by a State (Fletcher v. Peck, 6 Cranch, 87), or a grant made by a farmer to a railroad company of a strip of land for a right of way across his farm, the decision may be binding upon the people of the city of New York, but that case is no evidence at all of what the law is in Illinois, or in any other State in the Union. The Supreme Court of the

United States has ruled that an act of the Legislature of Massachusetts making a grant of the right to lay down and use street railroad tracks in a street in Boston, subject to a reserved power to alter or repeal, is not in the same class of acts as the act of a farmer making a grant of a strip of land across his farm. The latter is but an exercise by an individual of his natural and inalienable right to sell his own private property for money. The former act is an exercise by the supreme legislative body of a State of the sovereign law-making power of the State making a grant of a portion of its sovereign power to a street railroad company in trust, to be used for the ultimate benefit of the people, for the use of which power the grantee is at all times accountable to the legislative grantor, and the grantee must lay down the power, or stop using it, whenever the legislative grantor so wills, and must no longer encumber the streets with its material property, its rails and road bed, when the Legislature so wills by an act revoking the grant and authorizing a new corporation to construct and operate a street railroad right over the same ground (Greenwood *v.* Freight Co., 103 U. S., 105).

That is, I think, the true conception of the act of the city council of Chicago when, under the Constitution of 1870, it passes an ordinance making a grant of the right to lay down and use street railroad tracks in a street in Chicago (City of Belleville *v.* Citizens' Street R. Co., 152 Ill., 171). At least, it has got to be demonstrated that the judgment of the Supreme Court of the United States, and the opinion of Mr. Justice Miller, in the case cited, are wrong, before the conceptions of the personal pronouns mine and thine, as applied to a public street and the right to use if for street railroad purposes, under the doctrine of the Dartmouth College case and under a State's reserved legislative power to alter and repeal, incorporated into the law of New York by the decision in People *v.* O'Brien, 111 N. Y., 1, can get a permanent abiding place in the existing law of Illinois. (With Mr. Justice Miller's opinion compare Burke's exposition of the English phrase "Chartered Rights of Men," quoted in 8 Am. Law Rev., 226, and in 1 Ohio St., 634.)

XXVI. THE STREET RAILROAD TANGLE IN CHICAGO ARISES OUT OF A MISAPPREHENSION OF THE LAW OF ILLINOIS.

It results from the aforesaid views that the street railroad war in Chicago is based upon a wrong legal opinion, the legal opinion that the doctrine of the Dartmouth College case is now, and has been since August 16, 1858, a rule of law in Illinois applicable to the street railroad corporations of Chicago, and, consequently, that an ordinance making a grant of the right to lay down and use street railroad tracks in the streets of Chicago always did, and does now, grant special privileges irrevocable by legislative act. In other words, the whole war is based upon the idea that irrevocability by legislative act is a necessary ingredient of a franchise. That it is not is clear. The source of the error is probably the ninety-nine-year limitation in the act of 1865, and the twenty-year limitation in the Cities and Villages Act of 1872, and in the Horse and Dummy Act of 1874. That twenty-year limitation is not at all in harmony with the policy of the Constitution of 1870, in so far as it declares against irrevocable grants of special privileges. A just legislative carrying out of that policy requires that no maximum term of years at all be specified; that the grantees be allowed to hold, exercise, and enjoy their privileges just as the Judges both of the Supreme and inferior Courts of the United States hold their offices, that is to say, "during good behavior." If experience in Chicago has demonstrated anything, it has demonstrated that the street railroad business cannot be, or will not be, carried on honestly under twenty-year grants. Human nature being what it is, men who go into that business will get their money back within the twenty years, either by an excessive rate of fare for bad service, or by selling over-issues of stocks and bonds to investors, innocent very often in fact if not in law. As above stated, under our law, the operation and management of a street railroad by individuals and corporations is a trust. "And it is of the very essence of every trust to be rendered account-able, and even totally to cease, when it substantially varies from the purposes for which alone it could have a lawful existence. This, I conceive, sir, to be true of trusts of power vested in the highest hands, and of such as seem to hold of no human creature. But about the application of this principle to subordinate derivative trusts, I do not see how a controversy can be maintained" (Burke's speech, supra). The Constitution of Illinois of 1870, and the statutes of Illinois prior and subsequent to 1870, make the private owners and operators of street railroads in Chicago accountable to the local government of Chicago. Has Chicago ever had a local government that adequately and justly performed its functions in this regard?

XXVII. Revocable licenses under the law of Illinois and municipal ownership.

It also results that outstanding, unexpired ninety-nine and twenty-year grants of street railroad franchises or licenses to use the streets of Chicago present no real obstacle to a change, at any time, from the governmental policy of private ownership to the governmental policy of public ownership of street railroads in Chicago. I do not see how any court, without unpermissible legislation of its own economic views into our written Constitutions, could rule that a municipal legislative revocation of such outstanding, unexpired grants, made with a view to give effect to a popular vote in favor of such change was not based upon what the law deems a good and just cause.   Of course, after such revocation, the local government of Chicago could not be compelled to pay a dollar for such franchises or licenses to use the streets.   One might as well affirm that a private landlord, after exercising his reserved right to put an end to a lease, could not enter and use the premises covered by the lease without paying the tenant the value of the use of the premises for the unexpired term of years subsequent to the date of revocation.   Of course, the local government would have to pay the grantee of the revoked franchise or license for its material property, if it wanted to take it and to use it (City of Belleville *v.* Belleville Street R. Co., 152 Ill., 171, 188; Bridge Co. *v.* United States, 105 U. S., 470; Monongahela Nav. Co. *v.* U. S., 148 U. S., 312).

XXVIII. THE MUELLER MUNICIPAL OWNERSHIP LAW.

But does it now, or at any definitely assignable date in the future, lie in the power of the people of Chicago, however much they may desire it, to change from the established policy of the State, giving the local government of Chicago complete, sovereign, governmental control over the operation and management of street railroads in the streets of Chicago, to the policy of municipal ownership and operation of them?   The only act delegating power to Chicago to own and operate street railroads is the so-called Mueller Act, approved May 18, 1903, in force July 1, 1903 (Sess. Laws, 1903, page 285).

That act gives the city council power to construct new street railroads, or to buy ready-made ones, if the council can find the cash money.   But the act recognizes that the council of Chicago cannot, until there is a revolution in the administration of our tax laws, find the cash money by a use of its taxing power, and that resort must be had to its borrowing power.   Two modes of borrowing money are prescribed.   The first mode, an issue of bonds under authority of a two-thirds popular vote, may be laid to one side because, under existing tax laws and their administration, Chicago has quite reached the constitutional limit of its power to borrow money· by a sale of bonds.   The second mode seeks to enable a municipal corporation to avail itself of the familiar practice under which men have astonished all by acquiring railroads without spending any of their own money.   It provides a form of security denominated "street railway certificates."   These may be issued to an amount equal to the cost of a street railroad to be constructed new, or to be bought ready made, plus ten percent of such cost. In no event can these certificates become a personal liability of Chicago to be paid by general taxation.   They are payable only out of a particular specified fund, namely, the earnings of the street railroads to be constructed or bought.   To secure payment of the certificates, Chicago is authorized to pledge by way of deed of trust, or by way of mortgage, the street railroads to be constructed, or to be bought, with the certificates or with the proceeds of them.   The act then provides: "Any such mortgage or deed of trust may carry the grant of a privilege or right to maintain and operate the street railway property covered thereby for a period not exceeding twenty years from and after the date such property may come into the possession of any person or corporation as the result of foreclosure proceedings, which privilege or right may fix the rates of fare which the person or corporation securing the same as the result of foreclosure proceedings shall be entitled to charge in the operation of said property for a period not exceeding twenty years.   .   .   .   At a foreclosure sale the mortgagee or the holders of such certificates may become the purchaser or purchasers of the property and the rights and privileges sold, if he or they be the highest bidders."

Very plainly, I think, all that is a clear attempt to delegate power to Chicago to make an irrevocable grant of the right to operate a street railroad in the streets of Chicago for twenty years, and to charge a rate of fare irrevocably fixed for twenty years. Is the grant made revocable by this sentence following directly after the above quotation: "Any street railways acquired under any such foreclosure shall be subject to regulation by the corporate authorities of the city to the same extent as if the right to construct, maintain, and operate such property had been acquired through a direct grant, without the intervention of foreclosure proceedings?" In view of the object aimed at, the raising of money and the giving of security for repayment, in view of the source from which the mode of raising money was borrowed, and in view of the rate-fixing provisions, I do not think the last words quoted can fairly and reasonably be interpreted as a reservation of power to repeal the grant. Apt words for this purpose being at hand, I do not see how any court can say that the reserved power to prescribe "regulations" for street railways in the Mueller Act is tantamount to a reserved power to alter and repeal the grant of the right to use streets, and the grant of the right to charge a fixed rate of fare for a fixed term of years (Detroit *v.* Detroit Citizens Street R. Co., 184 U. S., 368, 383–385.) This view is somewhat supported by the fact that the aforesaid clause reserving power was taken from the fourth section of the Horse and Dummy Act, omitting the following very material words in that section, to wit: "to make all necessary police regulations concerning the management and operation of such railroad, whether such right is reserved in the grant or not." I incline to think, therefore, that the part of the Mueller Act referred to encounters the State constitutional prohibition against the making of irrevocable grants of special privileges, and is, therefore, void.

The act also provides that street railway certificates can be issued only on approval of a majority of the qualified voters of Chicago, voting on the question. Suppose such approval given, certificates issued, and new street railroads constructed, or old ones' bought, by Chicago. What can Chicago do with them? The act says Chicago must lease them, unless authorized to operate them by her own officers and employees by three-fifths of the electors voting on the question. The lease authorized to be made includes not only the material street railroad property acquired and owned by Chicago, but the intangible "franchise." The act says: "In case of the leasing by any city of any street railway owned by it, the rental reserved shall be based on both the actual value of the tangible property and of the franchise contained in such lease, and such rental shall not be less than a sufficient sum to meet the annual interest upon all outstanding . . . street railway certificates issued by such city on account of such street railway." What is "the franchise contained in such lease"? The intent was, it seems to me, that the lease should operate as an irrevocable grant of "the franchise contained in such lease" for the fixed term of years specified. It seems impossible to construe the words "lease," "grant," and "franchise," in connection with the whole act, considered in all its parts, otherwise than as meaning irrevocable lease, grant, or franchise. This part of the act, therefore, also encounters the State Constitution, and is void.

In so far as the act authorizes Chicago to acquire the material property of an existing street railroad company by a use of the power of eminent domain, before the required three-fifths vote to operate has been obtained, it seems difficult indeed to sustain the act. If it be conceded that the government of a State may lawfully use its power of eminent domain to acquire the property of an existing street railroad corporation, with a view to operating it immediately by its own officers and employees (In re Brooklyn, 26 L. R. A., 270), and even if it be conceded that a State government may use its power of eminent domain to reinvest itself with powers of legislation of which it had previously been deprived by irrevocable contracts, under the doctrine of the Dartmouth College case, I do not see how it is possible for a State government lawfully to use its power of eminent domain to acquire the material property of one street railroad corporation at a time when all that the government can do with the property when acquired is, first, to mortgage the material property, the mortgage containing a covenant binding the government to give the mortgagees an irrevocable grant of the right to use the streets of Chicago, and an irrevocable grant of the right to charge an irrevocably fixed street railroad rate of fare, and, second, to lease the property so mortgaged to another street railroad corporation for identically the same use. It would appear to be clear that a resort to the power of eminent domain, under the act, would be premature and unconstitutional, at least until the three-fifths vote to operate is obtained. It is too clear for discussion that the government cannot use its power of eminent domain merely to bring about a change in the private ownership of private property (Cary Library v. Bliss, 151 Mass., 304).

But if the aforesaid provisions of the Mueller Act be stricken out, it may be that the remainder can stand, and, if so, the act does give the local government of Chicago power to acquire street railroads, provided it can raise the cash money to pay for them, and power to operate them with its own officers and employees, provided the necessary three-fifths vote is forthcoming.

But it ought not to be forgotten that municipal ownership and municipal operation of street railroads are not in themselves ends for which the local government of Chicago was ordained and established. They are but governmental means for attaining a more ultimate end, the only end a government can rightfully aim to attain in dealing with street railroads, to wit: thè security and protection of the individual in the exercise and enjoyment of his right of person and of property to reasonably comfortable rides in street cars over and along the streets upon payment of a reasonable rate of fare (See the Declaration of Independence, second paragraph). There being little doubt that the local government of Chicago is not now, and is not likely to be for some time, in a position to avail itself of the means of municipal ownership and municipal operation to attain that end, should the available means be neglected, namely, the granting of revocable licenses to private individuals or corporations, and the passage of reasonable and just ordinances showing them "the way wherein they must walk," and holding them to a strict account of their trust? I do not see how it is possible, under the law of Illinois, by a use of those means, to prejudice the just rights of all those who are convinced in their own minds that our political safety requires a change from the policy of private ownership of street railroads to the policy of governmental ownership. The greatest obstacle to that change, outstanding franchises made irrevocable by legislative act by the doctrine of the Dartmouth College case, does not exist, and certainly no one supposes that any government ought ever to attempt to acquire the material property that goes to make a street railroad without money, or the means of raising money, to pay for it.

In my judgment, the Supreme Court of the State should be given an opportunity at the earliest possible moment to declare the meaning of the mandate in the Constitution that "No law making any irrevocable grant of special privileges or immunities shall be passed," and if it means what the men who wrote it intended, then the General Assembly ought, first, to revise the Horse and Dummy Act by at least striking out the words "not exceeding twenty years," and, second, to harmonize the Mueller Municipal Ownership Law with the cardinal principle that, within the limitations of our written Constitutions, the successful majority in a fair, stand-up fight must be permitted to rule.

It does look very much as if, in disregard of the law of Illinois as evidenced by the State Constitution, State statutes and decisions of the highest court of the State, and of the United States, the people of Chicago have been immolated for eight years upon the altars of those twin rival fetishes, so far as the present law of Illinois is concerned, the doctrine of the Dartmouth College case, and the abstract principle and policy of municipal ownership.

TOPIC VIII

THE POWER OF APPOINTMENT TO PUBLIC OFFICE

THE STATE CIVIL SERVICE ACT AND THE POWER OF APPOINTMENT

THE STATE CIVIL SERVICE ACT AND THE POWER OF APPOINTMENT [a]

The selection of persons to fill them is the essence of the power of appointment to public offices and employments. Election by the people is a mode of appointment, i. e., selection.[1]

The State Civil Service Act of 1911 lodges the power of appointment to "all the offices and places of employment in the state service," except those enumerated in section 11, in the State Civil Service Commission, to be exercised by that body on the basis of merit, ascertained by competitive tests, open to all, the highest man to have the office or employment in question.

In People *v.* McCullough,[2] the constitutionality of this act, as applied to the offices or employments known as "assistant chief clerk," "chief corporation clerk," and "bookkeeper" in the department of the Secretary of State, was assailed on the ground that this legislative grant of the power of appointment to the State Civil Service Commission collides with a superior constitutional grant of the power of appointment to the Secretary of State. Since the act prescribes the selection of the highest man, it collides with the constitution if it is true the constitution grants the power of appointment to the Secretary of State. Hence the question of constitutionality turned on the point whether the constitution grants the Secretary of State power to appoint the aids and subordinates

---

[a] [7 Ill. Law Rev., 329, January, 1913.]

[1] People *v.* Mosher, 163 N. Y., 32.

[2] 254 Ill., 9.

in his department.[3] Vickers, Farmer, and Cooke, JJ., speaking by Vickers, J., say the constitution does grant such power of appointment to the Secretary of State. Dunn, Hand, and Carter, JJ., speaking by Dunn, J., say it does not. Cartwright, J., takes a distinction, saying the constitution grants the Secretary of State power to appoint aids and subordinates who help him perform his constitutional duties, but not aids and subordinates who help him perform his statutory duties. The opinions of Vickers, Farmer, and Cooke, JJ., and Dunn, Hand, and Carter, JJ., destroy each other, and the opinion of Cartwright, J., alone stands as the law, controlling the practical administration of the State Civil Service Act. Neither the full power of appointment found by Vickers, Farmer, and Cooke, JJ., nor the partial power of appointment found by Cartwright, J., is expressed in the constitution, but only implied.

Under the opinions of Vickers, Farmer, and Cooke, JJ., and Cartwright, J., it seems a like or similar implied constitutional grant of the power of appointment to offices and employments in their respective departments must arise in favor of the Governor, the Lieutenant Governor, the Auditor, the Treasurer, the Superintendent of Public Instruction, the Attorney-General, and the Supreme Court.

Most exemptions from the merit system of the act claimed under this opinion of Cartwright, J., admit of debate and litigation. For example: Vickers, Farmer, and Cooke, JJ., say the rule of the opinion of Cartwright, J., exempts at least two of the positions in the case before

---

[3] It is held a Civil Service act avoids collision with a constitutional grant of the power of appointment when the act prescribes the selection of one of the three or four highest men. People v. Mosher, 163 N. Y., 32–43. Illinois is the pioneer for the rule of the highest man. Sixth Annual Report of the Illinois State Civil Service Commission, 8.

them, while Cartwright, J., holds it does not exempt any of them.[4]

It is hard to account on grounds of law for this diversity of judicial opinion. It seems to flow from a failure to separate the power of appointment from the power to create offices and employments, from confusion of thought on the difference between "offices" and "employments" for purposes of appointment, and from trying to decide a question in constitutional law without looking at the text of the constitution. The written text compels the result reached by Dunn, Hand, and Carter, JJ., denying altogether any implied constitutional grant of the power of appointment to the Secretary of State, et al.

The power of appointment and the power to create public offices and employments are different things. Only offices and employments in the state service with

---

[4] The case of positions under the Supreme Court figured in the argument at the bar. In point of fact all positions under the Supreme Court are exempt from the merit system of the act, as appears from the last report of the State Civil Service Commission. It is said the exemption of these positions is sustainable under the opinion of Cartwright, J., because janitors of the Supreme Court, the custodian of its building, the matron of its apartments, etc., are helping the court perform its constitutional duty to decide cases at law and in equity; and there is a Wisconsin dictum that lends support to that view. In re Janitor of the Supreme Court, 36 Wis., 410. A better reason for the exemption is that these positions are "offices" within the meaning of the exemption of "officers appointed by judges of any court" in section 11, the Illinois meaning of the word "office" for purposes of appointment appearing later on.

Though it does not appear in the printed report of the case, it is the fact that the opinion of Cartwright, J., was filed after the decision of the case by a four to three vote on the opinion of Dunn, J., Cartwright, J., being one of the four, and after the denial of a petition for rehearing with no announced modification of the filed majority opinion of Dunn, J., when nothing remained to be done in the case but the preparation and filing of opinions by the three dissenting judges. A filed opinion is, by statute, a part of the record, and is, as it seems to me, aside from this statute, unalterable in material particulars after filing and publication as in this case by any judge or by all the judges on his or their own motion, in the absence of fraud or imposition practiced on the court. See Houston v. Williams, 13 Cal., 24, 25, 27, Field, J. It is easy to imagine the protest if the Supreme Court of the United States should allow one of its members to change his published opinion in this sort of way.

salaries payable out of the state treasury need concern us. This excludes the office or employment of receiver and other like offices and employments with salaries or fees payable by the parties, created by courts in exercise of the judicial power to decide cases at law and in equity.[5]

The power to create salary-paying offices and employments in the state service is inherent in the people. Its exercise involves an exercise of the power of the purse, which the legislature alone can wield, as the constitution of Illinois expressly declares. Neither the Secretary of State, nor any other constitutional executive officer, nor the Supreme Court, can derive any implied constitutional grant of power to create salary-paying offices and employments in their respective departments from any necessity, however real, as adapted and appropriate means to aid them in the performance of duties imposed on them by the constitution, by statute, or by the common law, because such means, involving as they do the expenditure of public money, are prohibited, and therefore cannot be adapted and appropriate means in a legal sense, unless authorized by the legislature expressly or impliedly by the mode of an appropriation. There are but two legal

[5] The Juvenile Court act creates the office of "probation officer" in Cook County, with a salary payable out of the county treasury, and vests the power of appointment in the Cook County Civil Service Commission. Windes, J., in the Circuit Court of Cook County recently held this act unconstitutional in so far as it disposes of the power of appointment, on the ground that it collides with a constitutional grant of the power of appointment to the Circuit and Superior Courts of Cook County implied in the expressed constitutional grant of "original jurisdiction of all causes in law and equity." This position of "probation officer" falls between the receiver on the one side and the janitor on the other side, resembling the office of public administrator, where by statute the Governor appoints. The court has no constitutional power to create such a position, and therefore has no constitutional power to appoint. However, such is the judicial tendency in Illinois, acquiesced in and encouraged by the legal profession and by the people, to contract and discredit the legislative power, the ruling of Windes, J., is likely to be approved by the Supreme Court.

sources from which public offices and employments can flow: the constitution and a statute, the people and the legislature.[6]

The power of appointment, like the power to create offices and employments, also is inherent in the people, and belongs to the state legislature unless the state constitution otherwise provides.

"The power to appoint is by no means an executive function (or a judicial function), unless made so by the organic law or legislative enactment."[7]

For purposes of appointment the constitution of Illinois divides all positions in the state service into two classes: offices and employments.   If a position in the state service is an office, the power of appointment is in the Governor, acting by and with the advice and consent of the Senate, unless the legislature otherwise provides, but the legislature itself cannot make appointments to offices.   If a position in the state service is an employment, the power of appointment is in the legislature, to be exercised by itself, unless the legislature otherwise provides.

[6] Constitution, Article 4, Sections 17, 18, 19; Field v. People, 2 Scam., 79. Though the constitution says "Each general assembly shall provide for all the ordinary and contingent expenses of the government," this command involves no limitation on the legislative power nor expansion of the executive and judicial powers.   The duty prescribed is not a legal duty enforceable by a court.   It has been held no court can coerce the Governor, because he is the co-ordinate executive.   People v. Bissell, 19 Ill., 29; People v. Cullom, 100 Ill., 472.

[7] People v. Morgan, 90 Ill., 558, 562.   Vickers, J., expressly, and Cartwright, J., impliedly, deny this proposition, founding their opinions on such denial.   They are in error, and their opinions fall to the ground.   Vickers, J., says the power of appointment is inherently an executive function.   His words are: "When the constitution conferred all of the executive powers of the state on the state officers enumerated, it necessarily by clear implication conferred upon such executive officers the executive power to appoint such necessary assistants as would enable them to discharge duties required of them."   He cites Mechem, Public Officers, Sec. 104, where the author says: "So it is said appointments to offices, whether by judicial, legislative, or executive officers or bodies, are in their nature intrinsically executive acts," adding the qualifying clause overlooked by Vickers, J., "though it by no means follows that the appointing power is inherent in the executive."   In Field v. People, 2 Scam., 79, 109, the court discusses and denies

The legislature may prescribe the mode of appointment to all offices and employments in the state service. It may itself make appointments to employments, but not to offices. This general rule does not apply to offices and employments in the state service established by the constitution with modes of appointment expressly prescribed by the constitution, as e. g., the clerk of the Supreme Court to be elected by the people, and the reporter of the Supreme Court to be appointed by the Supreme Court.[8]

There is a judge-made qualification of the above general rule, which says the legislature cannot devolve the power of appointment to offices in the state service upon a private corporation by a local or special law, because, it is said, the power of appointment falls within Blackstone's definition of a franchise, "A royal privilege or branch of the king's prerogative subsisting in the hands of a subject," and the constitution says:

"the next political maxim relied upon . . . that the right of appointment and of removal from office are executive functions, and, as such, belong to the executive." See the cases collected in 29 Cyc., 137; 23 Am. and Eng. Ency. of Law, 2d Ed., 340, 343.

Under all authorities worthy of credit, the clear fixed general principle lying back of the text of the written state constitution is as stated by Walker, J., in People v. Morgan, 90 Ill., 558, first laid down in this state by Wilson, J., in Field v. People, 2 Scam., 79, 81, 82, 109, 110: The power of appointment is inherent in the people, and, on the division into departments, falls to the legislative department, not to the executive or judicial. The English king's prerogative of appointment under the English common law has no application, being unsuited to our condition. King George III is not the model of the American executive, state or federal. The chief object of the American Revolution was to get rid of George in particular and of kings in general. Hence, the power of appointment can become a constitutional function of the state executive or judiciary only by express constitutional grant, and, in the absence of such constitutional grant, can become a function of the state executive or judiciary only by legislative enactment. As shown in the text, the constitution of Illinois expressly ordains that the legislature may prescribe the mode of appointment to all offices and employments in the state service, except those established by the constitution with modes of election or appointment expressly prescribed by the constitution.

[8] Constitution, Article 6, Sections 9 and 10.

"The General Assembly shall not pass local or special laws . . . granting to any corporation, association, or individual, any special or exclusive privilege immunity or franchise whatever."[9]

Hence, by the express terms of the constitution of Illinois the power of appointment to offices and employments in their respective departments is not a constitutional function of the Secretary of State, the Lieutenant Governor, the Auditor, the Treasurer, the Superintendent of Public Instruction, the Attorney-General and the Supreme Court, and can become their function only by legislative enactment. The legislature may grant them the power of appointment and revoke the grant at pleasure. Even the power of appointment to offices given by the constitution to the Governor, acting by and with the advice and consent of the Senate, is made subject to the will of the legislature, under the written restriction that the legislature itself must not make appointments to offices, though it may itself make appointments to employments.

The rule of the constitution is expressed in article 5, sections 10 and 24. Section 10 says:

"The Governor shall nominate and by and with the advice and consent of the Senate (a majority of all the Senate elected concurring by yeas and nays), appoint all officers whose offices are established by this constitution, or which may be created by law, and whose appointment or election is not otherwise provided for; and no such officer shall be appointed or elected by the General Assembly."[10]

[9] Lasher v. People, 183 Ill., 226. Though the reasoning of this case is not sound, and therefore ought not to be extended, yet it suggests this observation: Inasmuch as the constitution declares it is one of the fundamental principles of civil government to which we should have frequent recurrence, that "no law making an irrevocable grant of special privileges or immunities shall be passed" (article 2, sections 14, 20), it is hard to believe the framers of the constitution themselves violated this fundamental principle of civil government by making an implied irrevocable grant of the power of appointment to the Secretary of State et al.

[10] This section goes back to the constitution of 1848, article 4, section 12, and

Section 24 says:

"An office is a public position, created by the constitution or law, continuing during the pleasure of the appointing power, or for a fixed time, with a successor elected or appointed. An employment is an agency, for a temporary purpose, which ceases when the purpose is accomplished."

These sections reaffirm the general disposition of the people's original power of appointment made in the constitution of 1848, as explained and applied in Bunn v. People,[11] wherein the legislature itself by act of 1867 selected the commissioners to build the State House. The act was sustained as a proper exercise by the legislature itself of the power of appointment, because the positions were employments and not offices. The framers of the present constitution drew their definition of "office" and "employment" from that case, and put it into the constitution with express reference to the power of appointment in order to fix with more precision the limit of the authority of the legislature itself to make appointments to employments, without going so far as to strip the legislature of power to select its own pages, clerks, etc.[12]

The view that the written text of the constitution excludes the idea of an implied constitutional grant of the power of appointment to offices and employments in their respective departments to the Secretary of State,

to that of 1818, article 3, section 20, the precedent being article 2, section 2, clause 2, of the federal constitution regulating the power of appointment to offices under the United States, the provisions in the two constitutions, state and federal, having to be viewed differently, and interpreted on different familiar principles, as shown in Field v. People, 2 Scam., 79, the federal constitution being a grant to all departments of the federal government, and the state constitution being a limitation on the legislature but a grant to the executive and judiciary.

[11] 45 Ill., 397.

[12] 1 Debates in C. C. of 1870, 779–781; 2 id. 1374; People v. Loeffler, 175 Ill., 585, 602, 603.

the other constitutional executive officers, and the Supreme Court, is supported by the practice and usage of the legislature, and by decisions of the Supreme Court. Numerous decisions sustaining acts of the legislature devolving upon judges the power of appointment to offices and employments in departments not connected with the judicial department affirm in the strongest possible manner the freedom of the legislature to dispose of the power of appointment at its own will and pleasure to all offices and employments in the state service except those established by the constitution with modes of appointment or election expressly prescribed by the constitution.[13]

If the meaning of these sections can be said to admit of any doubt, then, agreeably to the fixed pillar of our constitutional law that all power is inherent in the people to be exercised by the state legislature except as prohibited by the state and federal constitutions, the doubt ought to be resolved by a court in favor of the freedom of the legislature, i. e., the freedom of the people, acting through the legislature, to provide for the appointment, i. e., selection, of their officers and employees in the way that seems best to them.

"The idea cannot be entertained for one moment, that any intelligent people would have consented to so bind themselves with

[13] People v. Morgan, 90 Ill., 558; People v. Hoffman, 116 Ill., 587; Sherman v. People, 210 Ill., 552; People v. Evans, 247 Ill., 547. These cases reject the constitutional point, when raised in cases attacking the validity of appointments made by judges, that an act devolving upon judges the power of appointment to an office or employment outside the judicial department unconstitutionally imposes a non-judicial duty. When the point is made in a case to compel the exercise of the power of appointment by a judge who refuses to exercise it, the point is good, for it is clear a judge, qua judge, cannot be forced by the legislature against his will to exercise the power of appointment, though if he appoints, the appointment is valid. Hayburn's Case, 2 Dall., 409; United States v. Ferreira, 13 How., 40; People v. Morgan, 90 Ill., 558, 568, criticized in Lasher v. People, 183 Ill., 226, 235, 236. The Illinois Supreme Court might not sustain this distinction.

constitutional restrictions on the power of their representatives, as to prevent the adoption of any means by which to secure, if possible, honest and intelligent service in public office."[14]

The legal argument in support of the doctrine of an implied constitutional grant of the power to appoint aids and subordinates in their respective departments to the Secretary of State, the other constitutional executive officers, and the Supreme Court, rests on the proposition that subordinate positions established by existing law in these departments are not offices, but are employments.[15] This proposition is an irrelevant one. The question whether positions in the state service are offices or employments has no connection with the question of the extent of the authority of the legislature to prescribe the mode of filling them.

If subordinate positions in the state service are offices, it is agreed by all, as it must be, the authority of the legislature to dispose of the power of appointment to them is plenary and complete, except that the legislature itself cannot make appointments nor devolve the power of appointment on a private corporation by a local or special law.

As touching the authority of the legislature to prescribe the mode of filling them, it can make no difference whether subordinate positions in the executive departments and under the Supreme Court are offices or employments. The legislature may dispose of the power of appointment to employments in the state service just as freely as of the power of appointment to offices in the state service,

[14] Peckham, J., as quoted in People v. Kipley, 171 Ill., 44, 63.

[15] Most of the argument was, as the opinion of Dunn, J., says, a political complaint that the State Civil Service Act of 1911, under the guise of an extension of the merit system in the state service, centralizes the spoils system in the hands of the Governor, through the medium of a grant of the power of appointment of the State Civil Service Commission, mere wax-works of the Governor, it was said, because he may remove them at will.

the only difference being that the legislature itself may make appointments to employments but not to offices.

If positions in the state service are neither offices nor employments, the State Civil Service Act of 1911 does not apply to them, because that act does not dispose of the power of appointment to anything but "offices and places of employment in the state service." But there is no such thing as a position in the state service that is neither an office nor an employment for purposes of appointment.

To say that subordinate positions in the executive and judicial departments are not in the state service but in the private service of the head of the department, is to bring out and state as is done at one point in the opinion of Dunn, J., the reductio ad absurdum of the doctrine of an implied constitutional grant of the power of appointment to the Secretary of State, et al.

If the claim is made, and it is vaguely hinted, though not articulated in this case, that subordinate positions in the executive and judicial departments are "established by this constitution," it is enough to reply that the constitution does not prescribe any mode of filling them by appointment or election, and therefore they fall under the general disposition of the power of appointment in article 5, sections 10 and 24; and whether such subordinate positions are "offices" or "employments" "established by this constitution" can make no difference whatever in the extent of the authority of the legislature to prescribe the mode of filling them.

All of the opinions proceed on the footing of this irrelevant proposition that subordinate positions as established by existing law in the executive and judicial departments of the state service are not offices, but are employments. The reason given in the opinion of Dunn, J., for saying the subordinate positions in the department of the Secretary of State involved in the case before the court are not offices is this: they are not created by any law but the general appropriation bill for the ordinary and contingent expenses of the state government. This reason applies to most of the positions now existing de facto in the executive departments and under the Supreme Court, for only a very few of them, as e. g. librarian of the Supreme Court and private secretary to a judge of the Supreme Court, rest on any law but the general appropriation bill. This reason affirms that the legislature either did not as a matter of statutory construction, or cannot as a matter of constitutional power, provide for the creation of offices in the executive and judicial departments of the state service, but did or can provide for the creation of employments in those departments, in the general appropriation bill.

As already shown, it can make no difference for purposes of appointment under the State Civil Service Act whether positions are offices or employments. But a digression must be made to examine this idea at the basis of the whole case, that a position in the state service is not an office, but is an employment, because it rests on no law but the general appropriation bill.

If the words of the general appropriation bill are not enough to create positions in the state service that are offices for purposes of appointment, it is very hard to see how the same identical words can be enough to create positions that are employments for purposes of appointment, because it takes as many legislative words and as much constitutional power to create an employment as it does to create an office. But the place where a position is created, whether in the general appropriation bill or in a different and separate statute, has nothing to do with the question whether the position is an office or an employment for purposes of appointment.

This idea that a position in the state service is not an

office, but is an employment, for purposes of appointment, because it rests on no law but the general appropriation bill, apparently has its source in the dictionary meaning of the word "employment," and assumes the legislature has more power to prescribe the mode of filling offices than it has to prescribe the mode of filling employments, whereas the contrary is true, because the legislature itself may make appointments to employments but not to offices.

If there is no law but the general appropriation bill for the creation of positions in the state service, and the general appropriation bill is not enough to create them, either on grounds of statutory construction or on grounds of constitutional law, then the true legal consequence is that the positions have no existence de jure, and there is nothing to which appointments can be made by anybody; and the consequence is not that the Supreme Court must strain itself to magnify the offices of the Secretary of State, et al., through the medium of a judicially implied constitutional grant of power, first to create salary-paying positions in their respective departments, and then to fill them by appointment, all at their own will and pleasure, immune from legislative regulation and control.[16]

As a question in statutory construction, no reason is perceived why a legislative appropriation of a lump sum, say $30,000, "to the Secretary of State, for clerk hire and office expenses," may not be judicially construed, as it has been practically construed for years, as a legislative grant of authority to the Secretary of State to create positions in his department, to prescribe the duties, to

[16] Stott v. Chicago, 205 Ill., 281, and many cases following it. Neither the opinion of Vickers, J., nor that of Cartwright, J., expressly says the Secretary of State et al. have an implied constitutional grant of power to create salary-paying positions in their respective departments, but the opinions necessarily mean that.

fix the salaries, and to make the appointments, though it may be conceded the practice of itemizing the appropriations, begun in 1895, is a better legislative practice, and the practice of creating the more important positions by separate statute is a still better legislative practice. Decisions holding items in the annual appropriation ordinance of a city council not enough to create positions in the municipal service, are not necessarily decisive of the construction of the general appropriation bill of the legislature.[17]

As a question in constitutional law, of course the legislature, unless it is prohibited by the constitution, may create positions in the state service, whether offices or employments, in the general appropriation bill. The only constitutional prohibition pointed out is the one in article 4, section 16, which says:

"Bills making appropriations for the salaries of the officers of the government shall contain no provision on any other subject."

This forbids the familiar "congressional rider" in state general appropriation bills, but it has not been carried so far by judicial construction as to forbid the legislature to create positions of any kind whatever in the executive and judicial departments in the general appropriation bill and ought not to be carried so far in view of the contrary practice and usage of the legislature from the foundation of the state government. Ritchie v. People,[18] Mathews v. People,[19] and People v. Joyce,[20] saying legis-

---

[17] Moon v. The Mayor, 214 Ill., 40, followed in later cases. See Emergency Act of 1873, 1 S. & C. Ann. Stat., 2d ed., p. 826, overlooked in all these cases in the Supreme Court. By statute the County Board of Cook County is forbidden to create positions in the annual appropriation ordinance. Gridley, J., and Burke, J., so ruled in the Superior Court of Cook County. Hurd, R. S., 1909, p. 663, Sec. "ninth."

[18] 155 Ill., 98.

[19] 202 Ill., 389.

[20] 246 Ill., 124.

lative acts creating state offices and fixing the salaries are repugnant to this prohibition if they appropriate money to pay the salaries, do not necessarily expand the prohibition so far as to forbid the legislature absolutely and under all circumstances to provide for the creation of positions, i. e., offices and employments of any kind whatever, in the general appropriation bill. The prohibition was not intended to prevent all "tacking" in appropriation bills, but only unusual and objectionable "tacking." The error in the cases cited lies in assuming the acts in question were "appropriation bills" within the meaning of the prohibition.[21]

The distinction taken by Cartwright, J., between constitutional duties and statutory duties is good as related to the power to create positions, but bad as to the power to make appointments. When the legislature, whether in the general appropriation bill or in separate statutes, provides for the creation of positions in the executive and judicial departments of the state service, the legislature must provide expressly or by silent implication that the duties of such positions as are intended to aid the heads of departments in the performance of duties imposed on them by the constitution, shall be such as the head of the department in question may prescribe, because the legislature cannot relieve constitutional officers of their constitutional duties by the mode of creating new and independent positions, whether

[21] The logical consequence of the error was avoided in People v. Loyce, 246 Ill., 124, the well-known Board of Pardons case, by means of a medieval scholastical play upon the word "provide" in the phrase "provide compensation" in the title of the act, holding that it means "fix." See the provision in Sec. 537, Commonwealth of Australia Constitution Act of 1900: "But a proposed law shall not be taken to appropriate revenue or moneys, . . . by reason only of its containing provisions . . . for the . . . appropriation of . . . fees for services under the proposed law." Moore, Commonwealth of Australia, 2d Ed., p. 141.

offices or employments. For example: the legislature cannot relieve the Secretary of State of his constitutional duty to keep the great seal by the mode of creating the new and independent position of "custodian of the great seal." But the legislature may create the position of "custodian of the great seal" under and in subordination to the Secretary of State, with such duties as the Secretary of State may prescribe, to help him perform his constitutional duty to keep the great seal; and the legislature may make the position either an office or an employment as it pleases. And on this theory the statute creating the position of private secretary to a judge of the Supreme Court silently implies the duties of the position are to be such as the judge may prescribe. Hence the distinction of Cartwright, J., between the constitutional duties and the statutory duties of constitutional executive and judicial officers is well taken, and is well settled, as respects the authority of the legislature to provide for the creation of positions, i. e., offices or employments. The distinction has no relation whatever to the authority of the legislature to prescribe the mode of appointment, which was the only point before the court.[22]

[22] As a practical matter, no legislature ever has undertaken or ever can undertake to prescribe the duties of all the aids and subordinates in the departments, but must leave that to the heads of departments. The State Civil Service Act does not create positions, nor prescribe the duties of positions, nor authorize the State Civil Service Commission to create positions or to prescribe duties, excepting positions established to enforce the Act itself. The Act does not interfere with the relations between the head of a department and his subordinates as defined by the constitution, by statute, or by the common law. It requires the State Civil Service Commission to investigate and keep a record of the efficiency of officers and employees in the performance of their duties as a basis for determining their eligibility to promotional appointment. The Act deals only with the power of appointment, original and promotional.

Cartwright, J., derives his implied constitutional grant of the power of appointment to the Secretary of State et al., in part from their "independence," saying: "It is essential to the independence of the Secretary that he shall have perfect liberty of choice and full power of selection upon his own personal judgment and information of those through whom he discharges personal duties imposed upon

But the question, raised but not resolved by this case, whether the legislature did as a matter of statutory construction, or can as a matter of constitutional power, create positions, whether offices or employments, in the general appropriation bill, is quite beside the question of the authority of the legislature to dispose of the power of appointment. As above stated, if positions in the state service are not duly created by law, i. e., by the constitution or by legislative enactment, they have no existence de jure, and there is nothing to which appointments can be made; and it makes no difference whether the positions in question are offices or employments.[23]

The doctrine promulgated in this case, that the Secretary of State, the other constitutional executive officers, and the Supreme Court, have an implied constitutional grant of power to appoint aids and subordinates in their respective departments, overlooks the plainly written text of the constitution, and goes back for a constitutional limitation on the power of the legislature to the English common law of the days when all public officers, including judges, were paid by fees, and a public office was conceived of for many purposes as a private franchise to

him by the constitution." This does not warrant the learned Judge's distinction between constitutional duties and statutory duties, because executive and judicial independence extends equally to the performance of all duties, whether constitutional, statutory, or common-law duties. Moreover, it is clear on principle, and it is decided in those cases holding that a power of removal at will is not involved in a constitutional or legislative express grant of the power of appointment, that the power of appointment is not essential to the independence, dignity, and usefulness of constitutional executive and judicial officers. The idea that it is essential, or desirable, rather, is a private opinion, entertained by many, especially with reference to judicial officers, but it is not the law of the constitution, i. e., the idea of the people expressed in the constitution, which leaves the legislature free to enact this opinion into law if it wants to. Street v. County Commissioners, Beecher's Breese, 50; People v. Moberly, 1 Scam. 215; Field v. People, 2 Scam. 79, 97–101, 153, 154.

[23] Are subordinate positions in the executive and judicial departments of the state service, assuming them validly created by law, "offices" or "employments" for purposes of appointment? Though they are treated as employments by

take tolls from the people. The doctrine necessarily says these aids and subordinates are not in the service of the state, but in the private service of the head of the department. If they are in the service of the state, they must hold positions that, for all purposes of appointment, are either offices or employments, appointments to which, by the expressed terms of the constitution, must be made as the legislature may provide, and, in the absence of any provision by the legislature, by the Governor, acting by and with the advice and consent of the Senate, in the case of offices, and by the legislature in the case of employments.

The doctrine as promulgated by its terms does not extend to "offices" in the state service, but is confined to "employments." This distinction of an implied constitutional grant of the power of appointment to employments, but not to offices, cannot legally exist, because the Supreme Court decided in Bunn v. People[24] that the constitution of 1848 made the power of appointment to

___

the whole court in this case, it seems quite plain they are offices. The positions are permanent, i. e.,the work is steady, never ending. The constitution gives the word "office," for purposes of appointment, the broad, comprehensive, popular meaning of a permanent position or "steady job" in the state service, the dignity of the position as involving the exercise of "some portion of sovereign power" having no relation to the question whether it is an office or employment for purposes of appointment, whatever bearing the matter of dignity may have for purposes of indictment under a criminal statute, of quo warranto, or of impeachment under the constitution, as to which latter Scates, C. J., makes the suggestion in Dickson v. People, 17 Ill., 191, 194, that the legislature does not have to impeach every petty officer because the constitution says it may do so if it wants to. The framers of the constitution of 1870 intended their definition of "office" to apply to the word wherever it occurs in the constitution in connection with the state service, though it was drawn with special reference to the regulation of the power of appointment in Art. 5, Sec. 10. See citations in note 12, ante. As stated over and over in the text, if these subordinate positions are "offices," the power of appointment is in the Governor and Senate, unless the legislature otherwise provides; if they are "employments," the power of appointment is in the legislature, unless it otherwise provides.

[24] 45 Ill., 397.

employments in the state service a function of the legislature, and that decision was written into the present constitution by its framers and adopted by the people as a part of the fundamental organic law of the state.[25] Hence the power of appointment to employments, as well as to offices, can become a function of the Secretary of State, et al., only by legislative enactment, and there is nothing to the doctrine of an implied constitutional grant of the power of appointment to employments, but not to offices. The futility of the doctrine as a constitutional limitation on the power of the legislature comes out when it is borne in mind the legislature may free itself from the limitation by passing statutes establishing all subordinate positions in the departments as offices, if the dictum is correct that they now are employments because resting on no law but the general appropriation bill.

There is no excuse for the judicial acceptance of this doctrine in this case. The opinions in the case read in the light of the argument at the bar show the division in the Supreme Court is not along the line of law touching the limit prescribed by the constitution beyond which the legislature must not go, but is along the line of the policy of the extensions of the merit system in the state service made by the State Civil Service Act of 1911, the opinions reflecting the division of opinion outside the court between spoilsmen and merit-system men. The case is another of the numerous instances in the reports supporting the complaint that the judicial power to pass on the constitutionality of legislation, as exercised by state courts with reference to state constitutions for the last three or four decades, has degenerated into a legislative power of veto, inviting parties beaten in the

[25] See note 12, ante.

legislature to transfer their fight to the courts, converting the highest courts of the states into anomalous third legislative chambers, where political questions of governmental policy are debated and resolved by lawyers and judges under the guise of debating and resolving legal questions of governmental power, substituting the arbitrary will of judges for the expressed will of the people, undermining and destroying the principle of the supremacy of law, converting it into an intolerable supremacy of judges, where the will and not the law has dominion.[26]

[26] It must be borne in mind that our traditional Anglo-American principle of the supremacy of law involves the conception or ideal that all law is a just and reasonable expression of the will of the community. The supremacy of law and the supremacy of the people are convertible terms, the former being the lawyer's way and the latter the popular way of saying the same thing. The traditional Anglo-American principle of the supremacy of law was proclaimed in the Declaration of Independence, and was intended to have its highest and most striking realization and practical application in our written constitutions, prescribing limits beyond which governmental authorities must not go, enforceable by courts in ordinary actions between man and man like every other part of the law of the land. It is a great and dangerous error to suppose, as many judges, lawyers, and laymen do, that our system of constitutional law was designed to enable judges to control or check the people, acting directly or through the legislature. The error lies in confusing the causes of laws and institutions with their consequences as makers of public opinion and controllers of civil and political conduct.

The danger that the judicial power to discover, elucidate, declare, and enforce the law of the land may degenerate into a power to make it arbitrarily, substituting the will of judges or of others for the will of the community, always has been and always will be an ever-present danger. Every lawyer knows how the Stuart kings used the English judges to substitute the will of the prince for the law of the land, one of them losing his head and another his throne. The danger is really less in the department of constitutional law than in any other department of the law, because the will of the people is expressed in writing, but the temptation is greater because the conflicting interests are greater and feelings are aroused, and the consequences are vastly more serious to the state. There is no security against the merit system: "And thou shalt provide out of all the people able men, such as fear God, men of truth, hating covetousness; and let them judge the people at all seasons." "A government of laws and not of men" does not mean that a democratic government can operate and make progress by a danger except in an observance of Jethro's counsel to Moses, the basis of the process of automatic evolution without the labor of men.

TOPIC IX

DUE PROCESS OF LAW

Collected Comment

COLLECTED COMMENT

1. — POWER OF ILLINOIS, UNDER THE FOURTEENTH AMENDMENT, TO AID OWNERS OF WET LANDS TO DRAIN THEM FOR AGRICULTURAL PURPOSES[a] — On the merits, the Federal Supreme Court affirmed, in part, the State decision in Chicago, Burlington & Quincy R.R. Co. v. Illinois, 200 U. S., 561, 26 Sup. Ct. Rep., 341,[1] three Justices, White, McKenna, and Holmes, concurring specially in the judgment, but dissenting practically in toto from the opinion, and one Justice, Brewer, dissenting in toto from both the judgment and opinion. Just what was the question in the case, "of profound importance," as Mr. Justice Brewer said? The case was fought, and decided, solely upon the point of the right of the Company to just compensation for pecuniary losses that would result from obedience to the order of the Drainage District, the order making no provision for such compensation. The words "due process of law" in the Fourteenth Amendment require a State to make just compensation when it takes private property for

[a] [1 Ill. Law Rev., 116, June, 1906.]

[1] [For author's comment as to jurisdictional phase of this case, see ante, p. 113.]

public use (Chicago, B. & Q. Ry. Co., *v.* Chicago, 166 U. S., 226), and the word "deprive" in the Amendment perhaps means the same thing, certainly as much, as the word "taken" in the Fifth Amendment (whether it means more in Illinois, see Chicago *v.* Taylor, 125 U. S. 161, and Muehlker *v.* Harlem R. R. Co., 197 U. S., 544). The Company was a corporation created by the State, and it appears to have been taken for granted that the Company got its right to go across Rob Roy creek from the State, i. e., that the State created the right. But it may be doubted whether the Company's right to go across the creek, it being non-navigable, had, or could have, any other or different origin than the right of a natural person owning land on opposite sides of the creek to go across it. (But see Ry. Co. *v.* Moffit, 67 Ill., 524.) But accepting that proposition, that the State did, in a substantial sense, create the Company's abstract right to go across, it was noticed that the right was created, so far as appeared, durante bene placito, and that the right was not, as against the State, either a vested corporate contract right, under the obligation of contracts clause, or a right embraced within the meaning of the word property in the Fourth Amendment. The State was not attempting to take the abstract right of passage away from the Company. Compliance with the order of the State, acting by the Drainage District, would have left the Company in possession and enjoyment, as owner, of a heap of rubbish that once was a railroad bridge and culvert, and of the abstract right and, therefore, of course, of the correlative duty, to go across the creek in some way or other. The order of the State was held good, because it was not a State attempt to take private property without paying for it, but was only a State regulation of the use of private property. Obviously, however, since the pulling down of a bridge stops the use of it, the only private property the use of which could have been regulated by the order was, either the abstract, unrevoked right of the Company to go across the creek, or the real estate of the Company lying on opposite sides of, and at the bottom of the creek, or both. The majority did not say, however much the thought may have had to do with the result reached in the case, that the State's reserved, or unalienated, power to revoke, without pay, the Company's abstract right of passage over the creek, involved, necessarily, a power in the State to regulate the use of the abstract right by ordering, without any provision for pay, the Company to pull down an old, and build a new and bigger bridge and culvert; nor could the majority have said that in words, for the same reason that a State's power to pass a prohibiting liquor law (Mugler v. Kansas, 123 U. S., 623) does not, necessarily, involve a power in the State, whether for independent use or for use in aid of a prohibiting liquor law, to pull down, by the methods of a Carrie Nation, buildings used as saloons or breweries. (See Lawton v. Steel, 152 U. S., 133.) It should be observed also, that, so far as appeared, the Company's old bridge and culvert did not obstruct the natural channel of the non-navigable creek, or, if one pleases, the natural channel of the natural drain or ditch. Viewing the order of the State, then, as in all common sense it must be viewed, not as a regulation of the use of the Company's old bridge and culvert, which the order marked for destruction, but as an actual physical taking of them for the purpose of regulating the use of the Company's abstract right to go across the creek, and the use of the Company's realty on opposite sides of, and at the bottom of, the creek, the sole inquiry was whether the State's end, as evidenced by the order, read in the light of the surrounding conditions, justified, upon any rationally permissible view, the means employed by the State

to attain its end.   In plain English, the position of the
State in the case was that Illinois may, without violating
rights of private property protected by the Fourteenth
Amendment, give a combination of farmers the power
to drain their wet lands, for agricultural purposes, by
artificial means, and to compel other people, against
their wills, to pay a part of the cost, if such other people
happen to own a railroad in the neighborhood across
whose right of way the main, and most expensive, artificial drainage ditch must go.   A majority of the Justices
of the Federal Supreme Court thought the State's position was fully sanctioned by those familiar adjudications
giving full effect to State commands directing public
service corporations to make large pecuniary outlays to
alter the mode and manner of their exercise of their rights
to use public highways and public, navigable streams, by
elevating railroad tracks, pulling down and rebuilding
bridges and viaducts, shifting gas pipes, water pipes, sewer
pipes, electric lighting, telegraph, telephone, and trolley
wires and poles, and tunnels or bores, from one place to
another place on, over, or under the surface of the highway
or stream.   But in all those cases it appeared that the
State was confronted with the practical situation where
the prosecution of one admittedly governmental enterprise, in private hands on sufferance by the State, operated
as a blockade upon the prosecution of another and different admittedly governmental enterprise, either conducted by private persons as an agency of the State, by
the State itself directly, or by a municipal corporation
as a State agency, the blockade occurring on, over, or
under ground or water, if not owned by, at least under
the exclusive control of, the State.   In such cases, the
ultimate beneficiaries, that is to say, the people generally,
each one of the people having a right to use the property
("public use") employed in prosecuting each of the

governmental enterprises involved, of the removal of the blockade by command of the State really and in truth do, and must, pay the cost of removal, whether the State makes express provision for payment or not, because private persons carrying on a governmental enterprise have a right to charge rates, in fine, a right to lay and collect taxes, sufficiently high to bring in money enough to reimburse themselves for any expenses they may be put to, against their wills, by order of the State. The application of the rules of decision in those cases to this farm drainage case would appear, then, to hinge upon a solution of the question whether the artificial drainage of wet lands for agricultural purposes is, in Illinois, under the Fourteenth Amendment, a legitimate subject of governmental initiative and enterprise, and, if so, to what extent. That, then, was the question, not improperly called "of profound importance," down to which the case simmered. But that question was not discussed at all. The majority opinion says: "We assume also, without discussion, as from the decisions of the State Court we may properly assume, that the draining of this large body of lands so as to make them fit for human habitation and cultivation is a public purpose, to accomplish which the State may, by appropriate agencies, exert the general powers it possesses for the common good." (26 Sup. Ct. Rep., 346, column 2, bottom; Act 351, column 1, opening sentences of dissenting opinions.)

Now, has it not been settled that, under the Fourteenth Amendment, the artificial draining of wet lands, and the artificial wetting of dry lands, at other people's expense, to fit them for cultivation by their owners, are not legitimate subjects of governmental enterprise, except under extraordinary and unusual natural conditions, such as exist in the case of what used to be called "the great American desert"? Fallbrook Irrigation District v. Bradley, 164 U. S., 112; Clark *v.* Nash, 198 U. S., 361; Strickley *v.* Highland Boy Gold Mining Co., 200 U. S., 527; and see Eldridge *v.* Trezevant, 160 U. S., 452. Even there, a State, there can be little doubt, may not go so far as to acquire the wet or dry lands for the purpose of fitting them for cultivation, and cultivating them, by its own officers and employees. In the absence of such extraordinary and unusual natural conditions, has it not been settled also that the furthest a State government may go under the Fourteenth Amendment to aid the owners of wet lands to drain them for agricultural purposes is to compel unwilling owners whose lands inevitably must be benefited by the proposed drainage of their own lands by willing owners, to pay their just, proportionate part of the cost of the drainage, and to authorize the willing and unwilling owners, combined, of such wet lands to constuct, to a limited, reasonable extent, ditches, and to lay drain pipes, across the dry lands of others, against their wills, upon payment of just compensation for the involuntary easements? Wurtz *v.* Hoagland, 114 U. S., 66; Hagar *v.* Reclamation District, 111 U. S., 701; and see Head *v.* Amoskeag Mfg. Co., 113 U. S., 9; Otis Co. *v.* Ludlow Co., 201 U. S. 140, 26 Sup. Ct. Rep., 353, with which cases compare Gaylord *v.* Sanitary District of Chicago, 204 Ill., 576.[2] Under either rule, the owners of property

[2] The opinions of Mr. Justice Gray in the Wurtz and Head cases cited show clearly that the sole purpose of intervention by the Legislature is to prevent a "dog-in-the-manger" sort of an abuse of that incident of private ownership of land which Lord Selborne aptly called in Goodson *v.* Richardson, L. R., 9 Ch. App., 221, 223, 224, the "power of veto." In dealing with this power of veto, which is itself private property, "Parliament is, no doubt," said Selborne, "at liberty to take a higher view upon a balance struck between private rights and public interests than this Court can take." This power in Parliament "to take a higher view" was not cut away by our written Constitutions. The just compensation mandate does not apply to the situation at all, where the power is properly put forth. A proper use of the power does take private property, but does not take it for a public use, and, when the Legislature provides for reasonable

used or destroyed to make ways for the drainage or irrigation ditches, when not benefited through their ownership of adjoining lands by the drainage or irrigation,
are usually and doubtless must be paid in cash out of the
pockets of the willing and unwilling owners of the lands
benefited, or out of money put into the general public
chest by a use of the taxing power by the State. Under
the former rule, it may possibly be true that a railroad
company may be left by a State to recoup itself for pecuniary losses resulting from a forced adverse use or destruction of its railroad property to an exercise of its right to
charge reasonable rates, in other words, to levy taxes
upon the people generally. There, the advantage to
the people generally is so great, and so widely diffused,
that it may properly be said to amount, practically, to
a right in each one of the people generally to use ("public
use") the improved lands by paying for a part of their
food product, but never without pay, or "just compensation," rendered in one way or another by the ultimate
beneficiaries, the people, of the "public advantage."
But under the latter rule a railroad company cannot be
left to recoup itself by a use of its right to charge reasonable rates, unless it can be affirmed that a State may use
its general taxing power over other people to aid farmers
to drain their lands for agricultural purposes, which
brings one right round to the original question of the
proper application of the fundamental distinction between
legitimate subjects of individual enterprise, and of
governmental enterprise to the subject of "farm drainage" in Illinois. But see Heffner *v.* Cass & Morgan

and just compensation, private property is not even taken, in that substantial
sense meant by the constitutional limitation upon an otherwise omnipotent Legislature. Even the constitutional rights of private ownership against others involve
correlative constitutional duties, duties to others, the performance of which
duties may be forced by the Legislature consistently with full respect for the
correlative rights.

Counties, 193 Ill., 493; 58 L. R. A., 353; and compare Lowell *v.* Boston, 111 Mass., 454; State *v.* Osawkee Township, 14 Kans., 418, Brewer, J.; North Dakota *v.* Nelson County, 1 No. Dak., 88.

Do such extraordinary and unusual natural conditions exist in Illinois, as to make it reasonably and rationally permissible for the State government, consistently with the natural and constitutional, or chartered, rights of private property, to put forth, against the owners of a railroad, the full strength of "the general powers it possesses for the common good" to attain the end of converting wet lands into "good, tillable land, subject to cultivation," without seeing to it carefully that the owners of the wet lands, alone, be required to pay the cost of the work? So far as the Supreme Court of the United States is concerned, that would appear to be a question of fact.   But that Court had no evidence upon that question before it, and judicially noticed nothing but the very State laws and State decision drawn in question before it as being repugnant to the Federal Constitution.   Now, prior to the adoption of the Fourteenth Amendment on July 28, 1868, the State Supreme Court said that "farm drainage" was a private, and not a governmental, enterprise in Illinois.   Harward v. Drainage District, 51 Ill., 130; Hessler *v.* Drainage District, 53 Ill., 105; Houston *v.* Drainage District, 71 Ill., 318.   It said the same thing about the closely analogous subject of laying out roads connecting with public highways.   Nessbitt *v.* Trumbo, 39 Ill., 110; Crear *v.* Crossley, 40 Ill., 175; Winkler *v.* Winkler, 40 Ill., 185; see "Constitutionality of Private Ways," 6 Am. Law Rev., 196; Armsperger *v.* Crawford, 70 L. R. A., 497.   Then came the somewhat abortive attempt in the State Constitution, in force August 8, 1870, to reverse the State Supreme Court.   Article IV, Section 31, 1 Starr & Curtiss, Ill. R. S., Ed. 2, 139;

Updike *v.* Wright, 81 Ill., 49; Article IV, Section 30; Chicago Co. *v.* Wiltse, 116 Ill., 449; Sholl *v.* German Coal Co., 118 Ill., 427. Then, in 1877–78, Section 31 of Article IV was amended so as to read as it now stands in the State Constitution. In June, 1890, the State Supreme Court showed that there is a wide difference, under Section 31, between sanitary districts, and farm or mine drainage districts, and gave expression to a doubt whether the corporate authorities of the latter districts could be invested with power to make improvements "otherwise than by special assessment, because such purposes are, as intimated" in the cases cited supra, "private and not municipal." Wilson *v.* Sanitary District of Chicago, 133 Ill., 443, 475–476. In Moore, Executrix *v.* The People, 106, 376, 382, it was said that the rule of uniformity applicable to special assessments under Article IX, Section 9, did not apply, in its full extent, to special assessments to pay the cost of "farm drainage" under amended Section 31 of Article IV. There would appear to be little room for serious controversy about the proposition, that all that the amendment of Section 31 was designed to accomplish was to incorporate into the law of the State, so far as it could be done consistently with the Fourteenth Amendment, the rule in Wurtz *v.* Hoagland, 114 U. S., 66, enabling willing owners of wet lands to force unwilling owners of adjoining wet lands to help pay the cost of drainage, and also enabling owners of wet lands to lay out drainage ditches over the lands of others, upon payment of just compensation out of their own pockets. But see Heffner *v.* Cass and Morgan Counties, supra, and Wabash R. Co. *v.* Drainage District, 194 Ill., 310, 319; Chicago *v.* Reeves, 77 N. E. Rep. 237, 239, column 2; 242, column 2. Now where are "the decisions of the State Court," from which, a majority of the Federal Supreme Court said, "we may properly assume that" "farm drainage" is, in Illinois, "a public purpose to accomplish which the State may, by appropriate agencies (in this case a combination of owners of wet lands) exert the general powers it possesses for the common good?" Are cattle guard cases in point? Are public crossing cases in point? Are general expressions relied on in the State Supreme Court, in cases holding a railroad company liable in tort for injuries resulting from a tortious obstructing of the natural channel of a water course or slough in point? See R. R. Co. *v.* Horan, 131 Ill., 288, and R. Co. *v.* Thillman, 143 Ill., 127. Then what is left of the State decisions? Besides, how can State decisions control the meaning and application of the Fourtenth Amendment within the limits of the State?

The majority of the Supreme Court of the United States appear to say, in substance: "So far as our jurisdiction is concerned, we do not care what the State Supreme Court said about the case, but, so far as the merits of the case are concerned, we are bound by what the State Supreme Court said." (See the opening paragraphs of the dissent of Mr. Justice Brewer in C., B. & Q. R. Co. *v.* Chicago, 166 U. S., 226, 259.) What do the concurring Justices mean when, speaking by Mr. Justice Holmes, they say: "I suppose it to be plain, as my Brother Brewer says, that if an expense is thrown upon the railroad unlawfully, its property is taken for public use without due compensation"? Does Mr. Justice Brewer really say that? The trouble with the whole case appears to lie in the assumption that the right of the owners, as such, of these wet lands in Bristol township, Kendall county, to drain water into Rob Roy creek is just the same kind of a right as the right of a citizen, as such, to travel up and down a public street, or a public, navigable stream. It seems very clear that the Railroad Company was entitled to compensation, to be paid by the owners of the lands to be benefited by the system of drainage proposed. The decision appears to sanction one of the very things the Fourteenth Amendment forbids, a State legal fiat turning an enterprise, inherently individual in its nature, into a governmental enterprise. It may be doubted whether the decision ought to be accepted as final, based as it is upon a debatable, to say the least, but not debated, assumption, and even at that upon a practically five to four vote. See In re Tuthill, 49 L. R. A., 711, N. Y., and notes; Mound City Land Stock Co. v. Miller, 60 L. R. A., 190, Mo., and note.[3]

2. — Due Process of Law as Applied to Informing a Corporation that it Has Been Sued.[a] — In Nelson v. C., B. & Q. R. Co., 225 Ill., 197, 80 N. E. Rep. 109, Hand J., the State Supreme Court decided that that part of paragraph 5 of the Practice Act which permits a plaintiff to give a defendant corporation notice of suit "by publication and mail in like manner and with like effect as is provided in Sections 12 and 13 of" the Chancery Act, is consistent with the due process of law enjoined by Article II, Section 2, of the State Constitution, when such form and mode of procedure for giving notice is used by a plaintiff in an action to obtain a

[3] After the foregoing was written and in type, the report of West Chicago Street Railroad v. Illinois, 26 Sup. Ct. Rep., 518, appeared, wherein the Supreme Court of the United States, by a five to four vote, affirmed the decision of the State Supreme Court in 214 Ill., 9, sustaining an ordinance of the council of Chicago directing the Street Railroad Company to lower a tunnel under the Chicago River, making no provision for compensation. The ordinance had a close shave, for it is stated that Mr. Justice Holmes concurs in the judgment upon the authority of Chicago, B. & Q. R. Co. v. People. It is extremely difficult, for the writer at least, to appreciate the line of reasoning by which a judge could concur in the C., B. & Q. case, and dissent in the West Chicago Street Railroad case. The decision in the latter case seems clearly right, and the decision in the former just as clearly wrong. The failure of Mr. Justice Brewer to carry any of his associates with him in the C., B. & Q. case, — what is the true explanation of it?

[a] [2 Ill. Law Rev., 109, June, 1907.]

personal judgment for money against a railroad corporation organized under the laws of the State, and the action
is filed in a Court of a county through or into which the
railroad runs, the principal office of the corporation
being in a different county. See paragraph 2 of the
Practice Art. The Court does not consider, expressly
at least, the application of the Full Faith and Credit
Section, and the Fourteenth Amendment, of the Federal
Constitution, though it must be admitted that, at least
since the adoption of the Fourteenth Amendment, July
28, 1868, the ultimate tribunal on the question decided in
this case is the Supreme Court of the United States.
Pennoyer v. Neff, 95 U. S., 714, 733. As against a non-
resident, who is, and stays, off the soil of the State, no
form and mode of procedure for giving notice of suit,
whether by "personal service" or by "constructive
service," can give a Court of the State authority to entertain a proceeding for a personal judgment. Pennoyer
v. Neff, supra; Sirdar Singh v. Faridkote, 1894, A. C., 670.
The form and mode of giving notice by publication and
mail (See Bickerdike v. Allen, 157 Ill., 95, cited by the
Court), prescribed by Sections 12 and 13 of the Chancery
Act do look loose for use in a personal action ex contractu
or ex delicto, and the permissible administration of the
Act obviously may be very loose. But perhaps it may
be said fairly, that such looseness, real or only apparent,
is for the Legislature, not the Courts, to deal with. It
should be noticed, however, that the question before the
Illinois Court was national in its character, that the true
rule on the subject of notice of suit to people on the soil
of a State, so far as the irreducible minimum required
by due process of law goes, must be capable of substantially uniform and just application throughout the United
States, and that the Illinois Court deals with the question from an exclusively State point of view, seemingly

as if there were no such thing as a Constitution of the United States. The opinion of the Illinois Court proceeds upon the theory, not necessary to support the result reached, three Illinois cases being cited in its support, Bimelen v. Dawson, 4 Scam., 536; Welch v. Sykes, 3 Gilm. 197, 201; Smith v. Smith, 17 Ill., 482, that it is possible for a State Court to have jurisdiction sufficient to support a judgment enforceable in and by the State where rendered, but not sufficient to support a judgment enforceable, as of right, in and by any other State. The soundness of that theory remains to be proved, however, whenever the question properly arises. How can civil proceedings in a State Court be "judicial proceedings," unless every other State must give them "full faith and credit," or, as the Act of Congress of 1790 (R. S. U. S., Sec. 905) says, "such faith and credit as they have by law or usage in the Courts of the State from which they are taken?" See "The Doctrine of Haddock v. Haddock," 1 Ill. Law Rev., 219, 229 [ante p. 153]. As respects State criminal proceedings, see Huntington v. Attrill, 146 U. S., 657; Wisconsin v. Pelican Ins. Co., 127 U. S., 265, and note on this case, 1 Ill. Law Rev., 239 [ante p. 179].

3. — Does Legislative Power Exist to Confirm and Legalize a Majority Plan of Reorganization on Insolvency?[a] — The decree of the federal Circuit Court, Grosscup, J., confirming and legalizing against non-assenting creditors a plan for the reorganization of certain Chicago street railroad corporations, entered before, and without contemplating any judicial sale to get rid of liens, was reversed by the Circuit Court of Appeals, Brewer, Justice, Seaman and Baker, Circuit Judges, Saturday, September 7, 1907. The decree rested upon the proposition that a Court of Equity, bound by the existing

[a] [2 Ill. Law Rev., 189, October, 1907.]

laws of Illinois concerning street railroad corporations, has the power to compel creditors of such corporations, when insolvent, to give up the lien of their securities in favor of men ready to advance money needed to reconstruct the roads, to rehabilitate the properties, as it is called, and also to exchange their securities for new ones of less face value, thus parting with the right to put into force existing legal remedies to produce the money due on the old securities; in fine, to submit to a shave, whether they liked it or not.

Laying these Chicago street railroad corporations to one side, anyone acquainted with the history of the reorganization of insolvent public service corporations in this country, through the instrumentality of foreclosure and other creditors' suits, probably will have to agree with Judge Grosscup to this extent, namely: power to deal with persons financially interested in such reorganizations, without and against their consent, ought to reside somewhere.

If such power does reside anywhere, it must be in the Legislature, State or National. Does it reside in either?

The case of Canada Southern Railway Company *v.* Gebhard, 109 U. S., 527, is an interesting one and a very suggestive one upon this question. Chief Justice Waite there says that a Canadian Legislative Act confirming and legalizing a plan of a majority of the creditors for the reorganization of an insolvent railroad company is a species of Bankrupt Act, and "is no more than is done in bankruptcy, when a composition agreement with the bankrupt debtor, if assented to by the required number of creditors, is made binding upon the non-assenting minority" (pp. 535–536). On that view, perhaps Congress, under its delegated power "to establish uniform laws on the subject of bankruptcies throughout the United States," may have adequate power by a general law to authorize Federal Courts of Bankruptcy to confirm and legalize reasonable plans for the reorganization of purely local insolvent public service corporations assented to by a majority of creditors. See In re ·Klein, 1 Howard, 277, Catron, J.

In the absence of any National Bankruptcy Law covering the subject, has a State Legislature any reserved power to deal with it?

Mr. Justice Brewer suggests a negative answer, because of the obligation of contracts and property clauses of the Federal Constitution. Taking that as a general proposition, it is, at least, as respects the contract clause, in accord with prevailing legal opinion. See Gilfillan v. Union Canal Company, 109 U. S., 401, 404, Waitem, C. J.; Canada Southern R. Co. v. Gebhard, 109 U. S., 527, 540, Harlan, J., dissenting.

Such an Act of a State Legislature, however, would not collide with the property clause, the Fourteenth Amendment, so far as State Legislatures are concerned, and the Fifth Amendment, so far as Congress is concerned, if it be true, as Chief Justice Waite says in Canada Southern v. Gebhard, at p. 536, that "In no just sense do such governmental regulations deprive a person of his property without due process of law. They simply require each individual to so conduct himself as not unnecessarily to injure another."

The point that such an Act of a State Legislature would be repugnant to the contract clause is more intricate. Decided cases so apply the contract clause as to establish the doctrines, first, that a State Insolvency law is void so far as applicable to all contracts made before its passage, and second, that "certificates of discharge . . . granted under (a State Insolvency) Law, cannot be pleaded in bar of an action by a citizen of another State (upon a contract made after the passage of the Law) in the Courts of the United States, or of any other State than that where the discharge was obtained, unless it appear that the plaintiff proved his debt against the defendant's estate in solvency, or in some manner became a party to the proceedings." Sturgis v. Crowninshield, 4 Wheaton, 122; Ogden v. Saunders, 12 Wheaton, 213; Gilman v. Lockwood, 4 Wallace, 409, 410; Dewing v. Bennett, 128 U. S., 489, 497; Phoenix National Bank v. Batcheller, 151 Mass., 589, Holmes, J. These doctrines, unless modified, obviously bar the passage of any State Act confirming and legalizing any plan of reorganization, however reasonable, that would prevent, in invitum, the enforcement, not merely of existing contracts, but also of prospective cntracts with citizens of other States.

Congress, therefore, perhaps is the only Legislature we have competent to confirm and legalize reasonable majority plans for the reorganization of insolvent existing or prospective local public service corporations. Congress must act by a general bankruptcy law devolving the power upon Courts and regulating their use of it, as was done by the English Act of 1867 mentioned in Canada Southern v. Gebhard. The decree of the Federal Circuit Court in the Chicago street railroad cases really was an exercise of legislative power to pass a Special Bankruptcy Act like the Special Arrangement Acts of Parliament in England, and in Canada, for the reorganization of insolvent railroads, one of which was before the Court in Canada Southern v. Gebhard, and was enforced against non-assenting creditors who were citizens of New York. Only an amendment to the Federal Constitution, therefore, could legalize that decree. The Judges of the Circuit Court of Appeals evidently do not subscribe to the doctrine of amending the Constitution by the short-cut method of judicial interpretation.

4. — CONSTITUTIONALITY OF STATUTE PENALIZING DECEIT IN HIRING WORKMEN ABROAD.[a] — A statute that penalizes employers, criminally by way of fine and imprisonment, and civilly in damages with an attorney's fee, for suppression or concealment of the fact of a strike, and for misrepresentation concerning the compensation, the sanitary or other conditions of the employment, when hiring workmen in another state or in a place in Illinois other than the place of the employment, is held unconstitutional in Josma v. Western Steel Car Company, 249 Ill., 508, Dunn, J., writing the opinion, where the act of deceit was concealment of a strike. The ground of the decision is, that the statute drew discriminations (1) between hiring people abroad and at home, and (2) between workmen and non-workmen, that flowed from will and not from reason, and hence violated the rule of equality involved in the phrase "due process of law" in the prohibition of the state constitution, "No person shall be deprived of life, liberty, or property without the due process of law."

The Supreme Court says (p. 516): (1) hiring people abroad and (2) hiring people at home, are "cases not essentially different in kind"; the conditions of the employment enumerated in the statute are "as important to the (employee) who does not leave his home . . . as to him who does.

The difference in fact, as related to deceit by the employer, between hiring people abroad and at home is but a version of the proverbial difference in fact between offering a man a pig in a bag and a pig out of a bag, on which difference in fact the law always has rested legal distinctions touching deceit never heretofore thought arbitrary. In the case of a sale and purchase of labor,

[a] [6 Ill. Law Rev., 412, January, 1912.]

the employee at home on the spot in the place of the employment may investigate the conditions surrounding the job offered him; he does not need to rely on the honor of the employer for the truth about those conditions. Then, too, there is a difference in fact in the effect and tendency of an employer's deceit when hiring people abroad and at home; first on the victim of the deceit, and second on the people at large in the place of the employment. A man out of employment away from home is subject to misfortunes unlike those that afflict a man out of employment at home.

If the legislature had extended the burdens of this statute to employers when hiring people at home, then, in the view of the Washington Supreme Court, the statute would have been unconstitutional for not going further and embracing deceit in the purchase of other things in the home market, as well as labor. City of Spokane *v.* Macho, 51 Wash., 322; 98 Pac. Rep., 755; 21 L. R. A., N. S., 263. The Illinois Supreme Court intimates on p. 515, but does not decide, that there is no basis in fact for a rational legal distinction between deceit in buying labor and deceit in buying other things.

The Supreme Court also says (p. 516), the statute operated unequally in a constitutional sense, because its protection was confined to "workmen" and was not extended to "the stenographers in an office, the clerks in a store or a bank, the teachers in a school or any of the professional or semi-professional people who are employed by others."

The party before the court assailing the statute was an employer. No non-workman was making any complaint to the court. The burden was on the complaining employer to show the court just how and where he was hurt by the refusal of the legislature to extend the protection of the statute to non-workmen hired abroad.

(People *v.* Huff, 249 Ill., 164, 169.)   It is hard to see any reason in the complaint of an employer that the legislature ought to have abridged his common-law freedom to hire people more than it did.   But assuming that it was allowable for the employer before the court to take up the case of non-workmen outside the protection of the statute as against workmen within its protection, it is plainly impossible for a court to say, there is not enough difference in fact between workmen and non-workmen commonly hired abroad to give an adequate basis in fact for the judgment of the legislature that workmen hired abroad need, while non-workmen hired abroad do not need, the protection of this statute.   The members of the legislature are in a position to know more about the labor market than the members of the Supreme Court, and effect must be given to the fixed rule that reason must be judicially supposed to preside over the deliberations of the legislature (Claffy *v.* Chicago Dock Co., 249 Ill., 210).

Williams *v.* Fears, 179 U. S., 270, is against the Supreme Court's view that the statute was arbitrary   It was there decided that a statute exacting a specific license fee from "emigrant agents," i. e., persons engaged in the state in the occupation of hiring laborers to work outside the state, is good, though it does not subject the occupation of hiring laborers to work inside the state to a like tax. Like decisions in Georgia, Alabama, North Carolina, and South Carolina are cited in the case notes in 2 L. R. A., N. S. 859, and 21 L. R. A., N. S., 263.   In those cases the legislating state was the one from which workmen go, not the one into which they come, as in the Illinois case.   But no question was made in the Illinois court touching the extent of the power of a state to deal with the importation of workmen from another state.   It probably is the law, however, that deceit in hiring people in one state with a view to work in another state where the wrong takes

effect, falls within the legislative power of the latter
state, at least so long as Congress is silent, if Congress
may deal with the subject. But see the opinion of
Rogers, J., in Arkansas *v.* Kansas & Texas Coal Co., 96
Fed. Rep., 353,, affirmed on a point of federal jurisdiction
in 183 U. S., 155, where the State of Arkansas filed a
bill, not founded on any statute, to enjoin the importation of "armed men of the low and lawless type" to take
the places of striking coal miners. See the third section
of the Illinois statute in 249 Ill., p. 512.

The Illinois Supreme Court begins its opinion thus, on
p. 514: "No person can be deprived of life, liberty, or
property, without due process of law, and these terms
'life,' 'liberty,' and 'property' embrace every personal,
political, and civil right which any person within the
state may possess, including the right to labor, to make
and terminate contracts, and to acquire property."

This generality occurs over and over again in the
reports of the last two or three decades. Political
liberty, i. e., the right to vote and to hold office, religious
liberty, liberty of speech, and many other rights deemed
fundamental, secured by other parts of the state constitution, are not embraced by these words, unless much of
the rest of the state constitution can be held to be sur-
plusage. If "terminate" means "break," there is no
"liberty" to break lawful contracts. A corporation was
before the court complaining of an unconstitutional
abridgment of its right to buy labor. As related to
"property," corporations are "persons," it is held, because
they are "merely associations of individuals who are the
equitable owners of the property of such corporations"
(Pembina Mining Co. *v.* Pennsylvania, 125 U. S., 181,
189; Gulf, Colorado & Santa Fe Ry. Co. *v.* Ellis, 165
U. S., 150, 154); but as relatd to "liberty," corporations
are not liberi homines within Magna Charta, c. 39, the

original due-process clause, but artificial persons. "The liberty guaranteed . . . against deprivation without due process of law is the liberty of natural not artificial persons," just as "people" and "natural persons" alone have the privilege to refuse to give evidence against themselves (Western Turf Association v. Greenberg, 204 U. S., 359; Hale v. Henkel, 201 U. S., 43, 78; Wilson v. U. S., 220 U. S., 614). As "liberty" embraces more than freedom from restraint of the physical person of the liber homo, the spheres of "liberty" and "property" intersect and overlap. But the right to buy labor, as distinguished from rights arising out of the concluded contract, doubtless falls within the exclusive sphere of "liberty." But territorially considered, the sphere of "liberty" does not extend beyond the frontiers of the state. The right to buy labor in another state, in issue before the court, fell outside the sphere of "liberty"; it fell within the sphere of the privileges and immunities clauses of the federal constitution, Art. IV, Sec. 2; Amendment XIV, Sec. 1. But "citizens" only, and not corporations, are within the protection of those clauses (Williams v. Fears, 179 U. S., 270, 274; Western Turf Association v. Greenberg, 204 U. S., 359). Hence the legal capacity, not the "liberty," of the corporation before the court to buy labor in another state was not within the protection of the terms "life," "liberty," "property," and "due process of law" in the state constitution. Whether the corporation's right to hire people in another state fell within the protection of the equal-protection-of-the-laws clause of the fourteenth amendment need not be considered, because the court did not rely on that. That clause compels equality of treatment by a state in cases to which the equality tacitly involved in "due process of law" does not extend. But the protection of the constitutional terms "life," "liberty," "property," and "due process of law" flowed to the corporation before the court, not directly from those terms in the state constitution, but indirectly through the legislature, because the legislature saw fit to bracket corporations inseparably with "persons" or liberi homines in the familiar legislative formula at the head of the statute, viz., "Any person, persons, company, corporation, association, or organization of any kind." If the statute was unconstitutional as to "persons," it could not stand as to corporations. See Ives *v.* South Buffalo Ry. Co., 201 N. Y., 271, 290, 319, 320. But the statute was not unconstitutional as to "persons," as it seems to me, for the reasons stated.

5. — REMEDIAL OR CIVIL AND PUNITIVE OR CRIMINAL PROCEEDINGS FOR CONTEMPT OF COURT[a] — In Rothschild & Co. *v.* Steger & Sons Piano Co., 256 Ill., 196, Vickers, J., writing the opinion, it is held that a proceeding for the contempt of violating a preliminary injunction forbidding the use of the name "Meister" in advertising and selling pianos, resulting in a finding of guilty and a judgment of a fine payable to the state and a jail sentence for a definite term, may be classified and conducted as remedial or civil, and need not be classified or conducted as punitive or criminal. In the federal courts, under recent decisions of the United States Supreme Court, such contempt proceeding would have to be classified and conducted as punitive or criminal. Bessette *v.* W. B. Conkey Co., 194 U. S., 329; Re Christenson Engraving Co., 194 U. S., 458; Doyle *v.* London Guarantee & Accident Co., 204 U. S., 599; Ex parte Heller, 214 U. S., 501; Gompers *v.* Buck's Stove & Range Co., 221 U. S., 418; Re Merchants' Stock & Range Co., 223 U. S., 639. The case was taken from the Circuit Court of Cook County, Scanlan, J., direct to

a [8 Ill. Law Rev., 210, October, 1913.]

the Supreme Court, on the legal theory that Scanlan, J.,
did not conduct the proceeding as a punitive or criminal
proceeding agreeably to the above federal decisions; that
he thereby denied the accused contemners due process
of law; and hence the case involved the construction of
the constitution, state and federal, within the meaning of
the Illinois statute defining the direct appellate jurisdiction of the Supreme Court. On the facts as stated in
the report there was no basis of fact on which to rest this
legal theory, because, so far as appears, Scanlan, J., did
not deny the accused contemners any process of law due
to a man in a punitive or criminal proceeding for contempt
of court under these federal decisions, except the formal
process of entitling the proceeding in the name of The
People, the proceeding having been entitled in the name
of the party who obtained the injunction. The mere
failure, alone, to entitle a contempt proceeding in the
name of The People is without any legal significance, as is
expressly stated in Gompers *v.* Buck's Stove & Range Co.,
221 U. S., 418, 446; and there is nothing in these federal
decisions that invalidated or authorized the reversal of
the fine and imprisonment inflicted by Scanlan, J. The
Illinois Supreme Court, however, apparently assumes
there is something, not specified, in these federal decisions
that required the reversal of the judgment of Scanlan,
J., and accordingly devotes its opinion to showing that
the constitutional "due process of law" does not make
these federal decisions binding on Illinois courts, and
to stating that these federal decisions are not in harmony with Illinois decisions. Of course, the constitutional "due process of law" does not make these federal
decisions binding on Illinois courts. But since Illinois
courts and federal courts draw their law and practice on
this subject from the same sources, the true question is:
Are these federal decisions right?

When these federal decisions and the Illinois decisions referred to by Vickers, J., are examined and compared, there is no room for doubt that the doctrine of the United States Supreme Court is the only allowable one; which doctrine is, that a proceeding for the contempt of violating a negative order not to do a thing, as, e. g., not to use the name "Meister" in advertising and selling pianos, is essentially and dominantly punitive or criminal, when the object and result of the contempt proceeding is a fine payable to the state, or a jail sentence for a definite term. It is a plain abuse of ordinary language, and a palpable shock to the common sense of the community to call such a proceeding remedial or civil; and the common sense of the community and the law of the land are in harmony, as they usually are. See the remarks of Scott and Farmer, JJ., dissenting, in Barnes v. Typographical Union, 232 Ill., 424, 438, 439.

The most extended exposition of the Illinois Supreme Court's doctrine that such a contempt proceeding is remedial or civil is by Vickers, J., in the recent case of Hake v. People, 230 Ill., 194, where the learned Justice classifies contempts of court. The classification in Hake v. People, 230 Ill., 194, is based on the opinion of Scates, C. J., in Crook v. People, 16 Ill. 534, which in turn is based on 4 Bl. Com. 288, where the author divided the contempt of obstructing the course of justice otherwise than in facie curiae — which is quite different from the contempt of violating an order — into two species, viz.: (1) obstructing the course of justice in common-law courts, and (2) obstructing the course of justice in equity courts, the line of division being the right of purger by oath allowed by commn-law courts, but not allowed by equity courts. The facts of Crook v. People, 16 Ill., 534, are inadequately reported; but Vickers, J., in Hake v. People, 230 Ill., 194, overlooked the plain facts that the proceeding in Crook v. People was for the contempt of violating a preliminary prohibitive or negative injunction; that the proceeding was begun before, and concluded after, a final decree dismissing the bill for want of equity; that the proceeding was entitled in the name of The People; that it was conducted by the trial court as a punitive or criminal proceeding; that counsel on both sides agreed it was a punitive or criminal proceeding, and that the Supreme Court so held. Crook v. People, 16 Ill., 534, does not differ at all from Gompers v. Buck's Stove & Range Co., 221 U. S., 418.

When the object and result of a proceeding for the contempt of violating a negative order is to award to the party who obtained the order damages by way of compensation for the injury done him by the violation of the order, the proceeding is essentially and dominantly remedial or civil. Federal cases cited supra. The view of the Illinois Supreme Court, concurred in by the majority and dissenting judges in Barnes v. Typographical Union, 232 Ill., 402, 411, 412, to the effect that, in the absence of a statute, the trial court cannot award damages by way of compensation in such case, is plainly wrong on principle, is not sustained by the cases cited by the dissenting judges, and rests on a misunderstanding of the remarks of Scates, C. J., concerning the New York statute he alludes to in Crook v. People, 16 Ill., 534, 537, which New York statute is specified as 2 R. S., 538, Sec. 21, in People v. Spalding, 2 Paige 326, cited by Scates, C. J., and is, I assume, not substantially different from the statute in 1 Birdseye, Rev. Stats., Codes & Gen. Laws of N. Y., 3d ed., p. 703, Sec. 20. Of course, the trial court cannot give damages by way of compensation in such case without evidence of the quantum of injury done the party by the violation of the negative order; and the trial court cannot impose an arbitrary fine in exercise of its discretion, and then order the amount of the fine paid over to the party who obtained the injunction by way of damages to compensate him for the injury done him by the violation of the negative order. If that is all that is meant in Barnes v. Typographical Union, 232 Ill., 402, 411, 412, then it is correct.

The view of the United States Supreme Court that a contempt proceeding for violating an order of court, against a person who was not a party or privy to the order, is a punitive or criminal proceeding for the contempt of obstructing the course of justice (Bessette v. W. B. Conkey Co., 194 U. S., 324; Garrigan v. United States 23 L. R. A., N. S., 1295, 1298, C. C. A., 7th C.) is in accord with English rulings (7 Halsbury's Laws of England, 292); and clearly is better than the view of the Illinois Supreme Court that the whole world is a party to an "all-the-world injunction," and a proceeding for the contempt of violating such an injunction against a person who was neither party nor privy in point of fact, is a remedial or civil proceeding. O'Brien v. People, 216 Ill., 354, 356.

The right of purger by oath was allowed by English common-law courts in the case of a punitive or criminal proceeding for the contempt of obstructing the cou e of justice by acts done outside the court or its precincts, i. e., the "indirect" contempt of obstructing the course of justice; but was not allowed by the English chancery court in such case. The reason why the English common-law courts allowed the right of purger by oath in such case of "indirect" contempt was, as I understand it, because that kind of contempt of court was indictable as a misdemeanor. The refusal of the English chancery court to allow this right of purger by oath in the same kind of a case of "indirect" contempt in the chancery court is an historical anomaly of a kind not uncommon in English law. 4 Bl. Com., 288. The founders of the federal judicial establishment may have taken that view of it, and perhaps gave a preference to the rule of the English common-law courts when, in the federal Judiciary Act of 1789, they denied the federal courts authority to deal summarily with this kind of "indirect" contempt of court (R. S., Sec. 725), and in 1790 created the indictable "crimes against justice" enumerated in R. S., Sec. 5392 et seq.

It may be doubted whether this right of purger by oath extended to punitive or criminal proceedings for the contempt of violating either an affirmative (facere) or negative (non facere) order of a common-law court or of a chancery court. This kind of contempt of court, i. e., the contempt of violating an order of court, originated in English ecclesiastical courts, whence it was borrowed by the English chancery court, where it was conceived of as a contempt of the king amounting to rebellion and treason, and was later borrowed by the English courts of common law. Langdell, Eq. Pl., 2d Ed., pp. 28–31, and note 2 on p. 31. It is not clear the contempt of violating an order of a common-law or chancery court in a civil case was regarded as an indictable crime, the old idea that a violation of the chancellor's order was the high crime of rebellion and treason against the king having become obsolete for most practical purposes when it was clearly recognized the chancellor was running an ordinary, regular, established court of the realm. If the contempt of violating an order of court was not regarded as an indictable crime, then the reason of the English common-law courts for allowing the right of purger by oath for the contempt of "indirectly" obstructing the course of justice would not apply to the contempt of violating an order of court, whether a common-law court or a chancery court. It seems very plain that the

Illinois decisions, at least, compel us to say the right of purger by oath does not extend to a punitive or criminal proceeding for the contempt of violating an order of court, though the Illinois Supreme Court's reason for denying purger by oath in such case,· viz., that a proceeding for the contempt of violating an order of court is always and necessarily remedial or civil, is not a good reason, and is purely arbitrary, seemingly invented to meet the supposed necessities of particular cases, especially the recent strike-injunction cases.

The right of purger by oath did not extend, as I understand it, to the contempt of obstructing the course of justice in facie curiae, i. e., "direct" contempt. At least, that is the way I read Blackstone on direct contempt in facie curiae, 4 Bl. Com., 283–289. In that view, United States v. Shipp, 203 U. S., 563, 574, 575, — wherein the court denied the right of purger by oath in a proceeding against the sheriff and others for the contempt of lynching a prisoner in jail while his case was pending in the court for adjudication, — is right, because that was a case of direct contempt in facie curiae (7 Halsbury's Laws of England, 283; 3 Encyc. of the Laws of England, 502), though the opinion of Holmes, J., does not put the decision exactly on that ground. In Oster v. People, 192 Ill., 473, the right of purger by oath was allowed a receiver in a chancery suit in a punitive or criminal proceeding for his contempt of wrongfully removing the goods in his custody. That seems a wrong application of the right of purger by oath, for the contempt was direct in facie curiae. However, there is the opinion; it was overlooked or ignored in Hake v. People, 230 Ill., 194, and in all the recent strike-injunction cases in the Illinois Supreme Court, though the opinion certainly called for judicial notice and comment.

So far as I can see, there is really nothing in the

confused and confusing opinions of the Illinois Supreme
Court referred to by Vickers, J., as being in conflict with
federal opinions, that prevents an Illinois trial judge from
following the federal clearly correct and lucid classification of proceedings for the contempt of violating an order
of court into remedial or civil and punitive or criminal.
A trial judge is not concerned at all with the question
whether his judgment in such a contempt proceeding
should be taken up for review by way of appeal or by way
of writ of error. In point of actual precedent the decisions
of the Illinois Supreme Court allow the aggrieved party
in such case to invoke the appellate jurisdiction either
by way of appeal or by way of writ of error. The fact
that the Illinois Supreme Court allows the appellate procedure by way of appeal on the ground that a contempt
proceeding for violating an order of court is always and
necessarily remedial or civil, and can never be punitive
or criminal, does not appear to be of any practical importance to anybody, either by way of benefit or detri-
ment. But when it comes to fining men and sending men
to jail upon affidavits for violating injunctions, it is important for the presiding judge to recognize that the proceeding is essentially criminal, and to give the men their
due process of law, which, of course, does not necessarily
include jury trial, though the trial judge can allow jury
trial in such case. See generally the clarifying articles
on civil and criminal proceedings for contempt of court
by Professor Beale in 21 Harv. L. R., 161, and by J. C.
Fox, Esq., Master of the Supreme Court, Chancery
Division, in 7 Halsbury's Laws of England, 279; and see
Mr. Fox's historical articles in 24 L. Q. R., 184, 266, proving clearly that the undelivered opinion of Wilmot, J., in
Rex v. Almon in 1765, though accepted as law, is over-
charged with turgid eloquence and spurious history; that
the contempt of court by speeches and writings tending to

obstruct the course of justice is a modern test of contempt of court, about which the framers of the federal constitution and the founders of the federal judicial establishment could have known but little, if anything; that the summary process of committal for contempt of court is not of immemorial antiquity, as old as civilization, older than Abraham, flowing direct from God.

PART II
EQUITY

TOPIC I

SPECIFIC PERFORMANCE

I. The Word "Not" as a Test of Equity Jurisdiction to Enjoin a Breach of Contract.

II. Collected Comment.

I

THE WORD "NOT" AS A TEST OF EQUITY JURIS-
DICTION TO ENJOIN A BREACH
OF CONTRACT [a]

In two recent cases, Southern Fire Brick and Clay Co. *v.* Garden City Sand Co., 223 Ill., 616, and Carlson *v.* Koerner, 226 Ill., 15, the Illinois Supreme Court says that the jurisdiction of a Court of Equity to enjoin a breach of a contract may depend entirely upon whether the contract is expressly negative in point of form. The Court reaffirms, and apparently employs as a rule for resolving the cases, a distinction as respects equity jurisdiction made in the case of Consolidated Coal Co. *v.* Schmisseur, 135 Ill., 371, decided November 5, 1890. The distinction there made is this:

"In the one case (i. e., where there is an express negative) equity jurisdiction proceeds upon the ground of the express stipulation of the parties alone, irrespective of whether substantial injury will be incurred or not.

"In the other (i. e., where the contract is affirmative in form and the negative 'could fairly be implied from the stipulation of the parties'), the parties not having fixed in their agreement, by express covenant, what shall not be done, equity proceeds only to prevent irreparable injury. The party not having seen fit to expressly stipulate against the act in his contract, a court of equity will not by implication, insert it, and then enforce it, unless substantial injury is thereby to be prevented."[1]

Is this distinction supported by precedent? And if it is, do these three Illinois cases fall within the precedents? The Illinois Court in Consolidated Coal Co. *v.* Schmis-

---

[a] [2 Ill. Law Rev., 217, November, 1907.]

[1] 135 Ill., 371, 378–379.

seur, supra, extracts the distinction from three English cases: the well-known one of Lumley *v.* Wagner, decided in 1852 by the Chancellor, Lord St. Leonards, De Mattos *v.* Gibson, decided in 1858 on preliminary motion for an injunction by a Vice-Chancellor, Sir W·. Page Wood, afterward Chancellor as Lord Hatherley, and on appeal by Knight-Bruce, L. J., and Turner, L. J., and in 1859 on final hearing by Wood, V.-C., and on appeal by the Chancellor, Lord Chelmsford, and Peto *v.* Brighton, Uckfield & Tunbridge Wells Ry. Co., decided in 1863 by Wood, V.-C.[2]

The contract in Lumley *v.* Wagner was a contract of employment. Miss Wagner agreed to sing at Lumley's theater for a specified time, and agreed not to sing at any other theater or place during that time.[3] At the instance of Lumley, the Chancellor granted an injunction forbidding Miss Wagner to sing at any other theater or place during the space of her engagement with Lumley.

To get down to the significance attached to the express negative clause in Miss Wagner's contract, one or two things must be noticed and laid aside.

---

[2] The full text of the Illinois Court's citation of these cases is as follows: "Cases are much more rare, perhaps, where a court of equity has interfered to prevent the breach of a negative covenant which is implied from a positive stipulation. It is said by Wood, Vice-Chancellor, in Peto et al. *v.* B. U. & T. Ry. Co., 32 L. J. (N. S.) Eq., 1677: 'But in a case where the special contract is relied upon, and the negative is inferred from the positive contract, I think the case is weaker than where there is a distinctly negative contract, standing by itself, and the cases of De Mattos *v.* Gibson, 3 De Gex & J., 276 (28 L. J. Ch., 165), and Lumley *v.* Wagner are, so far as I am aware, the only instances in which the court has exercised such a jurisdiction.' The question in Lumley *v.* Wagner was, as we understand the case, not so much whether a negative covenant should be implied from Wagner's contract to sing, etc., for Lumley, and she be restrained from the breach of such negative covenant, but whether the Court would restrain her from singing elsewhere, when it could not compel her to perform her covenants with Lumley by singing under his management." 135 Ill., at p. 379.

[3] The negative clause was: "Mdlle. Wagner engages herself not to use her talents at any other theater, nor in any concert or reunion, public or private, without the written authorization of Mr. Lumley."

In the first place, if Lumley had refused to let Miss Wagner sing at his theater, the Chancellor could not have compelled him to do so. In other words, the employee was not entitled to the remedy of specific performance against the employer. But that objection, want of mutuality, is met and overthrown, at least after Lumley *v.* Wagner, in such a case thus:

"Where a person is ordered by injunction to perform a negative covenant of that kind, the whole benefit of the injunction is conditioned upon the plaintiff's performing his part of the agreement, and the moment he fails to do any of the acts which he engaged to do, and which were the consideration for the negative covenant, the injunction would be dissolved.[4]

"No doubt it might be very important to Mdlle. Wagner not to be compelled to sing unless she had every arrangement of the best kind to enable her to make as great an impression as possible; but then it was clearly Lumley's interest to afford her every facility in his power; and if he did not do so, she would have obtained all she wanted by being released from her agreement."[5]

In the second place, now confining ourselves strictly to Miss Wagner's side of the contract, the Chancellor "could not compel Miss Wagner to sing. Lord St. Leonards distinctly disclaimed any power in the Court of Equity to do anything of the kind."[6] "It is true that I

[4] Wood, V.-C., in Stocker *v.* Wedderburn, 3 K. & J., 393, 404 (1857). The learned Judge is referring to Dietrichsen *v.* Cabburn, 2 Phillips, 42, decided in 1846 by Lord Cottenham.

[5] Wood, V.-C., 1863, in Peto *v.* Tunbridge Wells Ry. Co., 1 H. & M., 468. See Fechter *v.* Montgomery, 33 Beav. 26, and Rice *v.* D'Arville, 162 Mass., 559, where injunctions against actors were refused because employers were in default. The view of Wood, V.-C., that an injunction conditioned on the plaintiff's performance of his side of the contract sometimes may furnish such adequate security to the defendant of performance by the plaintiff as to satisfy the requirement of mutuality is now generally recognized as sound. See "Mutuality in Specific Performance," Ames, 3 Col. Law Rev., 18. See Peto *v.* Tunbridge Wells Ry. Co., *infra,* where Wood, V.-C., thought such a condition would not afford adequate security to defendant of performance by plaintiff of plaintiff's side of the contract — to build a line of railroad.

[6] Kay, L. J., Whitwood Chemical Co. *v.* Hardman (1891), 2 Ch., 416, 431.

have not the means of compelling her to sing," said Lord
St. Leonards.[7]   The general principle that there is no
jurisdiction to compel a person to perform in specie a
contract for purely personal service is an old one.[8]

The proposition of counsel for Miss Wagner was this:

"The general principle on which we rely is, that this Court never
interferes to restrain the breach of the negative part (of the defendant's side of) a contract in any case where it cannot specifically
enforce performance of the positive part" (of the defendant's side
of the contract).[9]

The breach of the "negative part" in Miss Wagner's
case was a breach of the "positive part," so that the
proposition of counsel meant this:

This Court never interferes to restrain a defendant from breaking
a contract, when the Court cannot compel the defendant by decree
to perform the contract in specie."

The Court denied the proposition.   Lord St. Leonards
said:

"Wherever this Court has not proper jurisdiction to enforce
specific performance, it operates to bind men's consciences, as far
as they can be bound, to a true and literal performance of their
agreement; and it will not suffer them to depart from their contracts at their pleasure, leaving the party with whom they have
contracted to the mere chance of any damages which a jury may
give.   The exercise of this jurisdiction has, I believe, had a wholesome tendency towards the maintenance of that good faith which
exists in this country to a much greater degree perhaps than in any
other;[10] and although the jurisdiction is not to be extended, yet a
judge would desert his duty who did not act up to what his predecessors have handed down as the rule for his guidance in the
administration of justice."   .   .   .   "It is true that I have not

[7] 1 De G. M. & G., 604, 619.

[8] 26 Am. & Eng. Ency. of Law, Ed. 2, 102, cases collected in note 3.

[9] 1 De G. M. & G., 604, 609: Miss Wagner's counsel were Bethell, later Lord
Westbury, C., Malins, later V.-C., and Martindale.

[10] Miss Wagner was a German.

the means of compelling her to sing, but she has no cause of complaint if I compel her to abstain from the commission of an act which she bound herself not to do, and thus possibly cause her to fulfill her engagement. . . . Though . . . I disclaim doing indirectly what I cannot do directly."[11]

Whatever he might think about Lord St. Leonard's interpretation of the cases decided prior to Lumley *v.* Wagner, and relied on by him in the decision of that case,[12] certainly no English lawyer, after Lumley *v.* Wagner, could stand up at the bar of any English Court below the

---

[11] 1 De G. M. & G., 604, 619–620, quoted in Southern Fire Brick & Clay Co. *v.* Garden City Sand Co., 223 Ill., 616, 625. In applying the doctrine, that the Court may enjoin a breach of a contract which it is unable to compel performance of in specie, to a contract for purely personal service, Lord St. Leonards appears to have given away too much to a feeling of indignation at the way the wrong he had to deal with was done, and so to have fallen into the fallacy of mistaking a very likely, but wholly incidental, consequence of the remedy of specific performance for the ground of the right of an injured party to have the benefit of that remedy. "If he is committing a breach of the agreement," says Lindley, L. J., in Whitwood Chemical Co. *v.* Hardman, infra, "he is doing that which is wrong in point of law; but that is not the question. The question is as to the plaintiff's remedy." According to my understanding of it, the remedy of specific performance is a distinctively English invention (see Fry, Specific Performance, 3d Am. Ed., p. 3; Ames, Specific Performance, 1 Green Bag, 26; Ames, Cases in Equity Jurisdiction, 37, note 3, modifying a statement about the evidence of its age in 1 Green Bag) to give effect to then current English ideas about the ownership of land, and to the consequent presumed intent of an Englishman who contracted to buy land to have that land. That is to say, the remedy grew out of peculiar English ideas about landed property, and not, as Lord St. Leonards hints, supra, out of superior English ideas about morality. Of course, by reason of the nature of its remedial process — laying commands upon people which they must obey or go to jail — the Court of Equity has been, and still is, able to enforce accepted principles of morality that a Court of Law cannot — not because a Court of Law has any special hate for such principles, but because its remedial process is rigid and inelastic. But in order that the Court of Equity may enforce accepted principles of morality, it must appear that the enforcement of them by the Court of Equity will tend reasonably and substantially and practically to support, better than the Court of Law can do it, the difference between meum and tuum as applied to property, the enforcement and protection of property rights being the primary function of the Court, and the enforcement of principles of morality being only an incident, never the end to be attained. See the clear and compact account of the origin and nature of the judicial power of the English Chancellor in Langdell's Summary of Equity Pleading, Ed. 2, 27–42.

[12] "Specific Performance by Injunction," Ashley, 6 Col. Law Rev., 82.

House of Lords and deny the proposition that the Court
of Equity has jurisdiction to restrain a defendant from
breaking a contract which the Court cannot compel
the defendant by decree to perform in specie. He had to
acquiesce in that proposition as fixed law, and to confine
himself to its application. And after Lumley *v*. Wagner
the argument was frequently made that the jurisdiction
was confined to cases where the contract contained an
express negative clause binding the defendant not to
break it, and that, consequently, the presence of express
negative words in the contract was the test to be applied
to resolve the case in hand, the Court to exercise this
jurisdiction where the negative words are present, and
to refuse to exercise it where the negative words are
absent. But the argument did not prevail, even in cases
of contracts for purely personal service. The Court
acted on the theory of an implied negative not to break
the affirmative contract. After Lumley *v*. Wagner, it
first acted on that theory in the case of contracts for
purely personal service, and a little later in the case of
contracts with a different subject-matter. In 1891, the
English Court of Appeal overthrew the theory of an implied negative as a sole basis of the jurisdiction of a Court
of Equity to restrain a defendant employee from breaking
a contract for purely personal service. But the theory
perhaps has never been expressly overthrown in toto in
the case of other contracts, though it has at least been
said often by English Judges that neither an express
negative nor an implied negative has any direct relation
whatever to the question whether the case is a proper
one for the exercise of this jurisdiction, the doctrine of
express and implied negatives being merely an old and
simple doctrine of English grammar bearing only on the
question—quite separate and distinct from the question of
Equity jurisdiction, a question of remedy only — whether

the defendant has or has not broken, or is or is not threatening to break, his contract.[13]   In this country, the notion that the jurisdiction of a Court of Equity to restrain a defendant from breaking a contract which the Court cannot compel him by decree to perform in specie may hinge on the presence of negative words in the contract has not been taken seriously, though it is not always easy to tell upon what grounds our Courts do proceed in exerting, and refusing to exert, such jurisdiction.

The following authorities support the above, I think.

In the course of his opinion in Lumley v. Wagner, Lord St. Leonards said:

"In all sound construction, and according to the true spirit of the agreement, the engagement to perform for three months at one theater must necessarily exclude the right to perform at another theater.   It was clearly intended that J. Wagner was to exert her vocal abilities to the utmost to aid the theater to which she agreed to attach herself.   I am of the opinion that if she had attempted even in the absence of any negative stipulation, to perform at another theater, she would have broken the spirit and true meaning of the contract as much as she would now do with reference to the contract into which she has actually entered."[14]

On the authority of that passage in the opinion of the Chancellor in Lumley v. Wagner, in Webster v. Dillon (1857),[15] Wood, V.-C., and in Montague v. Flockton (1873),[16] Malins, V.-C., thought that a stipulation to act at a named theater for a certain time implied the negative not to act at any other theater during the ordinary hours

---

[13] "Whether they are negative words or affirmative words are very excellent reasons in considering whether it is meant that the thing should not be done, or whether it is not meant."   Lord Blackburn, Doherty v. Allman, L. R., 3 App. Cas., H. L., 709, 730, 1878.

[14] 1 De G., M. & G., 604, 619.

[15] 3 Jur. N. S., 432; s. c. 5 W. R., 867.

[16] L. R., 16 Eq., 189.

of theatrical performance during the time specified, and that such implied negative authorized the granting of an injunction against the actor. The case before Wood, V.-C., was ex parte, and the one before Malins, V.-C., a contested one inter partes. In Whitewood Chemical Co. v. Hardman (1891)[17] the defendant contracted to serve as manager of a manufacturing company for ten years, agreeing to give "the whole of his time to the company's business." His employer filed a bill to enjoin the defendant from connecting himself with a rival business. Kekewich, J., granted the injunction, resting his right to do it upon a negative implied from the affirmative agreement to give "the whole of his time" to plaintiff's business. The Court of Appeal, Lindley, L. J., and Kay, L. J., not denying that the affirmative agreement implied the negative one found by Kekewich, J., reversed the order. Lindley, L. J., said:

"I cannot read the decision of Malins, V.-C. (in Montague v. Flockton, supra), without seeing that he was under the impression that Lord St. Leonards in Lumley v. Wagner would have granted the injunction, even if the negative clause had not been in the contract. This was a mistake. Lord St. Leonards was very clear and explicit on that subject. He said, distinctly, he would not have done it in the absence of that negative clause. . . . We must therefore fall back and see if we can find any principle upon which he (Kekewich, J., below) has acted. Now, unquestionably, if the principle were that the Court would decree specific performance of all contracts, that would carry it; but the principle being the other way as regards contracts of service, it lies upon the plaintiffs to show that there is some recognized exception in this particular case, and that they fail to do. . . . I confess I look upon Lumley v. Wagner as an anomaly to be followed in cases like it, but an anomaly which it would be very dangerous to extend, I make that observation for this reason, that I think the Court, looking at the matter broadly, will generally do much more harm

[17] (1891) 2 Ch., 416.

by attempting to decree specific performance in cases of personal service than by leaving them alone; and whether it is attempted to enforce these contracts directly by a decree of specific performance, or indirectly by an injunction, appears to me to be immaterial."

Kay, L. J., said:

"That case (Lumley *v.* Wagner), certainly at the time it was decided, was understood to carry the power of the Court of Chancery in granting injunctions to the extreme limit to which it could go. . . . If a negative is to be implied, I do not see any case whatever in which it could be more clearly implied than in a case of a man's domestic servant, his butler . . . who has contracted to give the whole of his time to his master's service. We must tread with very great caution such a path as that which this application invites us to pursue."

In Davis *v.* Foreman (1894),[18] in a contract of employment as manager of the business of a carrier, the employer stipulated that "he will not, except in the case of misconduct or a breach of this agreement, require the manager to leave his employ." Kekewich, J., refused to give the employee an injunction forbidding the employer to dismiss him, saying that the employer's contract, though negative in form, was affirmative in substance, being equivalent to an agreement to retain the employee, and that Lumley *v.* Wagner could not be extended so as to work in favor of the employee against the employer.[19]

---

[18] (1894) 3 Ch., 654.

[19] Want of mutuality is fatal there. In Ryan *v.* Mutual Tontine Westminster Chambers Association (1894), 1 Ch., 116, the Court of Appeal reversed an order of A. L. Smith, J., giving a tenant of a residential flat building an injunction forbidding the landlord to break his covenant to provide a porter who should perform certain specified duties for the tenants. Lord Esher, M. R., said: "The contract . . . is not merely that the landlord should employ a porter, but that he shall employ a porter who shall do certain specified work for the benefit of the tenant. That is, in my opinion, one indivisible contract. The performance of what is suggested to be the first part of the contract, viz., the agreement to employ a porter, would be of no use whatever to the tenant unless he performed the services specified." See Welty *v.* Jacobs, 171 Ill., 624.

In Eberman *v.* Bartholomew (1898),[20] the defendant contracted to work as a traveler for the plaintiffs, wine merchants; to devote the whole of his time for ten years during usual working hours to the business of the plaintiffs, and not to engage in any other business during the ten years. Romer, J., refused to grant an injunction forbidding the defendant to work for anyone but the plaintiffs, on the ground that the express negative was unreasonably broad, and could not be limited to the business of a wine merchant.

In England, then, as the cases now stand, the jurisdiction of a Court of Equity to enjoin the employee's breach of his contract of employment may hinge upon the existence of express negative words in the contract. The reason of it is, that Lumley *v.* Wagner is "an anomaly which it would be very dangerous to extend."[21]

In 1881, Mr. Pomeroy laid down the following rule to determine the right of a plaintiff to an injunction like that in Lumley *v.* Wagner in the case of a breach of a contract of employment:

"Where a contract stipulates for special, unique, or extraordinary personal services or acts, or for such services or acts to be done by a party having special, unique, and extraordinary qualifications, as, for example, by an eminent actor, singer, artist, and the like, it is plain that the remedy at law of damages for its breach might be wholly inadequate, since no amount of money recovered by the plaintiff might enable him to obtain the same kind of services or acts elsewhere, or by employing any other person."[22]

[20] (1898) 1 Ch., 671.

[21] "Lindley, L. J., (in Whitwood Chemical Co. *v.* Hardman) took strong ground against the policy of enjoining breaches of negative covenants (in contracts of employment), and spoke of Lumley *v.* Wagner as an anomaly." 1 Pomeroy's Equitable Remedies, p. 520, note 65, by John Norton Pomeroy, Jr., published in 1905 as volumes 5 and 6 of Pomeroy's Equity Jurisprudence.

[22] Pomeroy's Equity Jurisprudence, Sec. 1343, first published in 1881.

"The rule is now generally accepted and applied in this country," says Mr. Pomeroy, Jr., in 1905.[23] The American cases show that that is true, if very materially qualified by striking out the word "generally," for very few American Courts of last resort have dealt with Mr. Pomeroy's rule as applied to a contract of employment.[24] This rule, of course, rejects the negative-words test of jurisdiction, and substitutes "the special, unique, and extraordinary qualifications" test, in the case of a contract of employment.[25]

As respects contracts other than contracts for personal service, and where the subject-matter is not land, the question whether a Court of Equity would imply a negative, and on that alone as a basis enjoin the defendant from breaking the contract, though the defendant's contract was such that, under established rules, the Court could not compel the defendant by decree to per-

[23] 1 Pomeroy's Equitable Remedies, Sec. 288, last sentence.

[24] The American cases are collected in 4 Pomeroy's Eq. Jur., Ed. 3, Sec. 1343, notes; 1 Ames' Cases on Eq. Jur., 123, note 1; 2 Scott's Cases, Eq. Jur., 106, note 1. Prior to Lumley v. Wagner, the current of decision here was all one way — against the jurisdiction of Equity, negative clause or not, "special, unique and extraordinary" employee or not. The early American cases are cited in 1 Ames' Cases, Eq. Jur. 93, note 1; see 2 Scott's Cases, 85, 86; in Rice v. D'Arville, 162 Mass., 559, 1895, note 5, supra, the Supreme Judicial Court, affirming a decree of Judge Holmes, now on the Federal Supreme Court, expressed itself quite strongly against enjoining a breach of a contract of employment. It appears from a note in 8 Harv. Law Rev., 172, that Judge Holmes rested his decision on that ground.

[25] The reason given by Mr. Pomeroy for saying that the remedy of damages is quite inadequate appears to assume that the employer cares for, and wants, the service in specie. The actual, or at least the presumed, fact is not so ordinarily. That may not be controlling, but the idea appears as relevant, at least, in the ratio decidendi of the early cases extending the remedy of performance in specie to a failure to deliver peculiar chattels in breach of contract, and to a tortious withholding of peculiar chattels. See a number of cases collected in 1 Ames' Cases, Eq. Jur., 39, note 2. "There is no showing whatever that appellants want it in specie," says the Illinois Supreme Court in Pierce v. Plumb, 74 Ill., 326, 332, affirming a decree refusing specific performance of a contract for the sale of stock. Other Courts have given the same reason for the same ruling. 1 Ames' Cases in Eq. Jur., 55, note 2.

form it in specie, first arose,[26] after Lumley v. Wagner, in
DeMattos v. Gibson, (1858–9),[27] one of the cases mentioned in the Illinois case of Consolidated Coal Co. v.
Schmisseur, supra. One Curry, as owner of a ship,
entered into a charter-party with the plaintiff, DeMattos,
to carry a cargo of coal from Newcastle to Suez. A
third person, Gibson, had a mortgage on the ship with a
power of sale after six months' default. When Gibson
advanced the money to Curry secured by the mortgage
on the ship, he knew of the charter-party between Curry
and DeMattos. The cargo of coal was put aboard the
ship. The ship started on the voyage to Suez, but
proved unseaworthy, and put into the port of Penzance
for repairs. The repairs went very slowly. The six
months having expired, Gibson was threatening to sell
the ship under the power of sale in his mortgage. De-
Mattos filed a bill against Curry and Gibson praying
(1) specific performance by Curry; (2) an injunction
to restrain Curry from permitting the ship and cargo
to remain at Penzance, or at any place other than Suez;
and (3) an injunction against Gibson, forbidding him to
sell the ship under the power of sale in his mortgage, or to
interfere in any way to interrupt the voyage to Suez.
The case came up before Wood, V.-C., on a motion by the
plaintiff for a preliminary injunction. Concerning specific performance by Curry of the agreement to carry coal,
the learned Judge said:

"I conceive that the specific performance of an agreement to
convey coals to Suez (which is in effect the operation of the charter-
party) is beyond the control of the Court. For what directions
could be given as to the navigation of the ship? By what process
could the hiring of sailors, the appointment of a proper master, the
victualing of the vessel, and the like be enforced?"

[26] Fry, Specific Performance, 3d Am. Ed., Sec. 836.
[27] 4 De G. & J., 276

Plaintiff's counsel appear to have rested their right to an injunction upon Lumley *v.* Wagner, and, there being no express negative, upon that part of the opinion on the authority of which Wood, V.-C., in Webster *v.* Dillon, *supra*, implied a negative and granted an injunction. But Wood, V.-C., refused to grant the injunction, saying:

"As regards the injunction, I consider the observations of Lord St. Leonards, in Lumley *v.* Wagner, to apply to cases in which the breach of a positive agreement involves specific damage beyond that of the mere non-performance of the agreement itself. He says: 'It was clearly intended that J. Wagner was to exert her vocal abilities to the utmost to aid the theater to which she agreed to attach herself. I am of the opinion that, if she had attempted, even in the absence of any negative stipulation, to perform at another theater, she would have broken the spirit and true meaning of the contract.' That is to say, a special damage would be done by her singing elsewhere at a rival theater — ultra, the non-performance of her contract to sing at the theater which had engaged her. The Court could not make her perform the latter engagement, but could prevent her doing anything which was an aggravation of her breach of it. This is more apparent if his Lordship's observations on Clarke *v.* Price (in p. 62 of the report in Lumley *v.* Wagner) are attended to. Indeed, at the close of his observations on that part of the case, his Lordship says he should not have granted any injunction on the affirmative part of the contract only in the case before him. Now in Clarke *v.* Price an injunction to restrain Mr. Price from writing any other (law) reports until he had written (law) reports for the plaintiff might have had the effect of compelling him to write for the plaintiff, but it was not in the nature of the contract, as Lord Eldon observed, that there should be such a restriction; so in the case before me, it is no part of the contract that the ship should not carry coals for others, nor will the plaintiff be at all the worse for her doing so, beyond the mere loss of his contract. Any other ship will carry the coals as well, or probably better, and the whole matter sounds in damages. He would gain nothing by the ship remaining idle, whereas, in all cases of negative contracts, there is a positive benefit from their observance."

On appeal, Wood, V.-C., was reversed. Knight-Bruce, L. J., though the agreement to carry coal to Suez implied the negative that Curry would not actively divert the ship from that use, and that he could be enjoined from doing so; that this negative was enforceable against Gibson by injunction, because he acquired his interest in the ship with notice of this implied restriction on its use. Turner, L. J., thought matters ought to be held in statu quo until final hearing on the questions: (1) Whether specific performance of Curry's affirmative agreement to carry coal could be granted; (2) whether that affirmative agreement implied a negative not to use the ship to carry coal for anyone else, enforceable by injunction; (3) whether such implied restriction on the use of the ship ran with the ship in the hands of a third person — Gibson — taking with notice of it.

On final hearing, Wood, V.-C., dismissed the bill, and, on appeal, the Chancellor, Lord Chelmsford, affirmed the decree, on the ground that the proof on final hearing showed that Curry's breach of the agreement to carry coal was a passive one, because he did not have the money to repair the ship and get her off into the water; that it was not a case "of Curry (actively) attempting tö employ a (seaworthy) vessel in a manner not in accordance with the terms of the charter-party," and that "Gibson has not in any way interfered with the performance of the charter-party until it was evident that Curry was wholly unable to perform it." Lord Chelmsford agreed fully with Wood, V.-.C., supra, that the Court could not compel Curry to sail the ship to Suez, but he disagreed with the view of Wood, V.-C., that the negative not to employ the ship in a manner inconsistent with the charter-party could not be implied and enforced by injunction. Lord Chelmsford said:

"When by this charter-party Curry undertakes to carry to Suez a full and complete cargo of coals for the plaintiff, it necessarily implies that if the plaintiff provides a full cargo, the vessel shall not be employed for any other person or purpose. . . . A person who hires a vessel under a charter-party does so not merely from a wish to have his goods conveyed to a particular place, but upon a careful choice of the vessel itself as best adapted for his purposes. Many considerations may influence him in the selection, and after these have determined him to bind himself and the owners of a particular vessel in a contract for its employment, he would be surprised to be told that all he wanted was to have his goods conveyed to their destination, and that it was immaterial to him in what manner or by what conveyance this was accomplished. I think that a vessel engaged under a charter-party ought to be regarded as a chattel of a peculiar value to the charterer, and that although a Court of Equity cannot compel a specific performance of the contract which it contains, yet that it will restrain the employment of a vessel in a different manner, whether such employment is expressly or impliedly forbidden, according to the principle so fully expressed in Lumley v. Wagner."

In Peto v. Tunbridge Wells Ry. Co. (1863),[28] the third of the English cases referred to by the Illinois Court in Consolidated Coal Co. v. Schmisseur, supra,[29] the plaintiffs were railroad contractors who had entered into a contract to build a line of railroad for the defendant company, the company agreeing to pay them in debentures and stock. The bill was filed to enjoin the company from letting the contract to other contractors, and the case came up on a motion for a preliminary injunction to restrain the company from dealing with the debentures and transferring the shares in question to others. Wood, V.-C., denied the motion, because the plaintiff's part

[28] 1 H. & M., 468.   One can see easily from the opinions herein, without looking further, that Wood, V.-C., deserved to be made Chancellor.

[29] See note 2 supra.   There are three reports of Peto v. Tunbridge Wells Ry. Co.: 32 L. J. Ch., 677, 11 W. R., 874, 1 H. & M., 468, all cited on appellant's brief in 135 Ill. at p. 374. The report in 1 H. & M. is evidently the correct one. The passage quoted, note 2, supra, by the Illinois Court is taken from 32 L. J. Ch. Lumley v. Wagner should read Webster v. Dillon.   Lumley v. Wagner and De Mattos v. Gibson, and their effect are considered at length in the second edition (1881) of Fry on Specific Performance, Ed. 2, Sec. 833, et seq.

of the contract, to build a line of railroad, could not be enforced specifically by suit by the defendant against the plaintiffs, and that a submission by the plaintiffs to perform would not be an adequate security to the defendants of performance in fact, within the rule, supra, for avoiding the objection of want of mutuality. As respects enjoining a breach of the company's affirmative contract on the doctrine of an implied negative, Wood, V.-C., said:

"I have every possible inducement to afford the plaintiffs as large a measure of relief as I can give them consistently with the established principles of this Court, but I feel the difficulties to be quite insuperable. If there were a distinct negative contract in this agreement, such as the contract which has now become usual in ordinary agricultural leases, that the lessee will not farm otherwise than according to the custom of the country, the Court might fasten upon that, and separating that from the rest of the agreement might enforce specific performance of that contract; but when a plaintiff comes into this Court upon an agreement which does not contain any such direct negative clause, and where you must infer the negative from the necessity of the case, the instances in which the Court has found it possible to act are very few and special. In DeMattos v. Gibson, where the plaintiff had nothing on his part to perform, the Lords Justices said, 'We will not permit the defendant to do that which will render it utterly impossible for him to perform his contract.' So, in a case which came before me some time ago (Webster v. Dillon, supra), where an actor had agreed to perform at a particular place on certain days, I thought myself justified in restraining him from acting elsewhere upon those days during the ordinary hours of theatrical performance. But I cannot bring this case within the principle involved in DeMattos v. Gibson, because the plaintiffs have to perform their part of this agreement by constructing the railway, whereas no difficulty existed (in DeMattos v. Gibson), inasmuch as in doing complete justice the plaintiff had nothing to do but pay the sum agreed upon by the charter-party, a condition which it was within the power of the Court to enforce. . . . Here I perfectly agree with Sir Hugh Cairns,[30] that these shares are of such a character that it is no

---

[30] Counsel for defendant.

consolation to the defendants to be told that if the plaintiffs should fail to perform their part of this agreement this injunction will go, and the shares thereby let loose; they might be depreciated by the very fact of their failure.   I do not lay any stress upon the fact that I should lock up the land of this company for an indefinite time.   In DeMattos *v.* Gibson the Lords Justices thought that the principle of Lumley *v.* Wagner made it right that the ship in question in that case should remain utterly useless if not used in performance of the contract; and I should be ready to act on the same principle here."

In section 838 of his second edition of "Specific Performance" (1881), after a full statement of DeMattos *v.* Gibson, Mr. Fry said of the principle of enjoining a breach of an affirmative contract, not enforceable specifically by decree, on the sole basis of an implied negative:

"It is not easy to see the limits to which the doctrine of an implied negative might be carried; for as A and not-A include the whole world, it follows that a contract to sell to A or to sing at A must imply a negative of a sale to not-A or a singing at not-A; and if injunction is to be granted where specific performance might be impossible, the logical conclusion of the doctrine would be a great and rather formidable enlargement of the jurisdiction of Equity."

In 1873, in Wolverhampton & Walsall Ry. Co. *v.* London & North Western Ry. Co.,[31] the plaintiff agreed to construct a line of railroad, and the defendant agreed to work it, and that certain specified kinds of traffic should pass over it.   The plaintiff constructed the road, put the defendant in possession of it, and the defendant now was diverting the specified traffic away from plaintiff's road to another road owned by the defendant. Lord Selborne enjoined the defendant, saying that the contract was virtually a lease, and that "the only question is, whether, being in possession . . . they (defendant company) are, or are not, at liberty to depart

[31] L. R. 16 Eq., 433.

from the terms on which it was stipulated they should have that possession." In response to the argument that there was no express negative, Lord Selborne said:

"With regard to the case of Lumley v. Wagner, to which reference has been made, really, when it comes to be examined, it is not a case which tends in any way to limit the ordinary jurisdiction of this Court to do justice between parties by way of injunction. It was sought in that case to enlarge the jurisdiction on a highly artificial and techincal ground, and to extend it to an ordinary case of hiring and service, which is not properly a case of specific performance; the technical distinction being made, that if you find the word "not" in an agreement — "I will not do a thing" — as well as the words "I will," even though the negative term might have been implied from the positive, yet the Court, refusing to act on an implication of the negative, will act on the expression of it. I can only say that I should think it was the safer and the better rule, if it should eventually be adopted by this Court, to look in all such cases to the substance and not to the form. If the substance of the agreement is such that it would be violated by doing the thing sought to be prevented, then the question will arise, whether this is the Court to come to for a remedy. If it is, I cannot think that ought to depend on the use of a negative, rather than an affirmative, form of expression. If, on the other hand, the substance of the thing is such that the remedy ought to be sought elsewhere, then I do not think that the forum ought to be changed by the use of a negative rather than an affirmative. But that class of cases, in which the Court has striven to enlarge, rather than narrow, its jurisdiction, seems to me to have no application at all in a case like this, where there is an agreement in substance for the leasing of a line of railway."

Of Lord Selborne's observation on Lumley v. Wagner, Mr. Fry said in Section 841 of the second edition of his "Specific Performance:"

"The doctrine in Lumley v. Wagner has been criticized[32] by Lord Selborne; and after his observations it is doubtful whether

---

[32] I. e., the extension of the jurisdiction to grant injunctions to the case of a breach of contract for personal service.

the mere presence of a negative stipulation can be relied upon,
if the contract is not such in its nature as to be the proper subject
of equitable jurisdiction."

In Fothergill v. Rowland (1873),[33] the plaintiff advanced
money to the defendant to help him extend his coal mine,
and procured the Taff Vale Railway Company to lay a
siding to the mine, and the defendant contracted to sell
to the plaintiff the whole of the output of the mine for
five years. Coal went up in price. The contract having
some three years to run, it was discovered that the defendant was selling coal to other parties, and was about to
sell the mine itself in order to avoid performance of the
contract with plaintiff. Jessel, M. R., refused an injunction on the ground that it was a contract for the purchase and sale of an ordinary chattel, coal, the proved
threatened breach of which would sound only in damages.
The learned Judge said:

"I cannot find any distinct line laid down, or any distinct limit
which I could seize upon and define as being the line dividing the
two classes of cases, that is, the class of cases in which the Court,
feeling that it has not the power to compel specific performance,
grants an injunction to restrain the breach by the contracting
party of one or more of the stipulations of the contract, and the
class of cases in which it refuses to interfere. I have asked (and
I am sure I should have obtained from one of the learned counsel
engaged in the case every assistance)[34] for a definition. I have not
only been able to obtain the answer, but I have obtained that
which altogether commands my assent, namely, that there is no
such distinct line to be found in the authorities."

In Donnell v. Bennett (1883),[35] Mr. Fry, as Judge, had
to decide a case which he thought just like Fothergill v.
Rowland, supra, except that there was an express nega-

[33] L. R. 17 Eq., 132.

[34] The question was put to Mr. Fry, author of "Specific Performance," counsel
for plaintiff. See L. R. 17 Eq., at p. 137.

[35] L. R. 22 Ch. D., 835.

tive in the contract. The defendant, a fish curer and
fish smoker, contracted to sell to the plaintiff, a manure
manufacturer, all fish and parts of fish not used by
defendant in his business of fish curer and fish smoker, for
the space of two years, agreeing expressly "that he would
not sell during the space of two years any fish or parts of
fish to any other manufacturer whatever." Fry, J.,
thought the contract was a contract for the purchase
and sale of an ordinary chattel, but granted an injunction
on the basis of the express negative. The learned Judge
said:

> "It appears to me that the tendency of the more recent decisions
> . . . is toward this view — that the Court ought to look at
> what is the nature of the contract between the parties; that if the
> contract as a whole is the subject of equitable jurisdiction, then an
> injunction may be granted in support of the contract whether
> it contain or does not contain a negative stipulation; but that if,
> on the other hand, the breach of the contract is properly satisfied
> by damages, then that the Court ought not to interfere whether
> there be or be not the negative stipulation. . . . But the
> question which I have to determine is not whether that ought
> to be the way in which the line ought to be laid down, but whether
> it has been so laid down by the authorities which are binding on me."

After an examination of the cases the learned Judge
concluded:

> "I have come to the conclusion, therefore, upon the authorities
> which are binding upon me, that I ought to grant this injunction.
> I do so with considerable difficulty, because I find it hard to draw
> any substantial or tangible distinction between a contract con-
> taining an express negative stipulation and a contract containing
> an affirmative stipulation which implies a negative. I find it
> exceedingly difficult to draw any rational distinction between
> the case of Fothergill v. Rowland and the case before me."

In Metropolitan Electric Supply Co. v. Ginder (1901),[36]
the plaintiff was bound by Act of Parliament to supply

[36] (1901) 2 Ch., 799.

electric energy to applicants. Defendant signed a statutory form of request, inserting the following term and condition: "The consumer agrees to take the whole of the electric energy required for the premises mentioned below from the company for a period of not less than five years." The consumer was not bound to take any. "It is competent to him to burn gas if he likes, and require no energy." Buckley, J., enjoined the consumer from taking electric energy from any other company for use on the named premises during the space of five years. The learned Judge said:

"The cases since that (Wolverhampton & Walsall Ry. Co. v. London & North Western Ry. Co., 1873, supra), I think, have gone to show that that which Lord Selborne there says (quoted supra) would be the true principle, if it should eventually be adopted by this Court, has really now been adopted by this Court."

After a review of the cases the learned Judge concluded:

"I therefore think that the fact that the contract is affirmative in form and not negative in form is no ground for refusing an injunction."

As above stated, in this country, the Courts generally have not attached any importance to the presence or absence of negative words as a criterion for deciding whether they could, or could not, enjoin a breach of a contract which they could not compel the defendant by decree to perform in specie. In Pomeroy's Equity Jurisprudence, the subject is dealt with in Section 1341, et seq. In Section 1341, it is said:

"The remedy of injunction is not confined to contracts whose stipulations are negative; it often extends to those which are affirmative in their provisions, where the affirmative stipulation implies or includes a negative."[37]

[37] See also Pomeroy's Equitable Remedies, Secs. 270, 271, 288-291; High on Injunctions, Ed. 2, Sec. 1109. It is not within my purpose to attempt to disentangle from the cases a rule, but it may be observed that, laying Lumley v. Wagner aside as "an anomaly" (Lindley, L. J., in Whitwood Chemical Co. v.

It is difficult to read the case of Welty *v.* Jacobs (1898),[38] without thinking that the Illinois Supreme Court then

Hardman, supra), and assuming the objection of want of mutuality overcome and put away, the breach enjoined generally is an active one; in other words, the defendant's sin is not one of omission merely, but of commission — actively diverting the substance of the contract away from the plaintiff to other people (Knight-Bruce, L. J., and Lord Chelmsford, in DeMattos *v.* Gibson, supra); that such active breach generally causes an injury to the plaintiff ultra the injury that a merely passive breach would cause (Wood, V.-C., in DeMattos *v.* Gibson, supra); that this injury ultra, for some reason or other arising out of the special circumstances of each case, does not sound wholly in damages, though the injury from a merely passive breach would so sound, ex vi termini the issue as to the remedy for an active breach; that, speaking practically, as men go and as they think and act ordinarily, the injunction forbidding the active breach is almost certain to secure performance by the defendant in specie. "Doing indirectly what cannot be done directly," is not thought a convincing argument against this jurisdiction; nor is it really true, the Courts say, that they act indirectly. When the nature of the case in which this jurisdiction has been exercised is kept in mind, the Court's process does seem more direct than an affirmative order of performance in specie would be. It coerces the defendant by a threat to lock up his property or business (see the remarks of Wood, V.-C., in Peto *v.* Tunbridge Wells Ry. Co., supra, about locking up the defendant's land). If the injunction is not likely to produce the only result the Court is, or ought to be, driving at — performance — it seems that it ought not to be granted. That seems to be the practical objection to the injunction in Lumley *v.* Wagner. Miss Wagner obeyed the injunction, but did not sing for Lumley. See Lumley *v.* Gye, 2 El. & Bl., 216. The refusal of the Court to order performance in specie is founded, not on any principle of justice that operates in favor of the defendant, but upon a practical necessity arising out of the nature of the work the contract calls for and the nature of an order for performance in specie, resulting in a rule of policy forbidding the Court to assume the position of general manager of the world's daily business with the duty of deciding daily applications by one half of the world to put the other half of it into the county jail. Singer Sewing Machine Co. *v.* Union Button Hole Co., Holmes, 253, 22 Fed. Cas., p. 220, is a good example of the usefulness of the jurisdiction to enjoin an active breach of a contract not enforceable in specie. The case is cited in Southern Fire Brick & Clay Co. *v.* Garden City Sand Co., on p. 625, but the two are quite dissimilar as respects Equity jurisdiction. The seeming disposition of some Courts to extend the jurisdiction appears to rest upon the obsolete idea — if it ever did exist (see Anson on Contracts, Ed. 2, pp. 9–13; Huffcutt's Am. Ed., p. 10, note a) — that the common-law remedy of damages means that a man has a right to break his contract (see the opinion of Coke quoted in Ames' Cases, Eq. Jur., note 3, p. 38). To-day, at least, one might as well think about the right of a man to commit murder if he is willing to be hanged. The text-books seem unsatisfactory on this jurisdiction. One does not say anything, when he announces it as a conclusion that the remedy of damages must be inadequate.

[38] 171 Ill., 624. The defendant agreed to furnish a theater; the plaintiff to furnish a company of actors to play the "Black Crook." An injunction to

thought very little of the idea that the jurisdiction of a
Court of Equity to enjoin the breach of a contract not
enforceable specifically by decree can depend on the negative or affirmative form of the contract. Indeed, in
point of reason, the idea may be dismissed with a sentence
from Lord Nottingham's celebrated opinion in The Duke
of Norfolk's Case.[39]

> "The . . . Rule given as a Reason by my Lord Popham in
> the Rector of Chedington's Case looks like a Reason of Art; but
> in Truth has no kind of Reason in it."

Where the subject-matter of the contract is land, the
jurisdiction of a Court of Equity to enforce performance
or prevent breaches of restrictions on the use of the land
is, of course, an old one. No one for some generations
back has ever heard it disputed that a Court of Equity
has jurisdiction to enforce a contract between an owner
of land and his tenant, or between an owner of land and
his neighbor purchasing part of, that the latter shall use
or abstain from using the land leased or purchased in a
particular way.[40] It is sufficient here to recall the remarks
of Lord Selborne in Walsall & W. Ry. Co. v. London &
N. W. Ry. Co., quoted supra, to the effect that the theory
of express and implied negatives that grew out of Lum-

---

restrain the defendant from letting the theater to a rival proprietor of a company
of actors playing the "Black Crook" was refused on the ground of want of mutuality. See Davis v. Foreman, supra; Ryan v. Mutual Tontine Westminster Chambers Association, note 19, supra. If the passage from Pomeroy quoted in 171
Ill. at p. 631, means anything, it is, as the Court says, a general rule subject to
exceptions — now numerous enough to destroy the rule, I think. Compare
High on Injunctions, Ed. 2, Sec. 1109, and read the following sections in Pomeroy
in elucidation of his proposition.

[39] 3 Ch. Cas., 14, 29.

[40] Lord Cottenham in Tulk v. Moxhay, 2 Phillips, 774, 1848, quoted in Frye v.
Partridge, 82 Ill., 267, 270; Story's Eq. Jur., Ed. 13, Sec. 721. And see the citations in the opinions of the Court and in the briefs of counsel in the three Illinois
cases herein; Bryden v. Northrup, 58 Ill. App., 233; Hovnanian v. Bedessern,
63 Ill. App., 353.

ley v. Wagner is a highly artificial and technical theory
to extend the jurisdiction of Equity, and is not properly
applicable when it is sought to limit its acknowledged and
established jurisdiction over breaches of stipulations in
contracts for the leasing or sale of land. In such cases,
so far as the subject in hand goes, it is conceded ordinarily
that the party thinking himself aggrieved coming into a
Court of Equity is in the right forum, and the question
is simply this: Has the defendant broken the contract as
alleged? When the jurisdiction of a Court of Equity
over a breach of contract is in issue, the breach is admitted
for purposes of argument, and the only question is whether
the plaintiff is in the right Court.[41] Where land is the
subject-matter of the contract, any theory that may appear in the cases as respects express and implied negatives
can rise no higher than a rule of construction for fixing
the meaning of the contract preliminary to determining
whether it has been broken in fact. An express negative
helps to fix the meaning of the contract. The absence of
it may leave a doubt that may be resolved in favor of
the free use of the land.[42] "I think . . . it would be
but seldom you could have it appear distinctly upon a
lease (or sale of land) that it was intended that a thing
should not be done unless there were negative words
used."[43] But if it does distinctly appear without the
use of negative words, the jurisdiction to give effect to
the stipulation in specie, regardless of the amount of
injury done by its breach, is plain and of long standing.[44]

[41] "The question is not whether Jacobs is justified in violating his contract, but
whether Welty's bill of complaint for equitable relief can be sustained, or he
should be remitted to his action at law." Welty v. Jacobs, 171 Ill., 624, 629.

[42] Downen v. Rayburn, 214 Ill., 342, 346, and cases cited.

[43] Lord Blackburn, Doherty v. Allman, L. R., 3 App. Cas., H. L., 709, 729.
Postal Tel. Co. v. Western Union Tel. Co., 155 Ill., 335.

[44] In Drury v. Molins, 6 Ves., 328 (1801), "Mr. Ainge moved for an injunction
to restrain a tenant from committing waste by plowing up pasture land. The

It only remains to state the three Illinois cases referred to at the outset.

In Consolidated Coal Co. *v.* Schmisseur [45] the plaintiff Schmisseur sold underlying coal to the Schuremans, and at the same time leased to them eleven acres of the surface "for the purpose of enabling the Schuremans to sink pits or shafts and successfully mine and remove said coal." The Schuremans sold their rights in the contract and lease to the defendant company. The bill was filed to enjoin the Company from removing through the entries and openings on the leased eleven acres, and from hoisting through the shaft or pit on the leased eleven acres, coal mined by the Company under adjoining land. The trial Court granted the injunction; the Appellate Court for the Fourth District affirmed the decree; and the Supreme Court reversed it. The Supreme Court's decision is, that the acts complained of were not a breach of any stipulation in the lease; that the statement in the lease of the purpose for which it was made neither expressly nor impliedly forbade the use of the entries, openings, and shafts on the premises for removing and hoisting coal mined under adjoining land; that this use of the eleven acres by the defendant was no more

---

lease contained no express covenant not to convert pasture to arable, but there was a covenant to manage pasture in a husbandlike manner. The Lord Chancellor (Eldon) said he thought that equivalent, and granted the injunction until answer and further order." See the third paragraph of the brief of Mr. Loesch in Postal Tel. Co. *v.* W. U. Tel. Co., 155 Ill., 335, 345, and cases cited; Bryden *v.* Northrup, 58 Ill., App. 233. In Doherty *v.* Allman, L. R., 3 App. Cas., 709, 720, Lord Cairns does intend, perhaps, to make a distinction, as respects Equity jurisdiction, between express and implied negatives in leases, sed quaere. In Pomeroy's Eq. Rem., Sec. 285, note 42, the author speaks of the "English rule," that "injunction is not a matter of course," "when the covenant in a lease is not negative in form," citing Harris *v.* Boots (1904), 2 Ch., 376, and in note 43 McEacharn *v.* Colton (1902) App. Cas., P. C., 104, but they do not proceed on any such "English rule," I think. The author in note 43 quotes from Consolidated Coal Co. *v.* Schmisseur, 135 Ill., 371, as giving a rule unlike either "the English rule" in note 42 or the rule in the text of Sec. 285.

[45] 135 Ill., 371.

inconsistent with the terms of the lease than planting corn or potatoes, or pasturing a cow, on the eleven acres would be. The distinction of the Court set forth at the beginning, as respects the jurisdiction of a Court of Equity, between express and implied negatives, therefore, was irrelevant and obiter.[46]

In Carlson v. Koerner[47] the plaintiff leased a farm to the defendant, the lease stipulating that the defendant would "allow" the plaintiff "to fall plow and haul out manure," and that plaintiff should have the "right to enter for viewing, seeding, or any other purpose." The defendant, the tenant, was let into possession. When the plaintiff, the landlord, went to the farm in the fall of 1905 to do fall plowing, the defendant locked the gates and would not let plaintiff enter. The trial Court granted an injunction; the Appellate Court for the Second District affirmed the decree; the Supreme Court reversed it. The Supreme Court said:

"There is no covenant or agreement that appellant (the tenant) will not interfere with appellee (the landlord) in her efforts either to plow the land or haul out the manure. The position of the appellee (the landlord) must be, that inasmuch as appellant (the tenant) covenanted to allow her to enter for certain purposes there is an implied negative covenant not to interfere with her doing so. The terms here used are not negative and can only become so by implication, and if they can be so treated, many affirmative or positive contracts may be construed to be negative and a Court of Equity given jurisdiction to enforce covenants either affirmative or negative. There is no negative covenant within the rule laid down by the authorities, and hence equity had no jurisdiction without proof of irreparable injury."

The Court goes on to say that plaintiff proved no irreparable injury from the breach of the covenant, and,

---

[46] In Postal Tel. Co. v. W. U. Tel. Co., 155 Ill., 335, 352, the case was used as laying down and applying a rule of construction.

[47] 226 Ill., 15.

finally, that the provision in the lease, securing to the landlord, in case of a breach of any of its terms, the right to declare the lease null and void and to retake possession of the farm was an adequate remedy, and excluded the jurisdiction of Equity. In Southern Fire Brick & Clay Co. *v.* Garden City Sand Co., 223 Ill., 616, 626 – 627, the Court says that a provision for liquidated damages in a contract will not oust the jurisdiction of a Court of Equity to enjoin a breach of it, unless it appears that such was the intention of the parties. It is thought generally, I think, that the usual provision in a lease securing to the landlord the right to declare the lease void and to re-enter for breach of any of its terms is a cumulative remedy, in the absence of evidence of a contrary intention.[48]

In Southern Fire Brick & Clay Co. *v.* Garden City Sand Co.[49] the salient facts were that one Lanyon owned certain fire clay land at Jonesdale Switch, Indiana. He knew nothing about the business of grinding and preparing fire clay for the market, and one purpose of the contract was to aid Lanyon to open up and extend the business of producing fire clay on this land of his in Indiana. The Garden City Sand Co. had an extensive business in the line of producing, and particularly of selling, fire clay. Lanyon agreed to erect and equip at his own expense on this land a new plant for the grinding and preparing of the clay. The Garden City Sand Co. agreed to make the greatest possible effort to sell all the fire clay produced at Lanyon's proposed new plant, and

[48] 1 Spelling on Injunctions, Ed. 2, Sec. 472, et seq., and cases in notes. The Supreme Court of Nebraska decided a case just like Carlson *v.* Koerner in favor of the landlord. State Bank of Nebraska *v.* Rohrer, 55. Neb. 223. The case is cited with others in Pomeroy's Eq. Rem. Sec. 285, note 246.

[49] 223 Ill., 616; s. c. in Branch Appellate Court for the First District, 124 Ill., App., 599. See also Stafford *v.* Swift, 121 Ill. App. 508.

to order and pay for at fixed prices not less than an average of forty tons for every working day for a period of eight years, and the Garden City Sand Co. also agreed to cease to operate a fire clay plant at Russell Switch, Indiana, but reserved the right to reopen this plant in case Lanyon's proposed new plant could not supply the demand, and further agreed not to buy fire clay produced at any other plant in Indiana, except at Lanyon's proposed new plant or their own Russell Switch plant. Lanyon agreed not to sell clay to anyone except the Garden City Sand Co., and also agreed not to operate any other fire clay plant on any land that he owned or controlled in Indiana during the eight-year space of the contract. The contract was signed October 26, 1901. It appears that Lanyon began the construction of the plant, but never completed it; the Branch Appellate Court's report says, "it was understood the plant would be completed about November 1, 1901." Just why Lanyon did not complete the plant does not clearly appear. The Supreme Court says Lanyon "claims himself that he failed to carry out his part of the contract because of his financial inability to do so" and "the record is full of evidence as to the financial irresponsibility of Lanyon," but there is no clear finding that Lanyon did not complete the plant for the want of money to do it. Just when the Southern Fire Brick & Clay Co. came into the business does not appear. But on September 17, 1902, nearly a year after the date (November 1, 1901) it was understood Lanyon would have his plant completed, the Southern Fire Brick & Clay Co. took from Lanyon and wife a warranty deed of ninety-three acres of the lands contained in the contract between Lanyon and the Garden City Sand Co. But prior to that and before May 28, 1902, the Garden City Sand Co. served notice on the Southern Fire Brick & Clay Co. that legal steps would be taken to restrain them from operating a plant or selling fire clay in violation of the contract between Lanyon and the Garden City Sand Co. The Branch Appellate Court says that the Southern Fire Brick & Clay Co. induced Lanyon to break his contract "with the evident purpose of robbing" the Garden City Sand Co. "of the benefit of the contract," and, but for the persuasion of the Southern Fire Brick & Clay Co., Lanyon certainly, or at least probably, would have completed the plant and performed his contract. The Southern Fire Brick & Clay Co. constructed a new fire clay plant, or completed Lanyon's abandoned plant, on the ninety-three acres, and placed its product on the open market for sale. April 4, 1903, the Garden City Sand Co. filed a bill for an injunction against Lanyon and the Southern Fire Brick & Clay Co. The Master reported against granting an injunction; the trial Court refused to grant one; the Branch Appellate Court for the First District reversed the decree; the Supreme Court affirmed the judgment of the Branch Appellate Court.

It may be conceded that the conduct of Lanyon and the Southern Fire Brick & Clay Co. merits the most vituperative epithet that counsel ever hurled at a faithless defendant. But vituperative epithets do not reach the question of Equity jurisdiction, the remedy to be applied to right the wrong. The law clearly gave the Garden City Sand Co. the remedy of an action for damages against Lanyon for breach of contract; and if the Southern Fire Brick & Clay Co. did persuade and induce Lanyon to break his contract, it is very probable that the law also gave the Garden City Sand Co. the remedy of an action in tort for damages against the Southern Fire Brick & Clay Co.[50] The Garden City Sand Co. did not want these ordinary remedies. They wanted the exceptional

[50] Lumley v. Gye, 2 El. & Bl., 216; Doremus v. Hennessy, 176 Ill., 608.

remedy of a Court of Equity. Did the law allow them
to have it, either as against Lanyon, the immediate party
to the contract, or as against the Southern Fire Brick
& Clay Co., a stranger to that contract?

"What is the contract for?" Is it for the sale of fire
clay, clay gotten, the get of the clay, the severed chattel,
or has it any relation whatever to a contract for the
sale of real estate?[51] This question is not answered very
clearly by either Court, but I think both Courts held the
contract to be for the sale of the severed clay, the chattel.
Counsel argued that the contract was an unlawful restraint
of interstate trade under the Federal Anti-Trust Act, and
fully one-half of the opinion in each Court is devoted to
answering that argument. Since the power of Congress
does not extend to the regulation of sales of real estate
inside the borders of a State, this part of the case must
proceed on the idea that the contract was for the
severed chattel. If that is the meaning of the contract
in its relation to the Federal Anti-Trust Act, it is
difficult to see how it could change to a contract for real
estate in its relation to Equity jurisdiction. That the
contract was for the severed chattel, and not for real
estate, would appear to be the true and only permissible
view of it. By the terms of the contract, the seller,
Lanyon, had to sever the clay, run it through the fire
clay plant, and deliver it to the buyer f. o. b. cars at
Jonesdale Switch. All the buyer had to do was to receive
the clay there, take it away, and pay for it.[52] Concern-

---

[51] Jessell, M. R., Fothergill v. Rowland, supra.

[52] The Branch Appellate Court cites Knight v. Indiana Coal & Iron Co., 47
Ind., 105–110, to the point that the Southern Fire Brick & Clay Co. bought the
land from Lanyon subject to the burdens of the contract. Doubtless Indiana
law should govern, but in the case cited the contract was a sale of underlying
minerals, with a right in the buyer to come and dig them, paying the seller a
royalty. It was conceded to be a contract for real estate, and the only issue was
whether it created an estate at will, in a higher estate.

ing the nature of the severed fire clay, it was found as a fact that it is not a peculiar chattel, but an ordinary chattel, easily obtainable in Indiana, Kentucky, Illinois, Ohio, and perhaps other States.   Hence, if it were not for the express negatives in the contract, it is not open to discussion that the remedy for the breach of the contract was, as against Lanyon, at Law and not in Equity.   And if there was no remedy in Equity as against Lanyon, there could be no remedy in Equity as against the Southern Fire Brick & Clay Co.

The Appellate and Supreme Courts seized upon Lanyon's express negatives, separated them from the rest of the contract, treated them as a contract standing by themselves, and enforced them by injunction not only against Lanyon but against the Southern Fire Brick & Clay Co.   It always has been, and still is, the law that a contract must be performed in its entirety if performed at all under compulsion of a Court of Equity.   "It often, therefore, becomes important to inquire whether a contract is entire or divisible, or, in other words, what is the whole contract which must be executed?"[53]   In their relation to the Anti-Trust Act, both Courts decided that Lanyon's negative stipulations could not be severed from the rest of the contract and dealt with by themselves.   Then how can they be severed, and held to form an independent contract, when considered in their relation to Equity jurisdiction?   Plainly Lanyon's negative stipulation not to sell fire clay to anyone but the Garden City Sand Co. was dependent upon, and inseparable from, his affirmative stipulation to erect a fire clay plant.   The negatives, standing alone as an independent contract by themselves, would appear to be either void,

<hr>

[53] Fry, Specific Performance, 3d Am. Ed., Sec. 802; English and American notes to Lumley v. Wagner.   6 Eng. Ruling Cas., 600; Welty v. Jacobs, 171 Ill., 624.

or at least of such dubious merit that a Court of Equity would have nothing to do with a breach of them even as between the parties to them, but would leave the parties to their remedy at Law.

Even if the negative stipulations were enforceable by injunction as between the Garden City Sand Co. and Lanyon, on what legal principle could they be enforced by injunction as between the Garden City Sand Co. and the Southern Fire Brick & Clay Co., a stranger to the contract? No principle is laid down by either Court, and there is no principle in the books that would carry it.

The subject-matter of the contract was a chattel found to be an ordinary one, and not a peculiar one. The idea that restrictions on the use of a chattel contained in a contract for its sale are, when enforceable in specie as between the parties to the contract, also enforceable in specie as against subsequent purchasers of the chattel with notice—run with the goods, as it is put tersely—appears to have the direct affirmative support of only two cases, and they are not decisions of a Court of last resort: Murphy v. Christian Press Association Publishing Co.,[54] and New York Bank Note Co. v. Hamilton Bank Note Co.,[55] the latter being cited in Southern Fire Brick & Clay Co. v. Garden City Sand Co. on p. 627. In each case the property was of a more or less peculiar kind; in the former, a set of electrotype plates of a copyrighted book, the restriction forbidding the buyer to sell books printed from the plates below fixed prices; in the latter, printing presses with attachments for printing strip tickets, the restriction forbidding the seller to sell printing

[54] 38 N. Y. App. D., 426.

[55] 83 Hun., 593; see the opinions of Knight-Bruce, L. J., and Lord Chelmsford in De Mattos v. Gibson, supra, and see also a recent highly instructive article by Professor Ames, entitled "Specific Performance For and Against Strangers to the Contract," 17 Harv. Law Rev., 174.

presses to anyone else for use with these strip ticket attachments.   In Willoughby v. Lawrence,[56] cited in Southern Fire Brick & Clay Co. v. Garden City Sand Co. on p. 627, the contract was for the erection and use of billboards on certain land, and it was held binding upon, and enforceable in Equity against, a subsequent purchaser of the land on the principle that it created an easement — the principle on which restrictions on the use of land are enforced in Equity by many Courts against strangers taking the land with notice, a principle inapplicable to personal property.   In Taddy & Co. v. Sterious & Co.,[57] a manufacturer of tobacco sold a quantity of tobacco done up in small boxes to a wholesaler, each box having affixed to it a label stating its retail price and forbidding its sale at retail at a lower price.   A retailer bought a lot of the boxes from the wholesaler, and was selling them at prices lower than the prices fixed in the labels.   Swinfen Eady, J., refused to enjoin the retailer at the instance of the manufacturer, giving as one of his reasons that, assuming the labels made a contract between the manufacturer and the wholesaler, "conditions of this kind do not run with the goods, and cannot be imposed upon them."[58]   I think that is a sound result[59] and applicable to Southern Fire Brick & Clay Co. v. Garden City Sand Co., where, it should be noted, the thing sold was not the very subject — the fire clay — but the land.

[56] 116 Ill., 11.

[57] [1904] 1 Ch., 354.

[58] See a note of the case in 17 Harv. Law Rev., 415, leaning against it, but proceeding, I think, upon a misapprehension of the views of Professor Ames in the article referred to in note 55.   Compare the statutes restricting the sale and use of empty bottles in Lippman v. People, 175 Ill., 101.   Can you blow the restrictions into the bottles and let Equity do the rest?

[59] Garst v. Hall & Lynn Co., 179 Mass., 588; 17 Harv. Law. Rev., 569; 55 L. R. A., 631, note, and the third resolution in Spencer's Case, there cited.

At the close of its opinion,[60] the Supreme Court says that the insolvency of Lanyon, even admitting that it did cause Lanyon's breach of the contract, operated for, rather than against, the jurisdiction to grant the injunction prayed for, because it showed that the remedy of an action for damages for breach of contract would be inadequate. But "by inadequacy of the remedy at law is here meant, not that it fails to produce the money — that is a very usual result in the use of all remedies — but that in its nature and character it is not adapted to the end in view."[61] Besides, it would appear to be plain that Lanyon's insolvency, if it really did render him incapable of performing his side of the contract, ought to have brought the case within the rule that "in contracts positive . . . , the defendant's incapacity to perform his side of the contract, whilst it furnishes no answer to an action for damages, affords a ground of defense against specific performance."[62]

Some expressions in, and the general tone of, the opinions of the Appellate and Supreme Courts indicate confusion of thought concerning the jurisdiction to enjoin the tort of inducing a man to break his contract, and the jurisdiction to enjoin the breach of the contract. The bill for injunction was not founded on the tort of the Southern Fire Brick & Clay Company—assuming that there was a tort within the principle of Lumley v. Gye—of inducing Lanyon to break his contract. The whole of the foundation of the bill was Lanyon's breach of contract, and the whole object of the bill could have been only to compel performance in specie of Lanyon's

---

[60] 223 Ill., 616, 628.

[61] Miller, J., in Thompson v. Allen County, 115 U. S., 550, 554.

[62] Fry, Specific Performance, 3d Am. Ed., sec. 969; De Mattos v. Gibson, supra, on final hearing.

side of the contract.[63]   The law regulating the specific performance of contracts was controlling without any doubt.[64]   The jurisdiction to enjoin the tort of inducing a person to break his contract, and the jurisdiction to enjoin the breach of the contract, are not identically the same thing.[65]   The two jurisdictions, at least as exerted to-day in many instances, do have a common origin, the adventures of Miss Wagner in London in the early part of 1852, but that is about all.

It is submitted, therefore, that the distinction between express and implied negatives laid down in Consolidated Coal Co. v. Schmisseur is not well enough supported by precedent to have a place in the law; that Carlson v. Koerner and Southern Fire Brick & Clay Co. v. Garden City Sand Co. show that its admission into the law would not add to the security of men's rights.

[63] The Master found as a fact "that the sole object of complainants is not to obtain fire clay .   .   . but to prevent" the Southern Fire Brick & Clay Co. "from entering the market in competition with complainants in the sale of fire clay" (124 Ill. App., 604).   Compare the last lines of the opinion of Kay, L. G., in Whitewood Chemical Co. v. Hardman, supra.

[64] See Welty v. Jacobs, 171 Ill., 624, 231.

[65] Arthur v. Oakes, 63 Fed. Rep., 310, 317–318, C. C. A., Harlan, J.; Franklin Union v. the People, 220 Ill., 335, 377, bottom.

II

COLLECTED COMMENT

1. — THE RULE OF MUTUALITY IN GENERAL.

2. — MUTUALITY—VALIDITY OF COVENANT IN BREWER'S LEASE TO SELL ONLY BEER OF LESSOR.

3. — MUTUALITY — EFFECT OF A POWER TO TERMINATE THE CONTRACT.

4. — MUTUALITY — OIL AND

GAS LEASE AS AN EXECUTED CONTRACT OR GRANT.

5. — MUTUALITY — OIL AND GAS LEASE AS AN EXECUTORY CONTRACT.

6. — RISK OF LOSS BY FIRE AS BETWEEN VENDOR AND VENDEE.

7. — ENFORCEMENT OF CONTRACT TO CONVEY FOREIGN REAL PROPERTY.

1. — THE RULE OF MUTUALITY IN GENERAL.[a] — The State Supreme Court, in common with many other Courts, appears to find want of mutuality as a defense to a bill for the specific performance of a contract a very difficult thing to deal with. See Lancaster v. Roberts, 144 Ill., 213; Welty v. Jacobs, 171 Ill., 624; Anderson v. Olsen, 188 Ill., 502; Tryce v. Dittus, 199 Ill., 189; Frothman v. Deters, 206 Ill., 159; Gage v. Cummings, 209 Ill., 120; Bauer v. Coal Co., 209 Ill., 316; Gibson v. Brown, 214 Ill., 330; Sayer v. Humphrey, 216 Ill., 426; Kuhn v. Eppstein, 219 Ill., 154. For a recent somewhat elaborate judicial examination of the subject, see Judge Cochran's opinion in Blanton v. Kentucky Distilleries & Warehouse Co., 120 Fed. Rep., 318, 350–361; aff'd, 149 Fed. Rep., 31, C. C. A. Professor Ames has done the service of demonstrating with admirable lucidity and brevity how easy of understanding and application the rule of mutuality is. Keeping in mind that the obligations of a contract are one thing; that the performance of those obligations is a

[a] [1 Ill. Law Rev., 548, March, 1907.]

different thing, and that it is with such performance that equity, in granting or withholding the superior justice of specific performance, is concerned, the learned author says: "The reciprocity of remedy required (by the rule of mutuality) is not the right of each party to the contract to maintain a bill for specific performance against the other, but simply the right of one party to refuse to perform, unless performance by the other side is' given or assured." After showing that "the soundness of this conception of mutuality is confirmed" by decided cases, he concludes: "It is hoped, too, that the preceding discussion of the cases will have proved the need of revising the common form of stating the principle of mutuality, and the propriety of adopting the form here suggested: Equity will not compel specific performance by a defendant, if, after performance, the common law remedy of damages would be his sole security for the performance of the plaintiff's side of the contract (and such common law remedy would be inadequate)." 3 Columbia Law Rev., 1, 8, 12. The words in parentheses are added at the instance of the author. The historical origin of equity as a system of remedies, because of the inadequacy of the common law remedies, must ever be remembered, particularly when legal rights are being dealt with. See Langdell, Summary of Equity Pleading, Ed. 2, 27–42. It is hard to make anything at all out of the Illinois cases, supra. Gage v. Cummings, supra, clearly is all wrong. See Fennelly v. Anderson, 1 Ir. Ch. R., 706. Though a very recent case, the Illinois Supreme Court itself has had to distinguish it twice, but each time pretending that there is something as obscure as a Delphic oracle left in it that must be respected. See Gibson v. Brown, 214 Ill., 330, 337; Kuhn v. Eppstein, 219 Ill., 154, 156. And see Sayer v. Humphrey, 216 Ill., 426, 430; Ullsperger v. Meyer, 217 Ill., 262.

2. — Mutuality — Validity of Covenant in Brewer's
Lease to Sell only Beer of Lessor[a] — In Fortune Bros.
Brewing Co. *v.* Shields, 137 Ill. App., 77, the Appellate
Court for the First District decided that a stipulation
in a lease of premises, "to be occupied for saloon and for
no other purposes whatever," saying that the lessee
"agrees to sell no beer but that manufactured by" a
named brewing company, is "not enforceable for want
of mutuality;" that is to say, is of no binding force or
effect as against the lessee, but is void and a nullity.
The case went to trial on an agreed statment of facts
substantially as follows: One Michael Allen, so far as
appears, an entire stranger to the brewing company, was
the lessor; the term was five years, May 1, 1905, to April
30, 1910; the rent was $100 a month; the lease was in the
form commonly used in Chicago, the Chicago Real
Estate and Renting Agents Association's form. Just
why the above stipulation for the benefit of the brewing
company was put into the lease does not appear. Payment of the rent and performance of all covenants by the
lessee was guaranteed by Peter Fortune, president of the
brewing company, the Fortune Bros. Brewing Company.
In January, 1906, the lessee stopped selling beer made by
the brewing company, and began to sell other beer.
Then the lessor, Michael Allen, assigned the lease to the
brewing company, but he did not grant the reversion of
the leased premises to the brewing company. Thereafter the brewing company brought an action of forcible
detainer against the lessee to get possession of the leased
premises, basing their right to the possession on the
lessee's breach of the above stipulation, a right of forfeiture reserved by the terms of the lease and claimed
under Sections 9 and 14 of the Illinois Landlord and

[a] [2 Ill. Law Rev., 402, January, 1908.]

Tenant Act, and the lessor's assignment of the lease. Judge Brown wanted to rest the judgment of the Appellate Court against the brewing company on the proposition that, under the Illinois Landlord and Tenant Act, the lessor's right of entry for the lessee's breach of the above stipulation did not pass to the brewing company by the lessor's assignment to it of the lease after breach of the stipulation, there being no grant to the brewing company of the lessor's reversion of the leased premises. Judge Brown thought that Sexton v. Chicago Storage Co., 129 Ill., 318, 332–333, supports that proposition, and renders Drew v. Mosbargar, 104 Ill. App., 635, Second D., of no value in point of persuasive force or authority. The other two judges preferred to express no opinion on that proposition[1] and accordingly the judgment of the Court was put upon the proposition stated at the beginning, in which apparently Judge Brown concurred. It will be noticed that the stipulation was made with Michael Allen for the benefit of a third person, Fortune Bros. Brewing Co. But the proposition laid down by the Court went to the root of the case, and rendered that fact of no significance. So the question whether it could be of any significance in the instant action of forcible detainer, or in any action by the brewing company against the lessee, may be laid aside here.

It is very evident from the opinion and the cases relied on — Keppell v. Bailey, 2 My. & K., 517, 535; Schlitz Brewing Co. v. Komp, 118 Ill. App., Second D.; Higbie v. Rust, 112 Ill. App., 218, First D. — that the Court did not get down to the true principles underlying the expression "want of mutuality." That expression, as used

---

[1] The question of the effect, if any, of Secs. 14 and 15 of the Illinois Landlord and Tenant Act, in force July 1, 1873, on 32 Hen. VIII. c. 34, s. 1, as construed by the English Courts, appears to be an open one in this State. See also Note 2, infra.

in the law of specific performance, where it goes to the
remedy for a breach of contract (see Keppell *v.* Bailey
and Schlitz Brewing Co. *v.* Komp, supra) had nothing to
do with the case, for the action was forcible detainer.
"Want of mutuality," as used in the law concerning the
formation of contracts, where it goes to the obligation
or binding force of the contract, is not exactly the same
thing as "want of certainty" in the terms of the contract
(see Higbie *v.* Rust, supra; Anson, Contracts, Huffcut's
Ed., 50, 108, 109; 1 Page, Contracts, Secs. 27, 28).
"Want of mutuality" as an objection to the obligation or
binding force of a contract, the only sense in which the
Court could have used the expression in the case before
it, means want of consideration (1 Page, Contracts, Secs.
302-309; Harriman, Contracts, Sec. 103). The Court does
not say that there was no consideration to support the
stipulation in the lease.[2] The chief reason the Court
gives for saying there was a "want of mutuality" in the
stipulation is that the stipulation did not bind the brewing company to supply its beer to the lessee; in other
words, that the stipulation was unilateral. Obviously,
when the Appellate Court's reason is shaken down to
that, there is nothing to it. "The objection to the
plaintiff's right to recover is, that the contract is unilateral.
I do not, however, understand what objection that is to
a contract. Many contracts are obnoxious to the same

---

[2] The Court does say that the beer clause in the lease "is not a condition subsequent, but an independent covenant of the lessees — a covenant not running
with the land, and which must find its consideration in and rely for support on
something else than the mere demise by the lessor of the leased premises." If
that means that the lessor's demise can be the consideration of only such covenants in the lease as are of a kind that run with the term or with the reversion,
obviously it is not true. It is true, however, that "the statute" (32 Hen. VIII,
ch. 34, in force in illinois, Fisher *v.* Deering, 60 Ill., 114) "applies only to covenants
of a kind that run with the term at common law" (Leake, Digest of the Law of
Contracts, Ed. 1, p. 1211, Hansen *v.* Meyer, 81 Ill., 321) — a very different proposition from the one, supra, laid down by the Appellate Court.

complaint" (Brett, J., in Great Northern R. Co. *v.* Witham, L. R., 9, C. P., 16, 19).

This sort of brewers' stipulation or covenant in a lease has been a familiar one in the English Courts for over one hundred years (see Hartley *v.* Pehall, 1 Peake's N. P. Cases, 131 (1792), and note). In Catt *v.* Tourle, L. R., 4, Ch. Ap., 659 (1869), Selwyn, L. J., said: "Every Court of justice has had occasion to consider these brewers' covenants, and must be taken to be cognizant of the distinction between what are called free public-houses and brewers' public-houses which are subject to this very covenant. We should be introducing very great uncertainty and confusion into a very large and important trade if we were now to suggest any doubt as to the validity of a covenant so extremely common as this is." It is well known that the English invasion of American breweries has made the English practice of tying public-houses or saloons to the brewery by means of this covenant a very common one here. The English Courts hold that this covenant, when found in a brewer's lease, is enforceable by and against transferees of the reversion and of the leased premises at Law and in Equity; in other words, that the burden of the covenant runs with the leased premises at Law and in Equity, and that the benefit of the covenant runs with the reversion. They also hold that the covenant, when found in a sale of premises, may be enforced in Equity against a subsequent purchaser of the premises with notice of the covenant, and that the benefit of the covenant may be enforced in Equity by a subsequent purchaser of the brewery; in other words, that the covenant falls within the doctrine of Tulk *v.* Moxhay, 2 Phillips, 774, approved and adopted in Illinois in Frye *v.* Partridge, 82 Ill., 267, and in numerous later cases. The English Courts also hold that the covenant is conditional on the brewer continuing ready

to supply good beer in quantities sufficient to meet the
wants of the lessee and at reasonable prices. (See Catt
v. Tourle, L. R., 4, Ch. Ap., 654; Clegg v. Hands, 44 Ch. D.,
563; White v. Southend Hotel Co. [1897], 1 Ch. D., 767;
Albergaw Brewing Co. v. Holmes [1900], 1 Ch., 188;
Manchester B. Co. v. Coombs [1901], 2 Ch., 608; Cases
in note to Hartley v. Pehall, supra; Luker v. Dennis, L. R.,
7 Ch. D., 227; Edwick v. Hawkes, L. R., 18, Ch., 199;
and cases cited in the opinions and arguments of counsel.
But see the observations of Lords Macnaghten, Davey,
and Lindley in Noakes v. Rice [1902], A. C., 24, 32, 35,
31. The Supreme Court of Nebraska enforced the
covenant in a lease by injunction in an action by lessor
against lessee. (Schlitz Brewing Co. v. Nielsen, 8 L. R.
A., N. S., 494). The Supreme Court of Indiana enforced
the covenant by injunction at the instance of the brewing
company against the lessee where the covenant was
found in a lease made by a stockholder of the company
as lessor (Ferris v. American Brewing Co., 52 L. R. A.,
305).

The Appellate Court lays it down quite peremptorily
that the covenant cannot "run with the land," repeating
the oft-quoted sentence of Lord Brougham in Keppell v.
Bailey, 2 My. & K., 517, 535: "It must not therefore be
supposed that incidents of a novel kind can be devised
and attached to property at the fancy or caprice of any
owner." Lord Brougham himself was not satisfied that
his sentence applied to this covenant in brewers' leases.
He expressly referred to this covenant on pp. 545–546.
As above stated, the doubt there expressed as to the
capacity of the burden of the covenant to run with the
leased premises has been resolved in England in favor of
the running of the burden.

The mere fact that this beer covenant may forbid the
use of land in competition with another, cannot in Illinois

bring it within Lord Brougham's "incidents of a novel kind." See Frye *v.* Partridge, 82 Ill., 267; Wakefield *v.* Van Tassell, 202 Ill., 41. It may be added that Tulk *v.* Moxhay, supra, and subsequent cases have overruled a part of Lord Brougham's opinion in Keppell *v.* Bailey. See Leake, Digest of the Law of Contracts, Ed. 1, p. 1209, note c; Luker *v.* Dennis, L. R., 7 Ch. D., 227, 235–237, Fry, J.; and that Lord Brougham's views on "want of mutuality" on pp. 530–551 of Keppell *v.* Bailey are against the Appellate Court and in harmony with later English decisions. See 2 Ill. Law Rev., 218–219.

The Appellate Court relied on Schlitz Brewing Co. *v.* Komp, 118 Ill. App., 566, Second D. There the owner of a saloon borrowed money from the brewing company, giving a mortgage of the saloon premises as security. By the terms of the mortgage the borrower was to repay the money in five years, or at any time before. The brewer's covenant to sell only the brewer's beer during the five years was inserted. The borrower paid the loan before the end of the five years. He then stopped selling the brewing company's beer, and began selling other beer. An injunction against the borrower forbidding him to sell other beer was refused on the authority of the phrase "want of mutuality." That is clearly not a good reason for the judgment (see Catt *v.* Tourle, L. R., 4 Ch. Ap., 659; 2 Ill. Law Rev., 218-219). In England, in 1898, the point made against this covenant in a mortgage was that, though valid so long as the debt remained unpaid, yet on payment of the debt the borrower was released from its binding force, because it then became an unpermissible "clog on the equity of redemption." All of the English Courts up to, and including, the House of Lords held the point good. See Rice *v.* Noakes & Co. [1900], 1 Ch., 213; [1900] 2 Ch., 445; [1902] A. C., 24. That would support the decision of the Appellate

Court for the Second District in Schlitz Brewing Co. v. Komp, in which case no such point was made.[3] In Rice v. Noakes the old but long dormant doctrine of clogging the equity of redemption was revived in England in a most brilliant manner. See the English cases before and since Rice v. Noakes in Wyman's Cases on Mortgages, Ed. 2, 323–349; Pomeroy's Eq. Jur., Ed. 3, Sec. 1193, and notes.

A point local to Illinois may be noticed. Does this brewer's covenant encounter the Illinois Anti-Option Act?

The fundamental principles applied by the English Courts in the above cases arising on this brewer's covenant unquestionably are a part of the law of Illinois. While Illinois Courts are not bound to follow these English decisions, yet it does seem that a refusal by an Illinois Court to follow them ought to be supported by reasons showing why the English Courts made either a wrong application of principles, or an application not suited to our conditions.

3. — MUTUALITY — EFFECT OF A POWER TO TERMINATE THE CONTRACT.[a] — In Watford Oil and Gas Co. v. Shipman, 233 Ill., 9, Vickers, J., the Supreme Court adopts the proposition that a power to terminate the contract existing in the party seeking the remedy of specific performance, but not in the party resisting that remedy, constitutes of itself an absolute bar to relief. There is probably only one decision to support that proposition, viz.: Rust v. Conrad, 47 Mich. 449, Cooley, J., overruled by the Michigan Legislature. See Grummett v. Gingrass, 77 Mich., 369; 3 Col. Law Rev., 10–11. But there are numerous dicta in decided cases seemingly in accord with

[3] I am indebted to my colleague, Mr. Pound, for this view of Schlitz Brewing Co. v. Komp.

[a] [3 Ill. Law Rev., 43, May, 1908.]

this Illinois decision. Singer Sewing Machine Co. *v.* Union Buttonhole and Embroidery Co., Holmes, 253, Fed. Cas. No. 12904, Lowell, J., and Philadelphia Baseball Club *v.* Lajoie, 202 Pa. St., 210, examine and expressly reject the proposition. With the last case compare the opinion of Dallas J., in Brooklyn Baseball Club *v.* McGuire, 116 Fed. Rep., 728. Franklin Tel. Co. *v.* Harrison, 145 U. S., 459, Brewster *v.* Lanyon Zinc Co., 140 Fed., 801, and St. Joseph Hydraulic Co. *v.* Globe Tissue Paper Co., 156 Ind., 665, 672–673, appear to be against the proposition. None of these cases are referred to by the Illinois Court.[4] In common with Cooley, J., in Rust *v.* Conrad, 47 Mich., 449, and the authors of the dicta above mentioned, the Illinois Court bases the proposition entirely upon Marble Co. *v.* Ripley, 10 Wallace, 339, and Express Co. *v.* Railroad Co., 99 U. S., 191, and especially upon the latter, the Illinois Court quoting a portion of the opinion of Swayne, J. In that case it was the defendant who had the power to terminate the contract. In pronouncing the judgment of the Court refusing the plaintiff the remedy of specific performance, Swayne, J., said that "a court of equity never interferes where the power of revocation exists," because the power may be exercised immediately upon the rendition of the decree, and "the action of the court will thus become a nullity." As above stated, Swayne, J., applied that principle to a case where the "power of revocation" was in the defendant, and evidently because it was in the defendant. That is the only sort of a case the learned Justice had in mind. As authority for the principle applied, he cites Fry, Specific Performance, Ed. 1, p. 64, Sec. 43 et seq., Ed. 2, p. 37, Sec. 72 et seq. Mr. Fry there states the principle, and the words of Swayne, J.,

---

[4] They are cited in Rose's Notes under Marble Co. *v.* Ripley, 10 Wallace, 339; and Express Co. *v.* Railroad Co., 99 U. S., 191.

are substantially the words of Mr. Fry. But Mr. Fry
confines the principle to cases where either the defendant
alone, or the plaintiff and the defendant, each separately,
has the power of revocation. This is evident from the
decided cases cited by Mr. Fry to illustrate the principle,
and from which he extracted the principle. And in
Sec. 47, Ed. 1, Sec. 75, Ed. 2, Mr. Fry expressly says:
"It is on the same reasoning that the court declines to
perform an agreement, if such covenants must be introduced into the instrument to be executed that *the party
resisting the performance* may immediately take advantage of them to deprive the other of all benefit under the
instrument; as, for example, an agreement for a lease
which is to contain a proviso for re-entry on breach of a
covenant, *which the plaintiff had already broken.*" (Italics
mine.) See Brewster *v.* Lanyon Zinc Co., 140 Fed. Rep.,
801, 812, C. C. A. 8th C.[5]

In the case before the Illinois Court the plaintiff only
had the power of revocation, and the defendant did not
have it. The rule, as stated and applied by Swayne, J.,
and Mr. Fry, was not necessarily applicable, and obviously the reason of the rule was quite inapplicable, for a
defendant can have no very good ground of complaint
because the plaintiff sees fit to let go of a decree in his
own favor, and what a plaintiff does with a decree in his
own favor cannot concern the Court ordinarily. And so,
in order to make use of the rule as stated by Swayne, J. —
"A court of equity never interferes where the power of
revocation exists" — in a case where the party seeking
specific performance has the power of revocation and

---

[5] The Illinois Court cites Page, Contracts, Sec. 1619. Mr. Page plainly suggests, if he does not state, a difference as respects specific performance between
(1) the case where the power of revocation is in the party resisting specific performance, and (2) the case where the power of revocation is in the party seeking
specific performance and is not in his adversary.

the party resisting specific performance has no such power, as a reason for denying to the plaintiff the remedy of specific performance, some other principle in the law of specific performance must be brought into play. In Marble Co. *v.* Ripley, 10 Wallace, 339, 359, the other case relied on by the Illinois Court, Strong, J., brought in the principle of mutuality in specific performance in a statement not necessary to support the judgment of the Court. There the party seeking specific performance (Ripley) had a reserved power of revocation, and the party resisting specific performance (the Marble Company) did not.

The contract before the Illinois Court was an oil lease, reserving to the lessee the right to terminate the lease at will. The lessor made a subsequent lease to other people, who apparently took with notice of the prior lease. The lessee under the first lease was seeking equitable relief against his lessor and his lessor's subsequent lessees with notice.[6] In Poe *v.* Ulrey, 233 Ill., 56, 63–64, Cartwright, J., it is said that such reserved power by the lessee in an oil lease does not of itself make the bargain a hard one as against the lessor. In connection with other provisions and surrounding circumstances such reserved power may have that effect. And of course a lessee with such reserved power must show, and be held to, a strict and prompt performance of his side of the lease. See Federal Oil Co. *v.* Western Oil Co., 121 Fed. Rep., 674, C. C. A., 7th C.; Brewster *v.* Lanyon Zinc Co., 140 Fed. Rep., 801, C. C. A., 8th C.; Eclipse Oil Co. *v.* South Penn Oil Co., 47 W. Va., 84. So far as the rule of mutuality in

[6] Plaintiff's lessor was one of three tenants in common, and also had a life estate in the premises. Plaintiff's lessor joined with the other two co-tenants in making the subsequent lease complained of. The plaintiff's somewhat peculiar prayer for partition was rejected. The whole of the rest of the case was controlled by the effect given to the reserved power to terminate.

specific performance is concerned, the books abound with
instances of decrees of specific performance, affirmative
and negative by way of injunction, in favor of a party to
a contract against whom no decree of specific performance
could go if he refused to perform his side of the contract.
The self-interest of the lessee in the usual fair and reasonable oil lease would appear to be enough to insure performance by him of his side of the lease. If the lessee
does not perform his side, the lessor at once would be
released from the contract and from any decree outstanding against him (Wood, V. C., quoted in 2 Ill. Law Rev.,
218–219).[7]   It is difficult to find in authority or in reason
any equity to resist specific performance arising in favor
of the lessor exclusively out of the lessee's reserved power
to terminate the lease. "The surrender clause" does
"not give to the lessors any option to compel a surrender."
(Cartwright, J., in Poe v. Ulrey, 233 Ill., 56, 64).   However, there is the decision that the lessor may lay hold
of the clause and with it alone drive the lessee to the
remedy of damages — which is no remedy at all in such
a case.   But one is justified in thinking and advising with
some confidence that the opinion of Lowell, J., in Singer
Sewing Machine Co. v. Union Buttonhole and Embroidery
Co., supra, correctly expresses the law of the Federal
Courts, viz.: A power to terminate existing only in the
party seeking the remedy of specific performance is not
enough to cut him off from that remedy, and to remit
him to the remedy of damages.   "I cannot think that the
(Supreme) Court (of the United States, in Marble Co. v.
Ripley, supra) intended to announce any general proposition that they would never enforce (specifically) a contract which one party (the plaintiff) had a right to put

[7] "The operator (i. e., the lessee in an oil lease) must have a fair chance to
perform his contract." — Hadley, J., in New Sun Oil Co. v. Wolff (Ind.), 76 N. E.
Rep., 253, 255.

an end to in a year. Everything must depend upon the nature and circumstances of the business." — Lowell, J., in the Singer Company's case, supra. And see Mutuality in Specific Performance, Ames, 3 Col. Law Rev., 1, wherein the inadequacy of Mr. Fry's statement of the rule of mutuality, applied by Mr. Justice Shay in Marble Company v. Ripley, supra, is shown.

4. — MUTUALITY — OIL AND GAS LEASE AS AN EXECUTED CONTRACT OR GRANT.[a] — In Ulrey v. Keith, 237 Ill., 284, 86 N. E. Rep., 696, Farmer, J., Watford Oil and Gas Co. v. Shipman, 233 Ill., 56, 84 N. E. Rep., 46, Vickers, J., was opened up and reargued, and, as a result of a re-examination of that case, the Court reaffirmed the ruling that the lessee's surrender clause in an oil and gas lease constitutes, of itself, a bar to the remedy of specific performance by lessee against lessor for an injunction to prevent an eviction of the lessee by the lessor. The ground of the ruling is that the surrender clause is a bar to the remedy of specific performance by lessor against lessee, because no decree of specific performance can go against a defendant who has a power to put an end to the contract (see 4 Pomeroy, Eq. Jur., Ed. 3, Sec. 1405, note 8 on p. 2771; 3 Ill. Law Rev., 43 [ante p. 782]), and, since the lessor cannot have the remedy of specific performance against the lessee, therefore, under the rule of mutuality in specific performance, the lessee cannot have that remedy against the lessor.[8]

The opinion contains the most extended exposition of the rule of mutuality in specific performance that has appeared in the Illinois reports. It declares the general rule more sweepingly, and applies it more literally, than

[a] [3 Ill. Law Rev., 601, April, 1909.]

[8] The word "lease" is a misnomer, for the instrument creates no tenancy, as appears hereinafter. But see Gillespie v. Fulton Oil and Gas Co., 236 Ill., 188, 206.

any previous opinion of the Court, except that in Gage
v. Cummings, 209 Ill., 120, which is not cited, was quickly
qualified, and perhaps may be regarded as overruled.
See Gibson *v.* Brown, 214 Ill., 330; Kuhn *v.* Eppstein,
219 Ill., 154; and see Mason *v.* Caldwell, 10 Ill., 196, 208,
209.   The opinion in Gage *v.* Cummings proceeds on
the footing that the requisite mutuality must be found
at "the time it (the contract) was entered into," while
this opinion fixes the date at "the time of the filing of
the bill in equity."[9]   The opinion shifts the Court's
authority for a correct statement of the general rule of
mutuality from Mr., now Lord, Fry on Specific Performance (see Lancaster *v.* Roberts, 144 Ill., 213; Gage *v.*
Cummings, 209 Ill., 120; Kuhn *v.* Eppstein, 219 Ill.,
154) to Mr. Pomeroy on Equitable Remedies, published
as volumes five and six of the third edition of Pomeroy's
Equity Jurisprudence, but written by the able and
learned son of the author of that work, and gives no
reason for the shift, though Mr. Pomeroy's rule differs
from Mr. Fry's.   Mr. Pomeroy gives as his reason for
attempting to restate the rule the fact that the rule as
stated by Mr. Fry "is open to so many exceptions that

---

[9] In Gage *v.* Cummings, the plaintiff agreed to exchange land, the title to a
part of which was in his wife, she not being a party to, or bound by, the contract.
She did, however, execute deeds of conveyance to the defendant, and the deeds
were tendered.   She was also a party plaintiff in the bill.   Specific performance
was refused, because the defendant could not have that remedy against the
plaintiffs.   The opinion rejected the leading case of Dresel *v.* Jordan, 104 Mass.,
407, but the case was taken up again in Gibson *v.* Brown, 214 Ill., 330.   The
decision in Gage *v.* Cummings is not sustainable, except possibly under a line of
English decisions holding that, under some circumstances, a vendee may repudiate
a contract for the sale of land, if he acts promptly and decisively as soon as he
finds that the vendor has no title.   See "Specific Performance of Contracts,
Perfecting Title After Suit Has Begun," Lewis, 50 Am. Law Reg., 522.   On p.
535 the author says: "I have been unable to find American cases discussing the
question of the right of the vendee to terminate the contract if he finds his vendor
has no title."   As sales of land are conducted ordinarily in Illinois, the question
cannot fairly come up.   And see cases in 1 Cases in Eq. Jur., Ames, 199, 200,
note 2.

it is of little value as a rule." Mr. Pomeroy gives four exceptions to his rule. Professor Ames previously had shown eight exceptions to Mr. Fry's rule (see 3 Col. Law Rev., 1). In Section 774, Mr. Pomeroy plainly shows that he does not regard his rule as capable of being applied to these Illinois oil and gas lease cases, regarding the leases as executory bilateral contracts. In Gibson *v.* Brown, 214 Ill., 330, 335, Mr. Justice Hand says: "The general rule thus announced (by Mr. Fry), however, like most general rules, has its exceptions." In Blanton *v.* Kentucky Distilleries and Warehouse Co., 120 Fed. Rep., 318, 351, affirmed in 149 Fed. Rep., 31, Judge Cochran quotes statements by Professors Pomeroy, Parsons, and Langdell pronouncing the rule artificial and hard to understand. I do not know of an instance where an English court has adopted Mr. Fry's general rule, or has attempted to formulate a general rule. But nearly all, if not all, American courts have taken up Mr. Fry's general rule, and, apparently, have swallowed it whole, without first testing it by the decided cases, and applied it literally. Professor Ames, however, has pointed out that American courts do not, except very rarely, in point of fact, in coming to their decisions, act on the general rule as they state it, and Mr. Pomeroy says the same thing. (2 Pomeroy's Eq. Rem., Sec. 769, note 31.) And Professor Ames expresses the hope that the whole doctrine will be judicially re-examined and rewritten, and gives us by far the best and simplest analysis and proposed restatement of the doctrine that has appeared in print. See " Mutuality in Specific Performance," 3 Col. Law Rev., 1. When the highest Court of a State decides that the lessor in an oil and gas lease having the legal effect of an executed grant of a freehold estate may use the rule of mutuality in specific performance as a weapon to make the lessee part with his property at a price to be fixed by a jury, by the method of ejecting the lessee from the premises vi et armis, that Court does the service, at least, of forcing the profession in that State to look into the rule to see whether it really is Rob Roy's "good old rule, the simple plan, that he may take who has the power, and he may keep who can," concealed behind the mask of a fetching arrangement of words.

The failure of the Court to observe the difference between (1) a bill for the "specific performance" of an executory contract to make a lease, or other deed of conveyance of property, and (2) a bill of "specific performance" to protect property, and enforce in specie contractual rights under the lease or deed of conveyance when made, so lucidly pointed out by Lord Selborne in Wolverhampton and Walsall Ry. Co. *v.* London and North Western Ry. Co., L. R., 16 Eq., 433, is the first proximate cause why the Court fell into a mischievous error of law in these oil and gas lease specific performance cases.

The bill before the Court was not the same as the bill in Rust *v.* Conrad, 47 Mich., 449, Cooley, J., cited by the Court, which was a bill to compel a landowner to specifically perform an executory contract to make an iron ore mining lease. The oil and gas lease had already been made before the bill was filed. In legal effect, the oil and gas lease made was not a mere executory contract giving the lessee a mere personal privilege of exploring the lands of the lessor for oil and gas; nor was it a mere executory contract for the purchase and sale of chattels — oil and gas when extracted from the earth; nor was the lease revocable at the will of the lessor. Under Illinois decisions, nearly contemporaneous with the decisions in these specific performance cases, an oil and gas lease, in terms and substance like that involved in these cases, is a grant of a freehold estate in real property.[10]

Under these decisions as to the legal effect of an oil and gas lease, these specific performance cases differed in no essential particular related to the point of equity jurisdiction to grant an injunction to prevent a forcible eviction of the lessee by the lessor from the case of Lynch *v.* Union Inst. for Savings, 158 Mass., 395, where a lessee of land refused to move off, and refused to come to the

[10] In Poe *v.* Ulrey, 233 Ill., 56, 62, where an oil and gas lease is set out in full, Ohio Oil Co. *v.* Indiana, 177 U. S., 190, is relied on, where oil and gas are spoken of as "minerals ferae naturae." As to a landowner's property in animals fera naturae, see Geer *v.* Connecticut, 161 U. S., 519. New York *v.* Hesterberg, 211 U. S., 31. These cases discuss the power of a State Legislature to deal with a landowner's property in oil and gas and animals ferae naturae. In Schulte *v.* Warren, 218 Ill., 108, it was held that a landowner has an exclusive right to hunt and fish within the limits of his land. That a landowner's right to explore, drill and operate for oil and gas within the limits of his land is exclusive is plain. The Supreme Court says an oil and gas lease is "a grant of such oil and gas as the grantee may find, and he is not vested with any estate in the oil or gas until it is actually found," and gives "to the lessee the right to operate on the premises, to enter upon them at all times for the purpose of drilling and operating, to erect and maintain all necessary buildings and structures, and to lay pipes necessary for the production and transportation of oil and gas," and is, therefore, "a conveyance of an interest in the homestead estate," and "is a freehold interest." Poe *v.* Ulrey, 233 Ill., 56, 62, Bruner *v.* Hicks, 230 Ill., 536, Watford Oil and Gas Co. *v.* Shipman, 233 Ill., 9, 12, 13. The right granted is expressed in the lease to be "exclusive," and is taxable as real property owned by the lessee, separate from the land owned by the lessor, under the denomination "mineral right" in an Act passed in 1861, now Hurd's R. S., 1905, p. 1399, People *v.* Bell, 237 Ill., 332, 86 N. E. Rep., 593, where Carter, J., says: "Manifestly the mining right created by this lease is property and should be taxed. . . . The Court has held, under provisions in a lease substantially like this, that it conveyed a freehold interest. Bruner *v.* Hicks, 230 Ill., 536, Poe *v.* Ulrey, supra. . . . Whatever may have been decided in other jurisdictions, it is clear under the decisions in this State that this lease conveys such a mining right in the land here in question that it can be properly taxed separately, and that as it involves a freehold it should be assessed as real property" of the lessee. In Ziegler *v.* Brenneman, 86 N. E. Rep., 597, it was held that an oil and gas lease made by a tenant in common to a stranger is void as against his co-tenants, but valid between the parties even while the premises remain undivided, just as in the case of a like grant of the land itself. The statute of 1861 at the basis of the tax case of The People *v.* Bell, supra, is not a revenue statute merely, but is primarily a conveyancing statute, only declaratory of the law as announced in 1849 in Woodward *v.* Seeley, 11 Ill.,

terms of the lessor, who wanted to put up a building on the land, and threatened to eject the lessee completely. Mr. Justice Holmes went to the root of the case thus:

"The result of denying the injunction is 'to allow the wrong-doer to compel innocent persons to sell their right at a valuation.' " . . . The defendant "simply is dispossessing or trying to dispossess a man of his land by willful wrong, and its argument that it should not be restrained in proceeding must be that it can make more money out of the plaintiff's property than the plaintiff can, if it is allowed to take it."

The only merit claimed for the decision in Ulrey *v.* Keith is the merit of implicit passive judicial obedience to local judicial precedent.[11] But the opinion does not give the name, book, and page of the precedent. It does,

159, and ever since adhered to. Entwhistle *v.* Henke, 211 Ill., 273, and cases cited on p. 279; McIntyre *v.* Harty, 236 Ill., 629. In Poe *v.* Ulrey, supra, on p. 64, the question whether the lessor in an oil and gas lease may revoke the lease before the lessee has done anything under it was noticed, and left open. Under Manning *v.* Frazier, 96 Ill., 279 (and see the uses made of this case in McConnell *v.* Pierce, 176 Ill., 627, 635, and in Catlin Coal Co. *v.* Lloyd, 210 Ill., 275, 282-3), the true consideration of the grant made by the oil and gas lease in Poe *v.* Ulrey, supra, would appear to be, not the $1 and the seal, as was argued in Poe *v.* Ulrey, supra, on pp. 62-3, but the covenants of the lessee to pay $100 for the gas produced at each gas well, and to give the lessor one-eighth of the oil produced and saved. See Gillespie *v.* Fulton Oil and Gas Co., 236 Ill., 188, 200. Cortelyou *v.* Barnsdall, 236 Ill., 138, wherein an oil and gas lease was rescinded at the suit of the lessor, does not fit in easily with the decisions, unless you can say it really was decided on the ground of fraud of the lessee in getting the lease. See Gillespie *v.* Fulton Oil & Gas Co., 236 Ill., 188. Compare the legal effect given to the Indiana oil and gas lease in Federal Oil Co. *v.* Western Oil Co., 112 Fed. Rep., 373, Baker, J., affirmed in 121 Fed. Rep., 674, Jenkins and Grosscup, JJ., and note the views expressed on, and use made of, "mutuality." See the observations on this case in 2 Pomeroy's Equitable Remedies, Section 773, p. 1298.

[11] A considerable part of the opinion in Ulrey *v.* Keith is devoted to proving that the bill before the Court fell under the general head of equity jurisdiction known as the specific performance of contracts. The decision that the bill was so classifiable cannot be doubted or questioned. But before dismissing the bill for want of jurisdiction under the head of specific performance, the question whether the bill did not present a case under the jurisdiction of equity to prevent the doing of tortious acts destructive of the plaintiff's property ought to have been considered. In Schulte *v.* Warren, 218 Ill., 108, the Court had no difficulty about the jurisdiction of equity to prevent tortious acts in disturbance

however, cite two cases to the point that the bill was a bill
for the specific performance of a contract, which prove
that the Court had jurisdiction, and that the rule of
mutuality had nothing whatever to do with the case.   The
cases are Chicago Municipal Gas Light Co. *v.* Town of
Lake, 130 Ill., 42, and East St. Louis Railway Co. *v.*
East St. Louis, 182 Ill., 433.   It is plain that a municipality cannot by a bill in equity for specific performance
compel a gas company to construct the gas plant contemplated by the terms of an ordinance ·operating as an
executed contract, or grant, of the right to use streets.
And it is equally or more plain that a municipality
cannot by a bill in equity for specific performance compel
a street railroad company to build the street railroad
contemplated by the terms of an ordinance operating as
an executed contract, or grant, of the right to use streets.
(Texas & Pacific Ry. *v.* Marshall, 136 U. S., 393; Peto *v.*
Tunbridge Wells R. Co., 1 H. & M., 468; Suburban Construction Co. *v.* Naugle, 70 Ill. App., 384; 26 Am. & Eng.
Ency. of Law, Ed. 2, 93.)   But no one has ever thought
that, therefore, the gas company, or the street railroad
company, cannot by a bill in equity prevent the municipality from evicting it out of the streets completely vi et
armis.   The bills in the above cases were bills of that kind,
though the injunctions prayed were denied, because the
plaintiff companies had been guilty of default, or laches,

---

of a man's exclusive property right to hunt and fish within the limits of his own
land.   And in Bruner *v.* Hicks, 230 Ill., 536, an injunction issued to prevent the
lessee in an oil and gas lease from disturbing the lessor's homestead estate.   And
see Espenscheid *v.* Bauer, 235 Ill., 172; Cragg *v.* Levinson, 238 Ill., 69; McGuire
v. Boyd Coal & Coke Co., 236 Ill., 69.   Gillespie *v.* Fulton Oil & Gas Co., 236
Ill., 188, decided less than two months before Ulrey *v.* Keith, appears to rule
exactly that the bill in Ulrey *v.* Keith should have been retained as a bill to prevent tortious acts.   The jurisdiction of Equity ex contractu is much more ancient
than most of its jurisdiction ex delicto, and a bill like that in Ulrey *v.* Keith may
be regarded now as sounding in contract or in tort according as the one basis
or the other will lengthen and strengthen the arm of the Chancellor to do justice.

about the work of building the gas plant in the one case, and the street railroad in the other.

In Leavers v. Cleary, 75 Ill., 349, and Consolidated Coal Co. v. Schmisseur, 135 Ill., 371, bills ex contractu by "lessors" in coal mining leases to prevent breaches of express or implied covenants in the leases were entertained. In Willoughby v. Lawrence, 116 Ill., 11, a bill ex contractu by the lessee or grantee or licensee of the right to erect and operate billboards on the defendant's land to enjoin a breach of the contract was entertained. In Postal Telegraph Co. v. Western Union Co., 155 Ill., 335, a bill by a lessee to enjoin a breach of the lease by the lessor was entertained. And see the briefs in this case. In all of these cases, the point of mutuality, as expounded in Ulrey v. Keith, was fatal, if it was applicable, but it was not raised or mentioned. And the contract involved in Wiggins Ferry Co. v. O. M. R. Co., 94 Ill., 83, plainly was enforceable by injunction in favor of the Ferry Company (see L. & N. R. Co. v. I. C. R. R. Co., 174 Ill., 448; Wiggins Ferry Co., v. O. & M. R. Co., 142 U. S., 396; Wolverhampton & W. R. Co. v. London & N. W. R. Co., L. R. 16 Eq. Cas., 433), though more plainly it was not enforceable specifically against the Ferry Company. (De Mattos v. Gibson, 4 De Gex & Jones, 276.)

What was the contract sought to be enforced specifically by injunction in these oil and gas lease cases? The Court does not attempt to define it. Plainly, it was not the whole of the lease in all its parts, but only a part of it, namely: The covenant for quiet enjoyment, either expressed by the word "grant" in the lease, under Hurd's R. S., 1905, p. 464, Sec. 8, or implied from all the terms of the lease and the relations to the subject-matter of the lease established and defined by its terms. For the purpose of enforcing it specifically by enjoining its breach by the lessor at the instance of the lessee, the covenant for quiet enjoyment is a divisible, separable covenant, and may be seized upon, extricated from the lease, and dealt with as a contract standing by itself. So seized, extricated, and dealt with, it is a unilateral executory promise. The tenendum clause of the lease (233 Ill., 58) reads: "To have and to hold for the term of five years,[12] and as much longer as oil and gas is found in paying quantities . . . on the following conditions," etc. In point of form, there is no promise by the lessee to explore, drill, pipe, and operate diligently for oil and gas, but only a condition, or conditions, the purpose of which is "to qualify and debase the purity of the donation," and reduce it to a qualified or base fee. "It is true the estate may not endure forever; it may be terminated by the (lessee's) failure to use and employ the rights and easements granted in the manner prescribed in the grant; but if they shall be so used and employed the grant is forever." See Wiggins Ferry Co. v. O. & M. R. Co., 94 Ill., 83, 93. Manifestly, then, so long as the lessee is using and employing the rights and easements granted in the manner prescribed in the grant, that is to say, so long as he is, actually, visibly, and diligently, exploring, drilling, piping, and operating for oil and gas, he is entitled to have the lessor keep his covenant for quiet enjoyment. That

---

[12] The bill for specific performance was filed before the expiration of the five years, but no point was made upon that. In the tax case of People v. Bell, supra, State v. South Penn. Oil Co., 42 W. Va., 84, 102, a tax case, was rejected. The West Virginia Court there took the point that the "lease" was executory until oil or gas was found in paying quantities, when it would become a grant or conveyance. And see the specific performance cases of Eclipse Oil Co. v. South Penn. Oil Co., 47 W. Va., 84, Federal Oil Co. v. Western Oil Co., supra. The doctrine of the Illinois Court appears to be that the estate vests in the lessee immediately on the execution of the lease, for purposes of taxation and for the purpose of affecting the homestead. Perhaps it is possible to say that the lease is "executory" until oil is found, for purposes of specific performance. But the Court has not said that, and I can't see how the distinction can be drawn. See note 10 supra.

covenant inheres in the property granted; in a sense, it is
the property granted, for it is the main prop, support, and
security of that property. The lessee has a right, therefore, to enforce that covenant specifically by an injunction forbidding the lessor to break it. All those cases,
familiar to everyone, of bills for injunctions by lessor
against lessee, and by lessee against lessor, to protect
rights growing out of the lease (1 Spelling Inj. & Extr.
Rem., Ed. 2, Secs. 498-501), and those cases between
vendor and vendee to specifically enforce restrictions on
the use of land, beginning in this State with Frye *v.*
Partridge, 82 Ill., 267, are applicable and controlling on
the point of jurisdiction, and prove beyond a doubt that
the Courts of Illinois have jurisdiction ex contractu in
these oil and gas lease cases to issue injunctions to prevent wrongful evictions of the lessees by their lessors;
that the remedy of damages is not the only remedy an
evicted lessee may avail himself of; and that in such
case the rule of mutuality is an inapplicable, negligible
thing.

Whether the lessee's surrender clause puts anything
into the lease, regarded as a grant, that would not be
implied, may be doubted. However that may be, the
expressed reservation by the lessee of the right to surrender the premises to the lessor cannot defeat the jurisdiction of equity to protect the lessee in the ownership,
exercise, and enjoyment of his rights, so long as he does
not choose to surrender them up to the lessor. To affirm
that it does, is to affirm that because A may give his
property to B whenever he (A) wants to, therefore B
may go and help himself to it against the will of A.
Where the jurisdiction of equity in specific performance is
invoked to protect property vested under a grant, and
having an existence apart from the grant, the power to
revoke the grant does not always defeat the jurisdiction,

even when the power of revocation is in the defendant. The partnership cases prove that. See Marble Co. *v.* Ripley, 10 Wallace, 339, 350, 351; and see Joy *v.* St. Louis, 138 U. S., 1, 50; Monongahela Nav. Co. *v.* United States, 148 U. S., 312, 343, 344; Willoughby *v.* Lawrence, 116 Ill., 11, 14, 21, 22. And see Fry, Specific Performance, Ed. 3, Secs. 824, 825.

The default or laches of the lessee in diligently exploring, drilling, piping, and operating for oil and gas, though falling short of such default or laches as would work a complete forfeiture of his rights under the lease, would defeat his right to the remedy of specific performance to enjoin his eviction by the lessor, under Chicago Municipal Gas Light Co. *v.* Town of Lake, supra. But it would not, I think, be in accordance with the injunction to "judge the people with equity" to use the surrender clause as a reason for holding the lessee to that degree of strictness in complying with the terms of the lease that is permissible when the holder of an executory option is seeking to bring himself within its terms, as in Estes *v.* Furlong, 59 Ill., 298, 308. That case shows that the rule of diligence bends to circumstances even in the case of executory options. That it bends more in cases like these oil and gas lease cases is shown and stated in I. C. R. Co. *v.* L. & N. R. Co., 174 Ill., 448, 458.

If the Legislature should pass a statute, singling out lessees in oil and gas leases as a class, shutting them off from the remedy of specific performance by injunction to protect themselves in the ownership and quiet enjoyment of their property as against their lessors, and confining them to the remedy of damages for the redress of wrongful evictions by their lessors, it could not be doubted for a moment that the Legislature would thereby do a thing that would encounter the prohibition in the Constitution of the United States — "Nor shall any State . . .

deny to any person within its jurisdiction the equal
protection of the laws." (Ex parte Young, 209 U. S.,
123, 145-8.) When the Supreme Court enacts identically
the same law in substance and in fact, though disguised
under a form of words, it thereby brings the State into
collision with that prohibition, for the act of the highest
Court of the State is the act of the State, just as truly
as the act of the Legislature is the act of the State. The
decision in Ulrey v. Keith is not res judicata as to the
property of the plaintiff lessee. It leaves his property in
him, untouched. It simply deprives him of a certain
remedy for the security and protection of his property.
The State declines, even refuses, to protect it, though
taxing it. The plaintiff lessee in Ulrey v. Keith may,
therefore, file another bill for an injunction in a State
Court, or in a Federal Court, I think, challenging the
decision and rule in Ulrey v. Keith as unconstitutional
and void, just as one may challenge on the face of a bill in
equity the constitutionality of an Act of the Legislature
saying the same thing that this decision says, and having
the same practical operation and effect.

5. — MUTUALITY — OIL AND GAS LEASE AS AN EXECUTORY
CONTRACT.[a] — Let us suppose the oil and gas lease in
Ulrey v. Keith, 237 Ill., 284, divested of its legal effect
as a grant of real property, corporeal or incorporeal, and,
treating it as purely personal executory contract, as the
Court appears to have done, and as the Federal Courts
for this Circuit treated the Indiana oil and gas lease in
Federal Oil Co. v. Western Oil Co., 112 Fed. Rep., 373,
121 Fed. Rep., 674, inquire how far the rule of mutuality
would apply in a suit for its specific performance by lessee
against lessor. The promise of the lessor is to allow
his premises to be used by the lessee for the purpose of

---

[a] [3 Ill. Law Rev., 608, April, 1909.]

exploring, drilling, piping, and operating for oil and gas. On the lessee's side, the surrender clause makes the contract unilateral, in point of performance, at least; the lessee may operate for oil and gas or not at his option, as suits his own convenience and profit. That a contract is unilateral is, of course, no objection to its validity, and, in itself, is no objection to its enforcement in specie. If there is no other objection to the specific performance of a unilateral contract, the rule of mutuality is idle and dumb as an objection, because the rule of mutuality has no application in suits for the specific performance of unilateral contracts. Perkins *v.* Hadsell, 50 Ill., 216; Adams *v.* Peabody Coal Co., 230 Ill., 469; Oswald *v.* Nehls, 233 Ill., 438, 445; 2 Pomeroy's Eq. Rem., Sec. 773; Ames, 3 Col. Law Rev., 9, 10.[13]

---

[13] It is true that Adams *v.* Peabody Coal Co. was put upon the footing of the usual option, where an acceptance gives rise to a bilateral contract of sale. But this seems to have been an oversight, as the terms of the option on p. 470 show the contract was unilateral throughout, and so within the reasoning in Perkins *v.* Hadsell, 50 Ill., 216, 219, where Lawrence, J., exposes the fallacy of "mutuality in a unilateral contract." Perkins *v.* Hadsell was cited by counsel in opposition to the mutuality point adopted by Cooley, J., in Rust *v.* Conrad, 47 Mich., 449, 450, cited in Ulrey *v.* Keith. It is against the reasoning of Judge Cooley in Rust *v.* Conrad and contains better reasoning than Judge Cooley's opinion. Bauer *v.* Lumaghi Coal Co., 209 Ill., 316, the principal local precedent relied on in Ulrey *v.* Keith to show the condition of the law of this State on the rule of mutuality, cannot be regarded otherwise than as wrong, in so far as it rests on the rule of mutuality, as the contract there was unilateral. The earlier case of Perkins *v.* Hadsell, supra, was overlooked, and the later case of Adams *v.* Peabody Coal Co., supra, is against it. Besides, as an authority on the rule of mutuality, Bauer *v.* Lumaghi Coal Co., is rendered worthless because of its reliance upon Beard *v.* Linthicum, 1 Md., Ch. 345, and Duvall *v.* Myers, 1 Md., Ch. 401, wherein Chancellor Johnson, following the well-known, and long since overruled, opinions of Lord Redesdale and Chancellor Kent, held that, for want of mutuality, a party who has not signed a contract within the Statute of Frauds cannot enforce it specifically against a party who has signed it, because the law on that point has been the other way in this State since the decision in Johnson *v.* Dodge, 17 Ill., 271, where the point first arose, the Court saying in Farwell *v.* Lowther, 18 Ill., 252, 255, that the contrary opinion of Lord Redesdale "has been repeatedly overruled." And see Ullsperger *v.* Meyer, 217 Ill., 262; Furthman *v.* Deters, 206 Ill., 159. And yet in Ulrey *v.* Keith the Court not only quotes the passage in Bauer *v.* Lumaghi Coal Co., taken from the previous case of Tryce *v.* Dittus,

Now let us suppose the lessee's surrender clause stricken out of the lease. It then stands as a bilateral executory contract, the promise of the lessee being to explore, drill, pipe, and operate them for oil and gas, the lessor to have one-eighth part of the oil produced and saved, and $100 per annum for the gas product of each well. When the rule of mutuality is applicable at all, it is applicable in suits for the specific performance of executory bilateral contracts. What is the rule?

In Ulrey v. Keith, it is said: "It should be borne in mind, also, that there is a distinction in equity between a mutuality in the obligation of contracts, and a mutuality of remedy under them."

First, then, what is "a mutuality in the obligation of contracts," i. e., as shown, supra, bilateral contracts? Dictionaries in general use define mutuality to mean

199 Ill., 189, 199, resting on those exceptional and anomalous Maryland Statute of Frauds cases, but also makes an independent citation of Chancellor Kent's opinion in Benedict v. Lynch, 1 Johnson, Ch. 370, on this point of mutuality under the Statute of Frauds, which Chancellor Kent himself overruled, as is shown by citations in Farwell v. Lowther, 18 Ill., 252, 255, and expressly in Ullsperger v. Meyer, 217 Ill., 262, 270. And, in addition, a comparison of other cases from other jurisdictions cited in Ulrey v. Keith with like cases adjudged in Illinois adds nothing to Ulrey v. Keith as an exposition of the rule of mutuality as heretofore understood and applied in this State. In Hissam v. Parish, 41 W. Va., 686, specific performance of a contract for the sale of shares of stock in a corporation was refused for want of mutuality. The contract there was either unilateral, or, if bilateral, then the plaintiff had fully performed his side of it. In this State, in that sort of a case, the only question would be: Are the shares of stock such peculiar chattels under the circumstances of the case that damages would be an inadequate remedy? See Pierce v. Plumb, 74 Ill., 326; Barton v. De Wolf, 108 Ill., 195; Kiels v. McMun, 232 Ill., 488; Oswald v. Nehls, supra. In Buck v. Smith, 29 Mich., 166, specific performance of an executory contract to enter into partnership was refused, the opinion giving want of mutuality as one of the reasons. A like decision was made in Clark v. Truitt, 183 Ill., 239, and, though Buck v. Smith, 29 Mich., 166, is cited on p. 246, the Court could not have been impressed with the want of mutuality argument therein, for its decision is put on the usual ground in such cases, that it would be quite as sensible to try to compel the specific performance of an executory contract to marry, as to try to compel the specific performance of an executory contract to enter into co-partnership.

"reciprocity," "interchange." "A mutuality in the obligation of contracts," therefore, must mean a reciprocity of interchange of promises, an exchange, or swapping of promises. That kind of mutuality goes to the legal existence of the bilateral contract alleged by the plaintiff. It is not peculiar to suits for specific performance. It comes up for discussion quite as often, if not more often, in actions of assumpsit, as in Plumb v. Campbell, 129 Ill., 101, 106, et seq. "Mutuality" in this sense exists in the oil and gas lease case, as now being considered, and the Court said it was present in Ulrey v. Keith, as viewed by the Court, and Ulrey v. Keith, therefore, went off on want of a "mutuality of remedy under contracts." And so Lancaster v. Roberts, 144 Ill., 213, Tryce v. Dittus, 199 Ill., 213, and Winter v. Trainor, 151 Ill., 191, cited in Ulrey v. Keith, were not applicable, for they plainly went off on want of a "mutuality of obligation under contracts," and so Ulrey v. Keith is left with no cited Illinois precedent to stand on (see note 13, supra), except Watford Oil and Gas Co. v. Shipman, and the Court is reconsidering that case de novo.

Second, what is "a mutuality of remedy under contracts?" A bill of specific performance can never be filed until after one of the parties has broken, or threatened to break, his contract. A defendant who has broken, or is threatening to break, his contract, therefore, cannot have any "remedy under the contract." He does not want any remedy. He wants to keep out of the reach of all remedies. So a "mutuality of remedy under contracts" can, in strictness, mean nothing to a Court. The Court, necessarily, can give a remedy only to the plaintiff.

Suppose, now, that the Court has determined in its own mind that damages would not be an adequate remedy for the breach by the lessor in an oil and gas lease of excluding the lessee from the premises, and that the plaintiff lessee, in justice, ought to have the remedy of specific performance in the form of an injunction forbidding the lessor to exclude the lessee from the premises. Having come to that mental determination, there can be no doubt that the Court must then take into view the plaintiff lessee's promise. But the reason why the Court must do that is important. That reason is this: The plaintiff's promise is the quid pro quo of the defendant's promise — the consideration, technically considered; and the actual performance of the plaintiff's promise is the quid pro quo of the actual performance of the defendant's promise — the consideration, substantially considered, as it must be in a suit for specific performance. Plainly, therefore, in point of equal and exact abstract justice, even though the defendant has broken his promise, the defendant, ordinarily, ought not to be compelled to perform his promise in specie, unless he gets the exact equivalent he bargained for, namely, performance of his promise in specie by the plaintiff. And so, if the plaintiff's promise is such in its nature that the plaintiff may be compelled to perform it in specie, such performance by the plaintiff will be secured to the defendant by provisions in the decree of specific performance that goes against the defendant. But the promise of the plaintiff lessee in an oil and gas lease, as now being considered, is such in its nature that performance of it in specie by the plaintiff lessee cannot be compelled, because, on grounds of policy and expediency, rather than on grounds of mere abstract justice operating between the parties, Courts will not undertake, on a bill for specific performance, to direct and supervise continuous work like that of exploring, drilling, piping, and operating premises for oil and gas. See 26 Am. & Eng. Ency. of Law, Ed. 2, p. 95, 12. Since therefore, compulsory performance in specie of the plaintiff lessee's promise is out of the question, and equal and exact abstract justice cannot be done, does it follow, necessarily, therefore, that the Court must dismiss the case, and remit the plaintiff lessee to the remedy of damages against the defendant lessor, the Court having already determined, and still believing, that the remedy of damages will not do complete and perfect practical justice to the plaintiff lessee as against the defendant lessor? The answer is — No. The Court may and must go further, and inquire whether, if the plaintiff lessee should, in the future, refuse to perform his promise, the remedy of damages would do perfect and complete practical justice in favor of the defendant lessor as against the plaintiff lessee. See note 19, infra. If it would, the decree of specific performance may and should go against the defendant lessor and in favor of the plaintiff lessee, the decree to cease to operate as soon as the plaintiff lessee breaks his promise, and the plaintiff to be liable in damages for such future breach to the defendant lessor, the effect of the decree being to repair the vinculum juris broken by the defendant, and so to enable the defendant to complain of its future breach by the plaintiff.

In this oil and gas lease case, as now being considered, the remedy of damages ought, I think, to be held an adequate remedy for the defendant lessor against the plaintiff lessee for any possible, but in fact quite unlikely, future breach by the plaintiff lessee of his promise to drill and operate for oil and gas.[14] The defendant lessor then would be released from the contract; that is what he wants; then he could make a new lease with other people; and the damages, on the basis of the contract, namely, $100 a year for the product of each gas well and one-eighth

---

[14] The lessee's attempt to appropriate all the oil found could be stopped and corrected in equity. See Parker v. Garrison, 61 Ill., 250, Manning v. Frazier, 96 Ill., 279.

of the oil produced and saved, could be computed with almost mathematical certainty.

If you now bring into the case the lessee's surrender clause, and can conceive of the contract as a bilateral contract as respects performance with that clause in it, plainly the effect of the surrender clause cannot be to cut off the plaintiff lessee from the remedy of specific performance, i. e., to strip the Court of jurisdiction to give it to him, if that remedy is otherwise in justice due to the plaintiff lessee. The intent of the clause is that there should be neither specific performance nor damages against the lessee. The whole of the effect that can be allowed to the lessee's surrender clause is on the question of the fairness of the contract under the rule that unfair contracts will not be enforced in specie. That is the only effect allowed to the plaintiff's power to terminate the contract in Singer Co. v. Union Co., Holmes, 233, 22 Fed. Cas., p. 220, where the contract was held to be a fair one, a case strongly approved of in Garden City Sand Co. v. Southern Fire Brick and Clay Co., 223 Ill., 616, 625.[15]

"Mutuality of remedy under contracts" is, therefore, a wrong, or misleading, phrase. It is mutuality, reciprocity, or interchange of performance under broken bilateral contracts that primarily concerns the Court in a specific performance case. If the defendant's promise ought to be, and can be, specifically compelled, and

---

[15] Observe the use made of the word "mutuality," and the so-called one-sided, or unilateral, character of an oil and gas lease, to prove it unfair, unjust, unreasonable, and "unconscionable" to the lessor in Federal Oil Co. v. Western Oil Co., 112 Fed. Rep., 373; 121 Fed. Rep., 674. While the lessor makes no technical promise to drill, yet the lease enables the lessor to confront the lessee with a condition, instead of an abstract theory of contracts, namely: drill or get off the farm. The lessee should have a fair chance to drill, work, and spend his money, according to the true intent and spirit of his contract. The contract is not unfair in itself. See Ulrey v. Keith, 233 Ill., 56, 63; Gillespie v. Fulton Oil & Gas Co., 236 Ill., 188.

specific performance of the plaintiff's promise cannot be compelled by the Court, then, if the remedy of damages would be an adequate remedy for the defendant against the plaintiff, if the plaintiff in the future should break his promise, then the plaintiff may have the remedy of specific performance; but if the remedy of damages would be inadequate for the defendant against the plaintiff, then the plaintiff cannot have the remedy of specific performance against the defendant. As Professor Ames states it: "Equity will not compel specific performance by a defendant, if, after performance, the common law remedy of damages would be his sole security for the performance of the plaintiff's side of the contract, and such common law remedy would be inadequate." 3 Col. Law Rev., 1, 8, 12. As to the last clause, see 1 Ill. Law Rev., 548, 549 [ante p. 774].

The celebrated case of Lumley v. Wagner — where the defendant agreed to sing at plaintiff's theater and not to sing at any other theater, and the defendant was enjoined from singing at any other theater, though the plaintiff was not compellable specifically to provide his theater for the defendant or to pay the defendant her wages or salary (Welty v. Jacobs, 171 Ill., 624) — is the case that proves most strikingly that the operation of the rule of mutuality of performance is as above indicated. See per Wood, V. C., in Peto v. Tunbridge Wells Ry. Co., 1 H. & M., 468, 487, and in Stocker v. Wedderburn, 1 K. & J., 393, 404; 3 Col. Law Rev., 1, 8, per Professor Ames. Lumley v. Wagner is cited in Ulrey v. Keith, but in an odd way that weakens the opinion as a whole. No one criticizes Lumley v. Wagner, either (1) in so far as it proceeds upon the principle that a decree of specific performance sometimes may go in favor of a plaintiff against a defendant, even though performance in specie by the plaintiff is not compellable in favor of the defendant, or

(2) in so far as it proceeds upon the principle that, sometimes, a defendant may be enjoined from actively breaking an affirmative contract by doing the same thing for
other people that the contract requires him to do for the
plaintiff, though the Court would not compel performance
in specie of the affirmative contract, or interfere in the
case of a merely passive breach.[16]   The criticisms of the
case have been (1) its application of these principles to
a contract for purely personal services, and (2) its trans-
cendental principle that a Court of Equity may act on
the expression of a negative — "not to sing' — but may
not act on the implication of a negative from the affirmative — "to sing."   See, for example, per Lord Selborne,
in W. & W. R. Co *v.* L. & N. W. R. Co., L. R. 16 Eq., 433.
In Garden City Sand Co. *v.* Southern Fire Brick and Clay
Co., 223 Ill., 616, the Supreme Court of Illinois acted
on every principle that was acted on in Lumley *v.* Wagner,
even up to the express negative principle, and cites and
relies on Lumley *v.* Wagner.[17]   Plainly, in that case, the
Garden City Sand Company was not compellable to
perform specifically its promise to take the defendant's
fire clay and market it, yet the defendant was enjoined
from selling the clay to other people.   That case has
never been disturbed or qualified by the Court.   In
Welty *v.* Jacobs, 171 Ill., 624, as I read the case, the

[16] This principle (2) of indirect specific performance by injunction was in no
way applicable to, or involved in, Ulrey *v.* Keith.   The remedy by way of prevention there sought was true specific performance, though, as Professor Langdell points out in "A Brief Survey of Equity Jurisdiction," 1 Harv. Law Rev.,
354, 355, it would be a more accurate use of words to denominate it "specific
reparation."   So far as I have found, Lumley *v.* Wagner has been cited four times
by the Supreme Court: Consolidated Coal Co. *v.* Schmisseur, 135 Ill., 371, 379;
Welty *v.* Jacobs, 171 Ill., 624, 630; Garden City Sand Co. *v.* Southern Fire Brick
& Clay Co., 223 Ill., 616, 625; Ulrey *v.* Keith, 237 Ill., 284, 291.

[17] In 2 Ill. Law Rev., 217, 237 [ante p. 739], the writer took exception to the
Garden City Sand Co. case for its adoption of the express negative principle of
equity jurisdiction only.

principles of Lumley *v.* Wagner, except the express negative principle, were recognized, and the Court only, but
very properly, refused to apply them to that case, the
defendant's promise being to provide a theater, and the
plaintiff's promise being to provide a company of actors,
which was a personal service contract, for a company of
actors would be of no use to the defendant unless they
could, and did, act the parts, and damages would be an
inadequate remedy for a breach of the plaintiff's promise,
even if the defendant's promise had been in its nature
enforceable in specie.[18]

The phrase "mutuality of remedy under contracts"
seems to have come into the law of specific performance as
a phrase to explain an apparent extension of equity
jurisdiction, and later seems to have got twisted and
inverted into a phrase to limit and restrict equity jurisdiction. The original specific performance cases were
bills by vendees to get the land in specie. Then vendors
were allowed to file such bills, until some one raised the
point that all a vendor of land was entitled to was a
sum of money, and he could get that at law. The answer
given to the point was: "The remedy of specific performance must be mutual," and, therefore, since the vendee
may file a bill of specific performance to get the land,
the vendor may file a like bill to get the money, even
though he can get the money in a common law action
just as well. This use of the phrase appears in Illinois
in Andrews *v.* Sullivan, 2 Gilman, 327, 332, 333; Robinson

---

[18] This must be remembered: (1) It is the law, that the remedy of specific performance cannot be had, unless the remedy of damages is "inadequate." (2)
It is not the law, that the remedy of specific performance can be had, whenever the remedy of damages is "inadequate." The plaintiff's promise in Welty
v. Jacobs was one of those promises where the remedy of damages, though "inadequate" as between the parties on grounds of private justice, yet is the only
remedy allowable by the law on grounds of policy and expediency, arising out of
the nature of the remedy of specific performance and the nature of the plaintiff's
promise.

v. Appleton, 124 Ill., 276, 281. But this use of the
phrase "mutuality of remedy under contracts" to extend
equity jurisdiction in specific performance is overthrown
and prohibited in Illinois by Anderson *v.* Olsen, 188 Ill.,
502, where it was held that, while the vendee of a patent
may file a bill of specific performance to get the patent
(Whitney *v.* Burr, 115 Ill., 289; Havana Press Drill Co. *v.*
Ashurst, 148 Ill., 135), yet the vendor of a patent, who
has so delivered the patent that nothing remains to be
done except the payment of the price by the vendee,
cannot file a bill of specific performance to get the money,
but must sue the vendee in assumpsit. The brief of
counsel for the vendor on p. 503 shows that Andrews *v.*
Sullivan, supra, was relied on to sustain the vendor's bill
in Anderson *v.* Olsen. The true ground of equity jurisdiction of vendors' bills of specific performance is that
the land, or other subject of the contract specifically
enforceable at the suit of the vendee, stands, so long as
the vendor has not conveyed or delivered, as security for
the unpaid vendor, and his bill of specific performance is
really a bill to realize on the security by a sale. See per
Breese, J., in Burger *v.* Potter, 32 Ill., 66, 73; per Ames,
3 Col. Law Rev., 1, 11–12.[19]

[19] In a suggestive note on "Specific Performance as a Primary and Secondary
Remedy," 2 Story's Eq. Jur., Ed. 13, p. 30, 32, Mr. Bigelow says: "As for the
converse case, of the right of the seller to enforce specific performance on the part
of the buyer, that is only a concession to justice, being based on the idea that the
remedy should be mutual." There is nothing at all in that "concession to justice" idea, except as indicated in the text, supra, whether "mutuality of remedy"
is used to extend, or to restrict, equity jurisdiction in specific performance, though
the books are full of it. What consideration of justice enters into a vendor's
claim to be allowed to file a bill of specific performance in a case like Anderson *v.*
Olsen, supra? "Specific performance" is neither a personal privilege nor a
personal burden, but a remedy only, i. e., a mode, means, or instrument of establishing justice. And "damages" is not a personal privilege — the purchase of
the right to break a contract — but a remedy only, ut supra "specific performance." "The principle which is material to be considered . . . is, " says Lord
Selborne in Wilson *v.* Ry. Co., L. R., 9 Ch. App., 279, 284, "that the Court gives
specific performance instead of damages, only when it can by that means do more

The first citation of Mr. Fry's general rule of mutuality in specific performance in an Illinois opinion appears to be in Lancaster *v.* Roberts, 144 Ill., 213, 233, in 1893. Whatever confusion there may be in the Illinois cases dates from that citation in that case. Post hoc, ergo propter hoc is, I think, in this instance, no fallacy, though I strongly suspect that American Courts have made a literal, ultra-automatic use of Mr. Fry's general rule that the learned and distinguished author never intended or dreamed of. But, so far as I have found, the Illinois Supreme Court has allowed the general rule of mutuality in specific performance to operate artificially and automatically in only two cases, Gage *v.* Cummings, and Ulrey *v.* Keith. Gage *v.* Cummings, as shown supra, is of doubtful authority. It is not cited in Ulrey *v.* Keith, though the only reported Illinois case that aids Ulrey *v.* Keith, if it does aid it, — and it does not aid it. And, besides, Ulrey *v.* Keith is stripped of its potentiality for mischief, injustice, and wrong, so far as oil and gas leases are concerned, by Gillespie *v.* Fulton Oil and Gas Co., cited in note 11, supra.

The view of mutuality in specific performance above given is that advanced by Professor Ames in 3 Col. Law Rev., 1. The view is drawn from the decided cases, harmonizes the overwhelming majority of them, and was suggested by the observations of Vice Chancellor Wood,

perfect and complete justice." If, therefore, "mutuality of remedy under contracts" cannot be used to extend the remedy of specific performance in a case like Anderson *v.* Olsen, why should it be allowed to restrict the remedy, and cut a plaintiff off from it as against a defendant, simply because the defendant could not have that remedy as against the plaintiff, when, in the future possible, but perhaps unlikely, contingency, of a breach of his promise by the plaintiff, the remedy of damages would give the defendant just as perfect and complete practical justice as the remedy of specific performance, and perhaps even more perfect and complete practical justice? The phrase "mutuality of remedy" cannot be used to restrict the remedy of specific performance in such case, consistently with the function of Courts "to establish justice" and defeat roguery and dishonesty.

later Chancellor as Lord Hatherley, on Dietrichsen v. Cabburn, 2 Phillips, 52, in Stocker v. Wedderburn, 3 K. & J., 393, 404, and on Lumley v. Wagner, 1 D. G. M. & G., 93, in Peto v. Tunbridge Wells R. Co., 1 H. & M., 468, 487. See 3 Col. Law Rev., 8. With candid respect, American judges ought to make an effort to extricate the rule of mutuality from the mountains of words under which they have buried it, and to bring the rule of mutuality within the reach of ordinary human understanding. It is safe to assume always that there is no rule of equity jurisdiction that is not, in origin and at bottom, a rule to advance justice by giving legal effect to some simple principle of common honesty and morality, generally accepted and acted on among men heretofore or now living on this earth outside the Courts, touching the difference between meum and tuum.

6. — RISK OF LOSS BY FIRE AS BETWEEN VENDOR AND VENDEE.[a] — The opinion expressed by Lord Eldon in Paine v. Meller, 6 Vesey, 346, that, where a contract of sale is silent on the subject, in equity the risk of loss by accidental fire is upon the buyer from the date of the bargain, probably is the law in Illinois. But, so far as I know, no case has arisen wherein the Supreme Court has made the buyer stand a loss by accidental fire occurring after the date of the contract. See 64 Ill., 477; s. c., 75 Ill., 271; Stevenson v. Loehr, 57 Ill., 509. And see the arguments of Professors Keener and Williston for and against the above rule, 1 Col. Law Rev., 1; 9 Harv. Law Rev., 106. In the recent case of Eppstein v. Kuhn, 225 Ill., 115, Farmer, J., on a bill for specific performance by the buyer against the seller, where the fire occurred after the date fixed for performance, the loss was thrown upon the seller, because, at the time of the

---

[a] [2 Ill. Law Rev., 274, November, 1907.]

fire, the seller was not able to convey a perfect title, there being an outstanding lease of the property.   The Supreme Court remanded the case "with directions to the Circuit Court to hear further testimony of the parties, or either of them, as to the difference in the value of the premises, if any, resulting from the encumbrance by virtue of the lease . . . and the deterioration in the market value caused by the fire.   If the proof shows that the market value of the premises has been diminished by one or both of these causes, the amount of the diminution is to be deducted from the $7,000 (the contract price) and a conveyance ordered made to the appellee upon payment of the balance."   Whether this direction for measuring the compensation for the fire loss should be taken literally, rather than as a rough sketch, may be doubted.   If the seller had set the fire, this direction taken literally would fit his case very well, but there is room for argument that the rule for fixing the amount of compensation is different where the fire is accidental, and the seller's title, though not perfect, is yet so far good that the buyer wants it, and can get it, with compensation for defects.   See Phinizy v. Guernsey, 111 Ga., 346, 354–355, cited by the Court in Eppstein v. Kuhn.

The seller had the property insured, and the contract was silent on the subject of insurance.   The logical result of the Supreme Court's decision that the seller must stand the loss doubtless is that the seller may keep the insurance, thus reversing the decree which made him accountable to the buyer for the $2,500 insurance he collected.   225 Ill., at p. 119.   Compare the Master's finding on the insurance, 225 Ill., at p. 118.   See Phinizy v. Guernsey, supra; Phoenix Co. v. Caldwell, 187 Ill., 73, 81; Gage Mill Co. v. Western Assurance Co., 118 Ill., 396; Rayner v. Preston, L. R. 18 Ch. D., 1, James, L. J., dissenting; cases cited in 29 Am. & Eng. Ency. of Law, Ed. 2, 714.

Eppstein *v*. Kuhn was before the court in 219 Ill., 154, where the seller's defense of want of mutuality was over-ruled. Taking the rule of mutuality as there stated, 219 Ill., at p. 157, it is obvious that one or more of the numerous exceptions to that rule must be brought into action to sustain the decision in 219 Ill., 154. See 3 Col. Law Rev., 1; 2 Ill. Law Rev., 42 [post p. 852].

7. — ENFORCEMENT OF CONTRACT TO CONVEY FOREIGN REAL PROPERTY.[a] — In Poole *v*. Koons, 252 Ill., 49, 53, Vickers, J., writing the opinion, being a writ of error to review a decree of specific performance of a contract to convey land in Arkansas, it is said:

"Plaintiff in error insists that while the court had the power to require plaintiff in error to execute the deed, it had no power to order the master in chancery to do so. We see no reason in this distinction. The alternative order requiring the master to execute the deed was only in furtherance of the relief sought, and insured the execution of the decree whether plaintiff in error was willing to carry out the order of the court or not."

The distinction taken by counsel is as old as the court of chancery. Sections 41 to 47 of the Chancery Act, which go back to sections 13 to 15 of the first Chancery Act of March 22, 1819, relieved Illinois courts of chancery of the limitation of the rule of procedure, aequitas agit in personam, so far as domestic property is concerned; but the limitation still applies to foreign property, and there is no constitutional mode of getting rid of it. An Illinois master's deed of land in Arkansas, in any other state of the Union, or in a foreign country, is waste paper. But in this case, plaintiff in error had no standing to object to the order directing the master to make the deed of the Arkansas land, because the order did not

[a] [6 Ill. Law Rev., 545, March, 1902.]

hurt him; it hurt the other side. It is enough to cite Fall *v.* Eastin, 215 U. S., 1, to prove how very important it is for a plaintiff who obtains a decree for a conveyance of foreign property to insist on getting the deed direct from the defendant personally under his own hand and seal.

TOPIC II

CONSTRUCTION, REFORMATION, AND RESCISSION OF WRITTEN INSTRUMENTS

I

SO-CALLED EQUITY JURISDICTION TO CONSTRUE AND REFORM WILLS [a]

In Miller *v.* Rowan,[1] Cartwright, J., writing the opinion, Vickers, J., dissenting, the sound but rather uncommon point is made that a collateral attack on a decree in equity for want of equity jurisdiction ordinarily must fail. The reason is that equity jurisdiction is not restrained by the subject-matter in controversy, but only by the adequacy of the remedy at law, there being no equity jurisdiction if the remedy at law is adequate. Hence an exercise of equity jurisdiction in a case where the remedy at law is adequate ordinarily involves no usurpation of ungranted judicial power, but only error of judgment in the use of granted judicial power on the question of the adequacy of the remedy at law. And Cartwright, J., says truly, there is great confusion of thought among men learned in the law on the difference between jurisdiction or judicial power and equity jurisdiction.[2]

The true nature of equity jurisdiction as a system of remedies for the enforcement and protection of rights is brought out clearly and pointedly by the fact that in most of our states since the Code Procedure commencing in 1848, and in England since the Judicature Act of 1873–5, questions in equity jurisdiction never arise under that name, because there is but one court and one form

---

[a] [6 Ill. Law Rev., 485, March, 1912.]

[1] 251 Ill., 344.

[2] In addition to the authorities cited in the opinion see Langdell, Equity Jurisdiction, 2d Ed., 22–24, for an explanation of the difference between jurisdiction as applied to a common-law court and equity jurisdiction.

of action wherein parties are given whatever relief the law of the land allows. In these jurisdictions, what used to be discussed as questions in equity jurisdiction now are discussed as questions of remedy. The change is one of form, and is not one of substance, though the change has been, is, and is likely to become more and more, of considerable import, good and bad, all depending on the bench and bar, to the actual administration of the law, and its orderly development as a coherent harmonious system. From the first establishment of the English High Court of Chancery and its accidental, not premeditated, master-stroke of adopting from the ecclesiastical courts the rule of procedure, Aequitas agit in personam, i. e., the rule of personal compulsion and coercion to do or not to do under pain of going to jail for disobedience, a question in equity jurisdiction always has been at bottom simply a question of remedy. The reason is historical, and is neither abstractly logical nor rigidly scientific, either in origin or in practical application, though the rise and final establishment of the English High Court of Chancery brought about the important practical result of realizing for English law in its full extent the great principle embodied in the maxim, Ubi jus ibi remedium.[3]

The historical line dividing remedies, not subject-matter, into "legal" and "equitable" was preserved for our federal courts by Section 18 of the Judiciary Act of 1789, later Revised Statutes, Section 723, now Section 267 of the Judicial Code, saying:

"Suits in equity shall not be sustained in any of the courts of the United States where a plain, adequate, and complete remedy may be had at law."

[3] Langdell, Equity Pleading, 2d Ed., 27–42; Maitland, Equity, Lectures 1 and 2; 3 Maitland, Collected Papers, 345–353; Spence, Equity Jurisdiction, 321–351, reprinted in 2 Essays in Anglo-American Legal History, 219; Ames, Origin of Uses and Trusts, 2 Essays in Anglo-American Legal History, 736.

and was preserved for our Illinois courts by Section 2 of the Chancery Act of March 22, 1819, now Section 1 of the present Chancery Act, saying originally:

"In all suits in chancery, . . . the rules and methods which regulate the High Court of Chancery in England shall, as far as the courts may deem the same applicable, be observed, except as hereinafter mentioned."

As the line between "law" and "equity" was not drawn with reference to subject-matter, so it was not drawn with reference to "justice" and "injustice," "equity" being devoted to the former and "law" to the latter. Both the common-law judge and the equity judge always have been equally bound to do justice. The word "justice," however, never was regarded by the sages of the law as denoting a loose abstract entity, from which every man might draw according to his taste, but always was regarded as denoting conformity to law, or the actual result flowing from an application of the law of the land to the case in hand, whether in a court of equity or in a court of law.

"In truth, law is itself the standard of justice. What deviates from any law is unjust with reference to that law, though it may be just with reference to another law of superior authority [as, for example, the law of God]. The judge who habitually talks of equity or justice — the justice of the case, the equities of the case, the imperious demands of justice, the plain dictates of equity — forgets that he is there to enforce the law of the land, else he does not administer that justice or that equity with which alone he is immediately concerned."[4]

An equity judge never had any more power to legislate to create rights than a common-law judge, who never had any such power at all. Neither ever had any right to substitute his own "common sense," "conscience," "discretion," "light of reason," or "justice," for knowledge

[4] Austin, Jurisprudence, Lecture 5, Sec. 179.

of the law of the land.   But the equity judge never was
at a loss for a remedy; and hence always has been able
to recognize and give legal effect to reasonable and en-
lightened customs which usage has approved, or is plainly
on the way to approving, that a common-law judge often
had to ignore, against his inclination, for want of an
appropriate remedy; and hence also the equity judge
was able to establish and develop whole branches of substantive law, now part and parcel of the common law
under the artificial name of "equity," as, for example,
the law of trusts, mortgages, etc.[5]

To exhibit the application to the case before the court
of the point that want of equity jurisdiction ordinarily
is not a good reason for a collateral attack on a decree
in equity, reference must be made to two Illinois doctrines, commonly stated as rules regulating the exercise
of equity jurisdiction, which doctrines constituted the
basis of the case of the defeated litigant, as the case was
presented for decision.

The first doctrine is the one saying, there is ordinarily
no equity jurisdiction to construe a will devising real
estate, unless the will devises it by way of trust — the "no
trust, no equity jurisdiction" doctrine.   The rise, long-
time fluidity, final judicial establishment, and quick
legislative fall of this doctrine must be had in mind.

Apart from statute, the bare averment alone by an
interested party that a will of real estate needs construction, is not enough to give any court of law or equity
jurisdiction or power to construe it.   The construction
of wills does not fall within the peculiar province or
power of courts of equity to the exclusion of courts of
law.   A court of law has as much jurisdiction or power
to construe wills as a court of equity.   Nor are wills

---

[5] Langdell, Equity Pleading, 2d Ed., 41.

construed one way in a court of law and another way in a court of equity. Apart from statute, the jurisdiction or power of any court of law or equity to construe a will can arise only when the will is exhibited to sustain a cause of action or defense pending in a court of law or equity. And whether a will can be exhibited to sustain a cause of action or defense pending in a court of law or in a court of equity, turns on the question of the adequacy of the remedy at law to deal promptly and efficiently with the cause of action or defense in question.[6]

When a will devises real estate by way of trust, the trustee or cestui may file a bill in equity, and thereby devolve upon the court the duty to construe the will. The foundation of equity jurisdiction is the trust, because there is no remedy at law to enforce or protect a trust.

When a will of real estate devises legal titles directly, what is the rule regulating equity jurisdiction to construe the will?

In 1874, in Whitman v. Fisher,[7] the Supreme Court said:

"Where purely legal titles are involved and no other relief is sought, a court of equity will not assume jurisdiction to construe the will, but will remit the parties to their remedies at law."

The rule purports to be a statement of the result of the opinion of Walworth, C., in Bowers v. Smith,[8] in 1843, and is good enough as a rule; all depends upon the application of the rule made by the courts in concrete cases. The rule was not applied in the case wherein

[6] Statutes making the bare averment by an interested party that a will needs construction enough per se to authorize a court to construe it are not uncommon now; they are natural, reasonable, and logical extensions of the Illinois quiet-title statute of 1869 hereinafter referred to. And there are like statutes on the subject of the validity of wills assailed for fraud, undue influence, or want of mental capacity. See note 9 infra.

[7] 74 Ill., 147.

[8] 10 Paige, 193, 200.

was stated, the court finding the will created a trust. In 1875, in Strubher *v*. Belsey,[9] where a will of real estate devised legal titles directly, the court applied the rule, dismissing the bill, and remitting the parties to "their remedies at law."

It does not appear from the report of Strubher *v*. Belsey whether the complainant was in possession or out of possession, or whether the land in question was improved and occupied, or unimproved and unoccupied. If the land was improved and occupied, and the complainant was out of possession, his remedy at law was ejectment, which was adequate and complete. If the land was improved and occupied, and the complainant was in possession, he had no remedy at law; and in that case of being in possession, when the court remitted him to his "remedies at law," they remitted him to the "dismal situation waste and wild" of the fallen angels cut off from remedy. On the hypothesis of either the complainant's possession of improved and occupied land, or the vacancy of the land as unimproved and unoccupied, the case was a plain one for equity jurisdiction to quiet title, on the principle of quia timet — because there was no remedy at law — both apart from statute and under the quiet-title statute of 1869, being Section 50 of the Chancery Act, which has been held, overlooking the apparently contrary dictum in Gage *v*. Rohrbach,[10] to be only declaratory of the prior chancery rule, except in so far as the statute dispenses with the necessity of possession by the complainant where the land is unimproved and unoccupied.[11]

It is believed the actual judicial practice in Illinois, in the trial courts at least, both before and after Strubher

[9] 79 Ill., 307.
[10] 56 Ill., 262, 266.
[11] Gage *v*. Abbott, 99 Ill., 366.

v. Belsey, in 1875, has been constant and steady, to construe wills of real estate devising legal titles directly, in suits in equity to quiet title filed by claimants in possession of improved and occupied land, and by claimants out of possession of unimproved and unoccupied land.[12]

Moreover, apart from the quiet-title statute of 1869, the chancery rule is that a holder of a future estate, such as a remainder-man, may file a bill in equity to quiet title, or to remove a cloud on title, when the life tenant is in possession.[13]

In Ewing *v.* Barnes,[14] in 1895, and in Strawbridge *v.* Strawbridge,[15] in 1906, on bills in equity to quiet title by claimants of future estates under wills, equity jurisdiction to construe wills was expressly sustained and exercised in the first case, and was exercised silently in the second case.

In Fletcher *v.* Root,[16] in 1909, where a bill to quiet title was filed by a devisee in possession claiming the fee simple, these two cases last named were overruled summarily, and the rule was laid down peremptorily, that equity jurisdiction to construe a will of real estate ordinarily can exist only when the will devises the real estate by way of trust. "Where there is no trust there is no jurisdiction," said the court, which declaration has the great merit of clearness and plainness of speech at any rate.

The sweeping rule of Fletcher *v.* Root was overthrown at the next session of the legislature by act of June 5, 1911, amending the quiet-title statute of 1869, or Section 50 of the Chancery Act.[17]

---

[12] Chapman *v.* Cheney, 191 Ill., 574, 580; Parsons *v.* Miller, 189 Ill., 107, 112; but see Mansfield *v.* Mansfield, 203 Ill., 92, 98

[13] 32 Cyc., 1337.

[14] 156 Ill., 61.

[15] 220 Ill., 61.

[16] 240 Ill., 429.

This act of 1911 turns the law back to the old chancery rule as embodied in the quiet-title statute of 1869, or Section 50 of the Chancery Act. It may be that the act of 1911 leaves a fair doubt whether the necessity of possession by the complainant in a bill to quiet title is dispensed with, where the will devises legal titles directly, and the land is improved and occupied. The constitutionality of a statutory provision dispensing with the necessity of complainant's possession of improved and occupied land in a bill to quiet title, as denying the right of trial by jury, was questioned and its constitutionality sustained recently in New Jersey.[18] The federal equity courts, however, decline to act on state statutory provisions dispensing with the necessity of complainant's possession of improved and occupied land in bills to quiet title, saying to do so would deny the right of trial by jury secured by the federal constitution to litigants in the federal courts.[19]

On the subject of the validity of wills challenged for fraud, undue influence, or want of mental capacity, the law is in a tangle like the construction-tangle prior to the Act of 1911, calling for curative legislation. Apart from statute, the bare averment alone by an interested party that a will of real estate is invalid, never was enough to give equity jurisdiction to determine the question. Forgetting that the ultimate test of equity jurisdiction always has been the adequacy of the remedy at law, and overlooking the difference between the case of a plaintiff in possession unable to bring ejectment, and the case of a plaintiff out of possession able to bring ejectment, the Supreme Court laid it down broadly in 1887, there is no

[17] Session Laws, 1911, 253.

[18] Brady v. Realty Co., 64 Atl. Rep., 1078; McGrath v. Norcross, 65 Atl. Rep., 998.

[19] Whitehead v. Shattuck, 138 U. S., 146, 150, 151; and see Scott v. Neely, 140 U. S., 106; Cates v. Allen, 149 U. S., 459; Holland v. Challen, 110 U. S., 15; Wehrman v. Conklin, 55 U. S., 314, 323.

equity jurisdiction to determine the validity of a will of
real estate. Luther *v.* Luther, 122 Ill., 558. Then in
1889 the court began to give a highly restrictive construction to the words "any person interested" in the 7th
Section of the Wills Act, allowing a suit in chancery to
determine the validity of a will. As the law now stands,
the remedy to determine the validity of a will of Illinois
land is not co-extensive with the substantive rights involved. Selden *v.* Ill. Trust & Savings Bank, 239 Ill.,
67. If the requisite diversity of citizenship and amount
involved are present in the case, the better place, under
existing law, to contest the validity of a will of Illinois
land would appear to be the federal equity courts, where
the Illinois statute as construed by the Illinois Supreme
Court probably cannot be allowed to control and restrict
the remedy. The remedy in Illinois Probate Courts to
determine the validity of wills, even under existing
statutes, never has been regarded as adequate and
complete.

The second Illinois doctrine regulating the exercise of
equity jurisdiction that lay at the basis of the case is
the one saying there is no equity jurisdiction to correct a
mistake in the government description of land in a will,
because such correction "is more than construction, it is
reformation," and there is no equity jurisdiction to reform
wills. The status of this doctrine in the Illinois cases at
the time this case came up for decision must be shown.

Of course, there is no equity jurisdiction to reform
wills. Indeed there is no judicial power to reform
wills, and, under existing law, an exertion of such judicial power by a court would be usurpation of ungranted
judicial power. No one ever has suggested that judicial
power to reform wills ought to exist, except Stephen in the
preface to the third edition of his Digest of the Law of Evidence,[20] which suggestion seems to have been dropped

[20] Thayer, Evidence, 437, note 2.

by Stephen from his later editions. The suggestion evidently was ill considered, though no doubt the legislature of Illinois has the power to authorize the courts to write wills for the dead, which legislative power may be exercised if enough people ever come to want it.

It often happens that a testator describing his land by the government description leaves out one of the points of the compass, puts in a wrong point, duplicates a point, puts in a wrong fraction, leaves out the right fraction, or duplicates a fraction, or puts in the wrong section number, and the question has arisen whether a testator's mistake of that kind can be corrected by the judicial process of construction. The question is not one in equity jurisdiction at all, but has arisen, and may arise, in courts of law as well as in courts of equity, without any regard to the form of the action at law or the nature of the bill in equity. The question first came up in Illinois in 1870, in Kurtz *v.* Hibner,[21] and has been coming up regularly ever since, the last case being Graves *v.* Rose,[22] in 1910, where the court divided four to three, Cartwright, J., writing the opinion, and Dunn, J., the dissenting opinion.[23]

[21] 55 Ill., 514.

[22] 246 Ill., 76.

[23] As is well known, the decision in Kurtz *v.* Hibner denying correction was assailed by Judge Redfield and defended by Judge Caton and by Mr. Julius Rosenthal. See the literature collected in 4 Wigmore, Evidence, p. 3517, note 6. The Caton-Rosenthal several and not joint defense was identical, viz.: that the court was powerless to insert words of ownership not written in the will by the testator, such as "my land" or "land owned by me," and in support of this point Mr. Rosenthal referred to the Roman-law rule of legatum rei alienae, permitting a Roman testator to leave by will not only his own property, but property of his heir and property of a stranger, the legacy of property of a stranger taking effect by way of a legal duty on the heir to buy the property and give it to the legatee. This Roman-law doctrine never had any place in our law, though it is said the doctrine of election in our law is founded upon it (2 Story, Equity Jurisprudence, Ch. 30, Swanston's notes cited), which may or may not be true, for coincidences are not foundations in comparative law, and in any event this doctrine is wholly irrelevant to this point of implying words of ownership in an Illinois will; and, besides, the Roman-law rule of construction apparently was that words of owner-

All the reported Illinois cases are cases where the practical effect of the mistake in the government description in the will was, on the face of things if the mistake was left uncorrected, to devise land the testator did not own instead of land that he did own, or to leave the testator intestate as to a parcel of land that he did own. To try to reconcile the Illinois cases involves a useless mental strain; they are irreconcilable; they stand about evenly divided, half correcting the mistake and the other half refusing correction, the cases of correction being most of the later ones, commencing in 1887, but the last case refuses correction. The doctrine prevailing now generally outside Illinois is, that a testator's mistake of the kind mentioned ordinarily is correctable by the judicial process of construction by a court of law or by a court of equity, by means of an application of the rule, falsa demonstratio non nocet, under which, striking out the words of mistake, it commonly happens in most cases that enough descriptive words are left in the will, when aided by evidence of proper extrinsic facts, to identify and pass the land in question the testator did own. But it is said over and over in the Illinois cases that such correction of such a mistake of description in a will "is more than construction, it is reformation," as by Bailey,

---

ship must be implied in a Roman will unless the text excludes them by a clear expression of intention to leave the property of a stranger by way of a charge on the heir to buy it. Institutes, 2, 20, 4. The right to leave property by will in Illinois flows from statute, and the statute always has authorized people to leave by will only their own property. Neither the Supreme Court, nor any judge thereof in a dissenting opinion, ever has adopted the Caton-Rosenthal defense of Kurtz v. Hibner, but, on the contrary, as it seems to me, the rule now is that a will necessarily speaks of the testator's own property at the time of his death; that words of ownership must be implied in every will, and it is not a question of inserting words of ownership, but of striking out words of ownership written in by the law, which striking out is not allowable, unless the text of the will excludes words of ownership, which never has happened and very likely never will happen. In 4 Wigmore, Evidence, pp. 3514, 3417, quaere whether the learned author has not given too much weight to the Caton-Rosenthal point.

J., speaking for the court, in Bingel v. Voltz,[24] in 1892, and by Vickers, J., dissenting in Gano v. Gano,[25] in 1909,[26] and in the last case of Graves v. Rose,[27] Cartwright, J., speaking for the majority said:

"That such a change in a deed, contract, or instrument other than a will, to make it conform to the intention of the maker, would be a reformation has never been questioned, and we do not see how it can be called anything different in case of a will."[28]

The difference, as related to the judicial process of construction, between a will and a contract is one of fact, not of law, and arises on the difference in the essential nature of the two instruments, as was pointed out by Blackburn in his "Contract of Sale."[29]

"The will is the language of the testator soliloquizing" about all his property and earthly affairs; but "the language used in a contract is the language used to another in the course of an isolated transaction."

[24] 142 Ill., 214.

[25] 239 Ill., 539, 547.

[26] Gano v. Gano was a four to three decision correcting the mistake. The case is unlike all the others preceding it in that the mistake did not occur first in the will, but occurred first in the deed to the testator over twenty years before, and was repeated in the will by the testator copying his deed apparently. This difference in fact was overlooked, but it is material: it rendered the rule falsa demonstratio non nocet inapplicable, because the description was not false in any particular, but was true in every particular. By the deed to himself as grantee the testator acquired an equity of reformation against his grantor, which equity of reformation passed to the devisee by the will repeating the same mistake just as the equity of reformation would have passed to a grantee by a deed of the testator repeating the same mistake. Dillard v. Jones, 229 Ill., 119; 34 Cyc., note 58. Moreover, treating the thing devised as the testator's adverse possessory title, the description used in the will signified the land in question to the testator, because he always knew the land by that description, and never knew it by any other description.

[27] 246 Ill., 76, 87.

[28] The words "a change," in connection with the whole opinion, show that the idea of the opinion is that the process of construction involves, first, the striking out of words, and, second, the insertion of fresh words. That is an error; fresh words are not inserted.

[29] 2 Ed., p. 47, note b.

And, under our recording act, the language used in a deed is the language used not only to another, but to third persons, or the world at large, to give them notice, which third persons must read the record of the descriptive part of the deed, and apply it on the surface of the ground, according to the government survey, when the government description is used in the deed to identify the property.

The question of construction in the case of a will is, What did the descriptive words signify to the testator? In the case of a contract, the question of construction is, What did the descriptive words signify to the parties? And in the case of a deed, under the recording act, the question of construction is, What would the descriptive words signify to third persons reading them in the record-books in the recorder's office? Hence the ambit of surrounding extrinsic facts that may be used to aid the construction of a will is much wider than the ambit of surrounding extrinsic facts that may be used to aid the construction of a contract, or of a deed under the recording act, in which latter case the auxiliary ambit of surrounding extrinsic facts is very circumscribed, ordinarily not extending beyond the government survey, when the government description is used in the deed in question, the government survey operating as the standard dictionary, so to speak, incorporated into the deed by reference.

The evidence of surrounding extrinsic facts that may be called the "stock evidence" to put the judicial process of reformation into play and action to correct a mistake of description in a contract or deed, i. e., evidence of "mistake of the scrivener,[30] ordinarily cannot be used at all to aid the correction of a like mistake in a will, deed, or other instrument by the judicial process of construction.[31]

[30] 34 Cyc., 910.

[31] 4 Wigmore, Evidence, Sec. 2471; 30 Am. and Eng. Ency. of Law, 2 Ed., 680.

And in so far as Kurtz v. Hibner and the other Illinois cases deny the right to use evidence of that kind of an extrinsic fact to aid construction, they are sound in principle.

Though the common statement in the cases — correction of mistake of description in a will "is more than construction; it is reformation" — is epigram mistaken for argument when used in cases like Kurtz v. Hibner and the cases after it in Illinois, where the practical effect of the mistake was, on the face of things, to devise land of another instead of land of the testator, or to leave the testator intestate as to part of his land, yet such is not always and necessarily the prima facie practical effect of a mistake, in the government description of land in a will; and in other cases, or in some cases likely to arise, the epigram may be entirely correct in point of law and applicable in point of fact. At any rate, the epigram as it stands there now in the cases is a clear authoritative judicial denial, not of equity jurisdiction but of judicial power, to reform wills for mistake.[32]

---

[32] The judicial construction of a will or other instrument involves only an intellectual process, and never was a coercive remedy, "legal" or "equitable." The judicial reformation of an instrument is both an intellectual process and a coercive "equitable" remedy. In construction, the outward written expression must stand; in reformation, the outward written expression must fall, because the whole end and aim of the party seeking reformation is to show that the outward written expression does not correspond with the true inner thought of the parties to the instrument, or the party where the instrument is an unilateral act as a deed of gift. When such want of correspondence has been shown and judicially found, the intellectual process of reformation is at an end, and the coercive remedy of reformation begins, and must be applied to give legal effect to the judicial finding, which coercive remedy is an order directing the parties to write, sign, and deliver a new instrument correctly expressing the true thought. The remedy of reformation is "equitable" simply because the court of chancery alone could apply it: the court of common law did not have the coercive machinery. The remedy of reformation is inapplicable to wills, because dead men cannot be made to write, though that might have been got over if the English people had not been opposed to letting the chancellor write wills. The modern practice, resting partly on statute and partly on usage apart from statute, of entering

The essential facts of the case of Miller *v.* Rowan[33] now may be stated. The owner of the "southwest quarter" of one section, i. e., 160 acres, and of one and one-half acres in another section, died in 1879, leaving a widow and five sons, James, Joseph, Samuel, Alexander, and McPharlin, devising a life estate in all his land to his widow by one provision of the will, and remainders in different parcels to four of his sons by two other provisions of' the will. In each of the three provisions of the will making the devises, the words "southwest quarter" were duplicated, reading "the southwest quarter of the southwest quarter of section 29," i. e., 40 acres, thus on the face of things devising only 40 acres of the 160 acres the testator owned. The provision of the will making the devise to the sons Alexander and McPharlin, on the second clause of which the controversy arose, shows the mistake in each of the provisions, and was as follows:

"At the death of my wife, Ellen Rowan, I give and devise unto my two sons, Alexander and McPharlin Rowan, their heirs and assigns, the south half of the southwest quarter of the southwest quarter of section 29 and one acre and a half of the northeast fourth of the northwest quarter of section thirty-two, all in township 10, south, range one west in Jackson County, Illinois, containing 81½ acres and half more or less.

"And in case of the death of said Alexander and McPharlin Rowan, said described lands shall revert to Joseph and Samuel Rowan. In case they should die leaving widow or widows, to the widow while she remains their widow or widows, then to their heirs if any living."

decrees in rem in cases of reformation for mistake, i. e., of dispensing with the execution of a new instrument by providing in the decree that "the instrument be and the same hereby is rectified" (Teel *v.* Dunnihoo, 221 Ill., 471, 477; 230 Ill., 476, 489; 34 Cyc., 993), does not bring reformation and construction to correct mistake any nearer together than they ever were. Of course there is always a danger of correcting a mistake in a will by reformation under the guise of construction; but that does not prove that correcting a mistake in a will by construction is reformation; it only proves that judges are but fallible men.

[33] 251 Ill., 344.

In 1881 the widow and three of the sons, Joseph, Alexander, and McPharlin, joined as complainants in a bill in equity to the Jackson Circuit Court asking the court to correct the mistake, and the court entered a decree correcting the mistake by striking out one of the phrases, "the southwest quarter of," from each of the three provisions of the will, finding and reciting in the decree the mistake was the "mistake of the scrivener," and also finding and reciting in the decree that Alexander and McPharlin "by virtue of the will took and had a fee-simple title" to the south half of the southwest quarter, i. e., the south 80 acres. Alexander died in 1906 and McPharlin died in 1909, neither leaving widow, child, or descendant. And then a bill for partition of the south 80 acres devised to Alexander and McParlin by the will as corrected was filed by some of the heirs of Alexander and McPharlin, to which bill for partition Joseph, the sole survivor of the four brothers, devisees under the father's will, was made a defendant, and he set up the claim, that, by virtue of the second clause of the provision of the will above quoted, Alexander and McPharlin took a base or determinable fee simple, and that Joseph and his brother Samuel took a remainder by way of executory devise over, and Joseph now claimed 40 acres of the 80 acres in his own right to the exclusion of all the other heirs of Alexander and McPharlin. In bar of Joseph's executory-devise claim the other heirs set up the above decree of 1881 as res judicata, relying on the finding therein that Alexander and McPharlin "by virtue of the will took and had a fee-simple title," to which plea of former adjudication Joseph replied by an attack on the jurisdiction of the court over the subject-matter of the decree.

The will did not create any trust but devised legal titles directly. The rule finally established by the Supreme Court by decisions rendered before this case came up, and standing unreversed when it came up, as above shown, was that there is no equity jurisdiction in a case like this to construe a will of real estate unless the will creates a trust; and under that rule the court clearly did not have equity jurisdiction to enter the decree in question. This rule, "no trust, no equity jurisdiction," evidently does not proceed along the historical equity-jurisdiction line of adequacy of remedy at law, but along the strict jurisdiction or judicial-power line of subject-matter. Hence, on sound general principle, the rule of "no trust, no equity jurisdiction" ought to be applicable and controlling on collateral attack, as it seems to me, in a case like this one, where the complainants in equity in the case where the former decree was rendered had no standing whatever, either in a court of equity or in a court of law in ejectment, and their bill in equity stated a case outside the jurisdiction of any court either of law or equity, and was but a private letter to the court, rising no higher jurisdictionally than an oral request to the court for an advisory opinion, which advisory opinion given by the court on oral request would have been a nullity for all purposes, direct and collateral. In Whitman v. Fisher,[34] 1874, the question of the collateral operation and effect of this rule, "no trust, no equity jurisdiction," was treated as a "most serious question," and was avoided by a ruling that the will before the court created a trust.

It must be borne in mind, however, that this rule of "no trust, no equity jurisdiction," is new in point of clear, authoritative, final promulgation, is anomalous in itself, sui generis, unsound and erroneous in point of principle, and had been overthrown by the legislature

[34] 74 Ill., 147, 153.

when the case came up for decision. An anomalous rule
admits of only anomalous application even to the future,
and hardly ever admits of any application at all to the
past. In at least two previous instances the Supreme
Court refused to allow parties who had not relied on the
rule in the lower court to rely on it in the Supreme Court
on direct appeal or writ of error.[35] Hence the majority's
refusal to sustain the collateral attack on the decree
for violation of this rule of "no trust, on equity jurisdiction," is right in point of authority, usage, and practice, and is right in point of special principle (jus singu-
lare), the special principle being that an anomalous rule
admits of only anomalous application to the future, and
of no application at all to the past, and the effort before
the court was to apply an anomalous legislatively ex-
ploded rule to the past to disturb titles.[36]

The decree corrected the mistake in the will by striking
out one of the phrases, "the southwest quarter of," and
recited that the court acted on the basis of "the mistake
of the scrivener." The rule that there is no equity jurisdiction to reform wills is not a rule regulating the exercise
of equity jurisdiction, but is a rule denying judicial
power to reform wills. Hence, if it affirmatively appeared
on the face of the decree that the court really and in
truth did reform the will, the decree was void collaterally

[35] Windsor *v.* McVeigh, 93 U. S., 274, 283; Curtiss *v.* Brown, 29 Ill., 201, 229.

[36] In Justinian's Digest, Monro's Translation, the Roman jurist Paulus says in
1, 3, 14: "Where a rule has obtained force which is against legal principle, no
analogous extension thereof should be made." And Celsus says in 1, 3, 39: "When
some rule has been introduced which was not arrived at by any legal principle,
but was founded on a mistake and subsequently maintained by mere custom, it
is not to be applied to similar cases." And Blackstone says in 1 Com., 69, 70:
"Yet this rule," stare decisis, "admits of exception where the former determination
is most evidently contrary to reason," which reason is not every man's natural
reason, but the reason, method, and science of the law, as Blackstone says, repeating the favorite and familiar teaching and preaching of Lord Coke.

as an exertion of ungranted, and, therefore, usurped, judicial power to write a will for a dead man.[37]

It cannot be said, however, from the case as reported, that it did appear affirmatively on the face of the decree that the court made the correction by the process of reformation and not by the process of construction. The mistake was unlike any of the mistakes in the reported Illinois cases, which, as already said, were mistakes in government descriptions in wills resulting on the face of things in passing land testators did not own instead of land they did own. The mistake in this instance resulted on the face of things in passing less land than the testator owned, or only 40 acres out of 160 acres. The case was a plain one admitting of an application of the rule, falsa demonstratio non nocet, because, striking out one of the phrases, "the southwest quarter of," the descriptive words left clearly were capable, in connection with evidence of proper extrinsic facts, of identifying and passing the land in question, or 80 acres instead of 40 acres of the 160 acres the testator owned. The descriptive

[37] In his dissent Vickers, J., who assumes the existence of equity jurisdiction to correct the mistake (but see his dissent in Gano v. Gano, 239 Ill., 539), cites Pomeroy, Equity Jurisprudence, 3 Ed., Sec. 871, where in addition to cases correcting mistakes in wills by construction in courts of law and courts of equity, the author cites cases of correction of mistakes in wills in probate courts. When a will is offered for probate the question is whether the instrument offered is or is not the last will of the deceased. If, for example, it is shown clearly and convincingly to the probate court that certain words were written into the instrument by mistake, accident, or fraud, as, for example, in violation of the instructions of the testator, who signed the instrument without reading it on the assurance of the scrivener that it was entirely in accord with testator's instructions, such wrong words may be struck out, and the rest of the instrument may be probated as the last will of the deceased. But fresh words cannot be added by the probate court. This kind of correction cannot be made in the court of construction, which must take the probated text. Bowen v. Allen, 113 Ill., 53, 56, perhaps may be regarded as an instance of the use of this kind of power of correction by an Illinois probate court, which power our probate courts have, I think. It may be that the same power may be exercised by a court of equity in Illinois under a bill to contest the validity of a probated will under Sec. 7 of the Wills Act.

words, ' in Jackson County, Illinois, containing 81½ acres and a half more or less," made the mistake an easy one to correct by the process of construction aided by evidence of proper extrinsic facts.[38] As above stated, evidence of "mistake of the scrivener" is not usable ordinarily to aid construction, and it was error to put into the decree the finding and recital of "mistake of the scrivener." However, rejecting that finding and recital, it may be presumed in this case on collateral attack that enough evidence of proper extrinsic facts was before the court to warrant the correction of the mistake by process of construction,

Hence, the majority's refusal to sustain the collateral attack on the decree for violation of the rule denying judicial power to reform wills, is correct on principle, and is not wrong on authority, — correct on principle, because it did not appear affirmatively on the face of the decree the correction of the mistake was made by the process of reformation, and not wrong on authority, because the Supreme Court, though on the way to the slough of wrong principle and error, confusing construction and reformation, has not yet arrived, and may not arrive at that destination. The mistake was capable of correction legitimately by the process of construction, unless the epigram about construction and not reformation may be taken and applied at its face value; on principle it ought not to be so taken and applied; and on authority now evidently it cannot be so taken and applied, retroactively at least to disturb titles. The majority's refusal to sustain the collateral attack on this ground of reformation, not construction, reacts back, and operates as a strong blow delivered by necessary implication and intendment of law at the "not construction but reformation"

[38] Myers v. Ladd, 26 Ill., 415, 417; Emmert v. Hayes, 89 Ill., 11, 17, 18.

epigram, and at the majority opinion in Graves v. Rose[39] and at the dissenting opinions in Gano v. Gano,[40] which opinions ought to be abandoned at the first opportunity; and Kurtz v. Hibner, and the other Illinois cases after it, completely discredited abroad since Patch v. White,[41] in 1886, except in so far as they deny the right to use evidence of the "mistake of the scrivener" as an aid to construction, ought to be regarded as overruled, and Kurtz v. Hibner was overruled in fact, in spite of the court's protest to the contrary, by Decker v. Decker.[42]

The jurisdictional attack, as described in the dissenting opinion of Vickers, J., was very peculiar, being aimed not at the whole decree, but at only part of it, i. e., the part finding that Alexander and McPharlin "by virtue of the will took and had a fee-simple title." The theory seems to have been that the decree was divisible into two parts for the purpose of jurisdictional attack, which parts may be called for convenience the "reformation part" correcting the mistake, and the "construction part" finding the fee-simple title in Alexander and McPharlin. The "reformation part" of the decree, being favorable to Joseph, was assumed at the bar and by Vickers, J., dissenting, to be immune from attack, or at least was not attacked. It seems, also, it was admitted at the bar, and the admission was accepted by the whole court, that the fee-simple finding was an adjudication of Joseph's executory-devise claim against him. On that jurisdictionally divisible theory of the decree and on that admission that the finding of the fee-simple title was an adjudication against Joseph's executory-devise claim, there is no objection to the majority's answer to the argument that there was equity jurisdiction to enter the "reformation

[39] 246 Ill., 76.
[40] 239 Ill., 539.
[41] 117 U. S., 210.
[42] 121 Ill., 341.

part" of the decree, correcting the mistake, but no
equity jurisdiction to enter the "construction part,"
finding the fee-simple title, which answer was, that
"equity jurisdiction to construe the will" follows necessarily from the admitted "equity jurisdiction to reform
the will," or to correct the mistake, because of the rule
that a court of equity having jurisdiction to determine
one controversy between parties may determine another
related and connected, though legally separate and
distinct, controversy between the same parties, in order
to prevent a multiplicity of suits.   But the whole juris-
dictionally-divisible theory of the decree was wrong,
arbitrary in fact and impossible in law.   The fee-simple
finding was not a separable or separate part of the decree,
but was intended and appropriate, if not necessary, to
effect the correction of the mistake.   The whole decree
flowed from the judicial power to quiet title or determine
titles, exerted erroneously, it is true, in violation of the
rule of "no trust, no equity jurisdiction," but not usurped
as above shown.   The decree was an indivisible unit,
both on the merits of the claim for correction, and jurisdictionally.   It did not purport to adjudicate two claims,
the claim to correction of the mistake and the claim of an
executory devise, nor did it flow from two pseudo-
jurisdictions, or judicial powers, one to reform wills and
the other to construe wills.[43]

The admission at the bar, accepted by the whole court,
that the "construction part" of the decree finding a fee-

---

[43] The only assignable reason for dividing the decree into two parts for jurisdictional attack seems to be the not ill-grounded fear that overthrowing the whole
decree for want of jurisdiction would have opened up and renewed the "construc-
tion-reformation" contest in Gano v. Gano, 239 Ill., 539, and Graves v. Rose, 246
Ill., 76, with possibly destructive consequences to Joseph, who was making the
attack, cutting down to 10 acres the 40 acres of the north 80 acres he got under
the will as corrected, and cutting down his executory-devise claim to 10 acres of
40 acres of the south 80 acres.   The dissent of Vickers, J., indicates rather clearly
that these possible consequences to Joseph of sustaining his collateral attack were
present to the mind of the court.

simple title in Alexander and McPharlin was an adjudication against Joseph's executory-devise claim, was ill-
advised, evidencing misapprehension and a consequent
abandonment of the point on which Joseph's right to
litigate his executory-devise claim depended, viz., the
scope of the thing adjudged by the decree. Jurisdiction
to adjudge is one thing, and the thing adjudged is another
and different thing. It is hard to see why the fee-simple
finding was not fully satisfied by a base or determinable
fee simple, or, in other words, by a fee-simple title with
an executory devise over. However that may be, still,
on the face of the report, it is very evident Joseph's
executory-devise claim was not in fact litigated in the
prior suit or adjudged by the decree. And there hardly
can be any fair doubt that Joseph's claim to have the
mistake corrected, and Joseph's claim of an executory
devise are legally separate, distinct, and divisible claims.
The rule above noticed regulating the exercise of equity
jurisdiction, i. e., the giving or refusing of remedies, permitting two or more legally separate and distinct claims
to be determined in one suit in order to prevent a multiplicity of suits, though it may be used, as it was used
by the majority, to expand the jurisdiction, i. e., the
remedies, of a court of equity, yet it cannot be used to
expand the scope of the thing adjudged by a decree to
include and embrace another separate, distinct, and
divisible thing that was not adjudged in fact. That rule
of equity jurisdiction permits, but does not compel,
people to submit more than one claim to a court
at a time. Though the law forbids a man to split a
single cause of action, the law does not compel a man to
unite two or more causes of action in one suit at law or in
equity. A man may file a multiplicity of suits at law or in
equity to settle a multiplicity of claims against the same
adversary, if he likes and has the money to pay the fees.
A man does not lose any substantial rights by refusing or

failing to unite two or more separate, distinct, and divisible claims in one suit, even though the law permits him to do it. The thing adjudged extends to and embraces a thing that might have been adjudged, only when the thing that might have been adjudged is one that ought to have been put in issue and litigated in the suit wherein the judgment or decree was rendered. An option but no legal duty to put in issue and litigate, is not enough to bring the might-have-been doctrine in res judicata into play to extend the scope of the thing adjudged to include and embrace another and different thing, legally separate and divisible, that was not adjudged. Joseph's executory-devise claim was a separate, divisible claim that was not adjudged by the decree relied on as res judicata, so far as appears from the report at least.[44]

The collateral attack on the decree deserved its fate, though the state of the decisions, issuing out of the same confusion of thought touching equity jurisdiction the court now exposes, perhaps invited and justified the attack. There is reason in the complaint of Vickers, J., dissenting, that Joseph Rowan was stripped of 40 acres of land without authority of law, but not any jurisdictional reason. It may be remarked that experience as recorded and preserved in the law reports teaches that it is wise, when a former judgment or decree seemingly bars the way to the merits of a case, to try to find a way to the merits, under, over, or around the bar, before trying the dernier ressort of smashing the bar. If that rule of caution had been observed in this case, the jurisdictional contest might have been narrowed and concentrated on the question of the scope of the thing adjudged by the former decree, and the result on that contest and on the merits might have been the one arrived at by Vickers, J., dissenting.

[44] 24 Am. & Eng. Ency. of Law, 2 Ed., 789.

II

COLLECTED COMMENT

1. — CONSTRUCTION OF WILL AS GIVING JURISDICTION TO DETERMINE RIGHTS IN FOREIGN REAL PROPERTY.

2. — MISTAKE OF LAW AS A TITLE TO PROPERTY.

3. — JURISDICTION TO CORRECT MISTAKE IN A VOLUNTARY DEED.

4. — DONOR'S MISTAKE OF FACT — CORRECTION FOR DONEE AFTER DONOR'S DEATH.

5. — RESCISSION OF CONTRACT FOR SELLER'S MISTAKE.

1. — CONSTRUCTION OF WILL AS GIVING JURISDICTION TO DETERMINE RIGHTS IN FOREIGN REAL PROPERTY.[a] — PER CURIAM OPINIONS. — In Bevans v. Murray, 251 Ill., 603, in a per curiam opinion, Dunn, Cartwright, and Hand, JJ., dissenting, it is decided that an Illinois court of equity has jurisdiction to determine the validity of a conveyance of Indiana land made by a testamentary donee of a power to convey Illinois land and Indiana land, when the question arises between a devisee named in the will and the grantee in the conveyance, and the devisee assails the conveyance on the ground that it was not authorized by the terms of the power.

The majority reached their jurisdictional result by the process of expanding, to include cases calling for the original construction of a will of foreign land, the English chancery exception to the general rule of the common law, that the courts of one country or state have no jurisdiction to determine and enforce rights in land in another country or state, which English chancery exception is,

a [6 Ill. Law Rev., 596, April, 1912.]

that courts of chancery in England or in a state have jurisdiction to enforce a contract between parties, or "an equity" between parties, touching land in another country or state.

This English chancery exception to the general rule of the common law is anomalous (Dicey, Conflict of Laws, 2 ed., pp. 201–206), and seems to admit of little, if any, expansion as between our states beyond the point where it stood when the constitution of the United States was adopted, and the independence and equality of each state over the title and possession of its own soil as against every other state was secured and protected by the tenth amendment.[1]

---

[1] In point of legal theory, this anomalous English chancery rule of foreign jurisdiction seems to flow from two mistakes: First, the mistake of overlooking the true nature of aequitas agit in personam as a rule of local English remedial procedure limiting, not expanding, the power of the English High Court of Chancery even inside of England; second, the mistake of supposing that the part of English law that goes by the artificial name of "equity" is a universal jurisprudence, the same everywhere. As between our states, this dead notion of the universality of equity has no application.

It is sometimes said this anomalous English chancery rule of foreign jurisdiction applies as between England and foreign countries just the same as between England and her colonies and dependencies like Ireland and Scotland. But that may be doubted. At any rate, the rule was originated and established in cases concerning property in English colonies, and dependencies at a time when the English colonial empire was arising, and the rule always has been applied most frequently in such cases by the English courts. As between England and her colonies and dependencies, the rule is defensible, and politically and constitutionally sound, as part and parcel of the English policy of employing and encouraging the superior courts in England to diffuse English legal ideas and methods throughout the British Empire, just as we now employ the Supreme Court of the United States to carry American legal ideas and methods into Porto Rico and the Philippine Islands. An original suit in the English chancery was, when this anomalous chancery rule was established, a highly convenient short-cut from "the plantations" to the English jurisdiction. This practical, political, and constitutional reason for the rule can have no application as between our states.

The majority opinion of McKenna, J. in Fall v. Eastin, 215 U. S., 1, throws doubt on the question whether a decree in one state entered in exercise of jurisdiction under this anomalous English chancery rule is valid and enforceable in any other state if the party bound by the decree refuses to perform it. The real trouble with Fall v. Eastin is, that the point that ought to have been con-

COLLECTED COMMENT 843

The majority cite no authority that supports their jurisdictional view. They admit their decree is brutum fulmen
in Indiana. The reason why it is brutum fulmen in
Indiana is, that Illinois courts, in this kind of a case, have
no jurisdiction over the subject-matter; the jurisdiction
of Indiana courts is exclusive, and it makes no difference
whether the will devises legal titles to Indiana land
directly or by way of trust, in combination with Illinois
land or separately, or whether the will is executed in
Illinois according to Illinois law or in Indiana according
to Indiana law. McCartney v. Osburn, 118 Ill., 403,
409–411; Ford v. Ford, 73 Wis., 19, 62–68; Clark v. Clark,
178 U. S., 186; Olmsted v. Olmsted, 216 U. S., 386;
Thormann v. Frame, 176 U. S., 350; Overby v. Gordon,
177 U. S., 214; Tilt v. Kelsey, 207 U. S., 43.[2]

The majority appear to have fallen into confusion of
thought over the different meanings of the word "equity,"

tested was not contested, viz., the jurisdiction of the Washington court to render
the decree touching Nebraska land that was brought into the Nebraska court
for enforcement. The case was argued on one side only, and that side had to
admit the jurisdiction of the Washington court. On the erroneous theory on
which the case proceeded, viz., that the Washington court had jurisdiction, the
dissenting opinion of Holmes, J., is much nearer the truth and sound law of the case
than the majority opinion.

[2] The majority opinion of White, J., in the divorce case of Haddock v. Haddock, 201 U. S., 562, expressly declares the idea that a state court has two jurisdictions, one jurisdiction to render a judgment or decree that is valid and enforceable at home and valid and enforceable in every other state, and another
jurisdiction to render a judgment or decree that is valid and enforceable at home
but valid and enforceable in another state according to the taste or "comity"
of the other state, every other state being free to respect the judgment or decree
or to disregard it at pleasure. This idea is not necessary to support the decision
in Haddock v. Haddock, plainly is obiter, is shaken by the later case of Fauntleroy
v. Lum, 210 U. S., 230, and is contrary to the clear rule of all the prior cases,
that there is no such thing as a judgment or decree valid in the state where rendered and depending for recognition in another state on the will of the other state.

When the fundamental law of a man's country secures to him a right to have
his controversy respecting the ownership of Indiana land adjudicated by the courts
of Indiana, it seems self-evident that an Illinois court has no jurisdiction to coerce
him, by a threat of imprisonment, to give up that right against his will, to submit
his controversy to the Illinois court, and to obey its judgment or decree.

taking "equity" in the construction of a will of land to be the same thing as "an equity" in the land itself. The will before the court devised legal titles to Indiana land directly and not by way of trust. On the merits the whole of the question was whether a power given by will authorized a certain conveyance of Indiana land, a question in the construction of wills. Construing the will according to "equity and good conscience," in the light of extrinsic facts surrounding the testator, the majority decided the conveyance of the Indiana land in question was not authorized by the terms of the power, and the land in question passed by the will to a devisee named therein. Hence the conveyance of the Indiana land made by the donee of the power was void both at law and in equity and passed nothing to the grantee, who, therefore, was not the legal owner of any Indiana land, and could not be subject to any equity or legal duty to convey any Indiana land to another. The case was an action of ejectment in an Illinois court by the devisee named in the will against the grantee named in the conveyance to try the title to Indiana land under the form and guise of a bill in equity in an Illinois court to quiet the title to Indiana land, for it seems the grantee in the conveyance was in possession of the Indiana land in question. As the dissenting opinion says clearly and pointedly, there was no equity to foreign property in the case anywhere, and the anomalous English chancery rule of foreign jurisdiction could not be applied — wholly aside from the question of its application where a will devises foreign land by way of trust. If the majority's "equity" in the construction of the will had brought them to the conclusion that the conveyance under the power was valid, could they have made a decree in favor of the grantee in the conveyance? Is the foreign jurisdiction here exercised a one-sided jurisdiction to dis-establish foreign titles but not to re-establish them?

The opinion is per curiam. There seems to be a variety of views among Illinois lawyers on the reason or reasons for anonymous opinions in this state and their authority. The per curiam practice does not obtain to any great extent, if at all, in the federal courts. It has been said that an opinion per curiam "does not receive as high respect as an opinion vouched for by some one judge and adopted by the court" (Wambaugh, Study of Cases, 2 ed., Sec. 45), though it is said "this is not so in English practice" (11 Law Q. Rev., 199). Whatever may be the practice in this state on this point, if there is any practice, this instant per curiam, with three named dissenters out of seven judges, evidently is of no practical value outside the case in which it was delivered. The prudent lawyer must decline to be guided by this per curiam, and must continue to keep in the middle of the beaten path to the courts of the state where the land lies to settle disputed titles under wills of foreign land, whether the will devises legal titles directly or by way of trust.

2. — MISTAKE OF LAW AS A TITLE TO PROPERTY.[a] — The inclination and tendency of Courts appears to be to restrict the use of the maxim, Ignorantia legis non excusat, as a muniment of title to money or other property, so far as it is possible to do so with due regard to the rule of stare decisis. But in Village of Morgan Park v. Knopf, 199 Ill., 444, 446, 1902, Mr. Justice Cartwright said: "This rule" — Money paid under a mistake of law ordinarily cannot be recovered back — "which is well settled as between individuals has been extended to municipal corporations under similar circumstances," citing People v. Foster, 133 Ill., 496, and the reporter's headnote to Village of Morgan Park v. Knopf states that as one of the points decided. See the same case in its

a [1 Ill. Law Rev., 335, December, 1906.]

final stage in 210 Ill., 452. In City of Sullivan v. Whitfield, 109 Ill. App., 120, 1903, the Appellate Court for the Fourth District, using People v. Foster as authority, allowed a lawyer (see Ex parte Moulton, 18 Wend., 586) to use the rule as the sole foundation of his title to money of the City of Sullivan illegally (see Chicago v. Williams, 182 Ill., 135) paid to him by officials of the City. Turning to the case of People v. Foster, I think I am safe in affirming, first, that the Court could not on the facts before it decide any such proposition, and secondly, that all of the cases there cited on pp. 509–511, in seeming support of that proposition have been explained away in the Courts where they were decided, except possibly Snelson v. The State, 16 Ind., 29, and I dare say if one searched diligently enough he would find the Indiana Courts have had something to say about that case. In Wisconsin Central R. Co. v. United States, 164 U. S. 190, 212, Chief Justice Fuller reviewed all the previous cases in that Court dealing with the right of the United States to recover money illegally paid by public officers and said:

"Reference was made to Barnes v. District of Columbia, 22 C. Cl. 366, 394, wherein it was ruled, Richardson, C. J., delivering the opinion, that 'the doctrine that money paid can be recovered when paid in mistake of fact and not of law does not have so general application to public officers using the funds of the people as to individuals dealing with their own money where nobody but themselves suffer for their ignorance, carelessness, or indiscretion, because in the former case the elements of agency and the authority and duty of officers and their obligations to the public, of which all persons dealing with them are bound to take notice, are always involved.' We concur in these views, and are of opinion that there is nothing on this record to take the case out of the scope of the principle that parties receiving moneys illegally paid by public officers are liable ex aequo et bono to refund them."

Other cases in agreement with the aforesaid ruling of the Supreme Court of the United States may be found cited by Mr. Woodward in his article on "Recovery of Money Paid Under Mistake of Law" in 5 Columbia Law Review, 366, 372, note 2, to which may be added County of Wayne v. Ellis, 126 Mich., 231, where County of Wayne v. Randall, 43 Mich., 137, cited in People v. Foster, is overruled, and Advertiser & Tribune Co. v. Detroit, 43 Mich., 116, also cited in People v. Foster, is reserved for future consideration. Though the above quoted remark of Mr. Justice Cartwright in Village of Morgan Park v. Knopf is probably obiter, repugnant to sound principles, adjudged cases, and provisions of the Illinois Cities and Villages Act of 1872, the Illinois Supreme Court may adopt it as the rule of decision. Counsel in a litigated case in an Illinois Court who wishes to contest that remark to the limit would do well to raise and save the Federal question whether a State judgment resting upon it is the due process of law which the Fourteenth Amendment enjoins upon the State Judiciary.

In Atherton v. Roche, 192 Ill., 252, 1901, the Court, by a vote of four to three, sustained a title to real estate resting exclusively upon a mistake of law, unaided by any equitable consideration whatever. Francis Atherton, having only one child, a daughter Margaret, wanted to settle ninety acres of land so that his daughter might enjoy it during her life and her children have the ninety acres after her death. Accordingly, acting as his own lawyer and scrivener, he drew up a deed of gift conveying the ninety acres to his daughter and her then husband, "to them and their bodily heirs." By the husband named in the deed, the daughter Margaret had one child, a boy. She also had a child, named Fannie Keeler, by a former husband. By a subsequent husband, named Roche she had three girls. Francis Atherton and his daughter Margaret died, and, of course, under the deed of gift the boy took the ninety acres, and his half-sisters, Fannie Keeler and the three Roche girls, took nothing. The case arose on a bill in equity filed by the Roche girls against the boy and Fannie Keeler to reform the deed of gift and for a partition of the ninety acres. It was proved and found as a fact that Francis Atherton did fall into a mistake of law in using the words "their bodily heirs" in his deed of gift. No rights of purchasers for value without notice, as in Fowler v. Black, 136 Ill., 363, were involved. Of previous decisions of the Court cited, Kyner v. Boll, 182 Ill., 171, seems the one most closely applicable. There a mistake of law in the words of a deed was corrected, and the writer of the opinion in that case, Mr. Justice Carter, dissented in Atherton v. Roche. Mr. Justice Hand distinguished Kyner v. Boll and Dinwiddie v. Self, 145 Ill., 290, thus:

"In both of these cases words were inserted in the deeds sought to be reformed without the procurement, knowledge, or consent of the grantees, which limited the title to a life estate in the grantee when it was the intention of the grantor to convey the fee, and the court in each case, upon well-recognized principles, properly expunged such words of limitation therefrom. In the case at bar the deed was written as the grantor intended it should be written. He knew its contents, but was mistaken as to the legal effect thereof. 'It is where parties intended to insert words in a contract which were by accident omitted that equity can reform the contract by inserting them or by expunging words they did not intend to have inserted. If the words are written as the parties intended they should be written or supposed they were written when they signed the contract, no matter how much they may be mistaken as to the meaning of those words, no relief can be granted either at law or in equity.' Sibert v. McAvoy, supra."

Turning to Sibert v. McAvoy, 15 Ill., 106, 109–110, we find the passage quoted, with no authority cited, as was the habit of Mr. Justice Caton, though he knew the cases, but followed by these three sentences: "The construction of words is a matter of law. The insertion of words is a

matter of fact.   It is for mistakes of fact alone that contracts may be reformed." The distinction between a
mistake as to the legal effect of words and that other mistake expressed as well as it is capable of expression by
Mr. Justice Caton in 1853 and Mr. Justice Hand in 1901
appears to go back to the opinions of Chief Justice
Marshall and Mr. Justice Washington in the leading case
of Hunt *v*. Rousmaniere, 8 Wheaton, 174, and 1 Peters, 1,
decided in 1823 and 1828.   Mr. Bigelow examined this
case at length and concludes that "Hunt *v*. Roumaniere
draws no such distinction in either of its stages" and
"such a distinction cannot be sound." See 1 Story's
Equity Jurisprudence, Ed. 13, note on Mistake of Law,
p. 108 and p. 112.   On Mr. Justice Hand's own statement of the distinction, even assuming it to be sound and
supported by decided cases, its application to the facts
in Atherton *v*. Roche is not made clearly manifest.   As
Mr. Justice Boggs, for the minority, points out, the central fact in Atherton *v*. Roche was that the deed sought to
be reformed was a deed of gift and not a deed of purchase,
a unilateral transaction and not a bilateral transaction.
Francis Atherton did not consult his donees or intended
donees as to the words he should use to give effect to his
intention, nor did he need to.   But the Court's attention
seems not to have been directed to the subject of the
jurisdiction of equity to.correct mistakes of fact and of
law of the donor in a deed of gift.   There are a number of
cases holding that such mistakes may be corrected in favor
of the donor, but not against him, while alive.   And
Kyner *v*. Boll, though the first deed was in truth a deed of
purchase, probably, rather indicates that Francis Atherton could have corrected his mistake at any time before
his death.   The evidence in Atherton *v*. Roche, so far as
reported, shows that Francis Atherton never changed
his original intention before he died.   There are cases

holding that after the death of the donor, on proof that he never changed his original intention, his intrument of gift will be reformed to correct a mistake of fact or of law made by him so as to give effect to his intention. Decided cases, pro and con, may be found in 2 Ames' Cases in Equity Jurisdiction, pp. 289–292, 245–247, and in 2 Pomeroy's Equitable Remedies, Section 679, notes 17 and 18. If the general expressions culled by Mr. Justice Hand from previous opinions of the Illinois Supreme Court are to be taken at their face value, then one would have to say that an Illinois Court has no power at all to relieve against a mistake of law; that, in Illinois, Lord Ellenborough's slip of the tongue in Bilbie v. Lumley, 2 East., 469, "Every man must be taken to be cognizant of the law," has grown up to be an old saw of the Courts like unto the law of the Medes and Persians that altereth not. But decided cases forbid one to say that. I think Atherton v. Roche was wrongly decided on principle and on authority. At any rate, since the Court did not articulate the proposition and three Justices dissented in Atherton v. Roche, and in view of at least two previous decisions (Dinwiddie v. Self and Kyner v. Boll) mitigating the rigor of the ancient statements of the mistake of law rule, I do not see how it can yet be said that, in Illinois, equity will not correct a donor's mistake of law as to the legal effect of the words used by him in his instrument of gift, no rights of purchasers for value without notice having intervened. Such a ruling would be distinctly reactionary to what Judge Redfield in his edition of Story's Equity Jurisprudence called "the enthusiasm manifested (by American Courts) to stigmatize the idea of asking relief, in a court of equity, from the consequences of a mistake of law, as a gross and puerile absurdity." (1 Story's Equity Jurisprudence, Ed. 12, Section 138g.)

Perhaps the Court did take that reactionary step in Strayer *v.* Dickerson, 205 Ill., 257. But the emphasis of the argument at the bar in that case was upon the point that the deed was upon a good and valuable consideration, a point that ultimately prevailed. Strayer *v.* Dickerson, 213 Ill., 414. Mr. Justice Ricks evidently overlooked the warning of Chief Justice Breese in Otis *v.* Beckwith, 49 Ill., 121, 134: "The general principle, advanced in the books, that a court of equity will not enforce a voluntary contract, is to be understood with proper qualification, for they abound in cases where such a contract has been enforced." But see the obiter dictum of Mr. Justice Hand in Henry *v.* Henry, 215 Ill., 205. See, however, the case of Deischer *v.* Price, 148 Ill., 383, per Mr. Justice Bailey, and the expressions of Mr. Justice Wilkin in Mason *v.* Mullahy, 145 Ill., 383. The remarks of Mr. Justice Ricks in Strayer *v.* Dickerson, supra, upon a proposition not relied on by counsel, as Mr. Justice Ricks says, and not necessary to support the result reached by the Court, certainly do not come within the rule of stare decisis. It is doubtful, to say the least, whether the Supreme Court is committed to the doctrine, that, if A, intending to give Blackacre to B, by mistake gives him Whiteacre, the Courts of Illinois are powerless, when the mistake is clearly proved, and no substantial rights of bona fide purchasers have intervened, to correct the mistake in favor of the donor, and thus act in favor of the donor's intention. The Illinois precedents leave it open to the Supreme Court to choose between rejecting and accepting that doctrine; in other words, between preserving and destroying an acknowledged jurisdiction. Boni judicis est ampliare jurisdictionem. "The true text is boni judicis est ampliare justitiam, not jurisdictionem, as it has been often cited," per Lord Mansfield, Broom's Legal Maxims, Ed. 3, star page 59, note 2. The true rule regulating the jurisdiction of equity to correct mistakes of fact and of law in an instrument of gift is stated in M'Mechan v. Warburton, L. R., Ireland, 1 Ch. D., 435, reprinted in Ames' Cases and cited by Pomeroy, supra, as follows:

"The elementary principle of this Court, that it will not interfere to enforce specific performance of an incomplete voluntary agreement, is subject to this exception, that after the death of the donor it will interfere to rectify a disposition which is clearly proved to have, through mistake, failed to carry out the proved intention. The principle is, I think, more correctly stated by confining it to this, that the Court will not rectify a voluntary disposition *against* the donor. That it will do so *in favor* of a donor is shown by the case of Lackersteen v. Lackersteen, 30 L. J. Ch. N. S., 5, where a voluntary settlement was rectified by Wood, V. C., at the instance of the settlor. This explains the view taken by Romilly, M. R., in Lister v. Hodgson, L. R., 4 Eq., 30, where he stated the exception I have mentioned in a case of a deceased donor, that upon clear proof of the intention of the donor, which, by mistake, was not correctly carried out by the instrument of gift according to such intention, the Court will interfere to correct the mistake, and thus act in favor of the intention. If the donor were living, it would have, of course, been competent for him to consent to such rectification, or to dissent from it. If the latter, it could not be reformed against his will, for a volunteer must take the gift as he finds it; but after his death, and in absence of proof of any change of intention, it cannot be assumed that he would have dissented, and it might even be presumed that he would not dissent. In this view Lister v. Hodgson, L. R., 4 Equity, 30, is not a departure from the true principle."

Compare the ruling of the Master, approved by the lower Court, and abandoned by counsel in the Supreme Court, in Strayer v. Dickerson, 205 Ill., 257, 263, 270.

3. — JURISDICTION TO CORRECT MISTAKES IN A VOLUNTARY DEED.[a] — Though the point appears not to have been argued, perhaps Finch v. Green, 225 Ill., 304, 80

[a] [2 Ill. Law Rev., 42, May, 1907.]

N. E. Rep., 318, in connection with other recent Illinois cases, overlooking some earlier cases and misapplying others, lets slip into the law of Illinois the proposition that a Court of Equity has no jurisdiction to correct mistakes in a voluntary deed, because the deed is voluntary. The injustice that would result from a logical application of that proposition was avoided in Finch *v.* Green, by a finding of fact by the Supreme Court, reversing the finding of the lower Court, that "there was a valuable consideration for the conveyance, which would authorize a Court of Equity to correct the mistake." The proposition rests upon a clear misapprehension of the scope of the rule, that a Court of Equity will not entertain a bill by donee against donor for the specific performance of an executory promise to make a gift. See Lynn *v.* Lynn, 135 Ill., 18; 1 Ill. Law R., 335–339 [ante p. 845]. In Finch *v.* Green, where the deed was absolute, with a reservation of a life estate to the grantor, the Court, speaking by Mr. Justice Cartwright, on the authority of Strayer *v.* Dickerson, uses these words: "If . . . the gift was unexecuted by reason of a mistake in the description." See Strayer *v.* Dickerson, 205 Ill., at pp. 266–267, Ricks, J., for the origin of that conception. In Lynn *v.* Lynn, supra, at p. 26, where the deed was in trust, the Court, speaking by Mr. Justice Craig, said: "Although it (the deed) may need reformation as to the description, it is not on that account, to be regarded as an executory contract." The present attitude of the Supreme Court appears to be to admit the above proposition into the law, and then to proceed immediately to knock it out by straining after "a valuable consideration." But with whatever dexterity and consistency the Court may be able to exercise its discretion it is plain that the Court is substituting the discretion of the Judge in the place of a rule that would attain the same beneficial object with more certainty.

4. — Donor's Mistake of Fact — Correction for Donee After Donor's Death.[a] — A strong-arm judicial determination that a deed of gift is a deed of purchase, made to avoid the hardship in a particular case resulting from an application of the rule in Strayer v. Dickerson, 205 Ill., 257, Ricks, J., that a donee cannot have a correction of his deceased donor's mistake of fact in the deed of gift, is an example of the kind of juristic process Roman lawyers used to call "inelegant" (inelegantia juris). The minority say the majority employed this inelegant process to save a donee in Legate v. Legate, 249 Ill., 359, Vickers, C. J., writing the opinion, Cartwight, Hand, and Dunn, JJ., dissenting.

The majority say the same process was employed to save a donee in the prior case of Finch v. Green, 225 Ill., 304, Cartwright, J., a case just like the present one, and because a valuable consideration was found in Finch v. Green a valuable consideration has got to be found in this case. The minority says Finch v. Green "is not like the case at bar," meaning there was a valuable consideration in Finch v. Green, but none in the case at bar. The truth appears to be, that the two cases are alike, as related to the common-law rule of "valueless valuable consideration," but their likeness consists in this, to-wit: there is no valuable consideration in either of them. The majority found the two cases alike in another particular, viz., as related to the difference between an "executory gift" and an "executed gift," or, in other words, the difference between compelling a man to give away his property and protecting a man in the ownership of what he already has, whether he acquired it by purchase or by gift. The majority say the instant case is "one to reform an executed contract," i. e., an executed gift. On that view, the ques-

---

[a] [6 Ill. Law Rev., 202, October, 1911.]

tion of valuable consideration vel non was irrelevant to
the question of the donee's right to have the deceased
donor's mistake corrected.

In Lynn *v.* Lynn, 135 Ill., 18, Craig, J., a donee got a
correction of his deceased donor's mistake in the deed of
gift, the Court resting the donee's right on the foundation
that the gift was executed and not executory. The
point was adjudged deliberately, as is plain on the face
of the opinion and as is made more plain by the reversed
opinion of Gary, J., in Lynn *v.* Lynn, 33 Ill. App., 299.
And see Lynn *v.* Lynn, 160 Ill., 307. It is true the deed
of gift in Lynn *v.* Lynn was not direct to the donee, but
was to a trustee in trust for the donee. That cannot make
any difference, however, because the reason of the decision,
viz., that the gift was executed, applies equally to a deed
direct to the donee. Lynn *v.* Lynn never has been questioned, and gives legal effect to the natural equity of
mankind under such circumstances. The case was overlooked in Strayer *v.* Dickerson, 205 Ill., 257, though it
was cited by counsel, and is just such a "well-grounded
case" as Ricks, J., on p. 266, challenged counsel to find.
Lynn *v.* Lynn is supported by cases in other jurisdictions.
Huss *v.* Morris, 63 Pa. St., 367, cited by counsel in Lynn *v.*
Lynn; Williamson *v.* Carpenter, 205 Pa. St., 164; Lister *v.*
Hodgson, L. R., 4 Eq., 30, 34; M'Mechan *v.* Warburton,
L. R., Ireland, 1 Ch. D., 435; Wyche *v.* Greene, 16 Ga.,
49; 2 Ill. Law Rev., 42 [ante p. 852]; 1 Ill. Law Rev., 335
[ante p. 845]. It is easy to drop Strayer *v.* Dickerson,
205 Ill., 257, without overruling it, because the deed in
question was not a deed of gift, but a deed of purchase,
as appeared later in Strayer *v.* Dickerson, 213 Ill., 257.
There can be no doubt at all that the sphere of the practical application of Strayer *v.* Dickerson, 205 Ill., 257, is
narrowed, if not wiped out, by Lynn *v.* Lynn, Finch *v.*
Green, and the instant case of Legate *v.* Legate.

As the cases stand, the lawyer must impress upon his donee client the supreme importance of "getting a witness to the valuable consideration," but when the evidence is closed he is not justified in admitting that a valuable consideration is indispensable to enable the donee to correct the donor's mistake after the donor's death in ignorance of the mistake when the mistake is one of fact. The case where a donor makes a mistake of law in his deed of gift admits of a difference in point of authority, though why that should be so in point of reason is hard to understand. Atherton v. Atherton, 192 Ill., 252; 1 Ill. Law Rev., 335 [ante p. 845]; Markby, Elements of Law, 1st Ed., Secs. 265 et seq.[3]

5. — Rescission of Contract for Seller's Mistake.[a] — In Steinmeyer v. Schroeppel, 226 Ill., 9, Cartwright J., the Supreme Court decided, as the third paragraph of the reporter's note says, that "A mistake by a dealer in adding up the various items of the selling price of material upon which he had been asked to furnish an estimate, does not justify a Court of Equity in canceling a contract to fur-

[3] There is a collection of gift cases in an article on "Mistake in the Formation and Performance of Contracts," 11 Col. Law Rev., 197, p. 203, note 29. In "Mistake of Fact as a Ground of Affirmative Equitable Relief," 23 Harv. Law Rev., 608, Mr. Edwin H. Abbot, Jr., says on pp. 619–621, "The better reasoning appears to be with the cases which deny the donee relief against the heirs or next of kin" of the donor, because, "if the donee had no equity against the donor in the donor's lifetime, it is hard to see how the death of the donor can raise one against those who take what the donor left." But the question is, What, on the facts of the case, did the donor have to leave by will or to pass by descent? The idea of Romilly, M. R., in Leister v. Hodgson, L. R., 4 Eq., 30, 34, that a gift though executory in the donor's lifetime, because of a mistake in the deed of gift, becomes executed on the donor's death in ignorance of the mistake, is a much better means to "do justice" than the idea that a moral obligation is a valuable consideration. See Austin's criticism of Lord Mansfield's tendency to arbitrary notions about "Equity." Jurisprudence, Lecture 5, Secs. 179, 180. In Legate v. Legate and Finch v. Green it is not clear whether the donee took possession in the lifetime of the donor. See the cases under part performances of oral executory gifts under the statute of frauds. 36 Cyc., 681.

[a] [2 Ill. Law Rev., 267, November, 1907.]

nish such material based upon the other party's acceptance of the proposition to furnish the same for the
amount represented by the erroneous total." The buyer,
a building contractor about to erect a building for himself,
left at the office of the seller, a lumber dealer, a list of
lumber containing thirty-four items. The seller's bookkeeper set down upon that list, opposite each item, the
price. The seller himself added up the column, making the
total $1,446. The correct total was $1,867 — a difference
of $421. The bookkeeper copied the list without the
prices, and wrote at the bottom "Above for $1,446."
The offer was made in this form, and the seller accepted it.
The buyer received bids from two other dealers, which
were for about $1,890. The seller's request for rescission
and cancellation was granted by Judge Burroughs, but
this ruling was reversed by the Appellate Court for the
Fourth District, and the reversal was confirmed by the
Supreme Court on appeal on certificate of importance.
On the case as reported, without any more evidence, perhaps the Court might have held that the buyer, when he
accepted the offer, knew or must be presumed to have
known or scented the seller's mistake, and hence that
the seller was entitled to a rescission under the rule
allowing it where there is a mistake on one side and a
dishonest or unfair attempt to take advantage of it on the
other. See Garrard v. Frankel, 30 Beavan, 450; Gun v.
McCarthy, L. R., Ir. 13 Ch. D., 304; McCormick v.
Miller, 102 Ill., 208. But no effort appears to have been
made by counsel either by evidence or by argument to
get the seller's case within this rule. The case is discussed
by the Court on the basis of fact that the buyer's conduct
in all respects came up fully to the high standard of
Courts of Equity in such cases. On that footing, the
case presented the question whether this mistake of the
seller, unaccompanied by any other equitable circumstance

in his favor anterior to the buyer's acceptance of the offer, furnished adequate ground for rescission. There is doubtless a difference between the moral delinquency of "snapping at an offer" with a suspicion that the offer is the result of a mistake like this, and the moral delinquency of insisting on holding the seller to an offer which the buyer now knows, after acceptance, to be the result of a mistake like this. But the practical effect upon the property interest of the parties is the same, if the mistake is allowed to operate, whether the buyer knows of the mistake before or after he accepts the offer. And that practical effect is to take property away from the seller and give it to buyer for nothing and against the seller's will. I take it to be plain, and the Court does not deny it, as such denial would put an end to the case,[4] that the minds of the parties were not ad idem concerning the price, the true thought of the seller being to fix the price at the correct total of the thirty-four items. Actual moral delinquency on the other side antecedent to the formal conclusion of the bargain hardly can be an indispensable requisite to relief by rescission for mistake of the complainant only (see Paget *v.* Marshall, L. R., 28 Ch. D., 255), when it is recalled that Courts of Equity do not concern themselves with the moral delinquencies of parties except when they touch, concern, and hurt the

---

[4] The decision is: Conceding that a want of correspondence between the outward expression, evidenced by the written contract, and the inner thought of the parties as respects the price has been proved, then the outward expression must stand for reasons which the Court gives. The Court does say on p. 15: "The contract was exactly what each party understood it to be and it expressed what was intended by each," and on p. 14 gets rid of the case of Harron *v.* Foley (62 Wis., 584) thus: "There was no agreement (in that case), for the reason that the minds of the parties never met." On the subject of mutual consent, the Court cites 2 Kent's Com. 477, and 24 Am. & Eng. Ency. of Law, Ed. 2, 618; quaere whether the opinion discloses a due apprehension of the basis for a bill for rescission of a contract for mistake, namely: An alleged variance between the outward, formal manifestation of consensus and the true inner thought of one or both of the parties.

property interests of others. The Court's opinion opens with the proposition that "The jurisdiction of Equity to grant the remedy of cancellation because of mistake of fact by one party to a contract is well recognized," and then proceeds to defeat the seller, first, because the mistake was due to his own want of care and caution, and, second, because the mistake did not affect the substance of the contract. This seems unsound, on principle and on authority. Clearly this mistake would defeat a bill for specific performance. Webster v. Cecil; 30 Beavan, 62; Chute v. Quincy, 156 Mass., 189; Mansfield v. Sherman, 81 Maine, 365. So far as going to the substance of the contract is concerned, there seems to be little difference between this mistake as a defense to a bill for specific performance and this mistake as a ground for the affirmative relief of rescission. See Garrard v. Frankel and Gun v. McCarthy, supra. As respects the rule, founded on reasons of policy rather than of justice between the parties, which says a buyer, or a seller, as the case may be when the mistake is on one side only, has no business to make certain kinds of mistakes concerning the thing sold (caveat emptor and caveat venditor), whatever may be its true application in the case of a prayer for rescission grounded on the alleged mistake, it would appear to be inapplicable to the particular mistake made by the seller in Steinmeyer v. Schroeppel. See cases supra. The court rests this part of its opinion on Bonney v. Stoughton, 122 Ill., 536. The subject there involved, however, was mistake as a ground for removing the bar of the Statute of Limitations, quite a different thing from rescinding a contract for mistake. The books are filled with cautions about applying the general statements in Bonney v. Stoughton and Story's Eq. Jur., Secs. 146–148, to the effect that, in the absence of fraud or concealment, a Court of Equity will never interfere on the ground of mistake unless the mistake is such as could not have been avoided by the exercise of ordinary diligence. See, for example, 2 Pomeroy's Eq. Jur., Ed. 3, Sec. 856, note 3; Bigelow's note on Mistake of Fact in his edition of Story's Eq. Jur., and cases cited by these authors. The court finally says its decision was required in order to maintain "stability in contracts." The force of that is not apparent, for the court evidently does not mean to impugn the whole doctrine of rescission for mistake. The doctrine is founded in part at least, on the good idea of harmonizing the law of contracts with accepted principles of common honesty and fair dealing. Mulkey, J., in McCormick v. Miller, 102 Ill., 208, 214. On the court's seeming full acceptance of the proposition that a mistake alone may be cause for rescission, its reasons for not giving the seller the benefit of the proposition in this case are quite unsatisfactory and unduly restrict the logic of the morality of the decided cases. I think Judge Burroughs' conclusion was in harmony with fixed rules and in accord with the general sense of right, and ought to have been sustained.[5]

[5] [Note by the then editor of the Ill. Law. Rev., Professor Roscoe Pound:] It is interesting to note that the new German Code, differing from the Roman law on this point, would clearly allow rescission in such a case, BGB, §119. It holds that errors are to be regarded as errors in the content where they are "of such a nature that from the point of view of practical affairs one ought to regard them as essential." This goes much beyond the Roman law. Digest, 12, 6, 65. 2, Baron, Pandekten, §50.

TOPIC III

RELIEF AGAINST TORTS

I. Equity Jurisdiction to Abate and Enjoin Illegal Saloons as Public Nuisances.

II. Right of Workmen to Enjoin a Threatened Strike — Comment on Kemp v. Division No. 241.

I

EQUITY JURISDICTION TO ABATE AND ENJOIN ILLEGAL SALOONS AS PUBLIC NUISANCES [a]

Stead *v.* Fortner[1] is believed to be the first ruling by a court of last resort that a saloon established in violation of a prohibitory liquor statute, and declared a public nuisance per se as being malum prohibitum, though in other respects an orderly house in the sense of the law, falls within the general jurisdiction of a court of equity to abate and enjoin public nuisances on information by the attorney-general.

The court cites Walker *v.* McNelly,[2] in 1904, as a like ruling. That seems an error. That Georgia case rests on the prior case of Lofton *v.* Collins,[3] in 1903, where the Georgia court puts the jurisdiction mainly on specified sections of the Georgia Civil Code of 1895. And section 5335 of the Georgia Civil Code of 1911, apparently re-enacting a Georgia statute of 1899, authorizes suits in equity to abate and enjoin "blind tigers," i. e., places where intoxicating liquors are sold in violation of law.

There are statutes in several of the states authorizing suits in equity to abate the present and enjoin the future use of premises for the illegal sale of intoxicating liquor. The Supreme Court says these statutes are "no more than a legislative declaration of an existing jurisdiction

a [8 Ill. Law Rev., 19, May, 1913.]
1 255 Ill., 468
2 121 Ga., 114
3 117 Ga., 434, 440.

of ancient origin and which has always existed without
any statute[4] and extends at least back to the reign of
Queen Elizabeth"[5] and "it would require a statute to
destroy such jurisdiction."[6] That is a good illustration
of the judicial fiction of making new law under the guise
of discovering old law in antiquity, so much condemned
as harmful intellectual dishonesty on the bench by Ben-
tham and by Austin after him, and recently by Gray in
his book on "The Nature and Sources of the Law."[7]

[4] 255 Ill., at p. 479

[5] 255 Ill., at p. 475

[6] 255 Ill. at p. 479.

[7] It is useless to talk about an attorney-general's bill in equity for an injunction
against a saloon-keeper to shut up and close an illegal saloon as a public nuisance
in the time of Elizabeth. Home-brewed ale was the English drink until the
Reformation, when, as it was commonly said, "hops and heresy" came in together
about 1525, beer fast becoming as popular as heresy. For a while after the
Norman Conquest in 1066, the Normans continued their native habit of drinking
wine, but they soon acquired a liking and preference for English ale and beer.
Bacon tells us Elizabeth's usual breakfast was beefsteak and beer. The drinking
of aqua vitae, or distilled liquors, "spirits," especially gin, began to be common
after the destruction of the Spanish Armada in 1588, the English soldiers having
acquired the habit in the Netherlands; and the habit grew to be a national evil in
1700-1750. The statute-books indicate there was very little drunkenness in
England prior to the last part of the reign of Elizabeth. The first statute against
drunkenness, making it crime, was in 1606, 4 James I, C. 5. In 1494, 11 Henry
VII, C. 2, and in 1503, 19 Henry VII, C. 12, Parliament, alarmed at the decline
of the practice of archery and the growing habit of loafing and tippling, i. e.,
drinking apart from meals, in public-houses for the sale of ale and beer, authorized justices of the peace to summarily stop the common selling of ale in 1494, and
of "ale or beer" in 1503. This power of summary abatement was continued in
1552, 5 and 6 Edward VI, C. 25, when all public-houses for the sale of ale and
beer were required to be licensed by justices of the peace, and in 1604, 1 James
I, C. 9; and the power was held by justices of the peace until 1830, when Parliament adopted the policy of free trade in ale and beer, but began to drop that
policy in 1869. Under the present Licensing Consolidation Act of 1910, 10
Edward VII, and 1 George V, English justices of the peace appear to have this
old power of summary abatement. Certainly since 1753, 26 George II, C. 31,
English justices of the peace have had a like power to summarily abate the
illegal sale of "spirits," commonly separated by Parliament from ale and beer
for licensing and taxing purposes. Until within the last forty years, as a general
rule, subject to occasional exceptions during the spasmodic crusades at long
intervals to reform the manners and morals of the "lower orders," English liquor

The fact is, equity jurisdiction to abate and enjoin public nuisances of any kind at the suit of the attorney-general is a rather modern subject.   It is true Story says in his Equity Jurisprudence,[8] "the jurisdiction of courts of equity [to abate and enjoin public nuisances on information by the attorney-general] seems to be of very ancient date, and has been distinctly traced back to the reign of Queen Elizabeth," citing as his authority Eden on Injunctions, ch. 11.   It appears Eden found one overlooked case in the time of Elizabeth, where on information by the attorney-general on the equity side of the exchequer, the court enjoined the erection of a pigeon-house by the lessee of a parcel of a manor, of which the reversion was in the queen, the court being of the erroneous opinion the erection was a common nuisance.[9]

---

laws appear to have been rather badly enforced, especially in cities. Dowell, infra, cites Bacon as Lord Keeper assisting James I's crusade against drunkenness and public-houses by entering, on his own motion, an order in the Court of Star Chamber to stir the justices of the peace to more activity in the enforcement of the liquor laws, but that is a very different thing from a chancellor's injurction against a keeper of a public-house, at the suit of the attorney general to abate the sale of liquor as a public nuisance.   There are instances of criminal informations and informations in mandamus by the attorney-general in the Court of King's Bench against justices of the peace to correct their enforcement of the liquor laws. See the modern case of Sharp v. Wakefield, 1891, A. C., 173, s. c. 21 Q. B. D., 66, and 22 Q. B. D., 239, and citations by court and counsel.   But no one in England ever seems to have thought of pushing the attorney-general off the beaten track of the law to apply to the chancellor for an injunction against a saloon-keeper to shut up and close an illegal saloon.   See generally, Webb, The History of Liquor Licensing in England, from 1700 to 1830; Webb, English Local Government: The Parish and the County, from 1689 to 1835, references under "Public-house" in the general index; 4 Dowell, History of Taxation and Taxes in England, 2d Ed., references under "ale," "beer," "wine," "port," "aqua vitae," "spirits," "gin," "usquebaugh," and "whiskey," in the general index.

[8] Sec. 921.

[9] Elizabeth Bond's Case, Moore, 293, in 1587.   Queen Elizabeth was a stranger to the scruples of present-day English royalty about lobbying the judges. Lord Burleigh was in the court when the case was on hearing, and told the judges it was the opinion of Plowden and of Montague, C. J., the pigeon-house was a common nuisance, when the injunction was ordered as a matter of course. 1 Waterman's Eden on Injunctions, 262-2, note a. Eden's book was published in 1821.

EQUITY

Eden's next precedent is a dictum of Lord Hardwicke in 1752 in Barnes v. Baker,[10] where Lord Hardwicke said the smallpox hospital in question was not a nuisance, but if it was a public nuisance the way to proceed in equity was on information by the attorney-general. Then after citing Mayor of London v. Bolt,[11] in 1799, where Lord Loughborough, though saying the Lord Mayor could apply a much more proper and effectual remedy, nevertheless gave an injunction to stop the use of old houses in London as temporary warehouses for sugar, two of the houses having actually fallen from overloading, Eden says:

"The author has not been able to find a precedent in which the court has actually interfered to restrain the carrying on of a noxious trade, destructive to the health and comfort of the neighborhood."

In Attorney-General v. Cleaver,[12] in 1811, being an information by the attorney-general to enjoin the manufacture of soap, Lord Eldon cites all the precedents he knew of. There is little in the equity reports on the subject of suits by the attorney-general to abate and enjoin public nuisances before Lord Eldon became chancellor in 1801.

As is well known, equity reports are few and far between prior to the restoration of the Stuarts in 1660, and down to the time of Lord Hardwicke a century later the practice of the court of chancery rested chiefly on oral tradition, or the unwritten custom of the forum. In Missouri v. Uhrig,[13] State v. Schweickhart,[14] State

[10] 3 Atk., 750.
[11] 5 Ves., 129.
[12] 18 Ves., 211.
[13] 14 Mo. App., 413.
[14] 109 Mo., 501.

v. Crawford,[15] and Oklahoma *v.* Robertson,[16] the courts refused to entertain suits in equity by the attorney-general to abate and enjoin illegal saloons simply because they were illegal, there being no statute authorizing such suits.   Mr. Edwin S. Mack's excellent article on "The Revival of Criminal Equity,"[17] notices the matter of suits in equity by the attorney-general to abate and enjoin illegal saloons and brothels, concluding that it is not a kind of work that ought to be put on the courts, properly belonging to the executive or administrative branch of the government.   Here the Illinois courts took the work without any compulsion by the legislature.   Let us examine the case.

It arose under the Local Option Act of 1907.   The City of Shelbyville lies within the limits of the township of Shelbyville.   At the regular township election on April 7, 1908, the township became "dry"; and at the regular city election a few days later on April 21, 1908, the city went dry, though it was already dry under the township dry vote of April 7.   At the next regular township election two years later on April 7, 1910, the township went "wet."   At once the question of law arose whether this township wet vote in 1910 made the city wet, or whether the city remained dry under its dry vote of April 21, 1908.   The city council thought the city was wet, while the state's attorney thought the city remained dry.   Acting on its view that the city was wet, the city council passed an ordinance authorizing the granting of saloon licenses, and saloon licenses were granted to Fortner and others, who established saloons within the city.   If the city was dry, as the state's attorney thought, the municipal saloon ordinance and licenses

[15] 28 Kas., 726.
[16] 19 Okla., 149.
[17] 16 Harv. L. Rev., 389.

were illegal and void acts of the municipal officers, ultra vires the corporate power of the city as a municipal corporation, by the express terms of section 11 of the Local Option Act; and each person who established a saloon under the saloon ordinance was guilty of setting up and maintaining a public nuisance, by the express terms of section 14 of the Local Option Act, which says that "all places where intoxicating liquor is sold in violation of any provision of this act shall be taken and held and are declared to be common nuisances and may be abated as such" — the word "may" doubtless meaning "shall," as the Supreme Court tacitly assumes, under the rule that "where the statute directs the doing of a thing for the sake of justice or the public good, the word may is the same as shall."[18] Acting on his view that the city was dry, the state's attorney tried to proceed criminally against the saloon-keepers for the misdemeanor of setting up and maintaining public nuisances. He could proceed criminally against them either by way of indictment in the circuit court, or by way of criminal information in the county court. Two grand juries refused to return indictments, refusing even to hear the state's attorney's witnesses. And the county judge refused to issue warrants on the state's attorney's criminal informations. Then the attorney-general was applied to, and he and the state's attorney filed an information in equity against one of the saloon-keepers and his landlord for the writ of injunction, mandatory to shut up and close the saloon, and prohibitory to prevent the future opening of the saloon. The trial court granted the writ, mandatory and prohibitory, and the judgment was affirmed by the Appellate Court and by the Supreme Court.

On the merits of the case the only question was the

[18] Rock Island v. State Bank, 6 Wall., 435; Brokaw v. Highway Commissioners, 130 Ill., 482.

one of law touching the construction and application of the Local Option Act. This question was decided in favor of the attorney-general and state's attorney, the Supreme Court holding the city became dry by its dry vote at the city election in 1908, and must remain dry until it goes wet at a city election, in spite of the township wet vote in 1910; that the Local Option Act of 1907 allows a dry city in a wet township, but does not allow a wet city in a dry township. The Supreme Court relied on Schwartz v. People,[19] where a similar question was decided the same way by a five to two vote.

Most of the Supreme Court's opinion is devoted to the question of the procedure chosen by the attorney-general, i. e., a bill in equity against one of the saloon-keepers and his landlord to abate the present and enjoin the future use of the premises for saloon purposes. The foundation of the bill was the violation of law by the saloon-keeper and its consequential effect upon public morals in the city of Shelbyville. Before taking up the opinion of the court on this question of procedure, we may usefully view the case from the foundation of the violation of law by the municipal officers by their illegal and ultra vires acts of passing the saloon ordinance and granting the saloon licenses. The attorney-general might have complained to the courts of this official violation of law and its consequential effect upon public morals in the city of Shelbyville, but he did not.

If the attorney-general had elected to try to reach and correct the violation of law by the municipal officers, the law permitted him to proceed against them criminally for their misconduct in authorizing the saloons and in neglecting and refusing to abate them as public nuisances.[20]

[19] 46 Colo., 239, and 47 Colo., 483.

[20] Criminal Code, Div. 1, Sec. 208; Cities and Villages Act, Part 1, Art. 2, Sec. 14; 4 Dillon, Mun. Corp., 5th Ed., Sec. 1599.

And the law permitted him to proceed either against the municipal officers, or against the saloon-keepers, by way of information in quo warranto to annul the illegal and ultra vires saloon ordinance and licenses.[21]   And also the law permitted him to proceed against the municipal officers by way of petition in mandamus to coerce them to exercise their discretionary powers to perform their imperative legal duty to shut up and close the saloons as public nuisances and to keep them shut up and closed.[22]

---

[21] People v. Board of Education, 101 Ill., 308; People v. Heidelberg Garden Co., 233 Ill., 290, 293.

[22] Brokaw v. Highway Commissioners, 130 Ill., 482; People v. Harris, 203 Ill., 272.   In this state any citizen of a municipality, as well as the attorney-general and state's attorney, may file a petition in mandamus to compel his municipal officers to perform their duty to the public.   County of Pike v. People, 11 Ill., 202.   In the cases cited, on citizen's petition in mandamus, municipal officers were compelled to abate public nuisances consisting of obstructions in the highway.   In People v. Dunne, 219 Ill., 346, and People v. Busse, 238 Ill., 593, the Supreme Court refused to entertain citizens' petition in mandamus to compel the mayor of Chicago to shut up and close all Chicago saloons, or two Chicago saloons owned by one saloon-keeper, open on Sundays in violation of the Sunday-closing law.   Criminal Code, Div. 1, Sec. 259.   The result in these cases perhaps may be sustainable as an allowable exercise of the wide judicial discretion to refuse the writ of mandamus in a purely public case, though the duty in que stion may be c lear and imperative in point of strict law.   But the Supreme Court did not put the result on that ground, but gave a reason that seems to be unsound in law, evidencing misunderstanding of the vigor of the power of the state as visitor of its public and private corporations, and of the origin and function of the writ of mandamus to give effect to that power.   The reason given was: "The court could not prescribe the particular act to be performed and enforce its performance."   The answer is, the court did not have to prescribe the particular act to be performed, and if it did have to, the court could prescribe the particular act to be performed, i. e., the particular means to be employed by the mayor of Chicago to attain the end of Sunday closing.   The Supreme Court's want of confidence in its ability to draw and enforce a saloon-closing mandamus order on the mayor of Chicago, and its complete confidence in its ability to draw and enforce a saloon-closing injunction order on a saloon-keeper in the city of Shelbyville, are not explainable or reconcilable on any known or knowable legal principle.   While municipal officers have some discretion in the choice of means to attain the end of Sunday closing, the discretion is very limited, and they have no discretion whatever as to the end itself.   The Supreme Court admits this fully, saying the law is imperative and clear that saloons must shut up and close on Sundays, and declaring the mayor of Chicago guilty of palpable omission of duty

In addition, the law permitted the attorney-general to proceed against the municipal officers by way of a bill in equity for an injunction, mandatory to undo the past and prohibitory to prevent the future enforcement of the illegal and ultra vires saloon ordinance. The jurisdiction of a court of equity on information by the attorney-general to issue the writ of injunction to undo past and prevent future illegal and ultra vires acts of public and private corporations and their officers that have a tendency to produce public mischief is an established jurisdiction. This equity jurisdiction is but a mode of exercising the power of the state as visitor of its public and private corporations. This power of the state as visitor of its public and private corporations was exercised in England in 1765, when Blackstone wrote, only in the Court of King's Bench on information

in not closing them, without reference to the question whether an open licensed saloon on Sundays is or is not a public nuisance. But it seems quite plain that an open licensed saloon on Sundays must be held to be a public nuisance, though the Sunday-closing law does not specifically so declare. The repeated and habitual illegal sale of liquor by a licensed saloon-keeper in his licensed saloon on Sundays ought to be enough to make the licensed saloon a public nuisance on Sundays, though not on Mondays, by reason of the repetition of the illegal sales and the continuity of the illegal practice. State v. Uhrig, 14 Mo. App., 413, 414; State v. Crawford, 28 Kas., 726, 732–733. In United States v. Hrasky, 240 Ill., 560, it was decided the habitual keeping of a licensed saloon open on Sundays is so far malum in se that an alien saloon-keeper in East Saint Louis, who habitually kept his licensed saloon open on Sundays, and frankly admitted that he intended to continue the practice at least until the constituted authorities stopped him, showed want of the good moral character essential to citizenship under the Naturalization Act. The leaning and tendency of that decision is to the result that an open licensed saloon on Sundays is a public nuisance. Quarles, J., made a contrary but verbally reconciled decision with reference to an alien saloon-keeper in Milwaukee in the case of In re Hopp, 179 Fed. Rep., 561. In State v. Wacker, 71 Wis., 672, the Wisconsin Supreme Court decided that an open licensed saloon on Sundays in LaCross, Wis., though forbidden by statute, is not a public nuisance, because not specifically made so by statute. One plain error in the reasoning of the opinion lies in overlooking that a thing may be a public nuisance on Sunday, though not a public nuisance on Monday, as e. g., a baseball game. McMillan v. Kuehnle, 76 N. J. Eq., 256. It is settled judiciary law in New Jersey that the habitual practice of keeping a saloon open on Sundays in

by the attorney-general in quo warranto and in mandamus.[23] About sixty years later in 1827 Kent said the state's power as visitor of its public and private corporations may be exercised in common-law courts in mandamus and in quo warranto, and added:

> "It is also well understood that the court of chancery has a jurisdiction over charitable corporations, for breaches of trust."

Then Kent said:

> "It has been much questioned whether it [i. e., the court of chancery] had any such jurisdiction over any other corporations, than such as were held to charitable uses. The better opinion, however, seems to be, that any corporation, chargeable with trusts, may be inspected, controlled, and held accountable in chancery, for abuses of such trusts."[24]

In truth, the attorney-general's information in equity for the writ of injunction to undo past and prevent future illegal and ultra vires acts of public and private corporations is, and always has been, the common-law mandamus and quo warranto rolled into one, the dif-

violation of the Sunday-closing law makes the saloon a public nuisance on Sunday, and the saloon-keeper is indictable for maintaining a public nuisance. Meyer v. State, 32 N. J. L., 145. Sec. 7 of the Illinois Dram-Shop Act declares "all places where intoxicating liquors are sold in violation of this act" to be common nuisances. The words "this act" very well may be held to include the Sunday-closing act as being in pari materia, or to mean "the laws of this state," a phrase used later on in said Sec. 7. And it is within the power, and fairly may be said to be the imperative legal duty, of a city council in this state to declare open saloons on Sundays to be public nuisances. Criminal Code, Div. 1, Sec. 221, Clause 9; Laugel v. City of Bushnell, 197 Ill., 20. The Chicago Municipal Code of 1911, in Sec. 1526, attempts to evade the Sunday-closing law by legalizing an open back-door on Sundays, but Sec. 1424 requires municipal executive officers to abate summarily all statutory and common-law public nuisances within the city as well as all municipally-declared public nuisances. People v. Dunne and People v. Busse give a bad reason for a result that may be sustainable on a different reason. The reason given unduly and seriously abridges and impairs the state's right under existing law to exercise in and through its courts the state's power as visitor of its public and private corporations.

[23] 1 Bl. Com., 480–481.

[24] 2 Kent Com., 304–305.

ference being the purely formal one that the remedies were given by different courts, i. e., were taken out of different pigeon-holes. To-day the line between these remedies, mandamus and quo warranto on the one side, and injunction on the other side, when employed by the attorney-general to correct illegal and ultra vires acts of public and private corporations, and to coerce the performance of corporate legal duty, is about obliterated everywhere, and is on the way to complete obliteration even in those jurisdictions that maintain either separate courts or only separate forms and modes of procedure for cases in law and cases in equity. Where public or private corporations or their officers are doing illegal and ultra vires acts that have a tendency to produce public mischief, there can be no question to-day that the attorney-general may proceed by way of bill in equity for an injunction to correct such illegal and ultra vires acts. In other words, in such cases to-day the state may make its power as visitor of its public and private corporations effective by means of the writ of injunction, whereas formerly the state was compelled to proceed either in quo warranto or in mandamus, or in both. That is the explanation of Attorney-General v. Cockermouth Local Board,[25] and Attorney-General v. Shrewsbury Co.,[26] cited by the Supreme Court on p. 478, and they are so explained in 3 Pomeroy, Equity Jurisprudence,[27] and by Judge Thompson in State v. Uhrig,[28] The cases cited by the Supreme Court would be in point

[25] L. R. 18 Eq., 179.

[26] L. R. Ch. D., 752.

[27] 3 ed., Sec. 1093, note 3.

[28] 14 Mo. App., 443. And see North American Ins. Co. v. Yates, 214 Ill., 272; Chicago Fair Grounds Association v. People, 60 Ill. App., 488; People v. Condon, 102 Ill. App., 449, 453, 454; 17 Halsbury's Laws of England, 227; Richardson v. Methley School Board [1893], 3 Ch., 510; 7 Encyc. of the Laws of England, 248–253.

if the attorney-general had founded his bill in equity
in this case on the illegal and ultra vires acts of the
municipal officers in passing the saloon ordinance and
granting the saloon licenses.   But that was not the foundation of his bill.[29]

The attorney-general complained only of the illegal

---

[29] By statute in this state trial by jury is commonly supposed to be demandable
as of right in all cases in quo warranto, and in all cases in mandamus begun in the
trial courts, whether the case is public or private; in equity cases trial by jury
is not demandable as of right; that is the chief procedural difference between
the attorney-general's information in quo warranto or mandamus, and for an
injunction.   By decision, trial by jury was demandable as of right in all cases in
mandamus begun originally in the Supreme Court until People v. City of Alton,
233 Ill., 542, a case in mandamus to enforce in the city of Alton the statute forbidding separate public schools for white and black children.   According to the
course of the common law of England as adopted by Illinois, the right of trial by
jury did not extend to public cases in quo warranto or in mandamus.   24 Cyc.,
129.   The Supreme Court made a mistake in extending trial by jury to original
mandamus cases.   They could have changed the practice for the future by rule
of court, — unless the words "as heretofore enjoyed" in the constitutional provision securing jury trial are held to mean, as enjoyed as a matter of statutory
or judge-made right as distinguished from a matter of constitutional right, when
the constitution of 1870 was adopted, on which the Supreme Court may rule
either way and be right as a matter of mere precedent, for its applicable decisions
are not consistent, — but the Supreme Court had no lawful right to change the
practice by decision in a litigated case retroactively over the objection of a party
claiming the right of jury trial.   In the above case, however, where the practice
was changed by decision, the court overlooked the fact that there was no issue to
submit to a jury, though the case was submitted to and tried abortively by seven
juries; and hence the objecting and overruled party in that case was not hurt by
the decision changing the practice of jury trial.   See 3 Illinois Law Review, 479
[ante p. 344].   It seems the right of jury trial in quo warranto and in mandamus
has never been examined by the Supreme Court.   Jury trial in quo warranto
seems to rest on Paul v. People, 82 Ill., 82; Puterbaugh, Pl. and Pr. at Common
Law, 8 ed., 593.   There are more like judicial declarations of the right of jury
trial in mandamus, but no considered opinion, so far as I know.   The distinction
between mandamus to enforce a public right and to enforce a private right was
not drawn with any clearness or for any practical purpose until 1901, in People
v. Chicago, 193 Ill., 507.   And the like distinction in quo warranto was not
drawn with any clearness or for any practical purpose until 1907, in People v.
Healy, 230 Ill., 280, followed the next year in People v. Healy, 231 Ill., 629.
Jury trial is not suited to either remedy in many cases, and defeats the purpose
for which the remedies were invented and designed.   It might be useful to try
the experiment of a rule of court, defining and limiting the right of jury trial in
quo warranto and in mandamus.

acts of one of the saloon-keepers, or, more precisely, of the result of his acts, i. e., his saloon, denounced by the Local Option Act of 1907 as a public nuisance. The attorney-general wanted an injunction against the saloon-keeper, mandatory to compel him to shut up and close his saloon, and prohibitory to restrain and prevent him from again opening his saloon so long as the city remained wet, i. e., an injunction to abate the saloon as an existing public nuisance, and to restrain and prevent its renewal in the future. If the attorney-general had made all the saloon-keepers and their landlords defendants, since there was nothing to be tried but a question of law in which all the saloon-keepers and their landlords had a common interest, perhaps his bill in that shape could have been sustained as falling within the sphere of equity jurisdiction as a bill of peace to prevent a multiplicity of litigation or to determine a single question of law in which many persons had a community of interest or privity of interest.[30]   But as the bill was directed against a single saloon-keeper and his landlord, it is not possible to sustain it as a bill of peace.

The bill as drawn could be sustained, and was sustained, as falling within the sphere of equity jurisdiction, only on the foundation of public nuisance. There can be no question at all about the general proposition that courts given general equity jurisdiction have the authority, on information by the attorney-general, to issue the writ of injunction against private individuals, commanding them to abate existing public nuisances set up and maintained by them, and to restrain and prevent them from renewing the public nuisances. The only question in this case was, whether a saloon set up and maintained in violation of a prohibitory liquor statute, declaring such

---

[30] North American Ins. Co. v. Yates, 214 Ill., 272, 283, 284; Chicago v. Collins, 175 Ill., 445; Mayor of York v. Pilkington, 1 Atk. 282.

saloon to be a public nuisance, but such saloon being in all other respects an orderly house in the sense of the law, fell inside that general proposition, or outside of it. It must be agreed, and is admitted in the case, that such saloon did not fall inside that general proposition, but fell outside of it, unless it appeared from the facts and circumstances of the case that other remedies provided by the law were not adequate, prompt, and efficient to shut up and close the saloon in question, and to keep it shut up and closed in the future so long as the prohibitory liquor statute remained in force.

Laying to one side the remedy of summary abatement by executive or administrative officers,[31] which is the most adequate, prompt, and efficient remedy there is to shut up and close an illegal saloon and to keep it shut up and closed, and considering only judicial or court remedies provided by the law, the only judicial or court remedy applicable to such illegal saloon as an existing public nuisance is the criminal one by way of indictment or criminal information against the saloon-keeper for the misdemeanor of setting up and maintaining the illegal saloon as a public nuisance. On a verdict or finding of guilty, the English common law adopted by Illinois authorized the Criminal court to give a judgment of fine or imprisonment, and, in addition, to order the defendant to abate the public nuisance at his own expense. The Criminal court could deal with disobedience of such an order as a contempt of court, and could order the sheriff or other proper officer to abate the public nuisance at the expense of the convicted person.[32] There seems to be little room for doubt that an Illinois Criminal court

[31] North American Cold Storage Co. *v.* Chicago, 211 U. S., 306; Laugel *v.* City of Bushnell, 197 Ill., 20; Earp *v.* Lee, 81 Ill., 193.

[32] Taggart *v.* Commonwealth, 21 Pa. St., 527, 530; Campbell *v.* State, 16 Ala., 144, 146, 157; 10 Encyc. of the Laws of England, 83.

always has had, and has now, the power to order a saloon-
keeper convicted of keeping an illegal saloon as a public
nuisance to shut up and close it, and to deal with his
disobedience as a contempt of court.[33] That is all a
court of equity can do under the attorney-general's information in equity for an injunction against the saloon-
keeper, so far as the saloon as an existing public nuisance
is concerned. The fact, if it be a fact, that such orders
are not usual in the Criminal court is of no significance.
The power and remedy are there, both as a common-law
and statutory power and remedy.

Perhaps the Criminal court cannot enter a preliminary
order on the accused saloon-keeper to stop selling liquor
in the saloon pending the trial of the indictment or
criminal information, though the Criminal court can put
the accused saloon-keeper under bonds to stop selling
liquor in the saloon pending the trial of the indictment
or criminal information.[34] And the Criminal court's
final shut up and close order entered on conviction perhaps can be only mandatory, to abate the existing saloon
as a public nuisance, and cannot be prohibitory, to restrain
and prevent the convicted saloon-keeper from again
opening the saloon or renewing the public nuisance in the
future. At least there is no instance that I know of
where a final prohibitory order of that kind was entered
on conviction by a Criminal court; though, on conviction,
the Criminal court may put the convicted saloon-keeper

---

[33] Illinois Criminal Code, Div. 1, Sec. 222; Div. 13, Sec. 8; Local Option Act of
1907, Sec. 14.

[34] The English Court of King's Bench used to grant writs of prohibition to
stop the continuance of public nuisances pending the filing and trial of an indictment, and perhaps when no indictment was contemplated. Jacob Hall's Case,
1 Mod., 76; 1 Ventr., 169; Rex v. Betterton, 5 Mod., 143; Skinner, 625. In Rex v.
Justices of Dorset, 15 East., 594, in 1812, the King's Bench refused to revive
this remedy, saying it was "confessedly new in modern practice." Russell on
Crimes, 7th Eng. ed. and 1st Can. ed., p. 1840; Waterman's Eden on Injunctions,
p. 262, note 8.

under bonds not to sell liquor again in the saloon. And
so it may be admitted that, in case of a renewal of the
saloon nuisance, the once convicted saloon-keeper must
be prosecuted criminally again as for setting up and maintaining a new and distinct public nuisance, though there
can be no question a saloon-keeper shown to be incorrigible
by indictment or criminal information may be dealt with
by injunction. Since, however, the illegal saloon, or the
use of premises for the illegal sale of intoxicating liquor,
is no stranger to the law, and there is no instance in
Anglo-American law where a court on an attorney-
general's bill in equity, not authorized by statute, issued
an injunction, either preliminary to control and regulate
the sale of liquor in the saloon pending the trial of an
indictment or criminal information against the saloon-
keeper, or final to restrain and prevent the saloon-keeper
from opening the saloon again, it is hard to see how any
court can say at this date that the remedy by indictment
or criminal information against the saloon-keeper is inadequate to shut up and close the illegal saloon as a public
nuisance, and to keep it shut up and closed in the future.
The rule that there is no equity jurisdiction on information by the attorney-general to issue the writ of injunction against a private individual to abate and enjoin a
public nuisance, unless it appears from the facts and
circumstances of the case that the remedy by indictment
or criminal information is not adequate, prompt, and
efficient to abate the public nuisance in question, and to
keep it abated, is a part of the law of the land, binding
on the courts, prescribing the limit beyond which they
must not carry the writ of injunction with its consequent
process of contempt of court and summary imprisonment
brevi manu without the restraint of jury trial. Subject
to applicable constitutional provisions, this rule of law
is under the control of the legislature, and the legislature

may repeal it entirely, or repeal its established application
to particular public nuisances, and may declare that the
remedy of indictment or criminal information shall no
longer be deemed adequate, prompt, and efficient to shut
up and close a saloon established in violation of a prohibitory liquor law, and may require the courts to apply the
remedy of injunction against the illegal saloon-keeper,
and such legislation will be binding upon the courts, con-
straining them to a new rule of judicial action in such
cases. But when the Illinois Supreme Court says such
legislation is but declaratory of an existing jurisdiction
to shut up and close illegal saloons as public nuisances by
the writ of injunction against the saloon-keeper, reaching
back to the days of Elizabeth, the court is simply going
against the whole current of English and American judiciary law. It always has been universally understood and
declared by judges, lawyers, and text-writers alike, that
these modern prohibitory liquor statutes in several of the
states authorizing and requiring the courts to issue the
writ of injunction against saloon-keepers, are innovating
statutes, introducing new doctrine on the point of the
adequacy of the remedy at law to shut up and close
illegal saloons as public nuisances simply because they
are illegal.[35]

[35] These prohibitory liquor statutes have been assailed for unconstitutionality
as being repugnant to state constitutional provisions securing the right of trial
by jury, but never successfully. See the arguments pro and con in Carleton v.
Rugg, 149 Mass., 350. In view of these constitutional decisions it may be said
well enough these statutes are but declaratory as related to the state constitutional
right of trial by jury; but it is a very different thing to say these statutes are
declaratory statutes on the subject of the adequacy of the remedy at law under
the rule there is no equity jurisdiction unless the remedy at law is inadequate.
The Supreme Court overlooked this plain difference. The courts sustained the
constitutionality of these statutes as related to jury trial on the theory that the
use of premises for the illegal sale of liquor so as to make a public nuisance, is one
thing; and the personal criminal act of illegally selling liquor is a different thing;
that the former may be dealt with by injunction as a proceeding in rem against
the premises; but the latter cannot be dealt with by injunction, for then the

All the Supreme Court says on page 475 concerning equity jurisdiction on information by the attorney-general to restrain and prevent a party from carrying out a threat to establish a public nuisance, has nothing to do with the case. This equity jurisdiction in the case of merely threatened public nuisances, rests on the fears of mankind, on the principle of quia timet, being an application of the old saying, "an ounce of prevention is better than a pound of cure." The fears of mankind, however reasonable, never have been regarded, and are not now

proceeding would be strictly in personam to enjoin a merely personal criminal act, as e. g., selling a glass of beer or whiskey. Public nuisances always have been subject to summary abatement by executive or administrative officers without any prior judicial investigation and determination of the question of nuisance or no nuisance by a court or by a common-law jury. Lawton v. Steele, 152 U. S., 133, 142. The filing of the statutory bill in equity brings the saloon in custodia legis, so to speak, as the subject-matter in litigation, and the court may control and regulate the use of the premises pendente lite by preliminary injunction as in other cases. The constitutional question of jury trial, therefore, really arises only on the final injunction, in so far as it is prohibitory to restrain and prevent future sales of liquor on the premises in question. This final injunction is in part a quia timet prohibitory order, and does in truth and in fact as it is commonly drawn enjoin the threatened or feared future purely personal criminal act of selling liquor in violation of the statute; and it is an abuse of language to say such final quia timet order only touches the use of the premises in question, and so is in rem and not in personam. The argument that such final quia timet order simply forbidding future selling, and the consequent process of contempt for disobedience, violate the right of jury trial has not been successfully answered; and it may be doubted whether the question has ever been well presented, or presented at all. The violation of such quia timet final order, unless it goes so far as to set up a new saloon, can be dealt with only by fine or imprisonment, which is essentially and wholly punitive in such case, and not remedial at all. Re Merchants' Stock, Grain and Provision Co., 223 U. S., 629. Of course, when a man has no issue of fact to be tried, or only a sham issue, his complaint of denial of jury trial has no foundation in fact. In these statutory-liquor-injunction cases, the constitutional-jury-trial point usually has been presented as a purely abstract, theoretical point in constitutional law, without reference to the actual facts of the case, and without distinguishing between jury trial on bill and answer, jury trial on violation of the preliminary injunction, and jury trial on violation of a quia timet prohibitory order in the final injunction. The rule is, though it is not always carefully observed by the courts, except the Supreme Court of the United States, that a litigant cannot assail the constitutionality of a statute unless it hurts him as applied to the actual facts of his case.

regarded, as enough to bring a man's mere threat to establish and open a saloon in violation of a prohibitory liquor law within the scope of this principle of quia timet. The common-law remedy of bonds to keep the peace always has been thought an adequate judicial way to deal with a man's threat to open an illegal saloon. Even in the states where statutes authorize suits in equity to shut up and close illegal saloons as public nuisances, the courts decline to entertain a suit unless it appears the saloon was in actual existence when the suit was begun.[36]

And all that the Supreme Court says on pp. 475, 476, concerning the so-called concurrence of the remedies by indictment or criminal information and by injunction to abate existing public nuisances, is wholly beside the point of the adequacy and efficiency of the remedy by indictment or criminal information in this case, It is not the law that the attorney-general may proceed by bill in equity to abate and enjoin any and every public nuisance at his own taste and choice. The remedy by indictment or criminal information extends to all public nuisances, but the remedy by injunction extends only to those public nuisances that cannot be adequately and efficiently abated by the remedy of indictment or criminal informa-tion. The two remedies are not applicable to all public nuisances, but only to some public nuisances; and when applicable to the particular public nuisance in question, they are not mutually exclusive, and the attorney-general does not have to make an election; he may pursue both remedies at the same time, or one after the other in succession, and the result reached by the court in one is not binding as res judicata in the other. This rule as to the so-called concurrency of the remedies throws no light on, and is of no aid to the solution of, the question whether a

[36] Sharp *v.* Arnold, 108 Ia., 203; State *v.* Saunders, 66 N. H., 39.

particular public nuisance may be abated by injunction;
that turns altogether and exclusively on the point whether
the remedy by indictment or criminal information is
adequate to abate the particular public nuisance in question and to keep it abated.

The only part of the court's opinion that is sound in
point of law is the repudiation, on p. 477, of the argument
that equity jurisdiction exists only to protect and enforce
public and private property rights.   There is a tendency
to misuse statements like that in Cope v. District Fair
Association,[37] saying: "It is no part of the mission of
equity to administer the criminal law of the state, or to
enforce the principles of religion and morality."   The
mission of equity jurisdiction is and always has been to
supply a remedy either where there is no remedy or the
remedy provided by the law is inadequate to the ends of
justice in the particular case in hand, and so to realize
the maxim ubi jus ibi remedium, so far as possible and
desirable consistently with sound public policy without
jarring the feelings, habits, and traditions of a people ac-
customed to the democratic, virile, and rigorous course of
the common law, and inclined to view with suspicion the
process of contempt of court as an alien and imperialistic
process, which it is in origin and development.   So far as
a question in equity jurisdiction is concerned, it makes
no difference whatever what the subject-matter of the
controversy is; the sole point in a question in equity jurisdiction is the existence or adequacy of another remedy
provided by the law.   As a general proposition, other
remedies provided by the law have been found adequate
in the past, and are likely to be found adequate in the
future, where no question of public or private property
rights is involved.   In controversies not involving such
rights, and in many controversies involving such rights,

[37] 99 Ill., 489, 492.

where people have only their bodies and souls to respond with, they cannot as a free people reasonably be expected to tolerate judicial extensions of equity jurisdiction, i. e., of the remedy of judicial personal compulsion and coercion to do or not to do what the law commands or forbids, under penalty of a judicial fine or imprisonment for disobedience, unrestrained by the common sense of the community voiced by twelve good men and true in the jury box.

The only reason given by the Supreme Court for declaring the remedy by indictment or criminal information inadequate to abate the illegal saloon in question as a public nuisance, and to keep it abated, is the refusal of the grand jurors to hear the state's attorney's witnesses and to return indictments against the saloon-keepers, and the refusal of the county judge to issue warrants on the state's attorney's criminal informations. The court censures the grand jurors and the county judge for lawlessness, and is equally severe on the municipal officers for passing the saloon ordinance and granting the saloon licenses, seeing in the facts of the case an evil combination and conspiracy of the municipal officers, the grand jurors, and the county judge to overthrow the Local Option Act of 1907 in the city of Shelbyville (pp. 476, 479, bottom). Accepting for the moment this judicially expressed view of the conduct of these men, it affords no legal reason whatever for judicially declaring the remedy by indictment or criminal information inadequate to abate the illegal saloon in question as a public nuisance and to keep it abated. The applicable rule of law is thus stated by Mr. Justice Hunt, speaking for the Supreme Court of the United States:

"The want of a remedy, and the inability to obtain the fruits of a remedy, are quite distinct, and yet they are confounded in the present proceeding. To illustrate: the writ of habere facias posses-

sionem is the established remedy to obtain the fruits of a judgment
for the plaintiff in ejectment.   It is a full, adequate, and complete
remedy.   Not many years since, there existed in Central New
York combinations of settlers and tenants disguised as Indians,
and calling themselves such, who resisted the execution of this
process in their counties, and so effectually that for some years no
landlord could gain possession of his land.   There was a perfect
remedy at law, but through fraud, violence, or crime, its execution
was prevented.   It will hardly be argued that this state of things
gave authority to invoke the extraordinary aid of a court of chancery.   The enforcement of the legal remedies was temporarily
suspended by means of illegal violence, but the remedies remained
as before.   It was the case of a miniature revolution.   The courts
of law lost no power, the court of chancery gained none.   The
present case stands upon the same footing.   The legal remedy is
adequate and complete, and time and the law must perfect its
execution."[38]

The Illinois Supreme Court thought it saw in this case
a war of the "wets" and "drys," carried on somewhat
after the manner of the old Wars of the Roses, when
the English chancellor, then running an executive
bureau of the government rather than a court of law
and justice, interfered as the alter ego of an absolute
monarch, conceived of as the parens patriae and ultimate
source and fountain of law and justice to the people,
whenever the regular processes of the law were strangled
by violence, corruption, or fraud.   In the times of the
Tudors the Court of Star Chamber gave a remedy in such
cases; but since the abolition of the Court of Star Chamber in the Puritan Revolution of 1640, and especially
since the Revolution of 1688, establishing the principle
of the supremacy of the people assembled in Parliament,
and the principle of the supremacy of law, the vir bonus
in the court of chancery has been subject to the rule
of law; and has had to keep within the sphere marked

[38] Rees v. Watertown, 19 Wall., 107, 124, 125; Thompson v. Allen County, 115
U. S., 550.

out for him by the rule that he must not interfere by his process of contempt of court, unless the remedy at law is inadequate; and the rule on the subject of the adequacy of the remedy at law as stated above by the Supreme Court of the United States always has been adhered to, in times of war and popular excitement as well as in times of peace. Inter arma silent leges does not apply to that rule of the adequacy of remedy at law limiting equity jurisdiction, and authorize judges to read the riot act and proclaim martial law in terrorem populi under the guise of issuing judicial writs of injunction.[39]

Moreover, the Supreme Court's charge of lawlessness against the municipal officers, the grand jurors, and the county judge is not warranted by the facts of the case as they appear in the report. The question of law whether the city of Shelbyville was wet or dry was one on which honest men might differ. The view of the municipal officers that the city was wet was not a frivolous view. The Supreme Court of Colorado divided five to two on a like question under a like statute. While in strictness of law the grand jurors ought to have heard the witnesses and ought to have returned indictments, and the county judge ought to have issued the warrants to facilitate the trial of the issue of law, yet in the higher forum of wholesome and sound public policy the refusal of the grand jurors to indict the saloon-keepers and the refusal of the county judge to issue warrants for their arrest are commendable on the ground that the state's attorney ought to have proceeded against the municipal officers for their illegal and ultra vires acts of passing the saloon ordinance and granting the saloon licenses, letting the

---

[39] "The Revival of Criminal Equity," 16 Harv. L. R., 389; "The Criminal Jurisdiction of the Court of Chancery," 1 Spence, Equitable Jurisdiction, 684; Pollock, The Genius of the Common Law, 38–46. See note on In re Debs at end of article.

saloon-keepers alone. The Supreme Court has laid itself
open to the retort of judicial lawlessness, for it is plain
the facts before the court did not bring the illegal saloon
in question within the authority of the courts of Illinois,
as defined and limited by existing law, to abate public
nuisances by the writ of injunction against private individuals.

It was for the legislature, not the Supreme Court,
to say the way to repair the notorious and wholesale
neglect and refusal of municipal officers throughout the
state to enforce the liquor laws fairly and impartially,
is to shift the burden of their enforcement from the
municipal officers to the judges by means of bills in equity
by the attorney-general and the state's attorneys for
writs of injunction against saloon-keepers. The Supreme
Court may or may not be right when it says "the hand
of equity" applied to saloon-keepers at the instance of
the public attorneys is "strong and efficient" to "uproot
the evil." That is a question in governmental policy
which the Supreme Court should have left to be decided
by the people acting in and through the legislature. The
Supreme Court missed its opportunity to exert its authority effectively under and through existing law to
"uproot the evil," when it said it could not mandamus
the mayor of Chicago to enforce the Sunday-closing law
because it "could not prescribe the particular act to be
performed and enforce its performance." [40] And there
can be no fair doubt the existing laws of this state authorize the courts to render a judgment in quo warranto
removing from office any mayor or other municipal
officer who directly or indirectly habitually sanctions
the illegal sale of intoxicating liquor.[41]

[40] See note 22, ante.

[41] Section 1 of the Quo Warranto Act authorizes the remedy of quo warranto
when "any person shall . . . unlawfully hold or execute any office or franchise

or any office in any corporation created by authority of this state;" and also when "any public officer shall have done or suffered any act which, by the provisions of law, works a forfeiture of his office. And section 6 authorizes a "judgment of ouster against any person . . . from the office." The Cities and Villages Act, Part 1, Sec. 14, and the Criminal Code, Div. 1, Sec. 208, make misconduct in office by a public officer a misdemeanor punishable by fine and removal from office. Under like legislation, in Bradford v. Oklahoma, 2 Okla. 230, a county clerk was removed from office in quo warranto for illegally issuing liquor licenses; in Commonwealth v. McWilliams, 11 Pa. St., 61, quo warranto was sustained as an appropriate remedy to inquire into and correct the alleged illegal exercise of his office by a de jure municipal officer; in State v. Rose, 74 Kan., 262, the mayor of Kansas City, Kansas, was removed in quo warranto for illegally exercising his office to protect "saloons and joints," and he was held guilty of contempt of court for attempting to exercise the office of mayor on re-election to it for the unexpired term after the judicial order of removal; in State v. Wilcox, 78 Kan., 597, the mayor of the city of Coffeyville was removed in quo warranto for a like reason. And see State v. City of Coffeyville, 78 Kan., 599. See note 29 ante on jury trial in quo warranto.

Any system must provide a method for recalling public officers for misconduct in office. The above quo warranto method of recalling public officers, like the method of impeachment and joint resolution on three-fourths vote for the recall of judges (Constitution, Art. 4, Sec. 24, Art. 5, Sec. 15, Art. 6, Sec. 30), is practically dead-letter law in Illinois The proposed recall of public officers and judges by popular vote proceeds frankly upon the idea that some laws ought to be enforced and other laws ought not to be enforced, and enables the majority to determine and select the laws to be enforced and the laws not to be enforced. Under the quo warranto method of recall, the public attorney makes the selection, i. e., practically, whether that is the law or not, — for it may be doubted whether the law makes the public attorney the czar he is commonly supposed to be over the machinery of justice in cases where the people are a party, to set it in motion, to control its operation, and to stop it, all at his will and pleasure, uncontrolled by the law defining his duty, first as public officer, and second as lawyer and officer of the court. See State v. Foster, 32 Kan., 14, removing a county attorney in quo warranto for neglecting and refusing to enforce a prohibitory liquor law.

Note on In re Debs: On p. 476, the Illinois Supreme Court cites and relies on the case of In re Debs, 158 U. S., 564, as lending support to the idea of judicial authority to extend equity jurisdiction for the sole purpose of getting rid of jury trial when judges think jurors cannot be relied on to do their duty. That case arose on habeas corpus, and the United States Supreme Court decided that the bill in that case by the attorney-general of the United States to enjoin striking workmen from obstructing railroad highways of interstate and foreign commerce fell inside the jurisdiction of a federal court as a court of equity. The Illinois Supreme Court intimates very plainly, though it does not directly and in words so say, that it thinks the decision in that case rests on the basis of a fear entertained by the judges of the United States Supreme Court that petit jurors could not be relied on to render just and true verdicts in criminal prosecutions against the striking workmen, because the case was one arising out of a controversy between capital and labor "on which there is a division of opinion among people who may serve as jurors." The United States Supreme Court did not put its decision on any such basis, and repudiated such basis as untenable and unpermissible. 158 U. S., on pp. 594, 595, 598. On the filing of the attorney-general's bill in that case, Woods, J., ordered a preliminary injunction, from which order no appeal was taken to the Circuit Court of Appeals. The preliminary injunction was issued, and later on Woods, J., found Debs and three others guilty of contempt of court for violating the preliminary injunction, and sentenced them to jail. 158 U. S., on pp. 572, 573. An application to the United States Supreme Court for a writ of error to review the sentence was denied on the ground the sentence was not a final judgment (158 U. S., on p. 572), though to-day the application would be denied on the ground that the sentence was a final judgment, but was a final judgment in a non-capital criminal case, and hence was directly reviewable only on writ of error issued by the Circuit Court of Appeals. Bessette v. Conkey, 194 U. S., 324; Re Merchants' Stock Co., 223 U. S., 639. Debs also petitioned the United States Supreme Court for the writ of habeas corpus, and the court heard the case on this petition. Debs' petition for the writ of habeas corpus was not a direct appellate attack on the sentence of Woods, J., but only an indirect and quasi-collateral appellate attack. No question in equity jurisdiction was open; i. e., no question was open touching the ruling of Woods, J., ordering the preliminary injunction, when the ruling is viewed solely as an exercise of equity jurisdiction or of judicial authority to apply the particular remedy of injunction, because, on the facts of the case, the ruling of Woods, J., ordering the preliminary injunction, if wrong as an exercise of his equity jurisdiction or judicial authority to apply the particular remedy of injunction, could be no more than an error of judgment in the exercise of his judicial power on the question of the adequacy of the remedy at law to abate the particular national public nuisance involved, i. e., the consequential effect on interstate and foreign commerce of the acts of the striking workmen congregated in the highways of interstate and foreign commerce. In re Tyler, 149 U. S., 164, 180, 181; In re Sawyer, 124 U. S., 200, 221. The only argument made on behalf of Debs touching the equity jurisdiction of Woods, J., i. e., the authority of Woods, J., to grant the writ of injunction in exercise of his judicial power to determine and select the remedy to be applied, was that the subject-matter of the case was but a casual, temporary, and admittedly lawless mob, acting without any claim of right in the highways of interstate and foreign commerce, and the judicial writ of injunction is not an appropriate and adequate remedy for such a case, the appropriate and adequate remedy being the bayonet of the soldier. 158 U. S., on pp. 596, 597. The Supreme Court answered this argument on behalf of Debs by saying: First, the argument does not prove a want of jurisdiction or judicial power to grant the preliminary injunction, but only an error of judgment in the exercise of jurisdiction or judicial power touching the adequacy of the remedy at law to abate the particular alleged national public nuisance; and, second, "this bill was not simply to enjoin a mob and mob violence. It was not a bill to command a keeping of the peace." 158 U. S., on pp. 597, 598. The Supreme Court concedes and says that no federal court as a court of equity can entertain a bill in equity by the attorney-general of the United States simply inviting a federal judge, under the guise of issuing the judicial writ of injunction, to read the riot act to a casual, temporary, and admittedly lawless mob, acting without any claim of right in the highways of interstate and foreign commerce. The mob in this case was not admitted to be a lawless mob as against the United States. The mob in this case was a casual and temporary mob, but it was in fact acting under a claim of right, as against the United States, to be where it was and to do what it was doing; it claimed to be a lawful mob, if I may say so, as against the United States, though perhaps not a lawful mob as against the state of Illinois; it claimed it owed no duty to the United States, and the United States had no right to restrain it or to put it down; it claimed, if it was acting against any peace, it was acting against the peace of the state of Illinois only, and not against the peace of the United States. The mob claimed that its own acts and the acts of its members fell entirely outside the sphere of activity of the United States as the national government. The authority of the government of the United States to deal with this particular mob and its members by the bayonet of the soldier, by criminal prosecution, or by any other method whatsoever, was denied altogether and was drawn in question in the case. This claim raised a question of jurisdiction in the true sense, that must be kept separate from the question of equity pseudo-jurisdiction to issue the writ of injunction. It cannot be said when the facts of the case are considered, that it was plain and clear law, statutory or judiciary, when the case arose, that the acts of the striking workmen were indictable criminal acts as against the United States, though it may have been plain and clear law that their acts were indictable criminal acts as against the state of Illinois, and fell within the Illinois Riot Act. No like riot act of the United States was cited or relied on. The only act of Congress referred to in the case, or considered applicable to the case in any way, was the Sherman Anti-Trust Act, relied on by Woods, J., as authorizing his order granting the preliminary injunction, but claimed to be wholly inapplicable by counsel for Debs, and laid to one side by the United States Supreme Court without passing on the question of its application to the case. 158 U. S., on p. 600. The only federal statutory law deemed applicable to the striking workmen was, so far as appears, the judicially established silent act of Congress declaring for the free and unobstructed flow of traffic over the highways of interstate and foreign commerce, i. e., free and unobstructed by the acts of states, or by the acts of individuals, though whether this judicially-established silent act of Congress applied to the acts of individuals, singly or collectively, was disputed in this case. Under this judicially-established silent act of Congress the acts of the striking workmen in this case were not criminal acts indictable by the United States. The United States could proceed only defensively to restrain the actors so as to prevent the consequential effect of their acts on the freedom of interstate and foreign commerce, but could not proceed offensively to indict and punish the actors as for crime against the United States, just as, e. g., the United States may guard and protect the person of the President while he is within the limits of a state, but may not indict and punish a person who shoots him, as in the case of President McKinley shot in Buffalo. The legal situation that confronted the United States attorney-general in this Debs case was not unlike the one that confronted him when he detailed a deputy marshal to act as bodyguard to the late Mr. Justice Field, though there was no act of Congress authorizing him to do it. In re Neagle, 135 U. S., 1. In addition to the striking workmen's claim of right as against the United States to congregate in the highways of interstate and foreign commerce, the consequential effect of their acts done in those highways on interstate and foreign commerce must be kept in view as the real alleged national public nuisance to be abated. Though the acts of the striking workmen were local, yet the consequential effect of their acts on interstate and foreign commerce was national and international. The attorney-general's bill, then, called upon the court to do more than to render mere judicial in terrorem physical assistance to the executive to restrain and put down a casual, temporary, and admittedly lawless mob in the highways of interstate and foreign commerce; the bill called upon the court for an exercise of its reason and judgment to give an authoritative judicial determination and definition of doubtful and disputed rights and duties of the United States on the one side, and the defendant workmen on the other side. The bill treated the striking workmen as rational men, and did not contradict the truism that courts cannot wield either the sword or the purse, but can only wield human reason and judgment. The bill was a bill of peace to adjust in a single litigation disputed and conflicting claims of rights, in the adjustment of which many people had a common interest, to prevent the disturbance of interstate and foreign commerce and a multiplicity of suits arising out of the acts of the striking workmen congregated in and obstructing the highways of interstate and foreign commerce. The bill presented a peculiar and exceptional case of a bill of peace sui generis, capable of arising only in the United States because of our dual system of government and the vitality of the erroneous political theory of state sovereignty, and hardly capable of arising in the United States more than once. The legal right of the United States government to employ the same means that any other government may employ to restrain and put down a casual, temporary, and admittedly lawless mob in the highways of interstate and foreign commerce having been adjudged and established in this case on the solid foundation of reason, judgment, and law, no second like occasion is ever likely to arise in the future for such an attorney-general's bill in equity, and any federal court may be expected to refuse to entertain a second like bill by the attorney-general of the United States for the reason advanced against the bill in this case by Debs, viz., that it is only a bill by the executive to restrain and put down by injunction a casual, temporary, and admittedly lawless mob, which is not within the sphere of the judicial writ of injunction, but falls within the sphere of the bayonet of the soldier. As in Donovan v. Pa. Co., 199 U. S., 279, the claim of right to be there and to do what it was doing and the consequential effect of what it was doing, as against the owner of the depot, brought the habitual and permanent multitude of cabmen congregated in front of the entrance to the Union Depot in Chicago within the judicial power and within its authority to grant the writ of injunction when the remedy at law is inadequate, so in this Debs case it was the claim of right to be there and to do what it was doing and the consequential effect of what it was doing, as against the United States, that brought the casual and temporary multitude of striking workmen within the judicial power and within its authority to grant the writ of injunction when the remedy at law is inadequate — and it was not the multitude itself, or the mob as Debs by his counsel styled it. Fear, entertained by the judges of the Supreme Court of the United States, that petit jurors could not be relied on to render just and true verdicts in criminal prosecutions against the striking workmen by the United States or by the State of Illinois, had nothing whatever to do with the decision of the court, and to say that it had is to put something into the opinion of the court that is not there, and that is repugnant to everything that is there, and is to impute to the court the suppression of the true reasons and the giving of false reasons for its judgment, i. e., to

say that the opinion in the Debs case is a judicial lie, which is the blackest kind
of lie there is. As the United States Supreme Court said, when all the circumstances in this Debs case are considered, the executive of the United States deserved praise, not blame, for submitting to the courts the determination and
definition of its questioned and disputed right to apply "the club of the policeman
and the bayonet of the soldier" to the misguided, striking workmen.

Since the attorney-general's bill fell within the federal judicial power and
within the authority of the federal court as a court of equity to grant the remedy
of injunction, it followed necessarily as a matter of law that Debs and the others
were not entitled, as a matter of constitutional right, to jury trial on any branch
of the case; though it seems to me that, in point of sound policy, jury trial ought
to be allowed on the question of the violation of an injunction like that in this
Debs case, when the accused want it and there is a fair issue of fact to be tried.
Legislation is not necessary to secure jury trial in such a case. It is error to say,
as Woods, J., said in 64 Fed. Rep., on p. 476, "the contempt can be tried and
punished only by the court." A judge sitting on the equity side of a court always
has had and has now a discretion to refer to a jury the decision of any issue of
fact, including the decision of the issue of fact whether an injunction has been
violated. If men do not get jury trial in such cases when they ought to have it,
it is not the fault of the legislature or of the law, but is the fault of the judges.
The contempt in this Debs case was not a mere violation of the injunction, but
was a violation of such a character and in such a manner as to bring the violation
under the head of obstructing the course of justice, as distinguished from the
procedural contempt of merely violating an order of a court. Bessette v. Conkey,
194 U. S., 324, 329; Article on "Contempt of Court" in Halsbury's Laws of England; Beale, "Contempt of Court, Civil and Criminal," 21 Harv. L. R., 161.

Obstructing the course of justice in courts of law or in courts of equity was
and is an indictable misdemeanor under the English common law as well as a
contempt of court; but whether the procedural contempt of merely violating an
order of a court, and especially of a court of chancery, was ever regarded as an
indictable misdemeanor under the English common law as adopted by us is not
clear. It is intimated in Russell on Crimes (7th Eng. and 1st Can. ed., p. 542),
that the procedural contempt of merely violating an order of a court is also an
indictable misdemeanor, but the author cites only one case (Rex v. Robinson,
2 Burr., 789, 804, in 1759), of an indictment for violating an order of a court of
quarter sessions directing a man to pay two shillings a week to support his infant
grandchildren. The practice of the English common-law courts was to allow a
person charged with any kind of a contempt of a common-law court, except
contempt in facie curiae, to purge himself of the charge by a denial of it under
oath. As Blackstone says, even to interrogate a man accused of crime is
contrary to the genius of the common law. Blackstone says this common-
law practice of purging contempt of a common-law court by denial under oath
never obtained in the court of chancery, even, as I read him, in the case of the
contempt of obstructing the course of justice in the court of chancery, which was
also an indictable misdemeanor. 4 Bl. Com., 288. The English common-law
practice of purging every kind of contempt of a common-law court, except in
facie curiae, by denial under oath, has been rejected, and the contrary English
chancery practice has been adopted and extended to all cases of contempt, both
of common-law courts and equity courts, by many of our American courts, includ-

ing the United States Supreme Court in United States *v.* Shipp, 203 U. S., 563, 574. These decisions fix beyond further discussion in the courts the scope of the right of trial by jury as a matter of strict constitutional right in all contempt cases; and this is so, though many of these decisions, including the recent one by the United States Supreme Court, proceed upon the erroneous idea that the only common-law remedy where a man purged himself of the contempt of obstructing the course of justice in a common-law court by a false oath was an indictment for perjury, forgetting that the contempt of obstructing the course of justice, at least, was an indictable misdemeanor according to the course of the English common law.   It must be borne in mind in this connection that nothing is indictable as a crime against the United States unless it is made so by act of Congress. See 5 Fed. Stats. Sum., p. 383, on the misdemeanor of "Obstructing Justice" in federal courts.   In this Debs case, though the contempt charged was the one of obstructing the course of justice, indictable as a misdemeanor under the English common law, and seemingly under the Act of Congress, supra, and though the accused denied under oath the charge of contempt of court, and an English common-law court of Blackstone's day would have remitted the case to an indictment for the misdemeanor, yet it seems quite plain there was no fair issue of fact for a jury, and it may be doubted whether the accused wanted a jury, as the claim of jury trial seems to have been a lawyer's claim interposed to make a record and save the point, which could be done only by a judicial denial of the claim of jury trial.   Hence it is plain under the course of the decisions at the time the case came up, Debs and the others were not entitled as a matter of law to a jury tria, on the charge of contempt in violating the injunction, and it seems equally plain on the facts of the case the refusal of jury trial was not an abuse of the judicial discretion to give or refuse jury trial on a fair issue of fact in such a case of contempt of court.

There is absolutely nothing in this Debs case from beginning to end that lends any support whatever to the Illinois Supreme Court's idea of judicial authority to expand the sphere of the writ of injunction on the basis of the notion that public officers and jurors cannot be relied on to do their duty.   The legislature, so long as it keeps within the lines of the constitution, may employ that notion if it wants to, as in the modern liquor statutes, as a reason for expanding the sphere of the injunction, but not the courts.   The inherited system expects every man to do his duty, marks out the sphere of his duty for him, and provides an adequate and efficient way for stamping out any man who does not do his duty, and forbids any man to extend the sphere of his duty on the notion that other men are not doing their duty or will not do it.   One of the chief troubles with the system to-day is that it has lost its balance and harmony, and has become lop-sided and court-heavy, through the voluntary and legislatively required efforts of courts to perform duties reserved to the people, to constitutional conventions, to legislatures, and to executive officers and boards.   Happily the failure and imminent danger of the complete collapse of the American experiment of the last three or four decades in government by courts, especially in the several states, are compelling more and more people to see and recognize that the right kind of executive officers and boards can enforce some kinds of laws vastly better than the best courts, without any danger and with better security to the stability of the traditional and cherished constitutional rights of the people.

II

RIGHT OF WORKMEN TO ENJOIN A THREA-
TENED STRIKE — COMMENT ON
KEMP *v.* DIVISION NO. 241 [a]

The comments in 7 Ill. L. R. 320, 323, on Kemp *v.*
Division No. 241, 255 Ill., 213, s. c. 153 Ill. App., 344, 637,
are confined to the proposition of substantive law on
which the judges of the Supreme and Appellate Courts
divided, and do not attempt to touch the case as related
to the procedural point of equity jurisdiction, i. e., the
remedy of injunction. The case arose on demurrer to
a bill in equity by non-union workmen to enjoin a labor-
union, its officers and members, from carrying out a
threat to call a strike and to strike to coerce the employer of the complaining non-union workmen to discharge them unless they joined the union. The Supreme
Court, in an opinion by Cooke, J., writing for himself
and Farmer and Vickers, JJ., and in an opinion by Carter,
J., specially concurring, Cartwright, Dunn, and Hand,
JJ., dissenting, sustained the demurrer and dismissed the
bill. The majority's result at least affirms the procedural point, that a non-union workman's quia timet
bill in equity to enjoin his fellow union workmen from
carrying out their threat to strike to coerce the employer
to discharge him unless he joins the union, does not fall
within the sphere of equity jurisdiction, i. e. within
the sphere of the remedy of injunction. And the majority's result dismissing the bill in this case seems to

[a] [8 Ill. Law Rev., 126, June, 1913.]

me to be the correct one — when it is put on the second
or purely procedural ground relied on in the last part of
the concurring opinion of Carter, J., on pp. 252–256;
viz.: the application of the non-union workmen for a
quia timet injunction was too precipitate, and they must
wait until they are discharged in fact, and then the discharged non-union workman's remedy at law of an action
on the case for damages against the coercing union workmen, and the People's remedy of indictment against
the coercing union workmen for the crimes of intimidation and conspiracy, will be adequate, complete, and
efficient to the ends of justice and its prompt administration; and hence there was no legal reason for giving
the non-union workmen in this case the remedy of a
quia timet injunction to protect them from the threatened
or feared discharge.

Cooke, Farmer, and Vickers, JJ., put their denial of
the remedy of injunction to the non-union workmen
on the proposition of substantive law, that a person or
corporation, acting singly or in combination with others,
that by a threat of a strike coerces an employer to discharge a workman for his refusal to join a labor union,
is not guilty of any actionable tort as against the discharged workman, or indictable crime as against the
People. And Mack, J., dissenting in the Appellate
Court, supports the same proposition of substantive
law. The dissenting judges in the Supreme Court intimate rather plainly on p. 256 they do not know where
Carter, J., stands on that proposition of substantive law,
though the first seventeen pages of his concurring opinion
are devoted to it. Since Carter, J., in the last part of
his concurring opinion puts his judgment on the procedural ground of the adequacy of the remedy at law,
this question of substantive law that divided his associates
three to three was not necessarily before him judicially

for decision; and with entire propriety he could have refrained from any expression of his views concerning it.

If this case had come up into the appellate tribunals of Illinois, after the actual discharge of these non-union workmen resulting from the union workmen's threat of a strike, to review a judgment for damages on a jury's verdict in an action on the case by a discharged non-union workman against the coercing union workmen, or to review a judgment of fine or imprisonment on a jury's verdict of guilty under an indictment of the coercing union workmen for the crimes of intimidation and conspiracy, it seems quite certain that no Illinois appellate judge would have voted to reverse such judgment for damages in the civil case, or such judgment of fine or imprisonment in the criminal case, on the ground advanced in this case by four Supreme Court judges and one Appellate Court judge for denying the non-union workmen the remedy of a quia timet injunction, which ground advanced is, that such coerced discharge of the non-union workmen would not be either an actionable tort as against the discharged non-union workmen, or an indictable crime as against the People. As to that reason of substantive law advanced by these judges in this case, it seems too plain for discussion that it is wrong in itself in point of law; and it is not shown to be necessary to support the result dismissing the bill. When this case arose, there can be no fair question whatever, as it seems to me, it was the established, existing, statutory, and judiciary law of Illinois, that any person or corporation, acting singly or in combination with others, that by a threat of a strike coerces an employer to discharge a workman for his refusal to join a labor union, is guilty of a tort, and is liable civilly to the discharged workman in an action on the case for damages, and is guilty of the

crime of intimidation or conspiracy, and is liable crimi-
nally to the People of Illinois in an indictment.　Doremus
v. Hennessy, 176 Ill., 608; London Guarantee Co. v.
Horn, 206 Ill., 493; Purington v. Hinchliff, 219 Ill., 159;
Gibson v. Fidelity & Casualty Co., 232 Ill., 49; Criminal
Code Div. 1, Secs. 46, 158, 159, 160; Franklin Union v.
People, 220 Ill., 355, 385, dissenting opinion of Boggs and
Scott, JJ.　That proposition seems wholesome and sound
in principle, and is supported by the best legal opinion in
Anglo-American law, whether that legal opinion is meas-
ured by count or by weight.

The explanation of the division in the Supreme and
Appellate Courts on the really non-debatable question
of substantive law they supposed was involved, and did
debate in fact, appears to lie in the way the case came up
and was presented at the bar.　The complaining non-
union workmen had not been actually discharged; they
only said they were afraid they were going to be discharged.　Their complaint was not based on any charge
of wrong done, but only on a charge of a wrong threatened,
feared, or anticipated.　The non-union workmen, proceeding on the basis of the threat of the labor union, its
officers and members, to call a strike and to strike in
futuro, wanted the court to issue a quia timet injunction
to restrain and prevent the labor union, its officers and
members from carrying out in futuro their threat to call a
strike and to strike.　The only reason given by the non-
union workmen for not waiting until they were discharged
in fact and then bringing an action on the case for
damages, was a general averment in their bill to the following effect as stated by Cooke, J., on p. 217: "The members,
officers, and executive board of Division 241, and also
Division 241, are unable to respond in adequate damages
for the injuries to the appellees [i. e., the plaintiffs] in the
event of their discharge, and that the causing of their dis-

charge or dismissal as employees of the Railways Company for the reasons above set forth will cause them irreparable injury." This generality in the bill, as admitted by demurrer, was assumed without question at the bar to be sufficient to bring the case within the sphere of the remedy of a quia timet injunction.   Accordingly, the whole discussion at the bar was shifted from the procedural point of the adequacy of the remedy at law, and was thrown back upon the point of substantive law, i. e. whether the discharge of the non-union workmen, if and when actually brought about in futuro by the threat of the labor union, its officers and members to call a strike and to strike, would give an in futuro discharged non-union workman a cause of action for damages against the labor union, its officers and members.   That question of substantive law so raised in this case evidently was rather speculative or abstractly philosophical, savoring of the moot-court in a law school; and carried the judges off the ground high up into the air, where there was plenty of room for the play and action of individual private opinion and bias, unrestrained by actual facts proven by evidence in the record, in a way that is entirely alien to and ordinarily is forbidden by the English and American system of administering justice in the courts, the chief distinguishing merit and glory of the system being its insistence on and respect for facts, established by evidence in the case in hand.   The judges had to, or did, assume the de jure and de facto possibility of a "peaceful strike"with its accompaniment of "peaceful persuasion"or "peaceful picketing" by union workmen to attain their ends.   The sources from which Cooke, Farmer, Vickers, and Carter, JJ., in the Supreme Court, and Mack, J., in the Appellate Court, drew their ideas on the abstract question of substantive law they elaborate in their opinions, may be illustrated by the dissenting opinion of Boggs and Scott, JJ., in Franklin Union v. People, 220 Ill., 355, 385, 386.   (And see the dissenting opinion of Scott and Farmer, JJ., in Barnes v. Typographical Union, 232 Ill., 424, 435.)   In the dissenting opinion cited, Boggs and Scott, JJ., took exception to a clause in an injunction granted to an employer against striking and picketing workmen, which clause forbade the striking and picketing workmen "from inducing by unlawful persuasion any of the employees" of the plaintiff-employer to leave his service; and the ground of their exception to this clause was, that the injunction did not precisely define "unlawful persuasion"; and, they said, there are two kinds of persuasion or picketing by striking workmen, viz., "lawful persuasion" and "unlawful persuasion"; and "lawful persuasion," i. e. "peaceful, platonic picketing" by striking workmen, cannot be enjoined by a court on the application of an employer.   Now, in point of actual fact, "lawful persuasion," i. e. "peaceful, platonic picketing" by the educational committee of a labor union, exists only in the minds of judges translated back among the highly speculative, ancient Greeks and up into Aristophanes' cloud-cuckoo town of the Sophists built by the birds twixt earth and sky; and is like the perfect man and the perfect woman that nobody ever saw, except a scared timid little woman at a prayer-meeting, who said she often heard about the perfect woman, and it was her husband's first wife.   But laying that matter of fact about "peaceful persuasion" entirely to one side, and taking up this abstract thing called "peaceful persuasion," when Boggs and Scott, JJ., and other learned judges at home and abroad say that "peaceful persuasion" by union workmen to induce other workmen not to enter or to leave an employment is "lawful" as against the employer, what they mean to say and do say is, that such "peaceful persuasion" cannot be enjoined by a court on the application of the employer; i. e. "peaceful persuasion" does not fall within the remedy of the writ of injunction when invoked by the employer against striking, picketing workmen. These judges are only laying down a rule of procedural law on the subject of the adequacy of the remedy at law, and not a rule 'of substantive law at all. They do not mean to say and do not say that "peaceful persuasion" by union workmen to induce other workmen not to enter or leave an employment is "lawful," in the sense that it cannot under any circumstances whatsoever constitute an actionable tort as against the employer, or an indictable crime as against the People. The reason why "peaceful persuasion" by union workmen to induce other workmen not to enter or to leave an employment cannot be enjoined by a court at the instance of the employer is, that the law does not permit the courts to use the remedy of injunction either to establish or to maintain the relation of employer and employee, an old, wise rule of procedure touching the adequacy of the remedy at law, resting on the most solid grounds of policy and statesmanship in a community where in theory of law all workmen are free and there are no slaves. Franklin Union v. People, 220 Ill., 355, 386, and cases cited; Barnes v. Typographical Union, 232 Ill., 424, 439, and cases cited; Kemp v. Division No. 241, 255 Ill., 213, 252, and cases cited. But it does not follow at all that such "peaceful persuasion" by union workmen is necessarily "lawful," always and under all circumstances, as against the employer, to say nothing at all about the non-union workmen in this case, in the sense that it can never under any circumstances give rise to an action on the case for damages by the employer against the "peaceful persuaders," or to an indictment of the "peaceful persuaders." Cooke, Farmer, and Vickers, JJ., and Carter, J., in the first seventeen pages of

his concurring opinion, and Mack, J., in the Appellate
Court, have simply mistaken an old rule of procedure
concerning the adequacy of the remedy at law for a rule
of substantive law, confused by the phrase "lawful
persuasion" as used by judges to explain their refusal to
give employers the remedy of injunction to compel workmen to enter into or to continue the relation of employer
and employee.

The averment in the bill in this case of the insolvency
of the labor union, its officers and members, though
admitted by demurrer, was not enough to bring the
quia timet case of these non-union workmen within the
sphere of the remedy of injunction. The mere insolvency, alone, of a tort-feasor is not enough to bring the
tort, committed or threatened, within the remedy of
injunction. If the insolvency, alone, of a tort-feasor,
whether he has actually committed the tort or is only
threatening to commit it, were enough to bring him
within the sphere of the injunction and its consequent
chance of summary punishment by fine or imprisonment
for violating it, there would be an invidious line of distinction drawn by the law between the rich and the poor
on the subject of remedies. Adequacy of remedy at
law never has meant that the remedy at law must always
produce the money. Thompson v. Allen County, 115
U. S., 550, 554, per Miller, J. In most cases arising out
of torts and breaches of contracts, the law allows only
the remedy of damages on grounds of policy, though
perhaps the remedy of injunction would be more adequate and efficient in actual practice and in point of
abstract justice between man and man, if in administering justice between man and man it were permissible for
the courts to consider only abstract justice between two
men on an island, like Robinson Crusoe and his man
Friday, leaving entirely out of view all considerations of

public policy, and the feelings, habits, and traditions
of a democratic community devoted to the ideal of the
equality of all men before the law.   The torts and
breaches of contracts that practically have to go unre-
dressed by judicial process are, and always have been,
far in excess of those that find their way into the courts.
The English and American systems never have attempted
to provide judicial relief for everything that happens to a
man in the course of his flight through this world.   The
popular stoicism, "It was coming to me and I got it,"
is all the practical relief obtainable in a lot of cases,
whether you are rich or poor; that may be barbarous and
unscientific, but it is the English and American way, and
has been for centuries.   Besides, the averment of insolvency in this case was too general, and was bad on demurrer; and a court ought to take judicial notice on
demurrer to such a general averment that it is not true
in point of fact ordinarily, that a modern labor union,
its officers and members, active and honorary, are all
paupers, unable to respond in damages for their torts of
the kind threatened in this case.   The bill in this case
showed that each member of the labor union in question
was assessed 75 cents a month; that the labor union had
collected $190,000 from its members and had $5,000 in its
treasury.   In the absence of any controlling decision
or statute to the contrary, it is fair to presume on the
question of the adequacy of the remedy in damages, that
the courts could and would reach the money in the
treasury of this labor union as well as the private property
of its officers and members.   The averment in the bill
that the discharge of these non-union workmen would
cause them "irreparable injury" is wrong as a legal
conclusion, for the injury caused a workman by his wrongful discharge is not ordinarily irreparable; and in any
event the averment of irreparable injury in this case was

bad on demurrer.   In addition, it must be remembered
that a quia timet injunction based on a threat to commit
a tort of the kind threatened in this case is a very rare
remedy in Anglo-American law; and a quia timet injunction is very rare in any case of tort outside the field of
nuisance, waste, and trespass to real property, and is
exceptional there.   Counsel on both sides and all of
the judges in the Supreme and Appellate Courts, except
Carter, J., in the Supreme Court, assumed with scarcely
any consideration whatever the general averment of
insolvency and irreparable injury foreclosed in the procedural question of the adequacy of the remedy at law.
This was error.   In spite of this error, however, the reasoning of the opinions, and especially the latter part of the
opinion of Carter, J., which actually disposed of the
case, making the rest of his opinion and all of the opinion
of Cooke, J., technically obiter, shows the case really
and in truth went off on the point of procedure that the
non-union workmen were too precipitate in asking for
a quia timet injunction, and must wait until they
are discharged, when the remedy at law in damages
would be adequate and complete.   As related to equity
jurisdiction, or the remedy of injunction, the case is nothing like the boycott-injunction cases of employers against
workmen, such as Wilson *v.* Hey, 232 Ill., 389, and
Gompers *v.* Bucks Stove & Range Co., 221 U. S., 418,
437, or the strike-injunction cases of employers against
striking and picketing workmen, such as Franklin Union
v. People, 220 Ill., 355, and Barnes *v.* Typographical
Union, 232 Ill., 402. And the hasty, unconsidered
citation of In re Debs, 158 U. S., 364, by Smith, J., in the
Appellate Court to sustain equity jurisdiction in this case,
only shows that judges in some way or other have got
the idea fixed in their minds that the Debs case authorizes
them to do anything they like in the way of governing
the world and sending people to jail by injunction.

It is to be regretted, and is somewhat surprising in view of the published dissent on the matter at different times lately by Boggs, Scott, Farmer, and Cooke, JJ., that the Supreme Court did not determine in this case to examine the foundations and limits of the quite recent, remarkable, and wholesale judicial extension in the United States of the remedy of injunction to industrial disputes between employer and employee, and between union workmen and non-union workmen, and decide to put its judgment in this case on the procedural ground that the case fell outside the legitimate sphere of the injunction, as it seems very clear that it did.   The dissenting opinion of Cartwright, Hand, and Dunn, JJ., is a model of straight thinking and reading of binding precedents on the question of substantive law it discusses, and says on p. 266: "Governments and courts would be useless if they failed to protect the laborer in the enjoyment" of his right under existing law "to dispose of his labor as he may choose for the support of himself and those dependent upon him."   That is true.   But no Illinois judge or lawyer can deny honestly, that the present admitted uselessness and impotency of government and courts in Illinois to perform that function of protecting the laborer in the exercise and enjoyment of his right to sell his labor, rests on the Illinois Supreme Court, and it is a heavy one.   The court's line of constitutional decisions commencing in 1886 in Millett v. People, 117 Ill., 294, incorporating into the life, liberty, and property clause of the state constitution the governmental policy of laissez faire of the "dismal science" of the political economy of David Ricardo, elevating that policy into a rule of constitutional law limiting the legislative power of the state, has made the Illinois legislature a legally insignificant and despised legislature, legally incapable of rising above the opening and division of a jack-pot if it wanted to, useless and impotent to pass adequate laws regulating the relation of employer and employee and of union workmen and non-union workmen. To maintain and enforce this constitutional, governmental policy of laissez faire in the relations of employer and employee fastened on to the people and the legislature of this state by the Supreme Court of the state, the remedy of injunction with its summary fines and imprisonments was judicially extended to industrial disputes. The uselessness and impotency of the judicial remedy of injunction to maintain and enforce the judge-made constitutional governmental policy of laissez faire between employer and employee is patent to everybody. Now three, and perhaps four, judges of the Supreme Court of the state are willing to turn this judge-made laissez-faire governmental policy over to the labor-unions, their officers and members, telling them to do as they please with non-union workmen under the name and guise of "peaceful persuasion," and telling non-union workmen they must bow to the "peaceful persuasion" of union workmen and join the union, or starve, so far as the existing law and courts of Illinois are concerned. This judge-made laissez-faire system of law and remedies, for the "protection" of the abstract "equal economic unit" called the workman, cannot stand; it is fundamentally wrong in point of law.[1]

---

[1] For concise statement of the fallacies and elements of truth in the governmental policy of laissez faire advocated by the older political economists, see the first lecture in Arnold Toynbee's Industrial Revolution in England, published in 1887. In reading the discussions of laissez faire by economists and philosophers, it must ever be kept in mind that the life, liberty, and property clause is centuries older than laissez faire; and that under it and without disturbing it, and in harmony with it, many systems of political economy and philosophy and legislative policy have had their day and ceased to be. It does not stand for the imperishable value of the individual as an end in himself, but it permits diverse experimental means of preserving that end. The labor union may be one of them; I do not know, and as a lawyer do not care till the legislature says so.

TOPIC IV

RELIEF AGAINST PROCEEDINGS AT LAW

I

IRREGULARITY IN AN EXECUTION SALE AS A FOUNDATION OF EQUITY JURISDICTION IN ILLINOIS[a]

The rule that gross inadequacy of price in an execution sale of real estate cannot give a court of equity jurisdiction to set aside the sale, unless there is an irregularity in the execution proceedings, is stated often in opinions of the Supreme Court. And it is said, in substance, that any irregularity, even the least spark of an irregularity, may be enough to give a court of equity jurisdiction to set aside the sale, if the inadequacy of price is gross.[1]

The recent case of Skakel v. Cycle Trade Publishing Company,[2] where $20,000 worth of land was sold on execution for $132.04, was presented to the Supreme Court on the basis of an accepted legal theory that made its decision turn on the single question whether the omission of the word "personal" before the word "property" in the copy of a constable's nulla bona return contained in the transcript of a justice's judgment filed in the circuit court as a basis for execution against real estate, was enough of an irregularity in the execution proceedings to give the court equity jurisdiction to set aside the

---

[a] [5 Ill. Law Rev., 203, November, 1910.]

[1] Thomas v. Habenstreit, 68 Ill., 115, 118; Davis v. Chicago Dock Co., 129 Ill., 180, 188, 189; Hobson v. McCambridge, 130 Ill., 367, 378; Bullen v. Dawson, 139 Ill., 633, 642; Miller v. McAlister, 197 Ill., 72, 79; Skakel v. Cycle Trade Publishing Co., 237 Ill., 482; and see Graffam v.Burgess, 117 U. S., 180; Schroeder v. Young, 161 U. S., 334.

[2] 237 Ill., 482.

sale. The Supreme Court divided four to three. The majority thought the irregularity was not enough, and the debtor's bill was dismissed.[3]

That decision breaks the notion that any irregularity, however slight, in execution proceedings, is enoguh to give equity jurisdiction.

The law is, it is believed, that either (1) any irregularity in execution proceedings that makes the sale void, or (2) the irregularity of a sheriff's sale en masse, gives a court of equity jurisdiction to set aside the execution sale; and that equity jurisdiction cannot be founded on any other irregularity, however grossly inadequate the price may be. The reason why either one of these two irregularities may be enough of a foundation for equity jurisdiction to set aside is that a court of equity in Illinois has, after fixed stages in the execution proceedings, the jurisdiction that normally belongs to the court of law that rendered the judgment to supervise and control its execution.

Before the adoption by New York of the policy of allowing a debtor to redeem from an execution sale of real estate,[4] the New York Court of Chancery, Kent, C., recognized the right or equity of a debtor to avoid an execution sale of his land, and entertained debtor's bills for relief from execution sales of land in Woods v. Monell [5] in 1815, in Howell v. Baker [6] in 1819, and in Tiernan v. Wilson [7] in 1822. And in 1796, in Lord Cranstown v. Johnston,[8] the English Court of Chancery, Sir R. Pepper

---

[3] The minority relied on other irregularities found in the abstract of the record, but I understand the transcript of the record removes them.

[4] On the origin of execution sales of land in the United States, see 4 Kent's Com., 428–430.

[5] 1 John, Ch. 502.

[6] 4 John, Ch. 118.

[7] 6 John, Ch. 410.

[8] 3 Vesey, 170; 5 Vesey, 277.

Arden, M. R., relieved a debtor from an execution sale of his land in St. Christopher's Island. All of these cases were cited with approval in Illinois in Day v. Graham [9] in 1844, twenty-three years after the state had adopted the redemption policy. The decisions of Kent, C., have spread through the states;[10] and in Graham v. Burgess,[11] in 1886, they were taken into the equity law administered by the federal courts in controversies between citizens of different states, and were applied in that case in favor of a debtor asking relief from an execution sale of land under a judgment of a state court, though the redemption policy prevailed in the state in question, i. e., Massachusetts.

The New York redemption act of April 12, 1820, was, perhaps, the first redemption act in the United States.[12] The first Illinois redemption act was passed January 27, 1821, and a redemption act has been in force in Illinois ever since.[13] February 19, 1841, the redemption policy was extended to foreclosure sales of mortgages executed before that date.[14]

The redemption act created a new right in favor of debtors, i. e., as it now exists, the right to redeem, to repurchase or purchase back, real estate sold on execution by paying the purchaser the amount for which it was sold with interest thereon from the date of the sale. A judgment debtor must exercise this right of redemption

---

[9] 1 Gilman, 435; 4 Gilman, 389.

[10] Mobile Cotton Press v. Moore, 9 Porter, 679; State Bank v. Noland, 13 Ark., 299; Blight's Heirs v. Tobin, 7 T. B. Monroe, 612; Schroeder v. Young, 161 U. S., 334.

[11] 117 U. S., 180.

[12] Elsworth v. Muldoon, 15 Abb. Pr. R., n. s., 440, 443; 4 Kent's Com., 431, and notes (a) and (g) on p. 432.

[13] Laws, 1821, 38, Sec. 3.   See the historical notes at the end of Ch. 77, Judgments and Executions, in 2 S. & C. Ann. Stat., 2d ed.

[14] Bronson v. Kinzie, 1 How., 311; Bradley v. Lightcap, 195 U. S., 1.

within twelve months from the date of the sale. Any decree or judgment creditor of the debtor may redeem after the expiration of twelve months and within fifteen months after the sale.[15] The time limited for the exercise of the right of redemption is not simply an inseparable ingredient of the definition of the right, but operates as a statute of limitations on the exercise of the right.[16]

The pre-existing common-law right of a debtor to avoid an execution sale of his real estate, i. e., to have it set aside by order of a court, and the new statutory right of a debtor to redeem from an execution sale, i. e., to repurchase or purchase back the property sold, are distinct, independent, substantive rights; that is to say, they do not stand in the relation of right and remedy. The right to redeem is not a remedy for the protection and enforcement of the right to avoid or set aside.[17] It is only when an execution sale is free from any infirmity that renders it void or voidable that the debtor's only course is to use his statutory right to redeem.[18]

The common-law right of a debtor to avoid an execution sale of his real estate arises, after the redemption act just as before it, either (1) from fraud, accident, mistake, or surprise occurring in the execution proceedings, or (2) from irregularity in the execution proceedings, i. e., from a failure to observe the terms of the law regulating the conduct of execution proceedings.[19]

[15] 2 S. & C. Ann. Stat., 2d ed., Ch. 77, Secs. 18, 20, pp. 2353, 2358.

[16] Mixer v. Sibley, 53 Ill., 61, 76; Briscoe v. York, 59 Ill., 484; Trotter v. Smith, 59 Ill., 240; Henderson v. Harness, 184 Ill., 520; Schroeder v. Young, 161 U. S., 334, 344.

[17] Day v. Graham, 1 Gilman, 435, and 4 Gilman, 389, and all the later cases show this.

[18] Miller v. McAlister, 197 Ill., 72, 79; McLean County Bank v. Flagg, 31 Ill., 290; Phelps v. Conover, 25 Ill., 309.

[19] Woods v. Monell, 1 John, Ch. 502; Howell v. Baker, 4 John, Ch. 118; Tiernan v. Wilson, 6 John, Ch. 410; Lord Cranstown v. Johnston, 3 Vesey, 170; Day v. Graham, 1 Gilman, 435.

Under the common-law line dividing remedies into remedies at law and remedies in equity a debtor had two concurrent remedies for the protection and enforcement of his right to avoid an execution sale for fraud, accident, mistake, or surprise, viz., (1) an application to the court of law that rendered the judgment invoking its inherent jurisdiction to supervise and control the execution of its judgments;[20] (2) an application to a court of equity invoking its equity jurisdiction to compel parties to surrender to their adversaries advantages gained in proceedings in a common-law court by fraud, accident, mistake, or surprise.[21]

The material differences between these two concurrent remedies lay (1) in the use the court applied to could make of irregularities in the execution proceedings, and (2) in the mode of administering the relief. Under the second remedy in the court of equity, the court could consider irregularities in the execution proceedings in the common-law court only as evidence of the fraud, accident, mistake, or surprise alleged; the court of equity could not grant relief on the basis of irregularity in the execution proceedings. And when it came to give relief the court of equity could not wipe out the execution sale; it could only order the defendant to reconvey the property to the debtor. Under the first remedy in the court of law that rendered the judgment, the court had all the equity jurisdiction invoked by the second remedy

[20] Schroeder v. Young, 161 U. S., 334, 345; Day v. Graham, 1 Gilman, 435. On the inherent power of the court of law to supervise the execution of its judgments, see Griffin v. Thompson, 2 How., 244, 257; United States v. Alfred, 155 U. S., 591, 595, 596; McLean County Bank v. Flagg, 31 Ill., 290, 295; Sandburg v. Papineau, 81 Ill., 446, 448, 449; Greenleaf v. Chesseldine, 4 Scam., 332; Swiggart v. Harber, 4 Scam., 364, 374; Beaird v. Foreman, Breese, 385, 386, 387, 388; cases in note 32 infra. That the power involves power to adopt forms and modes of procedure to make the jurisdiction effective, see United States Bank v. Halstead, 10 Wheat., 51, 64; Laws, Ill., 1819, 380, Sec. 27, now Ill. R. S., Chap. on Courts, Sec. 26.

[21] Schroeder v. Young, 161 U. S., 334, 345.

in the court of equity, and in addition had its inherent jurisdiction over its own officers, proceedings, and record, and by virtue thereof could consider irregularities in the execution proceedings not only as evidence of the fraud, accident, mistake, or surprise alleged, but as irregularities simply, because they were irregularities, regardless of whether they evidenced the fraud, accident, mistake, or surprise alleged or not. As to the relief under this remedy in the common-law court that rendered the judgment, the common-law court could wipe out the whole execution proceedings, expunge them from its record, and did not have to order the defendant to reconvey the property to the debtor.[22]

These differences between the two remedies come out pointedly when a federal court, sitting as a court of equity in a controversy between citizens of different states, is asked to set aside an execution sale under a judgment of a state court; or when a state court is asked to set aside an execution sale under a judgment of a federal court; or when a court of one state is asked to set aside an execution sale under a judgment of a court of another state, or of a foreign country. Equity jurisdiction, strictly so-called, to set aside an execution sale, is but an application, instance, or branch of the wider equity jurisdiction to interfere with judicial proceedings in a common-law court.[23]

[22] Day v. Graham, 1 Gilman, 435; cases in notes 20 and 10 supra. The decree of a court of equity never actually sets aside anything; it operates in personam, enjoining or compelling action by the parties. Local statutes and practice giving an in rem effect to a decree do not alter the principle, and have no application outside the jurisdiction. See Hart v. Sansom, 110 U. S., 151, 154; Ewing v. Ewing, L. R., 9 App. Cas., 34, 40; Arndt v. Griggs, 134 U. S., 216; Lynch v. Murphy, 161 U. S., 247; Fall v. Eastin, 215 U. S., 1.

[23] Marshall v. Holmes, 141 U. S., 589; Byers v. Surget, 19 How., 303; Graffam v. Burgess, 117 U. S., 180; Pearce v. Onley, 20 Conn., 544; Dobson v. Pearce, 12 N. Y., 156; Embry v. Palmer, 107 U. S., 3. That "all proceedings on the judgment are proceedings in the suit," see Wayman v. Southard, 10 Wheat., 1, 23;

A debtor's application by bill in equity to protect and enforce his common-law right to avoid an execution sale is sometimes called a bill to redeem.[24] But there is no such right as the equity of a debtor to redeem from an execution sale The only right to redeem from an execution sale a debtor has is the statutory right of redemption. As a condition of setting aside an execution sale, the court may impose such equitable terms on the debtor as the circumstances of the case may require. The terms imposed by the court flow from the principle that he who seeks equity must do equity. The law requires a debtor to pay a valid judgment promptly.[25]

There are two instances where a bill in equity by a debtor perhaps may be called correctly a bill to redeem from an execution sale, viz., (1) a bill by a debtor to be allowed to exercise the statutory right of redemption modo et forma according to the terms of the statute, but after the time limited, nunc pro tunc; in other words, a bill to suspend or remove the bar of the statute of limitations;[26] (2) a bill by a debtor for the specific performance of a contract extending the time limited for statutory redemption.[27] In these instances the ultimate relief asked by the debtor is to be allowed to exercise the statutory right of redemption; the debtor does not ask the court to protect and enforce his right to avoid the execution sale.

When a debtor's right to avoid an execution sale of his real estate is founded upon an irregularity in the

United States Bank v. Halstead, 10 Wheat., 51, 61; Leathe v. Thomas, 97 Fed. Rep., 136.

[24] Howell v. Baker, 4 John, Ch. 118; Roseman v. Miller, 84 Ill., 297.

[25] Ogle v. Koerner, 41 Ill. App., 452; Littler v. The People, 43 Ill., 188; 24 Cyc., 68.

[26] Cases in note 16 supra.

[27] Ross v. Sutherland, 81 Ill., 275; Davis v. Dresback, 81 Ill., 393; Chytraus v. Smith, 141 Ill., 237.

execution proceedings, then, under the common-law line dividing remedies into remedies at law and remedies in equity, the debtor's only direct remedy to avoid the sale is an application to the common-law court that rendered the judgment invoking its inherent jurisdiction to supervise and control the execution of its judgments.[28]

In Illinois, in Day *v.* Graham,[29] the line of the common law dividing remedies into remedies at law and remedies in equity was altered, so far as remedies for the protection and enforcement of a debtor's common-law right to avoid an execution sale of land are concerned. Day *v.* Graham is the first and leading case in Illinois on the subject of equity jurisdiction to set aside an execution sale. The case was taken up to the Supreme Court on a question of procedure, viz., whether a motion made on the common-law side of the court that rendered the judgment in the case wherein the judgment was rendered, as a continuation of, or appendix to, that case, or an entirely new suit begun by bill in equity filed on the equity side of the court, was the proper mode of procedure to enforce a debtor's right to avoid an execution sale for irregularity in the execution proceedings, the principal irregularity relied on being the irregularity of a sheriff's sale en masse. The Supreme Court decided that an entirely new suit begun by a bill in equity filed on the equity side of the court was the proper mode of procedure, and laid down this general rule.[30]

---

[28] Schroeder *v.* Young, 161 U. S., 334, 345.

[29] 1 Gilman, 435; 4 Gilman, 389.

[30] Illinois courts of general jurisdiction, like the federal circuit courts, have jurisdiction at law and in equity; and the equity side and the law side must be conceived of as two distinct courts, a court of equity and a court of law. The equity side is governed by the rules and methods of the English High Court of Chancery, except where altered by local statute, practice, or usage. See Laws, 1819, 170, Sec. 2, now Sec. 2 of the present Chancery Act; Greenleaf *v.* Chesseldine, 4 Scam., 332; Maher *v.* O'Hara, 4 Gilman, 424, 427.

"When the plaintiff in the execution is the purchaser, and before he conveys to another, the court would set the sale aside upon a motion. But after he conveys to a third person, and where a third person becomes the purchaser, the court will not determine, in this summary way, questions which may affect the rights of others, not before the court, and without opportunity of explaining away those circumstances which might destroy his title. Although the purchaser here was the attorney, and will be chargeable with notice of all irregularities, if any, yet he is a third person, and did not purchase as an attorney, but in his own right."

In Jenkins *v.* Merriweather[31] the Supreme Court re-examined the line drawn in Day *v.* Graham between the procedure by motion on the law side of the court, and the procedure by bill in equity on the equity side of the court, and, confirming Day *v.* Graham in all other respects, said:

"Under more recent decisions we should not go the length, even between the parties to the suit, of setting aside a sheriff's deed on motion."

And the court laid down this rule:

"The court [that rendered the judgment] may [on motion], on proper grounds, withdraw and quash executions and other writs, and no doubt set aside sales of real estate before they have ripened into titles; but it never has been the practice, on motion, in this jurisdiction, to set aside or divest title when the sale has ripened into a deed, and the title has vested, and all antecedent writs and processes have performed their functions, and have become functus officio. After a deed for real estate, under a sale on execution, has been made, it must be impeached, if at all, in equity."

The rule in Day *v.* Graham and Jenkins *v.* Merriweather is a rule of practice and procedure only. It does not abridge the common-law right of a debtor to avoid an execution sale for irregularity; nor does it abridge the power of an Illinois court to protect and enforce that right of a debtor. On the contrary, it enlarges the

[31] 109 Ill., 647.

power of an Illinois court, as a court of equity, or, rather, enlarges the power of the equity side of the court, to protect and enforce that right of a debtor, because it fuses or consolidates under one exclusive proceeding on the equity side of an Illinois court the equity jurisdiction of the court, and the inherent jurisdiction of the court as a common-law court to supervise and control the execution of its judgments. In short, the rule shifts the whole jurisdiction to set aside from the law side to the equity side of the court, (1) when a third person purchases at an execution sale, and (2) when the sheriff's deed is issued, in case the creditor purchases in his own name.[32]

When an Illinois court sets aside an execution sale under a domestic judgment, under the procedure by bill in equity, whether for fraud, accident, mistake, or surprise, or for irregularity only, the practice appears to be, if there is any established, uniform practice, to wipe out the sale; to make a decree in rem.[33] When the execution sale in question is one under a judgment of a foreign court, then there must be a decree in personam on the basis of fraud,

---

[32] Mr. Justin Butterfield made the motion in Day v. Graham, before Caton, J., in the La Salle Circuit Court. As the decisions then stood, it is not surprising that he decided to proceed by way of motion. See Greenup v. Brown, Breese, 252; Beaird v. Foreman, Breese, 385; Sloo v. Bank of Illinois, 1 Scam., 428; Russel v. Huginen 1 Scam., 562; Greenleaf v. Chesseldine, 4 Scam., 332. The procedure by motion was held improper, not because the law side of the court did not have jurisdiction, but on a reason of expediency, because the court thought the procedure by motion and affidavit was not well adapted to the nature of the case presented. Caton, J., brings that out in Watson v. Reissig, 24 Ill., 281, 284. And see Mason v. Thomas, 24 Ill., 285. In Coffey v. Coffey, 16 Ill., 141, it was contended, on the authority of Day v. Graham, that a bill in equity was the proper way to proceed to set aside a master's sale, but the point was rejected.

[33] See the decree in Day v. Graham, 4 Gilman, 389, 392. It is held to be reversible error to decree a reconveyance under a bill to remove a cloud on title where the land is in Illinois. Puterbaugh, Ch. Pr., 5th ed., 601; Clay v. Hammond, 199 Ill., 370; Casstevens v. Casstevens, 227 Ill., 547; Sugar v. Frolich, 229 Ill., 327. The practice appears to go back to Rucker v. Dooley, 49 Ill., 377, 384, a bill in equity to set aside a sheriff's deed issued twenty-nine years after the execution sale.

accident, mistake, or surprise only, ordering the defendant to reconvey the property to the debtor.[34]

To what irregularities in execution proceedings has the Supreme Court carried the doctrine established in Day v. Graham, that an irregularity in execution proceedings is enough, per se, to give a court of equity jurisdiction to set aside the execution sale?

When the irregularity relied on by a debtor is one that renders the sale void, it is said in the majority opinion in Skakel v. Cycle Trade Publishing Company[35] that this will not give a court of equity jurisdiction to set aside the sale, if the irregularity is apparent on the face of the execution proceedings. The minority opinion denies this. The minority are right. The majority statement is obiter. There are decided cases against it, and none for it, so far as I know.[36] The cases are supportable, as flowing from the jurisdiction of the court as a common-law court to supervise and control the execution of domestic judgments. An irregularity that makes an execution sale under a domestic judgment void is within the reach of the procedure by motion to set aside.[37] And the cases arising under the procedure by bill in equity after the sale, when a third person purchases, and after the sheriff's deed, when the creditor is the purchaser, are supportable as flowing from the strict equity jurisdiction of the court to remove a cloud on title, the case of an execution sale void for irregularity apparent on its face falling outside the scope of the rule that there is no equity jurisdiction to remove

[34] Cases in note 22 supra.

[35] 237 Ill., 482, 486, 488.

[36] Roseman v. Miller, 84 Ill., 297, Hobson v. McCambridge, 130 Ill., 367; Bullen v. Dawson, 139 Ill., 363; Merrick v. Carter, 205 Ill., 73; Schmitt v. Weber, 239 Ill., 377; Rucker v. Dooley, 49 Ill., 377.

[37] Weaver v. Peasley & Co., 163 Ill., 251; Beaird v. Foreman, Breese, 385, 388; Day v. Graham, 1 Gilman, 435, 451, 452; Jenkins v. Merriweather, 109 Ill., 647, 651, 652.

an instrument as a cloud on title when its invalidity is apparent on its face, either because of the color of official authority back of the execution sale, or because of the statute making the sheriff's deed prima facie evidence that the provisions of the statute regulating the conduct of execution sales were complied with.[38]

When the irregularity is one that makes the execution's sale void, the inadequacy of the price cannot affect the equity jurisdiction, so called, of the court to set aside the sale.   And the fact that the sale is void cannot deprive the court of power to impose terms on the debtor as a condition of having the sale set aside.   If the debtor is not willing to comply with the terms imposed, the court may leave the sale standing as a cloud on the debtor's title, to be got rid of by the debtor as best he can in some other proceeding, as, e. g., an action of ejectment against him, if he is in possession, or by him, if he is out of posession.[39]

Day *v*. Graham decides that the irregularity of a sheriff's sale en masse alone gives equity jurisdiction to set aside the sale.   This irregularity makes the sale voidable only, and not void.[40]

The irregularity of a sheriff's sale en masse arises when the sheriff does not observe, i. e., violates, the command now formulated in Section 12 of the Execution Act[41] in these words:

[38] Roby *v.* South Park Commissioners, 215 Ill., 200; 2 S. & C. Ann. Stat., 2d ed., Sec. 33, p. 2369; Pomeroy, Eq. Jur., 3d ed., and Student's Ed., Secs. 1398, 1399, and cases in the notes; Merrick *v.* Carter, 205 Ill., 73.

[39] Day *v.* Graham, 1 Gilman, 435, 451, 452; cases in note 37 supra.

[40] Day *v.* Graham, 1 Gilman, 435, 453; Palmer *v.* Riddle, 180 Ill., 461, 464.

[41] 2 S. & C. Ann. Stat., 2d ed., Sec. 12, p. 2344.   The statute law goes back to Laws, 1825, 155, top, and originally read: "Whenever any property, real or personal, shall be taken in execution, if such property be susceptible of division, it shall be sold in such quantities as may be necessary to satisfy the execution and costs."   This doubtless means the same as the present statute.   See Cowen *v.* Underwood, 16 Ill., 22, 23, 24.

"When real or personal property is taken in execution, if the same is susceptible of division, it shall be sold in separate tracts, lots, or articles, and only so much shall be sold as is necessary to satisfy the execution and costs."

This statutory provision is but declaratory of the common-law command to the sheriff having an execution against a debtor's personal property, extended and applied to the sheriff having an execution against a debtor's real estate when 5 George II, c. 7, allowed real property in English colonies to be sold on execution the same as personal property.[42] This rule is the basis of the law of the excessive levy and sale, and the sheriff's liability in damages in an action of tort therefor. The question whether the sheriff violated this statutory provision is not a question of form, but is a question of fact: Did the sheriff, in fact, sell more of the debtor's property than was necessary to satisfy the execution and costs? The regularity of the sheriff's return on the back of the execution, in point of form, as that he says in apt written words that he first offered the debtor's property in separate lots, tracts, or parcels, and then in two's and three's, etc., is not enough to decide this question of fact. The regularity of the sheriff's return in point of form is but prima facie evidence, at the most, that the statutory provision was complied with, shifting to the debtor the burden of showing that the sheriff did sell more property than was necessary to satisfy the execution and costs. It is very easy for the debtor to show this when several valuable tracts of land are sold en masse to pay a small judgment.[43]

[42] Day v. Graham, 1 Gilman, 435; Tiernan v. Wilson, 6 Johns, Ch. 410; and see note 4.

[43] Day v. Graham, 1 Gilman, 435; Cowan v. Underwood, 16 Ill., 22; Ballance v. Loomis, 22 Ill., 182; Morris v. Robey, 73 Ill., 462; Roseman v. Miller, 84 Ill., 297; Smith v. Huntoon, 134 Ill., 24; Miller v. McAlister, 197 Ill., 72; 2 Freeman, Executions, 3d ed., Secs. 196, 253. The rule as to first offering in separate parcels, and then in two's and three's, etc., was first announced in Phelps v. Conover, 25

But if the sheriff sells a single, indivisible tract of land, much more valuable than the amount of the execution and costs, it is harder for the debtor to show that the sale was a violation of the statutory provision. If it appears that the sheriff has been reasonably fair in his methods to collect the execution and costs, and resorted to the sale of a single indivisible, valuable tract as a last resort, and with an eye single to the collection of the debt, as the law contemplates, then the irregularity of a sheriff's sale en masse does not exist in fact.[44]

When a third person purchases bona fide at an execution sale, the irregularity of a sheriff's sale en masse is of no avail against him, unless it is made to appear that he had notice of it.[45] But this rule is of no practical importance, because bona fide third persons rarely purchase at execution sales since the redemption act. And, in addition, it is rather difficult for a third person purchasing at an execution sale to be ignorant of the irregularity of a sheriff's sale en masse. It is said in Roseman v. Miller [46] that a third person who pays ten dollars at an execution sale for land worth five thousand dollars cannot be a bona fide purchaser.

A third person may come in bona fide under an execu-

Ill., 309, a case arising on motion to set aside. In Ballance v. Loomis, 22 Ill., 182, 183, two parcels of land were levied on and sold, and it expressly appears they were first offered separately. In Roseman v. Miller, 84 Ill., 297, 299, it is said: "Notwithstanding they (i. e., the parcels of land) may have been previously offered separately without obtaining bidders, when the amount bid for them en masse is merely nominal, the officer should, ordinarily, postpone the sale and readvertise."

[44] Davis v. Pickett, 72 Ill., 483; O'Callaghan v. O'Callaghan, 91 Ill., 228; Dobbins v. Wilson, 107 Ill., 17, in which case the execution sale was on a federal judgment, but no point was made upon that.

[45] 2 S. & C. Ann. Stat., 2d ed., Sec. 15, p. 2350, says: "Nor shall any irregularity on the part of the sheriff, or other officer having the execution, be deemed to affect the validity of any sale made under it, unless it shall be made to appear that the purchaser had notice thereof."

[46] 84 Ill., 297, 299.

tion sale by purchasing the property from the purchaser at the execution sale; the irregularity of a sheriff's sale en masse is not available against such third person.[47] The debtor's possession of the property sold is, however, notice to the world of his rights and claims.[48]

The right of a debtor to use the procedure by bill in equity to avoid an execution sale for the irregularity of a sheriff's sale en masse is subject to the general rule of diligence that the laws aid the vigilant and not those who slumber on their rights. Subject to the qualification of a reasonable time limit hereinafter noticed, mere delay by a debtor, i. e., the mere lapse of time alone, is not fatal. But if innocent third persons have acquired rights, or if the purchaser has so changed his position in reliance on the debtor's delay that an order setting the sale aside would inflict damage or loss that money could not repair, the case is different. In short, the general equitable doctrine of laches governs.[49]

A debtor is not chargeable with negligent delay in the exercise of his common-law right to avoid an execution sale for the irregularity of a sheriff's sale en masse simply because he did not redeem from it, for the redemption act applies only to execution sales that are valid and unavoidable for the irregularity of a sheriff's sale en masse.[50]

The only suggestion there appears to be of a fixed time after which a debtor cannot proceed to have an execution sale set aside for the irregularity of a sheriff's sale en

[47] Prather v. Hill, 36 Ill., 402; Hay v. Baugh, 77 Ill., 501; see Smith v. Huntoon, 134 Ill., 24, 30, 31.

[48] Parker v. Shannon, 137 Ill., 376, 392, 393.

[49] Graham v. Day, 4 Gilman, 389, 394; Dickerman v. Burgess, 20 Ill., 266, 276.

[50] Day v. Graham, 1 Gilman, 435; 4 Gilman, 389; Morris v. Robey, 73 Ill., 462, 468. A judgment creditor of the debtor who redeems from a void execution sale acquires no title. Johnson v. Baker, 38 Ill., 98. And see Schmitt v. Weber, 239 Ill., 377; Merrick v. Carter, 205 Ill., 73.

masse, is the one in Swiggart *v.* Harber,[51] viz.: "After the lapse of a sufficient time to bar a writ of error, proceedings upon final process issued from circuit courts cannot be quashed for irregularity." A writ of error was barred in five years then, and now is barred in three years, except in enumerated cases of infants,[52] etc. This suggestion has never been applied, so far as I know. In Morris *v.* Robey [53] a suggestion of "two or three years after the sale" is repeated from the mortgage foreclosure sale case of Fergus *v.* Woodworth.[54]

Under a bill in equity to set aside an execution sale on an Illinois judgment for the irregularity of a sheriff's sale en masse, an Illinois court acts directly on the sheriff's violation of the rule of law that only so much of a debtor's property shall be sold as is necessary to satisfy the execution and costs; treats that violation of law as a tort by the sheriff; and specifically repairs the tort by setting aside the execution sale.

But the irregularity of a sheriff's sale en masse may fall within the reach of the jurisdiction of a court of equity, strictly so-called, to correct fraud. The court of equity cannot act directly on the sheriff's tort, for the court of equity cannot concern itself with the misconduct, violations of law, or errors of law, of the officers of a common-law court, from the judge down, though Kent, C., seems to have done it in Tiernan *v.* Wilson, but the court of equity can act on the sheriff's tort indirectly through the parties, through the medium of a personal equity attached

[51] 4 Scam., 364, 374, and last paragraph of the head-note; Day *v.* Graham, 4 Gilman, 389, 394.

[52] Laws, 1819, 146; R. S., 1833, 486; R. S., 1908, Hurd, 1637, Sec. 117.

[53] 73 Ill., 462, 468.

[54] 44 Ill., 374, 379. The rule in Day *v.* Graham and Jenkins *v.* Merriweather cuts off mere irregularities, making the sale voidable, other than the one of a sale en masse, when the sheriff's deed issues, and when the sale takes place, if a third person buys.

to the purchaser, or to a transferee of the purchaser taking as a volunteer or with notice of the sheriff's tort, binding the purchaser, or his transferee as a volunteer or with notice, to convey the property back to the debtor. The debtor's equity to a reconveyance by the beneficiary of the sheriff's tort, and the jurisdiction of the court of equity to compel the reconveyance, are founded on fraud, the view of the court of equity being that a purchaser at an execution sale, or his transferee taking as à volunteer or with notice, who appears at the bar of a court of justice striving to retain valuable property of the debtor acquired for a pittance by means of the sheriff's tort of an excessive levy and execution sale, now knowing the levy and sale were excessive, whether he knew it before or not, exhibits such a covetous desire to get the debtor's property for nothing, and such a willing spirit to commit a fraud on the debtor, as requires the court of equity to enlighten his conscience then and there at the bar of the court by fastening upon him an equity to convey the property back to the debtor on receiving the amount of his expenditures with interest.   The court of equity turns the sheriff's irregularity of a sale en masse into an irregularity of the purchaser's conscience, and thus brings the irregularity within its jurisdiction on the foundation of fraud to set aside an execution sale, the word "fraud" apparently meaning in this connection not actual fraud alone, but also the kind of fraud our law denominates constructive fraud, or fraud in equity.[55]

[55] Lord Cranstown v. Johnston, 3 Vesey, 170, and 5 Vesey, 277, approved by Eldon C., in White v. Hall, 12 Vesey, 321; Tiernan v. Wilson, 6 John, Ch. 410, where Kent, C., rested the decree on the sheriff's sale en masse, calling the sale fraudulent, and compelling the sheriff to pay part of the costs; Howell v. Baker, 4 John, Ch. 118; Woods v. Monell, 1 John, Ch. 502; Graffam v. Burgess, 117 U. S., 180, where the trial court refused to find the creditor-purchaser guilty of actual fraud, and counsel for the debtor did not rely on actual fraud.   The relief given was a removal of the bar of the time limited for redemption.   See pp. 183, 184,

The rule of Day *v.* Graham that an irregularity in execution proceedings making the sale voidable and not void, is enough, per se, to authorize the setting aside of the sale under a bill in equity after the sale when a third person is the purchaser, and after the sheriff's deed when the creditor is the purchaser, does not appear to have been extended to any irregularity in execution proceedings that makes the sale voidable only, and not void, other than the irregularity of a sheriff's sale en masse.

The decisions centralize on the rule declared in section 12 of the execution act, and make that rule the exclusive source and inspiration of the jurisdiction to set aside an execution sale for irregularity in the execution proceedings under the procedure by bill in equity, when the irregularity is one that makes the sale voidable only and not void.[56] The Supreme Court has said more than once, and with emphasis, that irregularities in execution proceedings making the sale voidable and not void, except the irregularity of a sheriff's sale en masse, are waived, if no attempt is made by the debtor to reach them by motion,[57] which means, under Day *v.* Graham, that such irregularities must be availed of by the debtor before the execution

185, 190, 197.   See Byers *v.* Surget, 19 How., 303; Schroeder *v.* Young, 161 U. S., 334.   Only actual fraud will authorize a court of equity to set aside a judgment of a common-law court.   Ross *v.* Wood, 70 N. Y., 8; Patch *v.* Ward, L. R., 3 Ch. App., 203; Story Eq. Jur., Sec. 1581.

[56] See the cases in note 42 supra.   Cases where rules of law designed to give the debtor notice of the execution sale have not been complied with, and where, in consequence thereof, the debtor had no notice of the sale until after the time for redemption, fall easily under the head of equity jurisdiction founded on fraud, accident, or surprise to set aside the sale, or to suspend or remove the bar of the time limited for redemption.   See Davis *v.* Chicago Dock Co., 129 Ill., 180; Parker *v.* Shannon, 137 Ill., 376; Miller *v.* McAlister, 197 Ill., 72.

[57] Prather *v.* Hill, 36 Ill., 402, 405; Fergus *v.* Woodworth, 44 Ill., 374, 378, 379; Hay *v.* Baugh, 77 Ill., 500, 503, 504; Fairman *v.* Peck, 87 Ill., 156, 163; Dobbins *v.* Wilson, 107 Ill., 17, 24; and see the early cases in notes 20 and 32 supra.   Day *v.* Graham allows the procedure by motion to be cut off by the device of a purchase by the creditor in the name of a third person.   The case has not been disturbed, nor has it been expressly affirmed, in that respect, so far as I know.

sale, when a third person is the purchaser, or takes by transfer from the creditor-purchaser, and, under Jenkins v. Merriweather, that such irregularities must be availed of by the debtor before the sheriff's deed issues, when the creditor is the purchaser, thus leaving no irregularity surviving the stage when the procedure by motion to set aside is cut off, except the irregularity of a sheriff's sale en masse, unless the irregularity is one that makes the sale void. And the common doctrine, that inadequacy of price is essential to a debtor's success under a bill in equity to set aside an execution sale, voidable for irregularity in the execution proceedings, means that the irregularity of a sheriff's sale en masse is the only irregularity in execution proceedings making the sale voidable and not void that can give a court jurisdiction to set aside the sale under the procedure by bill in equity.

In the case of an execution sale of a debtor's real property since the redemption act, the price is nearly always inadequate in an abstract sense, because the practical operation of the redemption act is to drive bidders away from execution sales, to stop competition at them, to leave the creditor as the only purchaser, and to fix a maximum price, viz., the amount of the execution and costs. The price in an execution sale can never be inadequate in a legal sense, unless it appears that more of the debtor's property was sold than was necessary to satisfy the execution and costs in violation of the rule declared by Section 12 of the Execution Act, i. e., unless the irregularity of a sheriff's sale en masse exists. The abstract inadequacy of the price can be of no legal significance except as evidence of a sale of too much of the debtor's property, i. e., of the irregularity of a sheriff's sale en masse.[58]

---

[58] Stone v. Gardner, 20 Ill., 304, 309, 310.

The case of Skakel v. Cycle Trade Publishing Company, wherein five lots, each worth $4,000, or $20,000 in all, were sold to the creditor for $132.04, the amount of the execution and costs, was argued and decided on the basis of the legal theory that the sale of these five·lots to satisfy an execution for $132.04 was regular and valid, simply because the sheriff's return on the back of the execution said that he first offered each lot separately, and then two of them, three of them, four of them, and finally en masse. The purchaser was a third person, but he was not a bona fide third person, for he purchased for the creditor. The majority of the court said the purchaser owed no duty to the debtor and had a right to bid as he saw fit. But that is a mistake. The law is the other way. A creditor's rights and duties as a bidder at his own execution sale are the same as they were before the redemption act, and are the same as they would be if that act were repealed to-morrow, leaving the rest of the execution act standing.[59] The rule of the common and statute law, that only so much of a debtor's property shall be sold as is necessary to satisfy the execution and costs, is a rule of substantial

[59] In Lord Cranstown v. Johnston, 3 Vesey, 170, 183, where a debtor's property in St. Christopher's Island, worth £20,000, was sold to the creditor for £2,000, Sir R. Pepper Arden, M. R., said: "I will lay down the rule as broad as this: This court will not permit him (i. e., the creditor) to avail himself of the law of another country to do what would be a gross injustice. It is said, what if the sale had been to a third person? I am glad I have not to determine that. A third person might have a great deal more to say than this defendant can. He might say, the law of the island authorizes a lottery; and, having bid, he has a right to retain it. But this defendant has no such right, except for the purpose of paying himself the debt." That is English law imposed on the creditor-purchaser, regardless of the law of St. Christopher's Island, the situs of the debtor's land. In White v. Hall, 12 Vesey, 321, Eldon, C., said: "I perfectly concur with the case of Lord Cranstown v. Johnston, which was decided upon the foundation of fraud." In Day v. Graham, 1 Gilman, 435, 443, Scates, J., said: "In the case of Lord Cranstown v. Johnston, 3 Vesey, Jr., 170, a sale was set aside because the circumstances of the proceedings showed that the party sought more to make an advantageous purchase, than a satisfaction of his debt."

justice; as Kent, C., said,[60] the rule "rests upon principles of obvious policy and universal justice;" the rule binds bidders at the sale, and especially the creditor bidding at the sale; and the rule requires something more substantial than a statement in writing by the sheriff, couched in apt words, that he performed the pantomime of first offering the debtor's property in separate parcels, and then in two's and three's, etc.   Ballance v. Loomis [61] is against the legal theory on which Skakel v. Cycle Trade Publishing Company was argued and decided.[62]

The only difference between an excessive levy and sale of a debtor's personal property, and an excessive levy and sale of a debtor's real property, is in the remedy.   In the former case, the remedy is an action for damages against the sheriff.   In the latter case, the superior efficiency of the remedy of specifically repairing the sheriff's tort by setting aside the sale has made the

[60] Tiernan v. Wilson, 6 John, Ch. 410, 414.

[61] 22 Ill., 82.

[62] In Ballance v. Loomis, 22 Ill., 82, the bill was filed one month after the time for redemption, and prayed (1) for a new trial at law, and (2) to set aside the execution sale.   The bill in Skakel v. Cycle Trade Publishing Co., 237 Ill., 482, prayed the same things, and was filed two months before the time for redemption.   That the primary prayer of the bill was a trial at law, the judgment having been taken by default, see Ballance v. Loomis, 22 Ill., 82; Thomas v. Habenstreit, 68 Ill., 115; Henderson v. Harness, 184 Ill., 520.   On equity jurisdiction to grant trials at law, see Frink v. McClung, 4 Gilman, 569; Propst v. Meadows, 13 Ill., 157; Ballance v. Loomis, 22 Ill., 82; How v. Mortell, 28 Ill., 478; Hilt v. Heimberger, 235 Ill., 235; 2 Freeman, Judgments, 4th ed., Sec. 22; 16 Am. & Eng. Ency. of Law, 2d ed., 374.   The debtor's primary prayer for a trial at law was lost sight of completely in the Supreme Court, and the court censured the debtor severely for going into the courts at all to resist a claim that he must have honestly believed to be ill-founded.   The prayer for a trial at law was not disposed of until six years after the filing of the bill.   It seems to me the act of filing the bill suspended the efflux of time under the redemption act, though, of course, a frivolous, vexatious, or dishonest bill could not have that effect.   The debtor had to elect between his right to redeem and his equity to a trial at law, for he could not pursue both rights at the same time.   Treating the bill as one to set aside the sale only, it was the only procedure available, though filed before the end of the time for redemption, under Day v. Graham, because a third person was the purchaser.

action for damages against the sheriff obsolete, so far as an excessive levy and sale of a debtor's real estate are concerned.

The jurisdiction invoked by a bill in equity filed on the equity side of an Illinois court to set aside an execution sale of land on an Illinois judgment, is not the limited jurisdiction of the English High Court of Chancery to interrupt and turn aside the course of the jurisdiction of a common-law court, on the foundation of actual fraud, accident, mistake, or surprise, occurring in the proceedings in the common-law court, but is rather the wider inherent jurisdiction of the court that renders a judgment or decree to supervise and control its execution, partly to prevent the scandal that inevitably and properly arises whenever the property of a party is sacrificed under the process of a court in contravention of the clearly expressed policy and spirit of the law, and partly to establish justice between party and party, by keeping the execution act from being perverted from its true purpose, the compulsory payment of debts, into a means or instrument of stripping debtors of their property for the unjust enrichment of creditors. The rule of substance and not form controls; and the merely technical, formal regularity or irregularity of the execution proceedings on their face, is not a test of the jurisdiction, unless the technical, formal irregularity is one that makes the execution sale void, or is the technical, formal irregularity of a sheriff's sale en masse. The technical, formal irregularity of a sheriff's sale en masse, i. e., the mere failure of the sheriff to say in apt written words in his return on the back of the execution that he first offered the debtor's property in separate parcels, and then in two's and three's, etc., and finally en masse, apparent on the face of the sheriff's return, ought to be, and doubtless is, removable by extrinsic evidence, showing that the sale was, in fact, a fair one under all the circumstances. When an execution sale is not a void one, then the general principle ought to be that an execution sale will not be set aside after the time limited for statutory redemption, unless it is made to appear to the satisfaction of the court that the sale was not a fair one within the policy and spirit of the execution act, as declared by its terms. This principle reduces all merely technical, formal irregularities in the execution proceedings to the subordinate position of evidençe, like the price, i. e., the amount of the debt, to show that the sale was not a fair one in fact. That such is the expressed general principle of the earlier cases cannot be doubted.[63]

[63] NOTE ON INADEQUACY OF PRICE. — The most generally accepted statement of the rule as to the effect of inadequacy of price on a private contract for the sale of land is that of Lord Eldon in the specific performance case of Coles v. Trecothick, 9 Vesey, 234, 246: "Unless the inadequacy of price is such as shocks the conscience, and amounts in itself to conclusive and decisive evidence of fraud in the transaction, it is not itself a sufficient ground for refusing a specific performance." See Zemple v. Hughes, 235 Ill., 424, 434; and see the statement of the rule by Eyre, C. B., in the rescission case of Griffith v. Spratley, 1 Cox, 383, 388, 389. In Story's Eq. Jur., Secs. 244 to 249, the rule is compared with the rule of the Roman law enacted by Diocletian, allowing the seller to avoid a contract for the sale of land when the price was less than one-half the value. The French rule, allowing a seller of land who has received less than seven-twelfths of the true value of the land to avoid the sale, does not apply to judicial sales. French Civil Code, Secs. 1674, 1684. So far as I can see, English judges never have made any real use of Lord Eldon's rule as an aid to solve the question whether the court ought to allow a master's sale to stand, either before or since the Sale of Land by Auction Act of 1867. All that Bradley, J., says, in Graffam v. Burgess, 117 U. S., 170, about the English practice is taken from the opinion of Kent, C., in Williamson v. Dale. In 1818, in Williamson v. Dale, 3 Johns, Ch. 290, Kent, C., rejected the English chancery practice of "opening the biddings," i. e., of allowing an advance bid on motion to confirm a master's sale (see 2 Daniel, Ch. Pr., 6th Am. ed., star page 1285; Graffam v. Burgess, 117 U. S., 180), and used Lord Eldon's rule as an aid to the decision of a petition or motion to confirm or set aside a master's mortgage-foreclosure sale, taking the rule from the specific-performance case of Livingston v. Byrne, 11 John, Ch. 555, 556, wherein it was taken by Yates, J., from the specific performance cases of White v. Damon, 7 Vesey, 34, Eldon C., and Burrowes v. Lock, 10 Vesey, 475, Grant, M. R. The opinion of Kent, C., was adopted in the guardian's chancery-sale case of Ayers v. Baumgarten, 15 Ill., 444, 447 (and see Cooper v. Crosby, 3 Gilman, 506, 508; Coffey v. Coffey, 16 Ill., 141, 144; Garrett v. Moss, 20 Ill., 549, 554; Comstock v.

Purple, 49 Ill., 158, 168), and was carried over to execution sales by an incidental citation of Ayres *v.* Baumgarten, by Breese, J., in Dickerman *v.* Burgess, 20 Ill., 266, 281.

In the case of a private sale of land, the point of inadequacy of price raises the question whether the contract is fit to be enforced by a court, either by way of an action for damages, or by way of a bill for specific performance; but in the case of a master's sale, the point of inadequacy of price, on motion to confirm, or on motion to set aside after an uncontested confirmation, raises the question whether the contract is fit to be made by a court and imposed upon the owner of the property. This difference seems to have been overlooked by Kent, C., in Williamson *v.* Dale. It is the constant habit in judicial opinions to throw all kinds of sales, private and under legal process, into one mass, regardless of the purpose of the sales and of how they come before the court, as respects the application of Lord Eldon's rule, as in Graffam *v.* Burgess, 117 U. S., 180, and the state opinions there cited by Bradley, J. Breese, J., did this in Comstock *v.* Purple, 49 Ill., 158, a contest over the confirmation of a master's partition sale, and produced an opinion that caused the legislature to pass the act of March 24, 1869, now Sec. 24 of the Partition Act, fixing a minimum reserved price equal to two-thirds of the appraised value in partition sales. Compare the English Sale of Land by Auction Act of 1867, and the practice of settling a reserved price under it, as stated by Malins, V. C., in Delves *v.* Delves, L. R. 20 Eq., 77, 81, 82. The fluidity of the law of the decisions purporting to apply Lord Eldon's rule to solve applications to confirm or set aside masters' sales, is illustrated by the four to three decision in the partition-sale case of Stivers *v.* Stivers, 236 Ill., 160, and the cases relied on by the majority and minority. With Stivers *v.* Stivers compare the specific-performance case of Twining *v.* Morrice, 2 Brown Ch. Cas., 326, Kenyon, M. R.

An execution sale differs from a master's sale in that it does not have to be confirmed by the court, in Illinois at least, and comes before the court only on the debtor's application to set aside. The rule that only so much of a debtor's property shall be sold as is necessary to satisfy the execution and costs, covers the same ground as Lord Eldon's rule, the only difference being that it acts on the property given up by the seller, while Lord Eldon's rule acts on the price paid by the buyer. Whenever Lord Eldon's rule produces the result, in the case of a private contract sale, that the buyer is an equity rogue, it at the same time produces the result that the seller is a common-law fool for giving up so much of his property for the money. See the old cases cited by Fuller, C. J., in Hume *v.* United States, 132 U. S., 406. In the case of a master's sale, or of an execution sale, the judge presides at both ends of the bargain, and is supposed to be Aequitas personified in flesh and blood, and his function is to exclude equity roguery and common-law folly from the bargain altogether, so that the property of the party may not be sacrificed by any act of the court. There is no need of bringing in Lord Eldon's rule as a guide to the decision of a debtor's application to set aside an execution sale. If that rule must be taken as a universal rule, applicable to all kinds of sales, judicial as well as private, in whatever way they may come before the court, then Sec. 12 of the execution act is much older than Lord Eldon's rule and must be taken to declare how Lord Eldon's rule must be applied to the particular case of a debtor's application to set aside an execution sale.

"The public policy of giving stability to judicial sales," so often given in opinions of the Supreme Court as the reason why inadequacy of price, alone, cannot be a ground for setting aside an execution sale, is but a way of stating the reason for rejecting the former English chancery practice of "opening the biddings," the opinion of Eldon; C., and his predecessors for fifty years (Williams v. Attenborough, T. & R., 70, 74, 75; Barlow v. Osborne, 6 H. L. C., 556) having prevailed with Kent, C., that the practice discouraged competition at masters' sales, and caused the sacrifice of property at judicial sales. In point of fact, the redemption act put an end to competition at execution sales, and it is even held that the highest bidder cannot be allowed to raise his own bid, when the bid is less than the amount of the execution and costs. See Cooper v. Crosby, 3 Gilman, 506, with which compare Ontario Bank v. Lansing, 2 Wendell, 200; Sullivan v. Jennings, 44 N. J. Eq., 11. But when there is any conflict between the public policy of giving stability to judicial sales, i. e., encouraging competition at them and the public policy of selling no more of a debtor's property on execution than is necessary to satisfy the execution and costs, the latter policy must prevail. See Garrett v. Moss, 20 Ill., 549, 554, and note that this case arose out of a mortgage executed September 14, 1840, to which the redemption act of February 19, 1841, could not apply. See Bronson v. Kinzie, 1 How., 311. After the redemption act, execution sales quickly ceased to be sales, in point of fact, but they are sales sui generis in contemplation of law, especially when a debtor applies by bill in equity to set one aside, because the redemption act did not alter the general legal theory or terms of the execution act.

II

JURISDICTION TO SET ASIDE JUDGMENT IN PROCEEDINGS UNDER TULEY ACT— COMMENT ON WEST CHICAGO PARK COMMISSIONERS *v.* RIDDLE [a]

In West Chicago Park Commissioners *v.* Riddle, 245 Ill., 168, 91 N. E. Rep., 1060, Farmer, J., writing the opinion, Carter and Dunn, JJ., dissenting without giving their reasons, it was decided that an allegation that a judgment rendered in a proceeding under the Tuley Act is erroneous for an error of law, does not give a court equity jurisdiction to examine the allegation of error— when, at least, equity jurisdiction is sought on the foundation that the alleged error of law is the result of fraud, partiality, and prejudice exhibited by the judge, and the charge of fraud, partiality, and prejudice is not made out in fact.   The case is the subject of a circular letter to the profession by Mr. H. S. Mecartney, the attorney in the case for the West Park Board, wherein it appears to be thought that the case is a bad precedent in that it opens up a way whereby municipal officers may use the Tuley Act to legalize illegal claims on the municipal treasury.

These were the salient facts: Mr. Francis A. Riddle was duly appointed attorney for the West Park Board, and his salary was duly fixed at $3,000 per annum.   After the expiration of his term of office, Mr. Riddle presented to the Board a claim for $27,624.50, as extra compensation

a [5 Ill. Law Rev., 245, November, 1910.]

for legal services rendered to the Board during his term of office.   The claim was submitted to the Circuit Court of Cook County, Honore, J., under the Tuley Act. Honore, J., allowed Mr. Riddle $20,583.53, and entered judgment for that amount.

The point against the judgment on the merits was this: The judgment of Honore, J., is against the rule of law that allows a public officer to get for his services only the salary fixed by the terms of some statute or ordinance, which rule goes so far that a public officer cannot get any pay at all for his services unless he can point to a statute or ordinance fixing his salary.   The framers of the constitution of 1870 put this rule into the constitution as a limitation on every branch of the state government.   See Constitution, Art. 4, Sec. 19; Art. 9, Sec. 11.

This point against the judgment is only the ordinary allegation of error of law that is made in every case that ever was taken to the Appellate and Supreme Courts by the process of appeal or writ of error.   But there is no established mode of procedure for getting an examination and correction of an alleged error of law of a judge sitting under the Tuley Act.   The West Park Board first moved to vacate the judgment, which motion Honore, J., denied, and then the Board filed in the Circuit Court of Cook County, Carpenter, J., a bill in equity to set aside the judgment, which was dismissed on demurrer.   On appeal, the Appellate Court for the First District affirmed this order of dismissal, granting a certificate of importance which carried the case to the Supreme Court, where the dismissal was again affirmed by a divided court by a vote of five to two.

The motion to vacate, and the bill to set aside, were presented on the theory that the judgment of Honore, J., was the result of his fraud, partiality, and prejudice in favor of Mr. Riddle and against the Park Board.   There was no claim that the successful party, Mr. Riddle, was implicated in the fraud, partiality, and prejudice charged against Honore, J. The Supreme Court found that this charge of judicial fraud, partiality, and prejudice had no foundation in fact; and it may be added the charge was as irrelevant in point of law under a motion or bill to set aside as it would have been under an appeal or writ of error to review the same alleged error of law if the same judgment had been rendered in an ordinary action of assumpsit. The charge of fraud, partiality, and prejudice was made in disregard of the difference between the bona fides and the scientia of a judge in the exercise of his office, which difference is emphasized in the maxim: De fide et officio judicis non recipitur quaestio, sed de scientia, sive sit error juris, sive facti.[1]

[1] "The law doth so much respect the certaintie of judgment, and the credit and authority of judges, as it will not permit any error to be assigned that impeacheth them in their trust and office, and in wilful abuse of the same, but only in ignorance, and mistaking either of the law or of the case and matter of fact." Bacon, Maxims, Regula 17, p. 63 of Ed. of 1636.

"It is, moreover, a general rule of very great antiquity, that no action will lie against a judge of record for any act done by him in the exercise of his judicial functions, provided such act, though done mistakenly, were within the scope of his jurisdiction." Broom, Legal Maxims, Ed. 3, star p. 61; on the penalties imposed on judges by Secs. 5 and 23 of the Habeas Corpus Act, see opinion of Kent, C. J., in Yates v. Lansing, 5 Johns, 291; affi'd, 9 Johns, 396; 23 Cyc., 567.

A court of equity has jurisdiction to set aside a judgment or decree on the foundation of actual misconduct by the successful party in procuring the judgment or decree; constructive misconduct is not enough. Story, Eq. Jur., Sec. 1541; Ross v. Wood, 70 N. Y., 8; Patch v. Ward, L. R. 3 Ch. App., 203. If the judge is implicated by collusion or otherwise in the active misconduct of the successful party, that will not oust equity jurisdiction. Sanford v. Head, 5 Cal., 297. In Hoskinson v. Head, 54 Ill. App., 59, where a judge of a probate court ordered a sale of an infant's lands, procured the same to be bid in by his wife for his use, approved the sale, and then sold the land at a profit, the judge was compelled by bill in equity to refund, with interest and costs.

The Change of Venue Act, R. S. Ch. 146, allows the bona fides of a trial judge to be drawn in question on error or appeal, if he denied a motion to change the venue, i. e., to send the case to another judge for trial. But the act has not been held to enlarge equity jurisdiction to set aside a judgment or decree; and the act was in no way involved in the case under comment.

Is the case, however, when stripped of its baseless and irrelevant charges of judicial fraud, partiality, and prejudice, within the equity jurisdiction lodged in the courts? By statute from the beginning, and by the constitution of 1870, Illinois courts of general jurisdiction have complete equity jurisdiction. The question in equity jurisdiction, presented by this case, was a question of remedy only. And the first point to be considered was whether there was any remedy on the law side of the court, and whether it was plain, adequate, and complete. And in considering this question, it must be borne in mind that a proceeding under the Tuley Act is a very exceptional institution, the constitutionality of which must be saved, if possible.[2]

Farwell *v.* Sturges, 165 Ill., 252, arose under the Tuley Act and was taken into the Supreme Court by writ of error. It was there adjudged: (1) that a proceeding under the Tuley Act "is not an arbitration, but is a proceeding in a court of general jurisdiction, before a judge thereof selected by the parties, . . . and one at law or in chancery, according to its nature;" (2) that "the right to prosecute a writ of error in cases submitted under this statute is recognized by the statute;" (3) that the release of errors mentioned in the statute need not be pleaded formally in bar of the writ of error; (4) that "it is, of course, true, that if the court did not have jurisdiction to render the [judgment or] decree no recital in the record that plaintiff in error had released all errors would avail."

Farwell *v.* Sturges establishes the right of the defeated party to sue out a writ of error under the Tuley Act, and plainly directed the West Park Board to the writ of

[2] Whether the judgment of Honore, J., was right or wrong is not relevant to the question of equity jurisdiction to examine its soundness.

error as an experimental speculative mode of procedure
to correct the error of law relied on. Under such writ of
error the West Park Board clearly would have been rectus
in curia, and could have forced the Supreme Court to
define with more precision the nature of the proceeding
under the Tuley Act, and the scope of the release of
errors, and the constitutional extent of the finality and
conclusiveness of a judgment or decree under the Tuley
Act. But this remedy by way of writ of error does not
exclude equity jurisdiction, unless it is a plain remedy;
and it seems very evident that the remedy by way of
writ of error under the Tuley Act cannot be pronounced
plain, as the law stood when this bill was filed. Boyce v.
Grundy, 3 Pet., 210, 215; Davis v. Wakelee, 150 U. S.,
680, 688; Story, Eq. Jur., Sec. 33. The record a judge
sitting under the Tuley Act is required to keep is likely,
ordinarily, to be insufficient for any useful purpose under
a writ of error; and the release of errors mentioned in the
Act must be given a scope and effect as a bar to a writ
of error that would not have to be given to it under a bill
in equity, just as the release of errors in a cognovit has an
operation as a bar to an appeal or writ of error that it
does not have on motion or bill to set aside the confessed
judgment. See the attempt to use affidavits in aid of
the record brought up by writ of error in Farwell v.
Sturges. And see Blackstone's remarks on the troubles
of parties and lawyers to get records in the days of oral
pleading. 3 Bl. Com., 407-411.

But if we assume that the appellate jurisdiction of the
Appellate and Supreme courts is cut off completely by
the Tuley Act by the indirect process of the release of
errors, then the case for equity jurisdiction becomes rather
easy. The right of a defeated litigant to invoke the
appellate jurisdiction of the Appellate Court, or of the
Supreme Court, as the case may be, can be cut off, or

abridged, only by the act or consent of the defeated litigant himself; it cannot be cut off, or abridged, by the act of the law alone, without reference to any act or consent of the defeated litigant. The reason is, that the right of a defeated litigant in an Illinois court of general jurisdiction to invoke the appellate jurisdiction of the Appellate Court, or of the Supreme Court, as the case may be, is a constitutional right. See Schlattweiler *v*. St. Clair County, 63 Ill., 449. But see Drainage Commissioners of Niles *v*. Harms, 238 Ill., 415, and the writer's comment on this case in 4 Ill. Law Rev., 202, 206, 211 [ante, pp. 374, 381, 389].

The finality and conclusiveness of a judgment or decree under the Tuley Act, then, must flow from the consent of the parties expressed in the agreement, submitting their controversy for decision, wherein they agree to release errors, for such finality and conclusiveness cannot flow from any other source. When, therefore, it is said in Farwell *v*. Sturges, that a proceeding under the Tuley Act "is not an arbitration, but is a proceeding in a court of general jurisdiction, before a judge thereof selected by the parties," the meaning must be that the proceeding falls within the judicial power lodged in the courts by the constitution in the sense that the judge selected by the parties cannot decline to hear and decide the controversy; that the judge must decide the controversy according to law and not according to his own opinion, and that the physical force of the state is pledged to carry the judgment or decree into execution against the defeated party immediately. But if the judge does not decide the controversy according to law, but decides it contrary to the law, and in disregard of the law, then it is evident the judge disregarded at once both the terms of the submission agreement and the terms of the Tuley Act, as construed in Farwell *v*. Sturges, The case then becomes one where the parties and the law did not, and the law alone could not, consistently with the Illinois constitution, make the judgment or decree final and conclusive.

If the agreement of submission under the Tuley Act is construed as binding the defeated party by contract to accept the judgment or decree as final and conclusive, however erroneous it may be in point of law, then the Tuley Act carries the right of freedom of contract to the height of a right vested in individuals to convert the judicial power granted to the courts by the constitution, into a power to make private opinion the rule of decision in the courts, and such construction brings the Tuley Act, at least as applied to this particular controversy between the West Park Board and Mr. Riddle, into a plain encounter with the constitution, for the constitution fairly construed and applied in all its parts, expressly forbids the legislature to authorize the officers of a municipal corporation to bind the corporation in advance by contract to pay one of its officers extra compensation for his service, if a third person, on or off the bench, says the municipal corporation ought to do it. Constitution, Art. 4, Sec. 19; Art. 9, Sec. 11.

On the view that the case fell outside the appellate jurisdiction of the Appellate and Supreme courts, because of the submission agreement and release of errors contained therein and that the proceeding was at the same time a proceeding at law in a court of general jurisdiction in the sense of the Illinois constitution, within the vague expressions in Farwell v. Sturges, then it seems that equity jurisdiction existed on the basis of contract simply, because the whole proceeding before Honore, J., was founded on, and limited by, contract, i. e., the submission agreement. On this view, the case, as related to equity jurisdiction, fell within the reason of the rules regulating the setting aside of awards made in disregard of established law, and not within the reason of the rules regulating the setting aside of common-law judgments, and the case is not unlike the case where a judgment, taken by confession, is not authorized by the terms of the warrant of attorney. Where parties submit a controversy to an arbitrator to be decided by him according to law, an allegation that the arbitrator did not decide the controversy according to law, but decided it according to his own opinion, will give a court of equity jurisdiction to examine the allegation, and, if the allegation is made out, to set aside the award; for to allow the successful party to retain the benefit of the award would force upon the defeated party a contract he never made, for he never agreed that the arbitrator's law should bind him; and the rule is the same whether the arbitrator disregarded the law intentionally or unintentionally. Young *v.* Walter, 9 Ves., Jr., 364, 365; Eldon, L. C., 3 Cyc., 740, 741, 742.

In the first part of its opinion in the case under comment the Supreme Court applied the rule that there is, sometimes, equity jurisdiction to set aside a common-law judgment when the judge exceeds the bounds of his authority, and no reason is perceived why the allegation that the judgment of Honore, J., was against the law and hence ultra the restraints of the Tuley Act and the submission agreement did not bring the case within the scope of that rule.

As related to equity jurisdiction, an ordinary common-law judgment and a judgment under the Tuley Act are not alike. There is not, and never was since the commencement of equity jurisdiction, any reason why the law should allow an equity to set aside an ordinary common-law judgment to arise out of an error juris of the judge, for such error juris is, and always has been, correctable under an application to the appellate jurisdiction. But in the case of a judgment under the Tuley Act, if that act is construed as cutting off the appellate jurisdiction of the Appellate and Supreme courts through the medium of the submission agreement and release of errors, an equity to set aside the judgment for an error of law of the judge, like the error alleged in this case, is necessary, to protect and enforce the contract of submission fairly construed, and as it is construed in Farwell *v.* Sturges, as requiring the rights of the parties to be determined according to law; to protect and enforce the supremacy, uniformity, and equality of the law; and to save the Tuley Act from an encounter with the constitution, as an attempt to authorize Illinois courts of original jurisdiction to adopt private opinion as the rule of decision, and as an abridgement of the appellate jurisdiction of the Appellate and Supreme courts. As between the policy of giving stability to judgments, right or wrong, under the Tuley Act—an exceptional, peculiar institution—and the policy of giving stability to lawful contracts, and to the law itself, the latter is the higher, paramount policy.

The Supreme Court's answer to this case for equity jurisdiction is this: "Appellant in its brief speaks of the bill as one to set aside an alleged award. On the contrary, it is a bill to set aside the judgment of a court of general jurisdiction in an action at law." The answer is perfect and complete, if it is true the judgment of Honore, J., was the judgment of a court of general jurisdiction in the ordinary sense; but that needed to be proved. To prove that it was the ordinary common-law judgment of a court of general jurisdiction, the passage quoted supra from Farwell *v.* Sturges was set forth by the court without comment. But Farwell *v.* Sturges plainly is not satisfactory proof of the point, unless Farwell *v.* Sturges is declared to mean that the error of law alleged in the bill in this case was open to examination and correction under a writ of error; and that the writ of error was the exclusive remedy. But the Supreme Court says nothing about that, but leaves us to make the best inference that we can, thus making it very clear that a writ of error under the Tuley Act is not, as the decisions stand, a plain remedy at all.

The decision of the Supreme Court in this case must be stretched unduly to make it mean that the defeated party is finally, conclusively, and irrevocably bound by a judgment or decree under the Tuley Act, however erroneous such judgment or decree may be in point of law. When it is held clearly that the Tuley Act means that, then its constitutionality must be drawn in question and assailed, as conferring power on the courts that is not judicial in the sense of the common law and of the Illinois constitution; and as abridging the appellate jurisdiction of the Appellate and Supreme courts, and the right of litigants to invoke it.

For the reasons stated, it seems that the case of West Chicago Park Commissioners v. Riddle, when stripped of its charges of judicial fraud, partiality, and prejudice, was within the equity jurisdiction of the courts as a remedy concurrent with the remedy by way of writ of error. But the courts could not take equity jurisdiction without noticing and dealing with those charges. They were false in fact, and irrelevant in law; in addition, they struck at the principle of the independence of the judiciary, tending to intimidate, and to impair public confidence in the fairness and impartiality of courts of original jurisdiction. There is a rule, that where a case for equity jurisdiction is presented on charges of fraud that are not sustained by the facts, the case will be dismissed, even though the facts of the case, with the charges of fraud eliminated, entitle the party to relief. The Supreme Court of the United States recently threw out a warning that this rule exists.

TOPIC V

SUBROGATION AND EXONERATION

COLLECTED COMMENT

COLLECTED COMMENT

1. — THE PRINCIPAL'S "PROM-
ISE IN LAW" TO INDEMNIFY HIS
SURETY.

2. — RIGHT OF HOLDER OF IN-
VALID TAX DEED TO BE SUBRO-
GATED TO LIEN OF THE PUBLIC.

1. — THE PRINCIPAL's "PROMISE IN LAW" TO INDEMNIFY HIS SURETY.[a] — Estate of Ramsey v. Whitbeck, 183 Ill., 550, 74 Ill. App., 524, 81 Ill. App., 210, was made to turn upon the proposition that, where the principal makes no promise of indemnity, upon payment of the debt by the surety, the principal comes under a "promise in law" to reimburse the surety. The opinion of the Supreme Court gives rise to two observations: First, that proposition had nothing to do with the case. Second, on the Court's view of the case, the law, and justice to the parties, required the Court to disregard the principal's "promise in law" as "a mere form," or "fiction of law," and to consider only "the real truth and substance of the thing." (Lord Mansfield, in Johnson v. Smith, 2 Burr, 950, 962, and see the quotation from this case in Union Traction Co. v. Chicago, 199 Ill., 579, 635.)

The case was this: Ramsay was elected State Treasurer in November, 1892. Certain Chicago men, being officers of five National Banks in Chicago, became Ramsay's official bondsmen, pursuant to an arrangement with Ramsay that he would deposit the State's money in his custody as State Treasurer in said five National Banks; that he would allow the depositary Banks to use the State's money in their business of making loans to their

a [1 Ill. Law Rev., 619, April, 1907.]

customers; and that the depositary Banks would pay
to Ramsay, for his own private use, interest on the
average daily balances of the State's money at the rate
of 2½ per cent. per annum. Ramsay died by his own
hand, a defaulter to the State for $478,539.51. This
amount was paid to the State. The Supreme Court
assumed that Ramsay's bondsmen paid his debt to the
State. But the truth appears to be, that the money of
the stockholders of the five depositary Banks went to pay
the State. Ramsay's bondsmen prosecuted, for the
benefit of the depositary Banks (183 Ill., at 566), a claim
against Ramsay's estate on the legal theory that, having
paid Ramsay's debt to the State, they were entitled,
under the doctrine of subrogation, to enforce the State's
rights to priority of payment out of Ramsay's estate
given by the Administration Act. General creditors of
Ramsay in his own proper person contested the claim,
Ramsay's estate being insolvent.

After using the doctrine of subrogation to get jurisdiction to re-examine the Appellate Court's finding of
facts (183 Ill., at 558-559), the Supreme Court laid the
doctrine to one side, and dealt with the merits on the
theory that Ramsay's bondsmen were seeking indemnity
against Ramsay. It is too plain for discussion, however,
that they wanted only the benefit of the doctrine of subrogation. And, of course, the Court could not give them
that without proof, by them, that they had paid, in a
substantial sense, that is to say, with their own money,
Ramsay's debt. Payment of Ramsay's debt by the
Banks could do Ramsay's bondsmen no good, because
such payment must have been either (1) voluntary (see
Young v. Morgan, 89 Ill., 199; Stearns on Suretyship,
Sec. 276), or (2) illegal (see Devine v. Holmes, 117 Ill.,
145; 27 Am. and Eng. Ency. of Law, Ed. 2, 204, note 6)
for two reasons: First, the Banks were forbidden by the

law of their being to bind themselves as sureties of the State Treasurer (Bowen *v.* Needles National Bank, 87 Fed. Rep., 439, aff'd C. C. A., 94 Fed. Rep., 925); Second, such payment by the Banks must have been, on the case as reported, pursuant to a term and condition of the arrangement—admittedly, in this case, forbidden by the law of the State—agreeably to which Ramsay's bond was underwritten. The bondsmen and the Banks, therefore, united or divided, had no case. And such was the result reached by the Supreme Court, but by a line of reasoning to which the second observation, supra, is applicable.

Counsel for the bondsmen, whether there was method in it or not, shifted the argument away from the doctrine of subrogation to the doctrine of indemnity. The point fatal to this argument (Shepard *v.* Ogden, 2 Scam., 257; Bonham *v.* Galloway, 13 Ill., 68), lying right on the surface of the case, inadequate proof that Ramsay's bondsmen had paid Ramsay's debt, was not taken. It was agreed by counsel on both sides, and by the Court, that, upon payment of Ramsay's debt by his bondsmen, the law imposed a promise upon Ramsay to reimburse his bondsmen, and that this promise in law related back to the contract of suretyship.[1] The whole of the argument was upon the question, whether Ramsay's promise in law, contemporaneous, by relation back, with the contract of suretyship, was a separable, or an inseparable, part and parcel of the said illegal arrangement, pursuant to which Ramsay's bond was signed. The Supreme

---

[1] Choteau *v.* Jones, 11 Ill., 300, was thought to support this. It is apparent, however, that Choteau *v.* Jones does not go the length ex contractu to which it was carried. The Court there only enforced the proposition (p. 318): "The relation of debtor and creditor between principal and surety, so as to entitle the latter to avoid a voluntary conveyance made by the former, commences at the date of the obligation by which the surety becomes bound, and not from the time he makes payment."

Court decided, that Ramsay's promise in law of indemnity, and the said illegal arrangement, were inseparable, and that, therefore, the maxim, ex turpi causa non oritur actio, applied, and, under it, the bondsmen had no case. To defend this use of the two legal notions of a "promise in law" and "relation back," a fiction upon a fiction, to impute such legal delinquency to the bondsmen as would bring them within the reach of the principle of policy on which the maxim ex turpi causa rests, the policy of enforcing the supremacy of, and obedience to, law, "which the defendant has the advantage of, contrary to the real justice as between him and the plaintiff, by accident, if I may so say," (Lord Mansfield, quoted in Pullman Car Co. *v.* Transportation Co., 171 U. S., 138, 150-151), the Court invoked the aid of another great first principle, the principle of equality before the law, or, as the Court put it, "The law is the same for all." (183 Ill., at 568.)

Obviously, the question — What is "the real truth and substance" of a principal's "promise in law" to indemnify his surety? — was a material one in Ramsay's case, on the view the Court took of the case. Lord Holt, who was quite opposed to entertaining actions of assumpsit founded upon promises in law, said, in Starke *v.* Cheeseman, 1 Ld. Ray, 538, that "the notion of promises in law was a metaphysical notion, for the law makes no promise, but where there is a promise of the party." We all know, however, that this "metaphysical notion" has long been "fixed in our law." (Ames, "The History of Assumpsit," 2 Harv. L. R. at p. 66.) As between principal and surety, the legal notion of a promise in law of indemnity does not mean, as the Supreme Court implies, if it does not say, in Ramsay's case, that a surety's right of indemnity is founded on promise or contract, actual or in law. A surety's right of indemnity is founded, in the absence of an express agreement of indemnity, on "a fixed principle of justice" (Lord Chief Baron Eyre, in Deering v. Earl of Winchelsea, 2 B & P., 270, 1 Cox., 319), — the principle that, where one man, upon compulsion, pays another man's debt, the latter ought, ordinarily, ex aequo et bono, to reimburse the former. The Court of Chancery first applied that principle in favor of a surety, and, in the beginning, and down to 1757, if not later, a surety had to go to the Court of Chancery to get the benefit of that, to us, elementary principle of justice. In that year, Lord Mansfield, at Nisi Prius, after conferring with "most of the Judges," used Lord Holt's "metaphysical notion" of a promise in law to put it in the power of a surety, who had paid his principal's debt, to get the benefit of that principle in a Court of Law by means of an action on the case on promises, that is to say, an action of assumpsit. A principal's "promise in law" of indemnity, then, is but a legal fiction whose function it is to liberalize the remedial procedure of a Court of Law. (Ames, "The History of Assumpsit," 2 Harvard Law Review, at p. 59, and cases cited, and cases printed in chronological order in Ames' Cases on Suretyship, 498; Judge Wilde, in Appleton v. Bascom, 3 Met. (Mass.), 169, 171; Vice-Chancellor Wood, in Newton v. Chorlton, 10 Hare, 646, 648, 649; Stearns on Suretyship, Sec. 296; 68 L. R. A. Note, 513, Sub-heads: "The Right of Action at Law," 517; "No Contract Right," 524. See the too general statement of Mr. Justice Breese in McConnel v. Dickson, 43 Ill., 99, 109, drawn in question, by implication, by the later Illinois cases; see Moore v. Topliff, 107 Ill., 241; Keach v. Hamilton, 84 Ill. App., 413.) "But the Court (will) not endure that a mere form, or fiction of law, introduced for the sake of justice, should work a wrong (as, for example, imputing moral or legal delinquency to a party, as in Ramsay's case), contrary to the real truth and substance of the thing." (Johnson v. Smith, supra.)

Taking now the Supreme Court's view of Ramsay's case, that Ramsay's official bond was good; that Ramsay's bondsmen paid his debt to the State; and that the bondsmen were claiming a right of indemnity, given by the law, against Ramsay, but resting the right of indemnity on its true foundation, the "fixed principle of justice," supra, is it not manifest that the result reached by the Supreme Court adverse to the bondsmen was wrong? Whatever may be thought, as a matter of abstract law, about the aforesaid arrangement between Ramsay and his bondsmen for the deposit of the State's money (see the applicable, but not adverted to, Act of 1893, and the way it was dealt with in Dreyer's Case, 176 Ill., 590, and in Wolf's Case, 221 Ill., 130), certainly it cannot be affirmed, that it was proven in Ramsay's Case that that arrangement, or anything done under it, caused, contributed to cause, or was in any way connected with, Ramsay's acts of defalcation. (See Deering v. Earl of Winchelsea, supra, a case not unlike Ramsay's Case in some particulars.) The reports of Ramsay's case are silent on the question as to just what Ramsay's acts of defalcation were. If, for example, the State had made Ramsay's bondsmen pay into the State Treasury the amount of the 2½ percent interest on the State's money received by Ramsey from the Banks, then, as to the amount of that interest, it could be said fairly that Ramsay's bondsmen, when they paid that amount to the State, paid their own debt, and not the debt of another, because, on the case as reported, they were particeps criminis to Ramsay's act of defalcation of keeping that interest for his own private use.

Ramsay's case appears to have been heard eight times, twice in the County Court of Clinton County, twice in the Circuit Court of the same County, twice in the Appellate Court of the Fourth District, and twice in the Supreme

Court. The way the case was dealt with by the courts is surprising, to say the least.

2. — RIGHT OF HOLDER OF INVALID TAX DEED TO BE SUBROGATED TO LIEN OF THE PUBLIC.[a] — In City of Chicago v. Pick, 251 Ill., 594, Vickers, J., writing the opinion, Cartwright, Hand, and Dunn, JJ., dissenting, general expressions in three prior cases are elevated to the rule of decision that "the holder of an invalid tax title is only entitled to reimbursement when his tax title is attacked and set aside in a proceeding brought for that purpose by the owner of the land." On that rule as a basis, it is decided that the holder of an invalid tax deed cannot be awarded, in a condemnation proceeding against the owner of the land, reimbursement of the purchase price and taxes paid.

The trouble in the court seems to have been to find a legal principle on which to rest the right of the holder of an invalid tax deed to recover back his cash paid out for the benefit of the owner of the property. What is the matter with subrogating the holder of an invalid tax deed to the lien of the public, keeping the public's lien alive for the benefit of the taxbuyer and his assignee to the extent of cash paid out for the benefit of the owner of the property?

The principle of subrogation was applied in Bruschke v. Wright, 166 Ill., 183, 194–198, in favor of a purchaser at an invalid foreclosure sale. As shown in Bruschke v. Wright, the principle has been applied often in this state in favor of purchasers at invalid execution and judicial sales. A tax sale in this state does not differ essentially from an execution or judicial sale, because a tax sale must be preceded by a valid judgment and proper precept authorizing the sale, as provided in the constitution of 1870,

[a] [7 Ill. Law Rev., 133, June, 1912.]

article 9, section 4. In 27 Am. & Eng. Ency. of Law, 2 ed., p. 239, it is said: "A purchaser of land at an invalid tax sale will be subrogated to the state's lien for the purchase price and all taxes paid by him." And see the statement of the law of Iowa by Gray, J., in Hefner v. Life Ins. Co., 123 U. S., 747, 750, 751.

The three cases relied on by the majority, Riverside Co. v. Townshend, 120 Ill., 9, Miller v. Cook, 135 Ill., 190, and Gage v. Eddy, 186 Ill., 432, are not against the view suggested. Riverside Co. v. Townshend only decides, at the most, that the holder of an invalid tax deed cannot enforce his right to reimbursement in ejectment, either by himself as plaintiff or against himself as defendant, especially when the ejectment case is one commenced before the act of July 7, 1885, hereinafter mentioned. Gage v. Eddy only decides, at the most, that the holder of an invalid tax deed cannot enforce his right to reimbursement in a burnt-record petition by himself to establish his title, especially when the burnt-record petition is filed after his tax deed has been adjudicated invalid in an action of ejectment by the owner of the property. And Miller v. Cook only decides at the most, that the holder of an invalid tax deed cannot enlarge his right to reimbursement under a bill by a prior mortgagee to set aside the tax deed, by the mode of compelling the prior mortgagee to collect his mortgage debt out of a different parcel of land covered by the mortgage and not covered by the tax deed; i. e., by the mode of compelling the prior mortgagee to marshall his securities for the benefit of the holder of an invalid tax deed covering only one of the securities. The taxbuyer recovered all money legally advanced for taxes as against the prior mortgagee.

The right of the holder of an invalid tax deed to reimbursement under an owner's bill to set aside was declared by statute taking effect July 7, 1885, 3 S. & C. Ann. Stat.,

2 ed., pp. 3494, 3495; Riverside Co. *v.* Townshend, 120 Ill., 9, 13.   It should be noticed that an owner's bill to set aside an invalid tax deed is not the same thing as an owner's bill to redeem from a valid tax deed under the constitution of 1870, art. 9, sec. 5.   See Wilson *v.* McKenna, 52 Ill., 43, 48, 49; Reed *v.* Tyler, 56 Ill., 288, 292, 293.

That statute of July 7, 1885, is but declaratory of the pre-existing common-law equitable right of the holder of an invalid tax deed to reimbursement, and is not creative of a new equitable right.   If that statute were repealed to-morrow, the holder of an invalid tax deed would be entitled to reimbursement under a bill filed by the owner to set the deed aside.   Reed *v.* Tyler, 56 Ill., 288, 291, 293, 294; Gage *v.* Rohrbach, 56 Ill., 262, 266, 267; Gage *v.* Billings, 56 Ill., 268.   The majority are in error if they mean to affirm that the right of the holder of an invalid tax deed to reimbursement rests on the statute of 1885.

Petty *v.* Beers, 224 Ill., 129, is on its face against the principle of subrogation.   In that case it was held that specific performance of a contract for an exchange of lands would be enforced without compensation for a vigintillionth tax deed on the plaintiff's parcel, because the tax deed was void as a conveyance on account of the infinitesimal quantity.   The court went on the rule in Roby *v.* South Park Commissioners, 215 Ill., 200, that a bill to remove a cloud on title is not a proper remedy where the invalidity of the instrument constituting the cloud is apparent on its face.   The court forgot that the bill before it was a bill for specific performance, and also forgot that tax deeds invalid on their faces are an exceptional class of instruments falling outside the rule in Roby *v.* South Park Commissioners.   It is hard to harmonize Petty *v.* Beers with the prior and subsequent vigintillionth tax deed cases.   See Roby *v.* Chicago, 48 Ill., 130; Glos *v.* Furman, 164 Ill., 585; Stimson *v.* Conn. Life Ins. Co.,

174 Ill., 125; Jackson *v.* Glos, 243 Ill., 280. The opinion in Jackson *v.* Glos, distinguishing Petty *v.* Beers, indicates that Petty *v.* Beers must stand as an exceptional case, vigintillionth tax deeds being obsolete now by statute. And Petty *v.* Beers is a weak authority against taxbuyers, whose interests were not represented in that case.

It seems an error to say, as in Petty *v.* Beers, 127 Ill. App., 593, 594, that St. Louis J. & C. R. R. Co. *v.* Mathers, 104 Ill., 257, decides that a purchaser at an invalid tax sale pays his money voluntarily within the meaning of the rule that money voluntarily paid ordinarily cannot be recovered back. The case does not so decide. It ought to be the law that the holder of an invalid tax deed may sue the owner of the land in assumpsit, on the basis of quasi contract, or contract arising ex aequo et bono, to recover back cash advanced by him for the benefit of the owner. See the recent discussion of this sort of contract by Vickers, J., in Board of Highway Comm. *v.* City of Bloomington, 97 N. E. Rep., 280, 283–286; 253 Ill., 164, 170–178.

On the whole, however, perhaps there may be some reason in the popular equity which says that tax buyers ought not to receive equity inside the courts until they have established a reputation for doing equity outside the courts.

TOPIC VI

ADMINISTRATION OF ASSETS

JURISDICTION OF FEDERAL COURTS TO MANAGE INSOLVENT
PUBLIC SERVICE CORPORATIONS — COMMENT ON RE MET-
ROPOLITAN RAILWAY RECEIVERSHIP.

JURISDICTION OF FEDERAL COURTS TO MANAGE INSOLVENT PUBLIC SERVICE CORPORATIONS—COMMENT ON RÉ METROPOLITAN RAILWAY RECEIVERSHIP[a]

"The mantle of the Federal Court," as it has been called in a somewhat misleading way, was thrown around the insolvent street railroads of Chicago by the process of giving a note to a creditor citizen of another State, entering judgment by confession on the law side of the Federal Circuit Court, and then filing a creditor's bill on the equity side of the same Court — all of these steps being contemporaneous and in pursuance of an antecedent agreed plan. See Blair *v.* Chicago, 201 U. S., 400. It is now decided in the case of the insolvent street railroads of New York — Re Metropolitan Railway Receivership, 208, U. S., 90 — that the taking of a judgment by confession on the law side of the Federal Circuit Court may be dispensed with, when, of course, the debt is bona fide due to a citizen of another State, and that a simple contract creditor who is a citizen of another state may file a bill right away on the equity side of the Federal Circuit Court asking the Court to take the management of the affairs of the insolvent debtor corporation. See the prayer in 208 U. S., on p. 65. The legal theory on which the taking of a judgment at law may be dispensed with is thus stated by Mr. Justice Peckham:

a [3 Ill. Law Rev., 385, January, 1909.]

"It is also objected that the Circuit Court had no jurisdiction because the complainants were not judgment creditors, but were simply creditors at large of the defendant railways. The objection was not taken before the Circuit Court by any of the parties to the suit, but was waived by the defendant consenting to the appointment of the receivers, and admitting all the facts averred in the bill. Hollins *v.* Brierfield Coal & Iron Company, 150 U. S., 371, 380. That the complainant has not exhausted its remedy at law, for example, not having obtained any judgment or issued any execution thereon, is a defense in an equity suit which may be waived, as is stated in the opinion in the above case, and when waived the case stands as though the objection never existed."

This way of stating the principle does well enought for a beginning. But ultimately, no doubt, the rule will have to be harmonized with established principles regulating the necessity of first establishing one's rights at law before seeking the superior remedies afforded by a Court of Equity. As the principle is stated by Mr. Justice Peckham, supra, no one can get any benefit out of it now except a creditor to whom the debtor's corporation is friendly; that is to say, a creditor who wants his money, and wants it now, cannot safely use the rule as it is now formulated. Perhaps such a creditor can never have much of any use for the rule anyway. However that may be, in point of actual, substantial fact, the rule as it now stands, and as it has been applied thus far, only enables an insolvent corporation to throw itself easily and comfortably into the arms of receivers, soft things judicially interposed as buffers and bluffers between the insolvent corporation and its adverse interests, that come rather high, but sometimes you have to have them.

The Court shows convincingly here and in other cases cited, that there is nothing in the idea that such suits in equity as those in the Chicago and New York insolvent street railroad cases are collusive in a legal sense; and that idea evidently issues out of a misconception of the relations, as respects controversies between citizens of different States, between State and Federal Courts established by the Federal Constitution and Acts of Congress.

The way Re Metropolitan Railway Receivership was got before the Federal Supreme Court is interesting, viz.: On original applications for leave to file a petition for a mandamus, or, in the alternative, for a prohibition, addressed to the Honorable E. Henry Lacombe, one of the Circuit Judges of the Second Circuit, commanding him and the Circuit Court to dismiss the whole of the proceedings against the New York street railroad companies. The Court did not pass upon this mode of procedure, saying:

"Without going into the question of the right of this Court to grant the remedy sought, we prefer to place our decision upon the ground that the Circuit Court had jurisdiction, and that its action in exercising it was, therefore, valid."

The wide sweep of the practically uncontrolled and unregulated discretion of the Judge in such cases is well illustrated by the following reports of proceedings upon interlocutory applications in the New York case: Pennsylvania Steel Co. *v.* New York City R. Co., 157 Fed. Rep., 440, 442, 443; Pennsylvania Steel Co. *v.* New York City R. Co., 158 Fed. Rep., 460; Pennsylvania Steel Co. *v.* New York City Ry. Co., 160 Fed. Rep., 221, 222; In re New York City R. Co., 160 Fed. Rep., 224, 226; Pennsylvania Steel Co. *v.* New York City R. Co., 161 Fed. Rep., 784, 786, 787; In re Receivership of Street Railways, 161 Fed. Rep., 879; Pennsylvania Steel Co. *v.* New York City R. Co., 163 Fed. Rep., 242.[1]

By way of admonition to lower Federal Judges, the Court closes its opinion in Re Metropolitan Railway Receivership, 208 U. S., 90, 1111–12, thus:

[1] I am indebted to Mr. Charles P. Abbey of the Chicago Bar for these citations.

"While so holding we are not unmindful of the fact that a Court is a very unsatisfactory body to administer the affairs of a railroad as a going concern, and we feel that the possession of such property by the Court through its receivers should not be unnecessarily prolonged. There are cases — and the one in question seems a very strong instance—where, in order to preserve the property for all interests, it is a necessity to resort to such a remedy. A refusal to appoint a receiver would have led in this instance almost inevitably to a very large and useless sacrifice in value of a great property, operated as one system through the various streets of a populous city, and such a refusal would also have led to endless confusion among the various creditors in their efforts to enforce their claims, and to very great inconvenience to the many thousands of people who necessarily use the road every day of their lives.

"The orders appointing the receivers and giving them instructions are most conservative and well calculated to bring about the earliest possible resumption of normal conditions when those who may be the owners of the property shall be in possession of and operate it. We have no doubt, if unnecessary delays should take place, the Court would listen to an application by any creditor upon due notice to the receivers, for orders requiring the closing of the trust as soon as might be reasonably proper, or else vacating the orders appointing the receivers."

It may be doubted whether such vague and elastic judicial generalities as the foregoing ever can be of any practical restraining force or effect. The suggestion made in 2 Ill. Law Rev., 189 [ante p. 717], may be repeated here, viz.: To clothe Federal Courts of Equity with adequate and plenary power to render complete and speedy justice in unraveling the tangled financial webs woven around so many public service corporations, it is necessary for Congress to exert its power "to establish . . . uniform laws on the subject of bankruptcies throughout the United States." The creditor's bill and the foreclosure suit as instruments to reorganize insolvent public service corporations ought to be done away with. In the brief of Mr. Joseph H. Choate in Canada Southern R. Co. v. Gebhard, 109 U. S., 527, it is stated that suits to foreclose railroad mortgages are not known in England.   Not the lest beneficial effect of a well-drawn Bankruptcy Act of Congress would lie in its protection of Federal Judges from much public criticism, quite apt to be ill-formed and therefore sometimes unjust and harmful, but always unavoidably provoked by the exercise of a practically unregulated judicial discretion to reduce a large, complicated, and sometimes rotten, insolvent quasi-public business from chaos to decent, respectable, efficient order and system.

INDEX-DIGEST

INDEX-DIGEST

BY MARGARET A. SCHAFFNER, OF THE CHICAGO BAR

Pages

Pages

Due Process of Law— *Continued*
criminal, when the object and result of the contempt proceeding is a fine payable to the state or a jail sentence for a definite term 728
When the object and result of a proceeding for the contempt of violating a negative order is to award to the party who obtained the order, damages by way of compensation for the injury done him by the violation of the order, the proceeding is essentially remedial or civil 729
The view of the United States Supreme Court that a contempt proceeding for violating an order of court against a person who was not a party or privy to the order, is a punitive or criminal proceeding for the contempt of obstructing the course of justice, is in accord with the English rulings, and clearly is better than the view of the Illinois Supreme Court . 730–731
The view of the Illinois Supreme Court that the whole world is a party to an all-the-world injunction and that a proceeding for the contempt of violating such an injunction against a person who was neither party nor privy in point of fact is a remedial or civil proceeding, has resulted in fining men and sending them to jail without due process of law in a proceeding essentially criminal in its nature 730–733
The mere failure, alone, to entitle a contempt proceeding in the name of The People is without any legal significance . . 726–734
Procedure in a state court — Form and mode of procedure for giving notice
Due process of law as applied to informing a corporation that it has been sued 715–717
The true rule on the subject of notice of suit to people on the soil of a state, so far as the irreducible minimum required by due process of law goes, must be capable of substantially uniform and just application throughout the United States . . . 716–717
Property rights and due process
Private property, not to be taken for public use without just compensation 21, 705–715
Principle is included in due process clause of 14th amendment 21, 705–715
Private property — contracts, impairment of
Within the protection of the due process clause of the 14th amendment 48, 85
The word "deprive" in the 14th amendment perhaps means the same thing certainly as much as the word "taken" in the 5th amendment 706
"Regulation" of property rights as distinguished from "taking" . 706
Government regulation of private property
Does legislative power exist to confirm and legalize a majority plan or reorganization on insolvency of public service corporations 717–720
Power of a state under the 14th amendment to aid private owners of wet lands to drain them artificially for agricultural purposes and to compel others against their will to pay a part of the cost, e. g., a railroad in the neighborhood across which the main drainage ditch must go 705–715
Question as to public purpose, to accomplish which the state may, by appropriate agencies, exert the general powers it possesses for the common good 705–715
Ordinance by municipal council, directing street railroad company to lower tunnel under navigable river, making no provision for compensation, is within due process . . . 715
Retroactive application of state law by a state court
When adjudicating upon private rights, without due process . 30

Pages

Pages